Bronchodilator Therapy:
The Basis of Asthma and Chronic Obstructive Airways Disease Management

Bronchodilator Therapy:
The Basis of Asthma and Chronic Obstructive Airways Disease Management

guest editor
T.J.H. Clark

coordinating editor
G.M. Cochrane

editorial advisory group
G.K. Crompton
Simon Godfrey
Ian Gregg
A.E. Tattersfield

ADIS Press Limited
USA • United Kingdom • Japan • Hong Kong • Australia • New Zealand

Bronchodilator Therapy:
The Basis of Asthma and Chronic Obstructive Airways Disease Management

National Library of New Zealand
Cataloguing-in-Publication data

Bronchodilator Therapy: the basis of asthma and
chronic obstructive airways disease management/
guest editor, T.J.H. Clark; coordinating editor,
G.M. Cochrane. – Auckland, N.Z.: Adis, 1984. –
1 v.

ISBN 0-86471-005-4
616.2306 19

1. Asthma—Treatment. I. Clark, T.J.H.
(Timothy John Hayes). II. Cochrane, G.M.

First printing

ADIS Press Limited
15 Rawene Road, Birkenhead, Auckland 10, New Zealand

Printed in Hong Kong by Toppan Printing Co. Ltd.

list of contributors

R.N. Brogden
Scientific Editor, ADIS Drug Information Services, Auckland, New Zealand

P. Sherwood Burge
Consultant Physician, Solihull Hospital, West Midlands, England

G.M. Cochrane
Consultant Physician in Thoracic Medicine, Guy's and New Cross Hospitals, London, England

R.G. Dent
Senior Registrar, Addenbrooke's Hospital, Cambridge, England

Simon Godfrey
Professor, Chairman Department of Pediatrics, Hadassah University Hospital, Jerusalem, Israel

M.R. Hetzel
Consultant Chest Physician, Whittington Hospital; University College Hospital, London, England

S.T. Holgate
Senior Lecturer in Medicine, Faculty of Medicine, Southampton General Hospital, University of Southampton, England

A.D. Milner
Professor of Paediatric Respiratory Medicine, Department of Child Health, Queen's Medical Centre, Nottingham, England

J.G. Prior
Senior Medical Registrar, Guy's and New Cross Hospitals; Brook General Hospital, London, England

G.M. Shenfield
Associate Professor, Department of Clinical Pharmacology, Royal North Shore Hospital, Sydney, Australia

J.E. Stark
Consultant Physician, Addenbrooke's Hospital, Cambridge, England

A.E. Tattersfield
Professor of Respiratory Medicine, The City Hospital, Nottingham, England

A. Ward
Scientific Editor, ADIS Drug Information Services, Auckland, New Zealand

J.D. Wilson
Associate Professor in Immunology, School of Medicine, University of Auckland, Auckland, New Zealand

foreword

Over the past two decades many new drugs for the treatment of asthma have both helped improve morbidity and provided clinicians with a wider therapeutic choice. An important advance has been the better treatments for the suppression of asthma and there has been special interest in the mode of action of sodium cromoglycate and the role of corticosteroids. The increasing use of these agents for asthma prophylaxis and the expanding role for inhaled steroids has inevitably distracted attention from developments in bronchodilator therapy.

Bronchodilators have come a long way since the early days when patients had to rely on non-selective adrenergic agonists or oral concoctions, usually of theophylline and ephedrine. Selectivity has been improved and there is now greater awareness of the importance of delivery systems whether by inhalation or oral formulation. Theophylline therapy has been virtually transformed by the developments largely carried out in the United States whereas on this side of the Atlantic inhaled therapy has been strongly developed with the introduction of longer acting bronchodilators capable of modifying both adrenergic and cholinergic activity. Bronchodilators are now recognised as being of value in the suppression of asthma as well as in the treatment of acute attacks and this has led to a change in attitude towards the scope of their role in the management of the disease.

The revived interest in corticosteroid treatment, and inhaled steroids in particular, prompted an earlier book, Steroids in Asthma, which was published in 1983. I was happy to act as its Guest Editor. The success of the publication, largely due to the extensive coverage of the subject and clarity of its presentation, prompted a suggestion from the publishers that bronchodilator therapy might lend itself to a similar approach. I thought it would indeed be helpful to review this subject at this juncture and once again have been happy to act as Guest Editor.

This book then can be seen as a companion volume to Steroids in Asthma. However, it has proved a more difficult task: bronchodilator therapy, inherently, is a far more diverse subject and the book was not conceived around a central theme as was the earlier volume which argued for a greater use of inhaled steroids. Although Bronchodilator Therapy lacks the unifying focus we found so useful in Steroids in Asthma I hope we have managed to achieve sufficient coherence for the book to be read as a whole rather than in parts. Once again we found ourselves with a degree of overlap in the contributions, inevitable when there is more than one author and the subject is somewhat artificially broken up into chapters. We have chosen not to eliminate this entirely bearing in mind those readers who will wish to read, or go back to, certain chapters rather than the book in its entirety.

We are conscious of the fact that this book is largely a reflection of the British school of asthma therapy but we have tried to achieve as much balance as possible. I hope we have given sufficient coverage to all bronchodilators especially to methylxanthines. The role of bronchodilators in relationship to other asthma treatments is inevitably touched upon in several subsequent chapters but by asking Dr Wilson to especially address this in chapter 3 we hope we have maintained some perspective.

As Guest Editor I have once more largely been responsible for selecting the authors and holding a ring between them. My task has been immeasurably eased by having Dr Mac Cochrane do most of the work of co-ordination and both of us are deeply indebted to our Editorial Advisory Group who have played such an active role in advising us about each chapter. All these endeavours would be without avail were it not for the work of our authors who have tackled this difficult subject with great skill.

This book could certainly not have been produced without the willing co-operation of all engaged in it. On behalf of Dr Cochrane and the Editorial Advisory Board I would like to thank again our authors and the publishers and also those who have helped and supported them. We all hope this book will enable bronchodilator therapy to be reconsidered in the light of recent advances so that we can not only provide better care for our patients but also plan the next generation of bronchodilators, so as to improve on the many advances made in recent years.

T.J.H. Clark
1 September 1984

list of contents

Guest Editor, Coordinating Editor, Editorial Advisory Group v

Contributors vi

Foreword vii

Chapter I
Bronchoconstriction
S.T. Holgate 1

Chapter II
Pharmacology of Bronchodilators
G.M. Shenfield, R.N. Brogden and A. Ward 17

Chapter III
The Role of Bronchodilators in the Management of Asthma:
An Overview
J.D. Wilson 47

Chapter IV
Getting the Best Out of Bronchodilator Therapy
P. Sherwood Burge 58

Chapter V
Bronchodilators in the Prevention of Asthma
A.E. Tattersfield 76

Chapter VI
Bronchodilators in Childhood Asthma
A.D. Milner 93

Chapter VII
Bronchodilators in Exercise-induced Asthma
Simon Godfrey 112

Chapter VIII
Bronchodilators in the Prevention of Nocturnal Asthma
M.R. Hetzel 131

Chapter IX
Bronchodilator Therapy in the Elderly
J.E. Stark and R.G. Dent 151

Chapter X
The Role of Bronchodilators in Severe Acute Asthma
G.M. Cochrane 167

Chapter XI
The Role of Bronchodilators in the Management of Chronic
Bronchitis and Emphysema
G.M. Cochrane and J.G. Prior 188

Appendix A
Structure-Activity Relationship of Bronchodilator Drugs
J.G. Prior 203

Appendix B
Dose Equivalents of Bronchodilator Drugs
J.G. Prior 209

Appendix C
Inhalation Devices
J.G. Prior 213

Index 226

Chapter I

Bronchoconstriction

S.T. Holgate

Bronchial asthma is a disease which has so far eluded any attempt at universal definition. From a clinician's point of view it represents diffuse airways obstruction which is reversible either spontaneously, or with treatment. The physiologist might describe bronchial asthma as airways obstruction in association with hyperinflation, and the pharmacologist, as enhanced reactivity of the airways to specific and nonspecific stimuli. Despite the variety of description it is evident that the cardinal feature of the disease is diffuse airways obstruction.

The difficulty in establishing a common definition of asthma can influence the findings of epidemiological surveys. Thus, although the reported prevalence of asthma in the United Kingdom is 2 to 4%, 11% of 2700 seven-year old children studied in northeast England (Lee et al., 1983), and 27% of 2000 adults studied in Hampshire (Mortagy et al., personal communication), had experienced intermittent wheezing during the preceding 2 years. The most likely explanation for this discrepancy is that asthma is underdiagnosed, and consequently, is undertreated.

Classifying Asthma

Allergic Asthma

In children and young adults there is a clear association between asthma symptoms and evidence of bronchial hyper-reactivity on exposure to common environmental allergens. Many of these patients exhibit features of an allergic diathesis which presents clinically as eczema, rhinitis, conjunctivitis and urticaria. Patients who experience an exacerbation of symptoms during, or just after, the 'hay fever season' (seasonal asthma), will demonstrate IgE-dependent sensitivity to grass pollen antigens. More persistent exposure to antigens from house dust mites *(Dermatophagoides pteronyssinus* and *D. farinae)* has been linked to perennial asthma. Although the airways may become hyper-responsive to various stimuli following sensitisation to allergens, this process alone does not precipitate asthma and other factors should be considered.

Infective Asthma

Frequently bronchoconstriction is associated with respiratory infection. Thus, children are often described as suffering from 'wheezy bronchitis', and adults as having 'asthmatic bronchitis' (see p.154).

Drug-induced or Occupational Asthma

There are also those patients with asthma in whom no allergic or infective process can be defined. Some of these may be unusually sensitive to non-steroidal anti-inflammatory drugs (NSAIDs), while in others, exposure to low concentrations of industrial chemicals, e.g. diisocyanates, may precipitate asthma (occupational asthma).

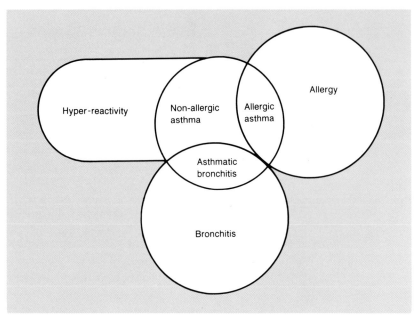

Fig. 1.1. Venn diagram to illustrate clinical and physiological associations in asthma (reproduced with permission from the Pharmaceutical Journal [London], 1983, 231: 412).

Intrinsic Asthma

This still leaves a group of children and adults for whose symptoms no cause can be found, giving rise to the descriptions 'intrinsic' or 'cryptogenic' asthma.

Bronchial Hyper-reactivity

The multifactorial nature of asthma and its various clinical associations may best be represented in the form of a Venn diagram (fig. 1.1). Although many aetiological factors contribute to diffuse airways obstruction in asthma, a common feature in all forms of the disease is enhanced bronchoconstrictor responsiveness to nonspecific stimulation. Clinically, this presents as attacks of asthma on exposure to noxious fumes, cold air, exercise and dust. Increased airway responsiveness has also been proposed as an explanation for the exaggerated diurnal variations in airway calibre in asthmatics, characterised by nocturnal wheeze and morning 'tightness' (see p.134). In the laboratory, bronchial reactivity may be defined by provocation testing with inhaled histamine, methacholine, sulphur dioxide, cold air, or more simply, by exercise. Close correlations have been found between the ability to cause bronchoconstriction of all these stimuli suggesting that hyper-reactivity represents a fundamental abnormality in all forms of asthma and distinguishing asthmatic from normal airways. Clinically, nonspecific airway hyper-responsiveness parallels the frequency and severity of asthma symptoms and also correlates with resting airway calibre.

It should, however, be emphasised that, although highly relevant, bronchial hyper-reactivity is only one feature of asthma and in itself does not constitute the disease. Enhanced airway responsiveness may occur with viral infections of the respiratory tract (Empey et al., 1976) or after exposure to ozone (Dimeo et al., 1981), but these provocations alone are insufficient to induce asthma. Moreover, a significant proportion of asymptomatic normal subjects exhibit bronchial hyper-responsiveness to nonspecific stimuli. This chapter will attempt to emphasise the cellular mechanisms in asthma which may contribute to bronchial obstruction and it is hoped unify some of the more controversial aspects of the disease.

The Pathology of Asthma

Diffuse obstruction of the airway lumen as the cardinal event of bronchial asthma has four elements (fig. 1.2):

1) Hypertrophy of bronchial smooth muscle

2) Increased secretion of mucus into the lumen of the bronchi

3) Oedema of the respiratory mucosa

4) Inflammatory cell infiltration of the airway wall and lumen with eosinophils and neutrophils.

An abundance of eosinophils in the airway wall and within the secretions distinguishes the inflammatory infiltrate of the asthmatic airway from that of chronic bronchitis, in which neutrophils predominate. Two additional pathological features which are characteristic of asthma are destruction of the respiratory epithelium, and thickening and fragmentation of the basement membrane underlying the remaining epithelium (Hogg et al., 1977). The pathological features of asthma have mostly been described from tissue obtained from patients who died during a severe attack, but recent studies suggest that similar changes also occur in less severe forms of the disease (Laitinen et al., 1982). Furthermore, the presence of numerous eosinophils, Charcot Leyden crystals (disrupted

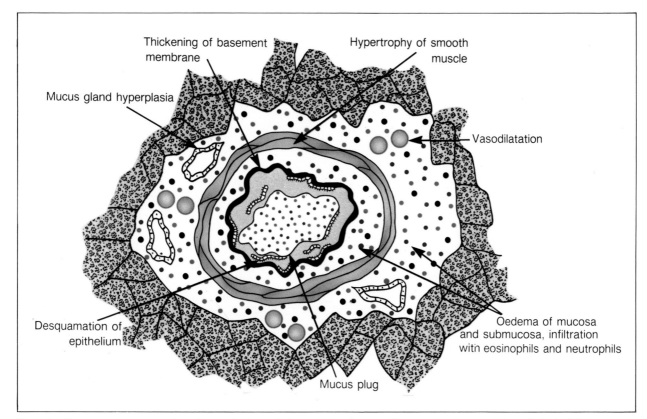

Fig. 1.2. Diagrammatic cross-section of a small airway in bronchial asthma to illustrate the characteristic pathological features (reproduced with permission of J. Linda Jackson).

eosinophils) and Curschmann spirals (coiled mucus plugs) in the sputum of asthmatic patients, is indicative of the inflammatory response.

The Physiological Changes in Asthma

During an acute asthmatic attack the large and small airways narrow. This is mainly due to an increase in bronchial smooth muscle tone, which, if left unopposed, would result in total airway occlusion. However, under static conditions, compensatory mechanisms operate to increase transpulmonary pressure and distend the intrathoracic airways. In a lung with limited elastic recoil the static transpulmonary pressure can only be increased by an increase in lung volume. The major difference between the asthmatic and normal lung is that in the asthmatic lung, closure of the airways occurs at a higher than normal transpulmonary pressure. Thus, the more severe the attack of asthma, the higher the transpulmonary pressure at which the airways close. This results in a decreased vital capacity, an increased residual volume and, on occasions, an increased total lung capacity. In patients with chronic asthma, where mucus impaction and oedema of the airways form an important component of airways obstruction, entrapment of air behind partially obstructed airways contributes to the increase in lung volume.

During an attack of asthma, diffuse airway narrowing causes non-uniformity of ventilation, and ventilation-perfusion mismatching which result in hypoxaemia. It should be stressed that patients with asthma have an increased rather than a decreased respiratory drive. During a moderate attack, the arterial blood gas picture is characterised by hypoxaemia from ventilation-perfusion inequality, and hypocapnia from hyperventilation. Attempting to increase ventilation at high lung volumes involves high expenditure of energy, demonstrated clinically by the involvement of accessory muscles in ventilation. If the asthma attack is prolonged, muscle fatigue occurs, and is eventually accompanied by ventilatory failure. Thus, an increase in arterial carbon dioxide tension in a patient with otherwise uncomplicated asthma is one of the most important clinical observations which should lead to urgent intervention with assisted ventilation.

Cellular Mechanisms of Bronchoconstriction

Airway inflammation is a central feature in the pathogenesis of asthma. However, the relationship of this pathological event to enhanced nonspecific airway reactivity has not been clearly defined.

Patients with seasonal asthma and, to a lesser extent, perennial asthma, notice an increase in their symptoms during particular times of the year; seasonal asthmatics during the late spring and early summer, perennial asthmatics during the autumn and early winter. It has been suggested that this seasonal variation in symptoms relates to increased exposure to particular environmental antigens. In classical allergic asthma, bronchial provocation with a specific antigen causes an immediate bronchoconstriction of rapid onset, reaching a maximum 15 to 20 minutes after challenge and slowly recovering over the following 2 hours (Fish and Kelly, 1979). This may be followed some 4 to 6 hours later by a second bronchoconstrictor response which is more prolonged and, on occasions, may reoccur over the following 2 to 3 days (Nagy et al.,

1982). These bronchoconstrictor responses are referred to as 'immediate' and 'late' reactions respectively. There is evidence to suggest that the late asthmatic reaction is associated with an increase in nonspecific bronchial hyper-reactivity (Boulet et al., 1983) which, as already noted, is one of the cardinal features of clinical asthma. Thus, insight into the nature of early and late phase reactions should shed some light on the pathophysiology of the disease.

The Mast Cell

Bronchoconstriction immediately following antigen bronchial challenge is an immediate hypersensitivity reaction characterised by the IgE-dependent release of inflammatory mediators into the airway wall. The mast cell initiates this response. Lung tissue contains 0.01 to 0.1% mast cells, over 80% of which are concentrated in the airways (Lamb and Lumsden, 1982). Bronchial mast cells are found free in the airway lumen, intraepithelially and beneath the basement membrane. Activation of mucosal mast cells by inhaled antigen stimulates the release of preformed and newly generated inflammatory mediators which are capable of initiating the bronchoconstrictor response.

Mast Cell Activation

It has long been known that challenge of IgE-sensitised human lung fragments *in vitro* results in the non-cytotoxic secretion of histamine and the *de novo* generation of prostaglandins and slow reacting substance of anaphylaxis (Lewis and Austen, 1981). Recently it has been possible to prepare virtually pure suspensions of dispersed mast cells from human lung tissue, thereby enabling their more detailed study (Caulfield et al., 1980). Figure 1.3 illustrates a typical human lung mast cell viewed by transmission elec-

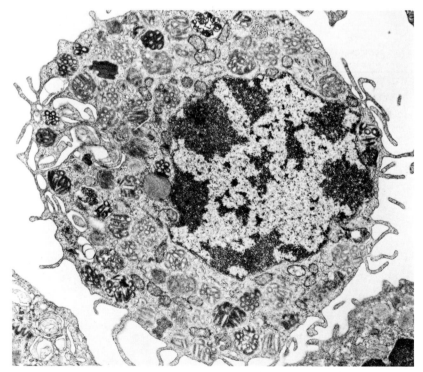

Fig. 1.3. Electron micrograph of a mast cell enzymatically dispersed from human lung tissue (reproduced by kind permission of Dr J.C. Caulfield and the Journal of Experimental Medicine).

Table 1.1. Preformed inflammatory mediators in human mast cells

Amines	Histamine
Exoglycosidases	Arylsulphatase B
	β-Hexosaminidase B
	β-Glucuronidase
	β-Galactosidase
Neutral proteases	Tryptase[1]
	Carboxypeptidase B
	Dipeptidases
Chemotactic factors	Eosinophil chemotactic tetrapeptides ⎫
	Eosinophil chemotactic oligopeptides ⎬ ECF-A
	⎭
	Neutrophil chemotactic factor - high molecular weight (HMW-NCF)
Other enzymes	Superoxide dismutase
Proteoglycans	Heparin

1 — Schwartz, 1984

tron microscopy. As with all mast cells, those from the human lung contain a large number of membrane-bound phagolysosomes which are modified for secretion. The secretory granules are characterised ultrastructurally by the presence of scrolls, lattices and gratings, which have a common periodicity of 75Å and 150Å. This subunit structure of the granule matrix indicates organisation of preformed inflammatory mediators stored within the secretory granule. A large number of preformed inflammatory mediators have now been identified within the mast cell granule (table 1.1) and are packaged in an orderly fashion along the acidic glycosaminoglycan side-chains of the proteoglycan heparin (Holgate and Church, 1982).

Human lung mast cells possess in excess of 10^5 high affinity receptors for the Fc fragment of IgE (Coleman and Godfrey, 1981). The binding of specific antigen to the Fab ends of two or more IgE molecules causes approximation of the Fc receptors (fig. 1.4a). This is the signal for cell activation (fig. 1.4b). This receptor-mediated cell surface interaction uncovers membrane channels which facilitate the passage of extracellular calcium ions into the cell (fig. 1.4c) to activate the energy-requiring secretory mechanism (Church et al., 1982). The preformed mediators within the granule are partially solubilised by passage of anions and water across the perigranular membrane, and the swollen granules move toward the cell surface. An approximation of the perigranular and plasma membrane results in membrane fusion and enables the granule contents to be secreted into the extracellular space by ion exchange with sodium (fig. 1.4d) [Holgate and Church, 1982].

Newly Generated Mast Cell-associated Mediators

Besides releasing preformed granule-derived mediators, the IgE-dependent activation of mast cells stimulates the *de novo* generation of additional proinflammatory mediators. A number of these are derived from the oxidative metabolism of arachidonic acid. Arachidonic acid, a twenty carbon polyunsaturated fatty acid, is present in large amounts in the mast cell plasma membrane,

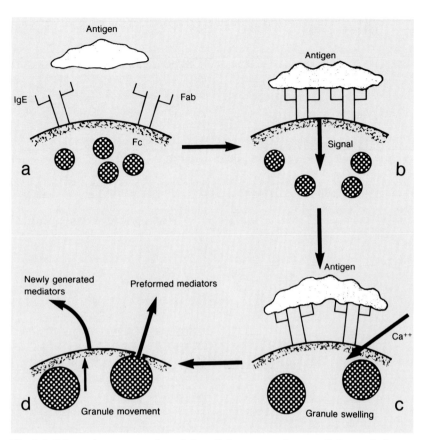

Fig. 1.4. Schematic representation of the cellular events of mast cell degranulation.

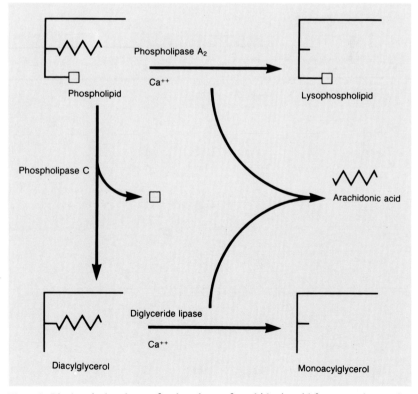

Fig. 1.5. Biochemical pathways for the release of arachidonic acid from membrane phospholipids in the mast cell.

chemically bound to phospholipids (fig. 1.5). The IgE-dependent activation of mast cells is associated with an influx of extracellular calcium which stimulates the degradation of phospholipids by membrane phospholipases, thus releasing large amounts of arachidonic acid. Arachidonic acid then undergoes metabolism by either the cyclo-oxygenase or the 5-lipoxygenase pathways (fig. 1.6).

The first products of cyclo-oxygenation of arachidonic acid are the endoperoxides, prostaglandin (PG)G_2 and PGH_2. These unstable intermediates then undergo further oxidation within the mast cell to its major prostanoid PGD_2, although smaller amounts of thromboxane (Tx)A_2 and PGI_2 are also synthesised (Holgate, 1983).

Oxidation of arachidonic acid by the 5-lipoxygenase pathway produces a potent group of inflammatory mediators including the components of slow-reacting substance of anaphylaxis (SRS-A) [Lewis et al., 1980]. The first intermediate compound in this reaction is 5-hydroperoxyeicosatetraenoic acid (5-HPETE), which is either transformed into a stable product, 5-hydroxyeicosatetraenoic acid (5-HETE) or to a further unstable intermediary, leukotriene A_4 (LTA_4). Leukotriene A_4 then either undergoes enzymatic conversion to a dihydroxy acid, LTB_4, or conjugates with the tripeptide glutathione to produce a series of 6-sulphidopeptide leukotrienes, LTC_4, LTD_4 and LTE_4 which comprise SRS-A (Samuelsson, 1983).

Dispersed mast cells from human lung have the enzymatic capacity to generate approximately equal amounts of PGD_2, LTB_4 and LTC_4, but whether a single population of bronchial mast cells has the capacity to generate all these products requires further def-

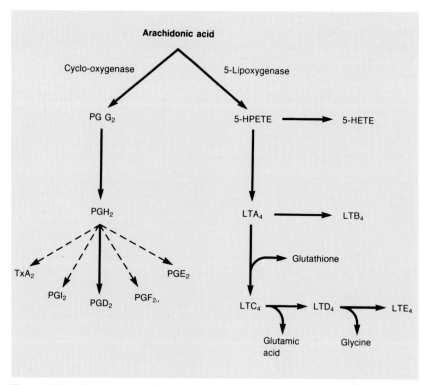

Fig. 1.6. The oxidative metabolism of arachidonic acid within the mast cell by the cyclo-oxygenase and 5-lipoxygenase pathways.

inition. Recent evidence suggests that mucosal mast cells have an enhanced capacity to generate LTC_4 (Razin et al., 1983), whereas the connective tissue mast cell preferentially generates PGD_2 (Lewis et al., 1982).

In addition to the oxidation of arachidonic acid, animal and human mast cells synthesise a potent platelet activating factor, which has been identified as acetylglyceryletherphosphorylcholine (AGEPC, PAF-Acether) [Demopoulos et al., 1979]. This mediator is also generated from membrane phospholipids by the action of phospholipase A_2 but the exact biochemical pathway for its synthesis awaits further definition.

Other Mechanisms of Mast Cell Activation

Although the immunological activation of mast cells by IgE [and possibly IgG_4 (Stanworth, 1983)] is clearly pertinent to allergic bronchoconstriction, other mechanisms may also activate mediator release from mast cells. The split products of complement, namely C3a, C4a and C5a (anaphylatoxins) activate mast cells for mediator release by a mechanism independent of the IgE-Fc receptor (Stimler et al., 1983). Additionally, certain bacterial lectins (complex carbohydrates) are able to directly cross-link IgE-Fc receptors. Both mechanisms may be relevant to asthma associated with respiratory infection and may also be implicated in the pathogenesis of intrinsic asthma (Norn et al., 1983). One particular form of non-allergic asthma is a hypersensitivity to non-steroidal anti-inflammatory drugs (NSAIDs) such as aspirin and indomethacin. Asthma, rhinitis and urticaria induced by NSAIDs may rarely be related to an IgE-dependent hypersensitivity reaction, but their inhibitory action on the cyclo-oxygenase pathway of arachidonic acid is probaby of more relevance. In susceptible individuals their administration may result in an increased production of bronchoconstrictor sulphidopeptide leukotrienes because of the diversion of arachidonic acid along the 5-lipoxygenase pathway (Szczeklik, 1982) [fig. 1.6].

Secondary Mediators in the Pathogenesis of Asthma

While mast cell activation with release of preformed and newly generated inflammatory mediators can account for many of the pathological features of bronchial asthma (see below), recruitment of secondary effector cells is of major importance in the overall inflammatory response. Histamine and other mast cell mediators cause the secondary release of prostanoids (Platshon and Kaliner, 1978) and adenosine (Mann et al., 1983) from contracting airway smooth muscle and activated inflammatory cells. The IgE-dependent activation of mast cells also releases a specific peptide, which is capable of stimulating the release of bronchoconstrictor prostanoids and which is therefore called prostaglandin generating factor of anaphylaxis (Steel and Kaliner, 1981). Released neutral proteases generate bradykinin and C3a from their circulating precursors, high molecular weight kininogen (Newball and Lichtenstein, 1981) and the complement component, C3 (Schwartz et al., 1983) respectively.

Evidence for the Role of Inflammatory Mediators in the Pathogenesis of Bronchial Asthma

Until recently, only indirect evidence was cited in support of a pivotal role of mast cells in the generation of immediate and late bronchoconstriction with antigen challenge. Cockcroft and co-workers have shown that the airway response to inhaled antigen is influenced by two components: nonspecific airway reactivity, and mast cell sensitivity to inhaled antigen (Cockcroft et al., 1979).

This observation has recently been confirmed more directly by showing that for a given airway bronchoconstrictor response, the increment in plasma level of histamine observed with antigen bronchial challenge inversely correlates with airway reactivity to nonspecific stimulation (Howarth et al., 1983). A number of studies have demonstrated the release of high molecular weight neutrophil chemotactic factor (HMW-NCF) [Kay and Lee, 1982], the 13,14-dihydrometabolite of $PGF_{2\alpha}$ (Green et al., 1974) and platelet factor 4 (an index of PAF activation of platelets) [Knauer et al., 1981]) into the circulation following antigen bronchial provocation.

The release of mast cell-associated mediators in asthma has also been incriminated in the pathogenesis of antigen-induced late reactions (Nagy et al., 1982). The intensity of late skin reactions observed following intradermal injection of a specific antigen is closely related to the strength of the antigenic stimulus (Bedard et al., 1983). It was originally thought that late reactions were the result of immune complex deposition, but it is now recognised that mast cell activation is more important (Solley et al., 1976). Histologically, the late response is characterised by oedema and inflammatory cell infiltration by neutrophils and eosinophils (Solley et al., 1976). Inflammatory cell infiltration is a consequence of the selective stimulation of neutrophils and eosinophils by mast cell-associated chemotactic factors. Chemotactic stimulation activates these cells to release their own preformed, and newly generated inflammatory mediators. The eosinophil chemotactic peptides and HMW-NCF preformed in the mast cell granule (table 1.1), and the newly generated products LTB_4 and 5-HETE (fig. 1.6), are all highly potent chemotactic agents, the release of which is considered to be important in the development of late phase responses.

The Role of Inflammatory Mediators in Bronchoconstriction

The release of inflammatory mediators into the airway from mast cells and other activated cells provides a mechanism which can explain many of the clinical, pathological and physiological features of asthma.

Smooth Muscle Contraction

One of the paramount features of bronchial asthma is the ease with which bronchoconstriction can be reversed by agents such as the β_2-adrenoceptor agonists and the methylxanthines, which relax bronchial smooth muscle. Contraction of airway smooth muscle both *in vitro* and *in vivo* may be produced by a wide variety of pharmacological mediators. These agents act directly, by an interaction of the inflammatory mediator with receptors on airway smooth muscle, or indirectly, through activation of local and vagal reflexes. Histamine, for example, contracts airway smooth muscle both by stimulating smooth muscle H_1 receptors, and also by stimulating sensory receptors in the airways to produce reflex bronchoconstriction (White and Eiser, 1983). The prostaglandins PGD_2, $PGF_{2\alpha}$ and TxA_2 are also potent contractile agonists. However, it is recognised that antagonism of histamine H_1 receptors or inhibition of prostaglandin generation have little overall effect on clinical asthma or bronchoconstriction induced by antigen challenge, suggesting that other mediators must be implicated.

Recently, interest has centred on the sulphidopeptide leukotrienes (Samuelsson, 1983). These 5-lipoxygenase products of arachidonic acid, are potent contractile agonists of airway smooth muscle, and also potentiate the bronchoconstriction produced by other mediators such as histamine. Leukotriene C_4, generated in large amounts by the activation of human lung mast cells, is at least 1000 times more potent than histamine as a contractile agonist (Dahlen et al., 1980). When inhaled by normal or asthmatic subjects, both LTC_4 and LTD_4 cause bronchoconstriction, with a preferential activity on peripheral airways.

The Role of the Vagus

In animals and man there exists a mild degree of airway smooth muscle tone which can be abolished by administration of systemic or inhaled muscarinic anticholinergic agents such as atropine methonitrate and ipratropium bromide. It has been suggested that a major component of bronchoconstriction in asthma is mediated by enhanced vagal reflex activity (Nadel, 1973). The airways contain stretch receptors (irritant or rapidly adapting receptors) which have myelinated nerve fibres in the vagi. Stimulation of the irritant receptors results in reflex bronchoconstriction, laryngoconstriction and airway mucus secretion (Widdicombe, 1983). Nerve impulses have been recorded in the afferent vagal fibres during anaphylactic bronchoconstriction (Mills et al., 1969) and following inhalation of a wide variety of irritants such as histamine, $PGF_{2\alpha,}$ sulphur dioxide, dust and cigarette smoke. It is likely therefore that at least some increase in vagal tone contributes to airway narrowing in asthma. It should be noted that atropine and related muscarinic cholinergic antagonists are relatively ineffective in the long term management of asthma. High concentrations of inhaled atropine compounds or ipratropium bromide have only a minor effect in reducing bronchoconstriction induced by inhaled antigens but are highly effective in antagonising bronchoconstriction with methacholine (Bendovakis et al., 1981). In contrast, by systemic administration atropine is effective in blocking antigen-induced bronchoconstriction in dogs but only at doses which exert profound cardiovascular and other unwanted effects (Holtzman et al., 1983). Clearly further investigation is required to clarify the role of the vagus in this complex disease.

Hyper-reactivity

Increased responsiveness of the airways to a variety of stimuli is characteristic of asthma, but the mechanism is poorly understood. One theory is that there is a fundamental alteration in the electrophysiological response of the smooth muscle of asthmatic airways compared to normal (Souhrada and Souhrada, 1981). However, in both animals and man *in vivo* bronchial hyper-reactivity is not reflected by enhanced smooth muscle responsiveness in airway preparations examined *in vitro*.

Other factors may also be important, e.g. an increase in permeability of the airway mucosa following exposure to inflammatory mediators may increase the access of inhaled antigens, and other stimuli, to effector cells lying deeper in the airway (Hogg, 1982). Antigen bronchial provocation testing in animal models and, more recently, in human subjects has demonstrated an increased mucosal permeability to large molecules. However, studies in patients with clinically active asthma have not shown a permanently increased mucosal permeability (Elwood et al., 1983). Nevertheless, it remains possible that intermittent changes in airway permeability, resulting from repetitive exposure to antigen or infection, are all that is required to enhance airway responsiveness.

Whatever the mechanism(s) of hyper-reactivity, airway inflammation is likely to have an important role since corticosteroids and sodium cromoglycate (cromolyn sodium), drugs which inhibit the inflammatory response, render the airways less reactive to non-specific stimulation and produce clinical improvement.

Mucosal Oedema

Immediate hypersensitivity reactions are associated with increased capillary permeability – as evidenced by the skin wheal reaction to an intradermal injection of antigen in allergic subjects. Mucosal oedema results from the interaction of inflammatory mediators. The sulphidopeptide leukotrienes, bradykinin and adenosine increase vascular permeability, which produces oedema when combined with the vasodilator actions of PGD_2, PGI_2 and histamine.

Hypersecretion of Mucus

Obstruction of the airways with copious viscid secretions is a pathological feature of severe asthma. An enhanced secretion of mucus has been observed in isolated airway preparations when stimulated by histamine, $PGF_{2\alpha}$, 6-keto $PGF_{1\alpha}$, PGD_2, the sulphidopeptide leukotrienes, and 5-HETE (Marom et al., 1981). Intraepithelial goblet cells are devoid of neural innervation, but the more complex submucosal glands are under both cholinergic and α-adrenoceptor control, stimulation of which enhances mucus secretion.

Epithelial Desquamation

Disruption and subsequent sloughing of the respiratory epithelium is another characteristic feature of asthma. Proteolytic enzymes from mast cells and neutrophils, together with cationic proteins from the eosinophil, have the capacity to disrupt the surface epithelium (Gleich et al., 1979).

Inflammatory Cell Infiltration

Activation of mast cells results in the release of chemotactic factors, including ECF-A, LTB_4, HMW-NCF and 5-HETE, which recruit eosinophils and neutrophils into the inflammatory zone. Chemotactic stimulation of these granulocytes activates them for mediator secretion and enhances their cell surface complement and immunoglobulin receptors (Kay et al., 1979).

Thickening of the Basement Membrane

Activation of mast cells in the respiratory tract releases a number of exoglycosidases and neutral proteases which have the combined capacity to break down the complex proteoglycans and glycoproteins of tissue ground substance. In addition, these enzymes disrupt the mucopolysaccharide components of the airway basement membrane. Multiplication of epithelial cells to repair the damaged membrane results in thickening and hyalinisation.

Immunopathological Events of Bronchial Asthma

Figure 1.7 illustrates the interaction of the inflammatory mediators with the effector cells concerned in the pathogenesis of bronchial asthma. In allergic asthma, it is considered that mast cells play an important role in the pathogenesis of bronchoconstriction, even though they constitute only a minor proportion of

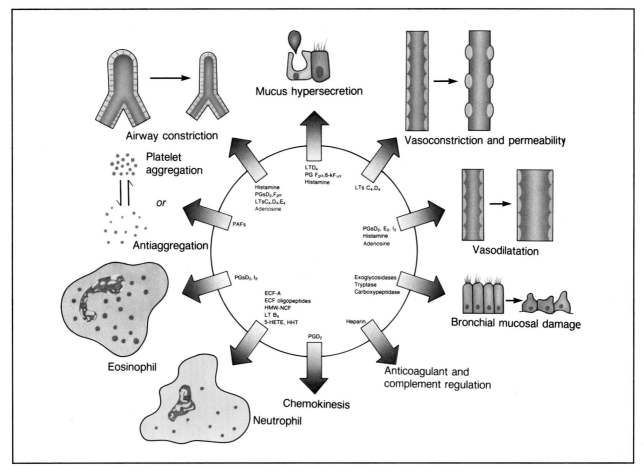

Fig. 1.7. The influence of mast cell-associated inflammatory mediators on the pathophysiological events of asthma.

the intraepithelial bronchial cells (Lamb and Lumsden, 1982). However, recent studies have suggested that mucosal mast cells form a discrete subgroup of mast cells. These are produced from bone marrow precursor cells under the influence of a T-lymphocyte growth factor (interleukin 3), the release of which is stimulated by chronic exposure to antigen (Ihle et al., 1983). Thus, an antigen-induced increase in the number of bronchial mucosal mast cells might contribute to the increase in bronchial reactivity observed in seasonal asthma.

In Summary

The mechanisms contributing to airway obstruction in asthma are complex, but inflammation of the airways, interacting with bronchial hyper-reactivity, must play a central role. Recognition of this fact has important therapeutic implications and emphasises the need for early diagnosis and positive therapeutic intervention if the natural history of the disease is to be altered.

References

Bedard, P.-M.; Atkins, P.C. and Zweiman, B.: Antigen-induced local mediator release and cellular inflammatory responses in atopic subjects. Journal of Allergy and Clinical Immunology 71: 394 (1983).

Bendovakis, J.; Cartier, A.; Roberts, R.; Ryan, G. and Hargreave, F.E.: The effect of ipratropium bromide and fenoterol on methacholine- and histamine-induced bronchoconstriction. British Journal of Diseases of the Chest 75: 295 (1981).

Boulet, L.-P.; Cartier, T.; Thomson, N.C.; Roberts, R.S. and Dolovich, J.: Asthma and increases in non-allergic bronchial responsiveness from seasonal pollen exposure. Journal of Allergy and Clinical Immunology 71: 399 (1983).

Caulfield, J.P.; Lewis, R.A.; Hein, A. and Austen, K.F.: Secretion in dissociated human pulmonary mast cells. Evidence for solubilization of granule contents before discharge. Journal of Cell Biology 85: 299 (1980).

Church, M.K.; Pao, G.J.-K. and Holgate, S.T.: Characterization of histamine secretion from mechanically dispersed human lung mast cells: Effects of anti-IgE, calcium ionophore A23187, compound 48/80 and basic polypeptides. Journal of Immunology 129: 2116 (1982).

Cockcroft, D.W.; Ruffin, R.E.; Frith, P.A.; Cartier, A.; Juniper, E.F.; Dolovich, J. and Hargreave, F.E.: Determinants of allergen-induced asthma: Dose of allergen, circulating IgE antibody concentrations and bronchial responsiveness to inhaled histamine. American Review of Respiratory Disease 120: 1053 (1979).

Coleman, J. and Godfrey, R.C.: The number and affinity of IgE receptors on dispersed human lung mast cells. Immunology 44: 859 (1981).

Dahlen, S.E.; Hedquist, P.; Hammarstrom, S. and Samuelsson, B.: Leukotrienes are potent constrictors of human bronchi. Nature 288: 484 (1980).

Demopoulos, C.A.; Pinckard, R.N. and Hanahan, D.J.: Platelet activating factor. Evidence for 1-O-alkyl-2-acetyl-sn-glyceryl-3-phosphorylcholine as the active component. (A new class of lipid mediators). Journal of Biological Chemistry 254: 9355 (1979).

Dimeo, J.R.; Glenn, M.G.; Holtzmann, M.J.; Sheller, J.R.; Nadel, J.A. and Boushey, H.A.: Threshold concentration of ozone causing an increase in bronchial reactivity in humans and adaptation with repeated exposure. American Review of Respiratory Disease 124: 245 (1981).

Elwood, R.K.; Kennedy, S.; Belzberg, A.; Hogg, J.C. and Pare, D.: Respiratory mucosal permeability in asthma. American Review of Respiratory Disease 128: 523 (1983).

Empey, D.W.; Laitinen, L.A.; Jacobs, L.; Gold, W.M. and Nadel, J.A.: Mechanisms of bronchial hyper-reactivity in normal subjects after upper respiratory tract infection. American Review of Respiratory Disease 113: 131 (1976).

Fish, J.E. and Kelly, J.F.: Measurement of responsiveness in bronchoprovocation testing. Journal of Allergy and Clinical Immunology 64: 592 (1979).

Gleich, G.J.; Frigas, E.; Oegering, D.A.; Wassom, D.L. and Steinmuller, D.: Cytotoxic properties of the eosinophil major basic protein. Journal of Immunology 123: 2925 (1979).

Green, K.; Hedquist, P. and Svanborg, N.: Increased plasma levels 15-keto-13, 14-dihydro-prostaglandin $F_{2\alpha}$ after allergen provoked asthma in man. Lancet 2: 1419 (1974).

Hogg, J.C.; Pare, P.D.; Boucher, R.; Michould, M.C.; Guerzon, G. and Moroz, L.: Pathologic abnormalities in asthma; in Lichtenstein, L.M. and Austen, K.F. (Eds) Asthma: Physiology, Immunopharmacology and Treatment, vol. 2, p.1 (Academic Press, New York 1977).

Hogg, J.C.: Bronchial mucosal permeability and its relationship to airways hyperreactivity. European Journal of Respiratory Diseases 63 (Suppl. 122): 17 (1982).

Holgate, S.T.: The leukotrienes and mast cell-associated mediators in asthma; in Flenley, D.C. and Petty, P.L. (Eds) Recent Advances in Respiratory Medicine, vol. 3, p.49 (Churchill Livingstone, London 1983).

Holgate, S.T. and Church, M.K.: Control of mediator release from mast cells. Clinical Allergy 12: 5 (1982).

Holtzman, M.J.; McNamara, M.P.; Sheppard, D.; Fabbri, L.M.; Hahn, H.L.; Graf, P.D. and Nadel, J.A.: Intravenous versus inhaled atropine for inhibiting bronchoconstrictor responses in dogs. Journal of Applied Physiology 54: 134 (1983).

Howarth, P.H.; Pao, G.J.-K.; Durham, S.R.; Lee, T.H.; Kay, A.B. and Holgate, S.T.: Influence of airway reactivity on circulating histamine and neutrophil chemotactic activity. Thorax 38: 705 (1983).

Ihle, J.N.; Keller, J.; Oroszlan, S.; Henderson, L.E.; Copeland, T.O.; Fitch, F.; Drystowsky, M.B.; Goldwasser, E.; Schrader, J.W.; Palaszynski, E.; Dy, E. and Lebel, B.: Biologic properties of homogenous interleukin 3. Demonstration of WEH 1-3 growth factor activity, mast cell growth factor activity, P cell stimulating factor activity, colony-stimulating factor activity and histamine-producing cell stimulating factor activity. Journal of Immunology 131: 282 (1983).

Kay, A.B.; Glass, E.J. and Salter, D.M.: Leucoattractants enhance complement receptors on human phagocytic cells. Clinical and Experimental Immunology 38: 294 (1979).

Kay, A.B. and Lee, L.T.: Neutrophil chemotactic factor of anaphylaxis. Journal of Allergy and Clinical Immunology 70: 317 (1982).

Knauer, K.A.; Lichtenstein, L.M. and Adkinson Jr, N.F.: Platelet activation during antigen-induced airway reactions in asthmatic subjects. New England Journal of Medicine 304: 1404 (1981).

Laitinen, L.A.; Kava, T. and Heino, M.: Ultrastructure of the airways and bronchial reactivity in asthma; in Nadel, J.A. and Pauwels, R. (Eds) International Conference on Bronchial Hyperreactivity, p.71 (The Medicine Publishing Foundation, Oxford 1982).

Lamb, D. and Lumsden, A.: Intraepithelial mast cells in human airway epithelium: Evidence for smoking-induced changes in their frequency. Thorax 37: 334 (1982).

Lee, D.A.; Winslow, N.R.; Speight, A.N.P. and Hey, E.N.: Prevalence and spectrum of asthma in childhood. British Medical Journal 286: 1256 (1983).

Lewis, R.A. and Austen, K.F.: Mediation of local homeostasis and inflammation by leukotrienes and other mast cell-dependent compounds. Nature 293: 103 (1981).

Lewis, R.A.; Drazen, J.M.; Austen, K.F.; Clark, D.A. and Corey, E.J.: Identification of the C(6)-5-conjugate of leukotriene A with cysteine as a naturally occurring slow reacting substance of anaphylaxis (SRS-A). Importance of the 11-cis-geometry for biological activity. Biochemical and Biophysical Research Communications 96: 271 (1980).

Lewis, R.A.; Soter, N.A.; Diamond, P.T.; Austen, K.F.; Oates, J.A. and Roberts II, J.L.: Prostaglandin D_2 generation after activation of rat and human mast cells with anti IgE. Journal of Immunology 129: 1627 (1982).

Mann, J.S.; Renwick, A.G. and Holgate, S.T.: Antigen bronchial provocation causes an increase in plasma adenosine levels in asthma. Clinical Science 65: 22P (1983).

Marom, Z.; Shelhamer, J.H. and Kaliner, M.: The effects of arachidonic acid, monohydroxyeicosatetraenoic acid and prostaglandins on the release of mucous glycoproteins from human airways in vitro. Journal of Clinical Investigation 67: 1695 (1981).

Mills, J.E.; Sellick, H. and Widdicombe, J.G.: Activity of lung irritant receptors in pulmonary microembolism, anaphylaxis and drug-induced bronchoconstrictions. Journal of Physiology 203: 337 (1969).

Mortagy, A.; Howell, J.B. and Waters, E.L.: Personal communication (1984).

Nadel, J.A.: Neurophysiologic aspects of asthma; in Austen K.F. and Lichtenstein L.M. (Eds) Asthma: Physiology, Immunopharmacology and Treatment, p.29 (Academic Press, New York, London 1973).

Nagy, L.; Lee, T.H. and Kay, A.B.: Neutrophil chemotactic activity in antigen-induced late asthmatic reactions. New England Journal of Medicine 306: 497 (1982).

Newball, H.H. and Lichtenstein, L.M.: Mast cells and basophils-effector cells of inflammatory disorders in the lung. Thorax 36: 721 (1981).

Norn, S.; Stahl Skov, P.; Jensen, C.; Koch, C.; Permin, H.; Bog-Hansen, T.C.; Lowenstein, H. and Hoiby, N.: Intrinsic asthma and bacterial histamine release via lectin effect. Agents and Actions 13: 210 (1983).

Platshon, L.F. and Kaliner, M.: The effects of the immunological release of histamine upon human lung cyclic nucleotide levels and prostaglandin generation. Journal of Clinical Investigation 62: 1113 (1978).

Razin, E.; Mencia-Heuerta, J.-M.; Stevens, R.L.; Lewis, R.A.; Lia, F.-T.; Coney, E.J. and Austen, K.F.: IgE-mediated release of leukotriene C_4, chondroitin sulfate E proteoglycan, and β-hexosaminidase from cultured bone marrow-derived mast cells. Journal of Experimental Medicine 157: 189 (1983).

Samuelsson, B.: The leukotrienes: Role in allergy; in Kerr J.W. and Ganderton M.A. (Eds) Proceedings of the XIth International Congress of Allergology and Clinical Immunology, p.23 (Macmillan Press Ltd, London 1983).

Schwartz, L.B.: Tryptase from human pulmonary mast cells; in Kay A.B.; Lichtenstein, L.M. and Austen, K.F. (Eds) Asthma: Physiology, Immunopharmacology and Treatment, vol. 3. In press (Academic Press, New York and London 1984).

Schwartz, L.B.; Kawahara, M.S.; Hugli, T.E.; Vik, D.; Fearon, D.T. and Austen, K.F.: Generation of C3a anaphylatoxin from human C3 by human mast cell tryptase. Journal of Immunology 130: 1891 (1983).

Solley, G.O.; Gleich, G.J.; Jordon, R.E. and Schroeter, A.L.: The late phase of the immediate wheal and flare skin reaction. Its dependence upon IgE antibodies. Journal of Clinical Investigation 58: 408 (1976).

Souhrada, M. and Souhrada, J.F.: The direct effect of temperature on airway smooth muscle. Respiratory Physiology 44: 311 (1981).

Stanworth, D.R.: IgG_4 antibodies in atopics and their families; in Kerr, J.W. and Ganderton, M.A. (Eds) proceedings of the XIth International Congress of Allergology and Clinical Immunology, p.337 (Macmillan Press Ltd, London 1983).

Steel, L. and Kaliner, M.: Prostaglandin-generating factor of anaphylaxis: Identification and isolation. Journal of Biological Chemistry 256: 12692 (1981).

Stimler, N.P.; Bloor, C.M. and Hugli, T.E.: Immunopharmacology of complement anaphylatoxins in the lung; in Newball, H.H. (Ed.) Immunopharmacology of the Lung. Lung Biology in Health and Disease, vol. 19, p.401 (Marcel Dekker Inc., New York 1983).

Szczeklik, A.: Aspirin and asthma. European Journal of Respiratory Diseases 63: 376 (1982).

White, J. and Eiser, N.M.: The role of histamine and its receptors in the pathogenesis of asthma. British Journal of Diseases of the Chest 77: 215 (1983).

Widdicombe, J.G.: Mediators and reflex bronchoconstriction. European Journal of Respiratory Diseases 64 (Suppl 129): 65 (1983).

Chapter II

Pharmacology of Bronchodilators

Gillian M. Shenfield, R.N. Brogden and A. Ward

For the purpose of this book bronchodilators have been defined as drugs with an anti-bronchoconstrictor effect. This is a readily demonstrated short term action and excludes drugs such as sodium cromoglycate (cromolyn sodium) and corticosteroids, which might with some justification be viewed as indirect bronchodilators in that their long term use may maintain airway patency. There are, therefore, three pharmacological groups to be discussed:

1) Adrenoceptor agonist drugs
2) Anticholinergic (antimuscarinic) drugs
3) Methylxanthines.

Historical Overview

The story of modern bronchodilator therapy began in 1900 when the use of adrenal extract to treat asthma was first described (Solis-Cohen, 1900). In 1924, ephedrine was introduced into Western medicine although its parent plant had been known to the Chinese for more than 5000 years. These drugs stimulated both α- and β-adrenoceptors which were defined by Ahlquist in 1948. Bronchodilatation is mediated by β-receptors and isoprenaline (isoproterenol) was the first adrenoceptor agonist to have exclusively β actions. It proved to be an extremely effective bronchodilator but had the disadvantage of producing cardiac stimulation also.

In 1967, Lands and his colleagues showed that β-adrenoceptors could be divided into β_1 and β_2 subgroups with the β_1-receptors being responsible for both chronotropic and inotropic effects on the heart and the β_2-adrenoceptors mediating bronchodilatation. A series of new agents was developed with relative 'selectivity', i.e. they have much greater effects on β_2-adrenoceptors than on β_1-adrenoceptors.

All of these drugs may be administered by inhalation and many of them can also be prescribed for oral or intravenous delivery. They have very similar actions and effects as bronchodilators but, as will be discussed later, they differ from one another in the way in which they are metabolised.

The success of the relatively selective β_2-adrenoceptor stimulants led to their widespread use as primary and often exclusive therapy for asthma in Britain, Europe and Australasia at a time when they were not available in the United States. Approval by the FDA was further delayed by epidemiological reports of increased death rates in asthma. These appeared to parallel sales of isoprenaline aerosols and a cause and effect relationship was assumed. Retrospective analysis suggests that some deaths may have been due to an unjustified reliance on the aerosols with an associated failure to seek medical help at an early stage.

A consequence of this delay was that until comparatively recently American physicians had available only adrenaline (epinephrine), ephedrine, isoprenaline, isoetharine, orciprenaline (metaproterenol) and theophylline as bronchodilators for the treatment of obstructive airways disease. During this time the use of theophylline was studied extensively in both adults and children and a relationship between the plasma theophylline concentration and its therapeutic and toxic effects was clearly established. This led to more rational use of theophylline and it became the mainstay of bronchodilator therapy in the United States. This situation is now changing as some of the selective β_2-adrenoceptor agonists are now marketed in the United States (see appendix B) although they are often used as adjuncts to theophylline therapy. Physicians elsewhere have tended to restrict the use of methylxanthines to intravenous aminophylline in severe asthma but, learning from the American experience, there is now some increase in the use of oral theophylline. The recent introduction of a variety of slow-release theophylline preparations which provide more consistent plasma drug concentrations and possibly fewer side effects, has also contributed to a wider use of theophylline.

Extracts of *Atropa belladonna* and *Datura stramonium* have been used in the treatment of asthma for several centuries. They were usually inhaled and 'asthma cigarettes', which contained related compounds, were available until very recently. Atropine was isolated in pure form in 1831 and has been used sporadically in the treatment of airways obstruction. Recent interest in the vagal control of airway function and the development of more selective drugs has resulted in a resurgence in the use of anticholinergic (more specifically antimuscarinic) drugs. Ipratropium bromide* is at present the most widely used of this group.

Mechanisms of Action of Bronchodilators

Anticholinergics

Bronchial asthma is associated with diffuse obstruction of the airway lumen. The nerve supply to the bronchi is from the parasympathetic nervous system via the vagus nerve. Reflex vagal activity has been proposed as a major component of bronchoconstriction in asthma but the exact role of the vagus has not been clarified (see p.11). The transmitter substance is acetylcholine and this, and its analogues, will cause bronchoconstriction. Atropine is a competitive antagonist of acetylcholine and will produce relaxation of bronchial smooth muscle and hence bronchodilatation. It also inhibits bronchoconstriction caused by dust and by histamine or cough reflexes in animals (Widdicombe et al., 1962; Simonsson et al., 1967).

Adrenoceptor Agonists

By contrast, there is little direct sympathetic innervation of human bronchial muscle although there are many β-adrenoceptors in bronchial smooth muscle. These are predominantly β_2-adrenoceptors but recent work in both animals and man suggests that there may also be a few β_1-adrenoceptors present (Engel, 1981). Stimulation of bronchial muscle by a β-agonist produces bronchodilatation. Figure 2.1 illustrates these opposing processes and indicates that they are believed to be mediated via the cyclic nu-

---

* For product availability in the USA, see appendix B.

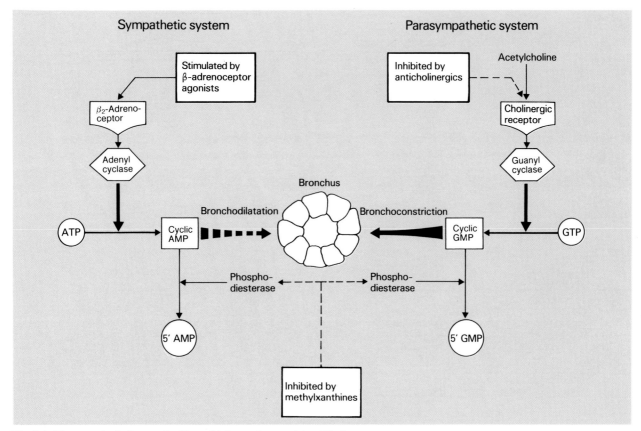

Fig. 2.1. Pharmacological control of bronchial muscle tone (simplified).

cleotides. Extensive biochemical studies have suggested that the β-receptor is closely related to adenyl cyclase and that the key substance in producing a dilator response is cyclic 3,5-adenosine monophosphate (cyclic AMP). Bronchoconstriction appears to be mediated by another nucleotide – cyclic guanosine 5-monophosphate (cyclic GMP).

The Molecular Pharmacology of the β-Agonists

Recent radioligand binding studies have increased our understanding of the mechanisms by which β-adrenoceptor agonists activate adenyl cyclase (Lefkowitz et al., 1981). These have shown that:

1) The formation of a receptor high affinity state (HRX) is a functional intermediate in the mechanism of hormonal activation of adenyl cyclase

2) Guanine nucleotides have an important role and that guanine nucleotide destabilisation of HRX results in the stimulation of adenyl cyclase; and

3) The intrinsic activity of an agonist correlates with its ability to stabilise the intermediate HRX.

It is proposed that there are three molecular components of the adenyl cyclase system; the receptors (R), the nucleotide regulatory proteins (N), and the catalytic moiety (C) and that these exist in active and inactive states (Lefkowitz et al., 1981). Figure 2.2 shows the general model for β-adrenergic agonist activation. The cycles of activation/inactivation of the components are shown

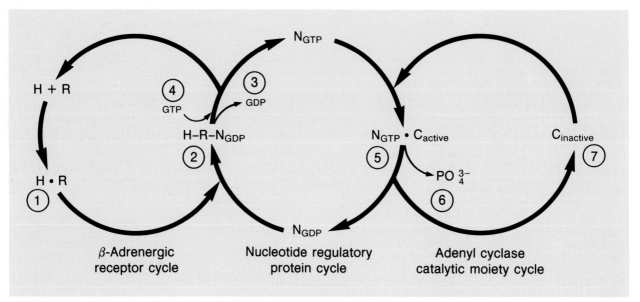

Fig. 2.2. Scheme for a proposed mechanism of adenyl cyclase activation by β-adrenergic agonists and GTP. The agonist (H) interacts with the receptor (R) and forms a binary complex HR (1); binding to the receptor promotes formation of a complex with the nucleotide regulatory proteins, HRN (2) and loss of tightly bound inhibitory GDP (3); GTP interacts with and stabilises HRN, freeing HR and N_{GTP} (4); N_{GTP} associates with the catalytic moiety (C) to form activated adenyl cyclase (5) which catalyses the conversion of ATP to cyclic AMP (6); $N_{GTP}C$ is hydrolysed (7) and the components return to the baseline state (after Lefkowitz et al., 1981, with permission).

as being interlocking and the nucleotide regulatory proteins are the crucial element coupling the receptor cycle to the cyclase cycle. In the membranes, at rest, each of the components is in its inactive state.

Methylxanthines

There is general agreement that the above mechanisms operate in both animals and man. However, the previously accepted mode of action of methylxanthines (also included in fig. 2.1) has recently been challenged. It has been known for many years that the methylxanthines inhibit phosphodiesterase and increase intracellular cyclic AMP concentration. It was assumed that this was the mechanism by which bronchodilatation was produced but there are now several reasons to doubt this. Firstly, the inhibitory action of phosphodiesterase is seen only at much higher concentrations of theophylline than those normally achieved therapeutically (Bergstrand, 1980) and *in vitro* studies have demonstrated a direct bronchial smooth muscle dilating action of theophylline. Also many drugs, e.g. dipyridamole, which have greater phosphodiesterase inhibitory activity than theopylline do not bronchodilate. Finally, as figure 2.1 indicates, inhibition of phosphodiesterase may also cause an increase in the bronchoconstrictor substance cyclic GMP. This might not be a problem since there is a range of different phosphodiesterases with different responses to drugs (Svedmyr and Simonsson, 1978).

Possible Mechanisms of Methylxanthine Bronchodilatation

Thus, the explanation for the bronchodilating effect of the methylxanthines in asthma is not known with certainty, but several other mechanisms have been proposed:
- Adenosine receptor blockade (Fredholm, 1980). At therapeutic concentrations theophylline is a potent adenosine receptor ant-

agonist (Andersson and Persson, 1980) but although this mechanism may account for the central nervous system stimulation, tremor and diuretic effects of theophylline it appears unimportant for bronchodilatation (Svedmyr, 1981). Recent new drug development has suggested that the bronchodilating effect of methylxanthines may be independent of adenosine antagonism (Persson, 1982).

● Stimulation of endogenous catecholamine release. Studies in animals and man have shown that theophylline increases adrenomedullary secretion of adrenaline and noradrenaline (Berkowitz and Spector, 1971; Higbee et al., 1982). Although it is possible that increased plasma catecholamines cause some of the pharmacological side effects of theophylline such as tremor and cardiovascular stimulation, further studies are needed to establish whether this is an additional mechanism for the therapeutic effect in asthma.

● Increase in the number and efficacy of suppressor T cells. In a group of asthmatic children with a significantly decreased number of suppressor T cells, one month's treatment with theophylline restored the number to normal (Shohat et al., 1983). The increase in suppressor T-cell levels after theophylline correlated with an improvement in asthma symptoms. It was suggested that theophylline probably restores the normal immune balance in asthmatic children by correcting the lack of suppressor T cells (Shohat et al., 1983). However, the role of suppressor T cell dysfunction in asthma remains controversial (Harper et al., 1980) and there is no direct evidence of a causative relationship between T cells and the actions of theophylline.

● Prostaglandin inhibition. Methylxanthines have been shown to antagonise the effect, but not the synthesis or release of prostaglandins PGE_2 and $PGF_{2\alpha}$ on smooth muscle in vitro (Horrobin, 1977). However, there is no evidence that prostaglandin inhibition is the mechanism by which methylxanthines produce bronchodilatation.

● Antagonism of calcium mediated processes of smooth muscle contraction and release of histamine and leukotrienes from mast cells. The principal elements of asthma – smooth muscle contraction, mast cell mediator secretion, mucous gland secretion, and vagal reflex activity – are all ultimately calcium-related phenomena. Middleton (1980) proposed that effective asthma drug therapy must reduce calcium availability to the essential contractile, secretory, and vagus nerve functions. The smooth muscle relaxant effects of theophylline have been attributed to increased calcium uptake into smooth muscle cells (Kolbeck et al., 1977) and the mechanism by which theophylline inhibits mediator release from mast cells may be due to altered extracellular calcium concentrations (Foreman et al., 1975) although this has been discounted by Sydbom and Fredholm (1982).

Other Actions of Bronchodilator Drugs

Vascular Effects

In asthma bronchoconstriction is a major element of diffuse airways obstruction (see p.2) and it is likely that bronchial muscle relaxation is the primary action of bronchodilator drugs although other actions such as inhibition of mast cell mediator release may play a role.

Bronchial wall oedema may be an additional cause of airway narrowing in asthma although little is known regarding either the frequency of occurrence of oedema during asthmatic attacks or its intensity and distribution along the bronchial tree. It might appear that adrenaline, with α-adrenoceptor vasconstricting activity, would be better than the other drugs at decreasing bronchial oedema because of its constrictor effect on arterioles. However, it also causes venous constriction and this effect could negate or even supersede any beneficial effect of arterial constriction. The result might be a worsening of tissue oedema and, certainly in clinical studies, adrenaline has never been shown to have any advantages over other adrenoceptor agonists in relieving airway obstruction. It is, therefore, theoretically possible that the vasodilatory effects of all the other bronchodilator drugs could be of benefit in the reversal of bronchial oedema produced by mediators. This would be the case if their effect on veins exceeded that on arterioles and there is some evidence to support this (Paterson et al., 1979).

Clearance of Mucus Secretion

In patients with stable asthma, a slowing of tracheal mucus velocity has been reported and thick sticky mucus is frequently found post mortem in the airways of asthmatic patients. The retention of viscous mucus is one cause of continuing obstruction in the small airways of some patients between attacks. Most of the bronchodilator drugs have some effects on mucus secretion or mucociliary clearance although the clinical significance of these effects has not been clearly defined. There is some evidence from animal studies that anticholinergic drugs reduce mucus secretion but they also impair mucociliary transport, and atropine has been shown to inhibit production of tracheobronchial secretions and decrease sputum volume (Lopez-Vidriero et al., 1977).

β_2-Adrenoceptor agonists stimulate mucus secretion and mucociliary transport in normal subjects and in patients with chronic bronchitis. The clinical significance of these properties for asthmatics is debatable and a recent study using inhaled terbutaline failed to show any enhancement of mucociliary clearance in a group of mild stable asthmatics (Bateman et al., 1983). The methylxanthines also increase the frequency of ciliary beating and stimulate mucus production in animals but no studies have yet been done in man.

Adrenoceptor Agonists

The structures of many of the numerous drugs in this category are shown in appendix A. The principal pharmacological and metabolic effects of stimulating α-, β_1- and β_2-receptors are shown in table 2.1. Both functionally and historically these drugs should be considered in three groups:

1) Drugs with α and β activity, e.g. adrenaline
2) Drugs with β_1 and β_2 activity only, e.g. isoprenaline
3) Drugs with predominantly β_2 activity, e.g. salbutamol (albuterol).

The rationale behind the development of these drugs has been to produce increasing selectivity of agonistic effect and to prolong the duration of action. The structure of the molecules has been modified to produce selectivity and alterations have been made to the metabolic pathways of the drugs. As a consequence, there have been major changes in the duration of action of the drugs and in

Table 2.1. The principal pharmacological and metabolic effects of α- and β-adrenoceptor agonists

Tissue or metabolic process	α effect	β_1 effect	β_2 effect
Smooth muscle			
Bronchial muscle	Constriction		Relaxation
Uterine muscle	Contraction		Relaxation
Alimentary tract	Contraction of sphincters Decreased motility and tone		Decreased motility and tone
Peripheral blood vessels	Constriction		Dilatation
Skeletal muscle (tremor)			Increased
Cardiac muscle		Increased chronotropic and inotropic effects	
Biochemical properties			
Glycogenolysis			Stimulated
Glycolysis			Stimulated
Lipolysis	Inhibited	Stimulated	
Insulin secretion	Inhibited		Stimulated
Lactic acidaemia			Stimulated

the routes by which they may be administered. These factors are, of course, closely interrelated but the general principles will be briefly discussed separately and the pharmacodynamic and pharmacokinetic characteristics of drugs in this group will be described in greater detail.

Selectivity

Adrenaline, the first adrenoceptor agonist to be used for asthma, has both α and β activity. Although it is an effective bronchodilator, the side effects caused by its α and β_1 actions – anxiety, tremor, hypertension, tachycardia, palpitations and cardiac arrhythmias – are undesirable. Ephedrine also has α-adrenoceptor activity since it acts principally by releasing noradrenaline from sympathetic nerve terminals. It also has a small direct action on both α- and β-receptors and its clinical effects are similar to those of adrenaline. Ephedrine's lack of selectivity and side effects limit its usefulness and it has been superseded by newer drugs and should no longer be used to treat airways obstruction.

The pharmaceutical industry has concentrated on producing molecules with exclusively β-adrenoceptor agonist activity (appendix A). Isoprenaline, the first such drug, was described in 1940. It has no α activity and proved to be an extremely potent bronchodilator, but has equal activity at β_1 and β_2 receptors. Table 2.2 outlines the 'receptor activity' of some of the adrenoceptor agonists but it must be understood that selectivity is always a relative property. The very marked β_2-selectivity of drugs such as salbutamol in isolated tissues is much less apparent in intact man because of reflex changes *in vivo*. At high plasma concentration any of the 'selective' drugs will produce cardiac stimulation and this effect is frequently seen with intravenous bolus administration of drugs such as salbutamol (Paterson et al., 1971).

Metabolism

Adrenaline is a naturally occurring catecholamine and therefore is rapidly and extensively metabolised and inactivated. Major mechanisms terminating its pharmacological effect are uptake into sympathetic nerve endings (uptake 1) and into any sympathetically innervated tissues, particularly smooth muscle (uptake 2). In the

Table 2.2. Selectivity and relative efficacy of some adrenoceptor agonists

Drug	Routes of administration			Relative efficacy *in vitro*[1] (compared with isoprenaline)	Mechanism of action (selectivity)		
	injection	inhalation	oral		β_2	β_1	α
Ephedrine			✓	0.5	✓	✓	✓✓✓
Catecholamines							
Adrenaline	✓	✓		0.7	✓✓✓	✓✓✓	✓✓✓
Isoprenaline	✓	✓	✓	1.0	✓✓✓	✓✓✓	
Isoetharine		✓	✓	0.6	✓✓✓	✓✓	
Rimiterol	✓	✓		0.6	✓✓✓	✓	
Hexoprenaline	✓	✓	✓	0.6	✓✓✓	✓	
Resorcinol derivatives							
Orciprenaline	✓	✓	✓	0.7	✓✓✓	✓✓	
Terbutaline	✓	✓	✓	0.8	✓✓✓	✓	
Fenoterol	✓	✓		0.9	✓✓✓	✓	
Saligenin derivatives							
Salbutamol	✓	✓	✓	0.8	✓✓✓	✓	
Salmefamol[2]	✓	✓	✓	0.9	✓✓✓	✓	

1 – In man β-agonists are equally efficacious.
2 – Never been marketed.

nerve endings the major route of metabolism is oxidation by monoamine oxidase (MAO) to 3,4-dihydroxymandelic acid. In tissues innervated by sympathetic nerves, catechol-*O*-methyltransferase (COMT) is the dominant enzyme. This converts adrenaline to 3-*O*-methyladrenaline. The combined effect of both enzymes is to form 3-methoxy-4-hydroxymandelic acid (VMA). The enzymes MAO and COMT are widely distributed in organs such as gut, liver, kidney and lung.

By contrast, the next drug to be developed, ephedrine, is not a catechol and is therefore resistant to COMT. An additional methyl group on the α carbon also makes it resistant to MAO. Its kinetics are therefore very different to those of adrenaline. All the other drugs listed in table 2.2 have substituent groups on their amine head and are therefore resistant to MAO. The majority are also resistant to COMT but isoprenaline, isoetharine, rimiterol and hexoprenaline are all catechols and are metabolised by COMT. Hexoprenaline appears to be metabolised more slowly than isoprenaline and its 3-*O*-methyl metabolite is probably an active bronchodilator whereas the 3-*O*-methyl metabolite of isoprenaline is not.

In addition to these rapid phase 1 types of metabolism, all the drugs, other than adrenaline, undergo slower phase 2 metabolism or conjugation. This is mainly to sulphates or glucuronides and takes place in both the liver (the main site) and the gut wall. There is also evidence that if drugs are given by inhalation some metabolism may occur in the lung. Thus, isoprenaline and rimiterol are metabolised by COMT in the lung but salbutamol and terbutaline are not metabolised by the lung, probably because the lung does not have the potential to perform conjugation reactions. There is also evidence that salmefamol undergoes some form of metabolism in the lung (Shenfield et al., 1976).

Relationship of Route of Administration, Metabolism and Duration of Action

Drugs which are metabolised by MAO or COMT are relatively ineffective when given orally because they are metabolised in the gut wall and liver. In addition, the bioavailability of oral isoprenaline is reduced by its sulphation in the gut wall. Ephedrine, together with the resorcinol and saligenin derivatives, may be given orally (table 2.2). All the drugs in this group (except ephedrine for reasons of formulation) may be given by inhalation or by intravenous injection. The latter route allows the catechol drugs to circulate and reach the lungs before being metabolised by COMT. The inhalation route, of course, allows direct delivery to the bronchi before any metabolism can occur.

It is also clear that unless metabolites are active, as in the case of hexoprenaline, the drugs that undergo phase 1 metabolism will have shorter half-lives and thus shorter duration of action than the other compounds. As will be discussed later, the bronchodilating effects of compounds such as salbutamol last very much longer than those of drugs such as isoprenaline.

Thus, by making structural changes to produce selectivity, the pharmaceutical industry has synthesised drugs such as salbutamol which may be given by various routes and has a prolonged duration of action. The newer drugs do, therefore, have several additional advantages.

Properties of the Individual Drugs

Before discussing the comparative properties of the adrenoceptor agonists it is necessary to define the terminology that will be used:

1) Potency is the amount of drug necessary to produce a given effect.

2) Efficacy is the maximal effect that can be produced by a drug.

In figure 2.3, which shows stylised log-dose response curves, drug A is more potent than either drugs B or C because it produces its peak effect at a lower dose than the other two drugs. However, drugs A and B are equally efficacious and both have greater efficacy than drug C, which never achieves the same peak effect as the others, even at very high doses. These differences are of critical importance in comparing drugs, since what matters for clinical use is always the efficacy. In general, drugs are marketed in equipotent doses which is why the actual dose in milligrams or grams often varies widely.

3) Pharmacokinetics is the science of describing the processes of absorption, metabolism, distribution and excretion of a drug, i.e. it is what the patient does to the drug.

4) Pharmacodynamics describes the effects (desirable or undesirable) produced by the drug, i.e. it is what the drug does to the patient.

Assessing Clinical Trials

Great care is needed when interpreting studies making comparisons between different drugs in this group as there are problems both with pharmacological aspects of drug delivery and the physiological aspects of patient response. In order to make true comparisons the drugs should be given in equipotent doses and by the same route. If the chosen route of administration is by inhalation then comparable devices should be used. Only 10% of the dose from a metered pressurised aerosol is inhaled, the rest being

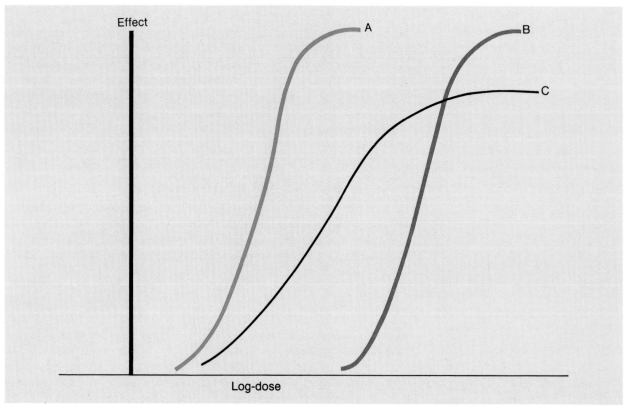

Fig. 2.3. Stylised dose-response curves for the bronchodilator effects of 3 drugs to illustrate the difference between potency and efficacy.

swallowed (Davies, 1975). With a nebuliser a similar proportion of the dose will enter the lungs, although this will vary with the type of nebuliser and the way in which it is used (Shenfield et al., 1974; Cushley et al., 1983; see p.86). Very little drug is swallowed following nebulisation; most is lost in the apparatus and atmosphere.

Airways obstruction is by definition a variable condition and care must always be taken to match subjects. Even the same subject may respond very differently on different days. It has been observed that in many attacks an inhaled β_2-agonist does not completely reverse airways obstruction.

The pattern of response to bronchodilators in relation to basal lung function has been described as 'bell-shaped' (Hume and Gandevia, 1957). This is because response is poor when lung function is greatly impaired, maximal when lung function is about 50% reduced and falls again at better levels of lung function simply because there is less potential room for improvement. As a result, clinical estimates of both efficacy and selectivity will vary according to the severity of airways obstruction in the individual being studied. Trial patients should be carefully selected and precautions such as ensuring that the patients are capable of responding to bronchodilators and that baseline values vary by no more than 15% on different study days should be taken.

Efficacy

When assessing the efficacy of adrenoceptor agonists, isoprenaline is usually taken as the standard for comparison. Although *in vitro* results (table 2.2) suggest that isoprenaline has a greater efficacy than other β-agonists, efficacy in man has not been shown to be different for any β-agonist.

It should be emphasised that in clinical practice potency is irrelevant since the dose of each drug is adjusted accordingly. Any claim that a drug has an advantage because of its greater potency should be countered by a request for information about its efficacy in relation to isoprenaline or one of the β_2-selective agonist drugs.

Table 2.2 also indicates the relative selectivities of the various agents. Selectivity in man is often very different from that demonstrated in animals. This may be due to the compensatory reflex mechanisms which exist in man rather than to any direct cardiac stimulating effect of the drugs. The response to β_2-mediated vasodilatation *in vivo* is a fall in blood pressure which induces reflex vagal withdrawal and tachycardia. Studies in man suggest that salbutamol, terbutaline and rimiterol are equally β_2-selective while orciprenaline and fenoterol are slightly less selective (Gray et al., 1982; Kennedy and Simpson, 1969).

Routes of Administration and Duration of Action

Inhalation

The number of routes by which bronchodilators may be given (see appendix B) is dependent on their metabolism; this in turn greatly influences both their pharmacokinetics and pharmacodynamics. The clinical advantages of the inhaled route are considered elsewhere (chapters IV and V) but there are clear pharmacodynamic advantages. By delivering drugs directly into the target organ, a much more rapid effect is achieved (fig. 2.4). When given by inhalation all β-agonists achieve a measurable bronchodilator effect within 5 minutes, and by 10 minutes, 80 to 90% of the maximal response has usually been achieved. The onset of action is usually slightly faster with isoprenaline and rimiterol.

Metered dose pressurised aerosols are by far the most popular and effective way of giving inhaled bronchodilators. Even though only 10% of the dose reaches the lungs this produces near maximal bronchodilation in most subjects. However, pressurised aerosols do require a certain degree of coordination and sufficient inspiratory flow. Some pharmaceutical companies are now marketing 'spacer' devices which both simplify the inhalation process and increase drug delivery to the lung (appendix C).

In certain circumstances 'spacer' devices can be of benefit in both adults and children, particularly in the management of an acute attack when nebuliser therapy is unavailable (see p.179). In general some form of wet nebulisation is preferable for small children, adults who cannot use other devices, or very sick patients. More recently, dry powder inhaler devices have been introduced for β_2-agonists. Although these devices have not been shown to have any clinical benefit over aerosol preparations [higher doses may be required because of different deposition profiles in the bronchial tree (Hartley et al., 1977)], they can be used by many patients who are unable to operate aerosols correctly (Crompton, 1982).

The advantage of giving bronchodilators by inhalation is that they do not have to be distributed to the rest of the body and therefore may be given in very much smaller doses. In general the dose from 1 puff of a metered aerosol is 40 times less than the oral dose necessary to produce equivalent bronchodilatation. This

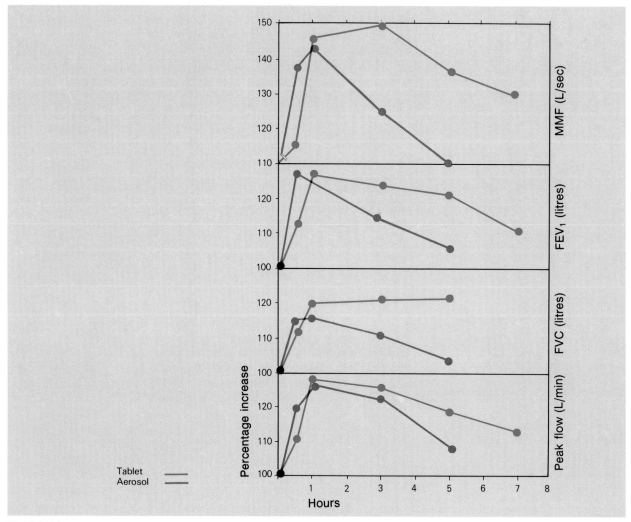

Fig. 2.4. Mean percentage changes from control value (taken as 100%) in peak flow, forced vital capacity (FVC), forced expiratory volume in 1 second (FEV₁) and maximum mid-expiratory flow rate (MMF) after fenoterol, tablet (5mg) and aerosol (200μg) [Plit et al., 1972].

has been termed 'therapeutic selectivity' as opposed to pharmacological selectivity (Paterson and Shenfield, 1974). The major advantage to the patient is a considerable reduction in side effects. With the exception of minor degrees of tremor these are very rare after aerosol delivery. They are more commonly seen after nebulised drug delivery, principally because the dose used is considerably higher than that from a pressurised aerosol.

The duration of action of bronchodilators after inhalation varies greatly but depends mainly on the dose given. The catecholamines have a shorter duration of action than the saligenin or resorcinol derivatives.

Intravenous Administration

Many of the selective drugs may be given intravenously and adrenaline, terbutaline and salbutamol can be given subcutaneously (appendix B, table III). A β_2-selective drug is now the treatment of choice in the emergency therapy of asthma (chapter X).

Intravenous drugs may be given by bolus injection or by infusion. Often a combination of the two is used to obtain a therapeutic plasma concentration quickly and to maintain it. This route of administration has the advantage of a rapid onset of action. There has also been a suggestion that by reaching the lungs via the systemic circulation, a drug will have a greater effect on small airways than if it is given by inhalation (Svedmyr and Simonsson, 1978). Whether this is of clinical importance remains to be determined.

The disadvantage of bolus injections is that very high early plasma concentrations are achieved which may produce quite marked side effects, e.g. tachycardia. The pharmacokinetics of the bolus injection are such that the drug is rapidly distributed throughout the body and effective plasma concentrations are available only for a short time. Thus, it is advisable to follow the bolus with a maintenance infusion if this is the desired route of administration. Details of specific administration regimens are discussed in chapter X.

Oral Administration

The oral administration of bronchodilators may result in a greater effect on small airways compared to the inhaled route, but the place of this route of administration in the maintenance therapy of asthma is probably limited and is discussed in chapters IV and V. The pharmacokinetics and quantitative pharmacodynamics of orally administered drugs are very different from those of the same drugs when given by other routes.

After oral administration, improvement in pulmonary function parallels the plasma drug concentration. Thus, in the case of salbutamol, peak bronchodilatation occurs between 2 and 4 hours after ingestion, at the same time as peak plasma concentrations (Paterson and Shenfield, 1974). The duration of action is determined by the pharmacokinetics of the individual drug. It varies from 2 to 4 hours for the non-catecholamine selective β_2-agonists, but is less with orciprenaline and considerably shorter for catecholamines such as rimiterol. Side effects are greater after oral therapy than after inhalation simply because of the higher plasma concentrations that are achieved (fig. 2.5).

Bronchodilator Response

Despite animal work suggesting that some β-agonists may have a greater maximum bronchodilator response than others, there is no evidence that this occurs in man, i.e. bronchodilator efficacy appears to be similar. Differences resulting from variable disease states or individual patient factors are likely to be considerably greater than any differences between drugs.

Side Effects

Other than hypersensitivity reactions, which are extremely rare with this group of drugs, the side effects are a predictable extension of their pharmacology. The frequency of side effects is directly proportional to the plasma concentrations achieved and therefore depends on route of administration as well as on selectivity. Side effects, such as hyperglycaemia, hypokalaemia and hyperinsulinaemia. Hypertension, an α-effect, is produced by adrenaline and monest complaint is skeletal muscle tremor. As this is a β_2 effect it occurs with all available drugs in this group, as will metabolic effects, such as hyperglycaemia, hypokalaemia and hyperinsulinaemia. Hypertension, an α-effect, is produced by adrenaline and ephedrine. Although cardiac effects are more common with the non-selective agents, tachycardia will occur with selective agents

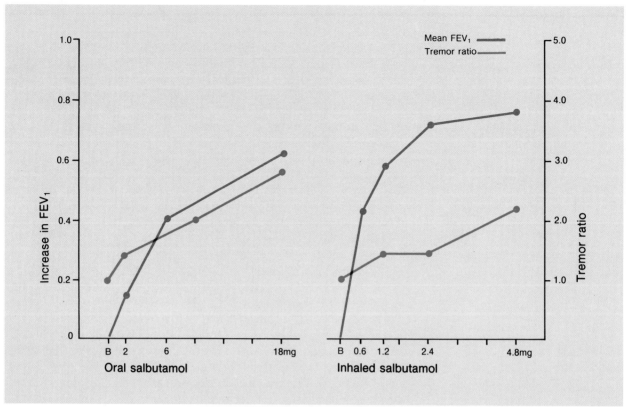

Fig. 2.5. Effects on the mean FEV₁ and tremor ratios of increasing oral and inhaled doses of salbutamol (Larsson and Svedmyr, 1977).

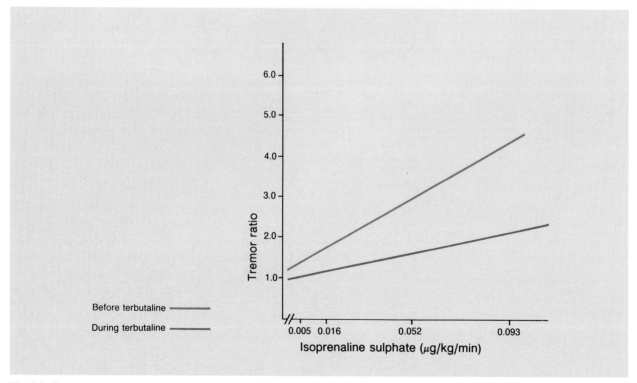

Fig. 2.6. Tremor response to isoprenaline sulphate infusion recorded before and during terbutaline therapy (after Larsson et al., 1977).

at high plasma concentrations. Thus, a β-selective drug should be the treatment of choice, given by inhalation whenever possible.

Effects on Arterial Oxygen Tension

Asthma is associated with considerable ventilation-perfusion imbalance. This phenomenon of ventilation-perfusion inequality, termed the shunt effect, results in low PaO_2 and hypoxaemia.

All bronchodilators have been reported to decrease arteriolar PaO_2 (Paterson and Clark, 1971) but β-agonists have two pharmacological actions which may affect PaO_2 in different directions. Firstly, they may decrease PaO_2 by causing pulmonary vasodilatation, which increases perfusion of the poorly ventilated areas and thus increases the shunt effect. Secondly, β-agonists will increase cardiac output and decrease peripheral resistance (Iodice et al., 1980) and providing the shunt remains constant, this will increase PaO_2. The net effect on PaO_2 will be the balance of these two effects.

The significance of any bronchodilator-induced fall in PaO_2 will depend on the initial oxygen tension of the patient. In patients with an initially low PaO_2 the fall in oxygen tension with the β-agonists may produce dangerous hypoxaemia and oxygen should always be given concurrently with bronchodilator therapy in severe acute asthma (chapter X). There is little evidence that any one drug is safer than another in this respect.

Tolerance (Tachyphylaxis)

It has been postulated for over 20 years that β-agonist drugs might cause worsening of asthma by inducing 'resistance' to their own action. The ultimate outcome of this process would be asthma completely unresponsive to both endogenous and exogenous β-stimulation. A reduced bronchodilator response following long term administration of β-agonists has been demonstrated in animals and *in vitro* studies suggest that tolerance might be a problem.

Using radioligand binding, measurements of β-receptor numbers on lymphocytes of both normal and asthmatic subjects showed a marked reduction following treatment with oral and inhaled β-agonists (Tashkin et al., 1982; Conolly et al., 1982; Galant et al.; 1978) and human bronchial smooth muscle strips showed tolerance to the relaxant effect of isoprenaline after incubation with isoprenaline for 1 hour (Davis and Conolly, 1980).

Although of considerable theoretical interest these results are not relevant to the clinical situation. Studies of the long term bronchodilator response of the airways of asthmatic subjects and the implications of the findings on clinical practice are discussed in chapter V. Interestingly, one study showed that following prolonged treatment with oral terbutaline the bronchodilator response was maintained but treatment did produce tolerance to isoprenaline-induced tremor (Larsson et al., 1977; fig. 2.6). This means that the effect could be a beneficial rather than a harmful one although the underlying mechanism is not fully understood.

Anticholinergic Drugs

Atropine (*dl* hyoscyamine) is a plant alkaloid occurring in *Atropa belladonna* (deadly nightshade) and in *Datura stramonium* (thornapple). It is an organic ester formed by the combination of an aromatic acid, tropic acid, and an organic base, tropine (appendix A). Atropine has been used for many years in the treatment of airways obstruction and is a competitive antagonist at muscarinic, cholinergic receptors. These are not only present in the smooth muscle of the bronchi but also in the gastrointestinal tract and in various secretory glands, including the pancreas and the salivary, lacrimal glands, bronchial and sweat glands. In addition, muscarinic receptors mediate pupillary constriction and ciliary muscle contraction in the eye and have effects on cardiac rate and conductivity.

The lack of selectivity of the atropine compounds has led to intensive efforts to discover similar drugs with more selective effects. Atropine as the sulphate is well absorbed when taken by mouth, most of the drug being excreted in the urine within 12 hours with approximately 15 to 50% excreted as unchanged atropine. The metabolites have not yet been identified. The quaternary ammonium compounds atropine methonitrate and ipratropium bromide (appendix A) differ from atropine mainly in their kinetics. They are poorly and unreliably absorbed after oral administration and do not cross the blood-brain barrier readily because of lower lipid solubility. They also have a more prolonged action than atropine sulphate.

Ipratropium bromide is the newest available anticholinergic agent and is now the most commonly used drug in this group. Only about 30% is absorbed after oral administration and, of this, 7% is excreted as unchanged drug. After intravenous administration in man, 70% of the dose is excreted in the urine (Pakes et al., 1980). As with atropine, the major metabolites have not been identified.

When ipratropium is given intravenously to the dog there appears to be some selectivity, as bronchodilatation occurs at approximately one-tenth of the dose required to cause inhibition of salivation and approximately one sixty-sixth of the dose required to cause tachycardia (Engelhardt and Klupp, 1975). In clinical practice these drugs are always given by inhalation which further increases the selectivity. This is the 'therapeutic selectivity' already described for β-adrenoceptor agonists and is clinically of great value.

Clinical Efficacy

If reflex vagal bronchoconstriction is important in asthma, anticholinergic drugs should be effective treatment. In experimental situations they are effective against cholinergic challenges but give little protection against serotonin- or histamine-induced bronchoconstriction. They are less effective than selective β_2-agonists or sodium cromoglycate in protecting against exercise-induced asthma (chapter VII).

Clinical studies have mainly used single doses and many suffer from problems of definition of diagnosis of individual patients. However, Altounyan made an important observation that has been confirmed by a number of other workers using both atropine preparations and ipratropium bromide (Altounyan, 1964; Ullah and Saunders, 1980). He found that in an exacerbation of extrinsic asthma in patients requiring steroid therapy, the response to atropine was very small when compared to the response to inhaled isoprenaline. When the same patient's asthma was in remission, the atropine response was restored.

A more recent extension of these findings has shown that even in their responsive phase, asthmatics (particularly those whose disease has an allergic component), will always respond better to a β_2-agonist than to an anticholinergic drug (Petrie and Palmer, 1975).

Table 2.3. Anhydrous theophylline content of various preparations

Preparation	Anhydrous theophylline content (%)
Various anhydrous theophylline preparations – tablet, capsule, elixir	100
Aminophylline	80
Choline theophyllinate (oxtriphylline)	65
Theophylline monohydrate	90
Theophylline calcium salicylate	48
Theophylline sodium glycinate	50
Theophylline monoethanolamine	75
Diprophylline (diphylline, glyphylline)	None[1]
Proxyphylline	None[2]

1 – Diprophylline is a stable theophylline derivative. It is excreted in the urine unchanged. It is about one-tenth as potent as theophylline w/w.
2 – Proxyphylline is also a stable theophylline derivative, about one-fifth as potent as theophylline w/w.

In contrast, chronic bronchitics will usually respond equally well to both groups of drugs (chapter XI; Crompton, 1968).

Routes of Administration

Ipratropium bromide is not given orally or by injection. It is available in pressurised metered dose aerosols and as a nebuliser solution.

Onset and Duration of Action

Even when given by inhalation, the onset of action of anticholinergic agents is slower than that of the β_2-agonists. It often takes 15 to 30 minutes to achieve appreciable bronchodilatation, and the peak effect may not be seen for up to 2 hours. This is an additional reason for using ipratropium in combination with a β_2-agonist and the usual recommendation is to use the anticholinergic agent second, after some bronchodilatation has been achieved with the β_2-agonist. Some combined metered dose inhaler preparations are now marketed but only if there is an advantage to the combination should a 'mixed' inhaler be prescribed (Shenfield, 1982).

Side Effects

In spite of the multisystem actions of anticholinergic agents, side effects are not a major problem because of the inhaled route of administration. As with β_2-agonists, nebulisation tends to lead to the use of higher doses and thus higher plasma concentrations, but side effects are still extremely uncommon. No significant decrease in bronchial secretions has been seen in long term studies and there is no tendency towards a higher incidence of bronchial infections. With the exception of transient local effects, e.g. dry mouth, 'scratching' in the trachea or an unpleasant taste, and the rare occurrence of bronchoconstriction (see p.176) adverse effects are uncommon with ipratropium bromide.

Methylxanthines

The methylxanthines are plant alkaloids of which a number, including caffeine, are available as therapeutic agents. Most methylxanthines are theophylline derivatives which either dissociate to, or are metabolised to theophylline *in vivo* (table 2.3).

Table 2.4. Factors altering theophylline clearance[1]

Increased clearance	Decreased clearance

Enzyme-inducing drugs, e.g.
    ethanol
    phenobarbitone
    rifampicin
    sulphinpyrazone, etc.
Tobacco
Marihuana
Barbecued meat
High protein, low carbohydrate diet
Youth
Cystic fibrosis
	Enzyme-inhibiting drugs, e.g.
	    cimetidine
	    oral contraceptives
	    β-blockers
	    erythromycin compounds
	    troleandomycin
	Caffeine
	
	High carbohydrate diet
	Obesity
	Age
	Antiviral vaccines

	Factors altering hepatic blood flow and/or oxygenation, e.g.
	    cirrhosis
	    congestive cardiac failure
	    pulmonary oedema
	    chronic obstructive airways disease
	    cor pulmonale
	    fever
	    viral infection

1 – Antacids may alter the rate of absorption of theophylline from slow-release preparations by increasing gastric pH.

Others, such as diprophylline, are substituted theophylline derivatives which do not form theophylline. Enprophylline, a non-methylated xanthine, is a recently developed bronchodilator. At present the anhydrous theophylline formulations are the most commonly used oral preparations. Aminophylline, a combination of theophylline and ethylenediamine (which increases its solubility), is the only preparation generally available for intravenous injection, and is also used orally. Table 2.3 lists the anhydrous theophylline content of the various methylxanthines. It is important to consider this when comparing formulations or evaluating clinical trials of different drugs in this group.

Metabolism

Theophylline is extensively metabolised in the liver before excretion in the urine. Only 7 to 13% is excreted unchanged and the major metabolites are shown in figure 2.7. The transformation of 1,-methylxanthine to 1,-methyluric acid is mediated by xanthine oxidase. However, serum uric acid concentrations do not increase with theophylline treatment and the drug is not contraindicated in the presence of gout. Allopurinol produces an alteration in the relative ratios of urinary metabolites but at a dose of 300mg daily does not alter theophylline clearance. One study has suggested that at very high dosage (300mg twice daily) in patients whose theophylline elimination is already compromised, allopurinol might increase theophylline half-life (McElnay et al., 1982). Theophylline is mainly metabolised by hepatic microsomal enzymes, cytochrome P-448 in particular, and is subject to alteration by a wide variety of factors.

Table 2.4 lists some of the factors which have been reported to alter theophylline metabolism. When hepatic metabolism is in-

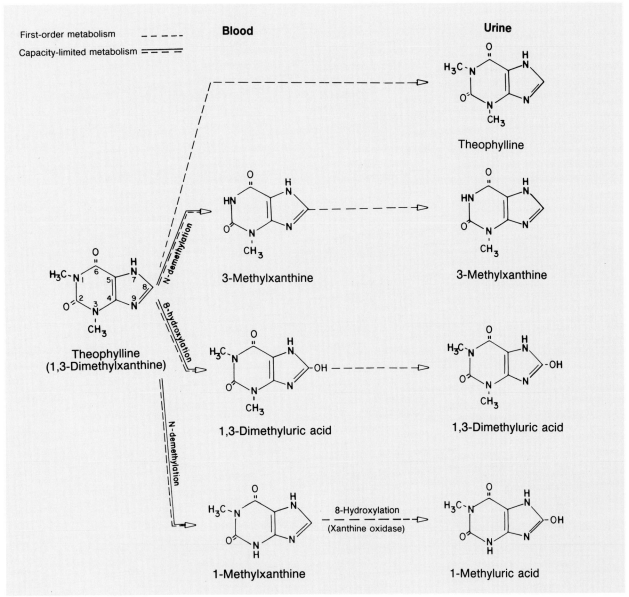

Fig. 2.7. Proposed scheme for the hepatic biotransformation of theophylline by first-order and capacity-limited processes. The pathway for 7-methylation to caffeine is important only in neonates.

creased, theophylline clearance is increased, half-life is decreased and the plasma concentration is reduced. In contrast, when clearance is decreased, half-life is increased and a higher plasma concentration is seen. Factors which can influence theophylline kinetics have been the subject of a recent review (McElnay et al., 1982).

Cigarette smoke, which contains polycyclic hydrocarbons, such as 3,4-benzpyrene, induces cytochrome P-448 and is one of the most powerful inducers of theophylline metabolism. It has an additive effect to that of marihuana. Smokers, therefore, usually need higher and more frequent doses of theophylline than non-smokers. When patients with chronic bronchitis give up smoking their plasma theophylline concentrations may rise into the toxic range with no change in dose. Barbecued (or charcoal broiled) meat has been shown to induce theophylline metabolism as has a high protein diet. Some drugs which are themselves metabolised by the liver may induce the microsomal enzymes and influence the rate of theophylline clearance (table 2.4).

Age has a marked effect on hepatic enzymes. Neonates metabolise the drug very slowly but children have much faster metabolism than adults and in children reaching puberty a toxic plasma concentration of theophylline may develop with no change in dose. A recent report has suggested that neuroticism is associated with rapid theophylline metabolism (Hartzema et al., 1982) but the reasons for this remain speculative and a single study cannot be taken as definitive.

An even greater number of factors may decrease theophylline clearance by reducing its rate of metabolism. Drugs which inhibit hepatic microsomal enzymes have this potential and cimetidine, which is not uncommonly prescribed with theophylline, is the most consistent inhibitory drug. This seems to be due to specific binding of cimetidine to microsomal enzymes rather than to any H_2-receptor antagonist effect, as ranitidine, a more potent H_2-receptor antagonist, does not appear to inhibit hepatic drug metabolism. Erythromycin compounds have been shown to reduce theophylline clearance. Methylxanthine derivatives such as caffeine and theobromine are found in tea, coffee, chocolate and cola drinks. Caffeine is metabolised by the same enzyme pathways as theophylline and acts as a competitive inhibitor thereby slowing theophylline metabolism. The effect is most marked if a high caffeine intake is suddenly reduced allowing an abrupt increase in theophylline metabolism. Obesity and high carbohydrate diets have been reported to be associated with the impairment of theophylline clearance and elderly patients also seem to have reduced clearance. Virus infections may be associated with decreased clearance and patients should be told to halve the dose when febrile.

Hepatic metabolism is an oxygen-dependent process and therefore any disease state which reduces hepatic blood flow or tissue oxygenation will diminish the rate of metabolism. Any severe illness may have this effect, as indicated by table 2.4.

Pharmacokinetics

It is clear from the above that theophylline pharmacokinetics vary considerably between patients and one of the most constant features of all pharmacokinetic studies of this drug is the very large intersubject variation. The plasma half-life may vary from 4 to 12 hours although the volume of distribution is fairly constant in adults, being about 0.5 L/kg, which is approximately equal to body water. The mean volume of distribution in premature newborns, adults with cirrhosis and the elderly is slightly larger because of reduced protein binding. This wide intersubject variation in half-life is of considerable clinical importance and it must be appreciated that the various published nomograms for intravenous infusions can only be approximate and that plasma theophylline concentrations must be assayed to achieve the optimum dose in any individual.

Controversy now exists about the elimination kinetics of theophylline (Lesko, 1979). It is likely that after oral dosing, and with plasma concentrations within the therapeutic range, theophylline follows first-order kinetics, i.e. a constant proportion of the dose is excreted in a given time. If this is true, there will be a simple relationship between any change in dose and the resultant plasma drug concentration (Koëter et al., 1981). However, there is some evidence that at higher doses or after prolonged intravenous infusion, theophylline obeys zero-order or saturable kinetics, i.e. a constant proportion of drug is not eliminated in a given time. The result of this is that a small increment in dose may result in a much larger increment in plasma drug concentration. This situation is familiar to most doctors in the context of ethanol metabolism and is also true of the anticonvulsant drug phenytoin. For theophylline the available evidence is conflicting and detailed studies of urinary metabolic ratios have produced contradictory results. As a therapeutic guide it is probably best to consider that saturable metabolism is a possibility in children or after prolonged intravenous infusions of aminophylline. With oral therapy it is unlikely to be a problem (Brown et al., 1983).

Duration of Action

As will be discussed below both the bronchodilator effects and side effects of theophylline are directly related to its plasma concentration. Its duration of action will therefore be dependent on all the metabolic and kinetic factors outlined above and must be established for individual patients. It will also be influenced by the route of administration and the particular formulation used.

Routes of Administration

Intravenous Therapy

Intravenous aminophylline is the route of choice for severe attacks of asthma. It is usual to give a bolus loading dose followed by a maintenance infusion. Details of doses used are described in chapter X. It is very important to remember that patients who are already on maintenance oral theophylline therapy do not need a bolus dose. If there is any doubt, blood should be taken for theophylline assay and a maintenance infusion alone used until more information is available. Aminophylline is a basic substance and should not be mixed in an infusion solution with acidic drugs such as penicillin, heparin, ascorbic acid or vancomycin.

Oral Therapy

It has proved difficult to produce a formulation of theophylline which gives consistent and reliable plasma levels. Theophylline was erratically or incompletely absorbed from early formulations and this was thought to be due to its low solubility and hence low dissolution rate in the stomach. Attempts to circumvent these problems included complex or salt formation to increase solubility, the synthesis of derivatives, and, a few years ago, the micronisation of theophylline. However, it has recently been demonstrated that theophylline is in fact well absorbed after oral administration of salts or micronised formulations as long as the drug is released completely from its tablet. The rate of its appearance in the systemic circulation is predominantly dependent on its rate of release from the administered formulation.

Furthermore, the incidence of local side effects, such as gastric irritation, is also influenced by the rate of drug release in the stomach. For these reasons, traditional theophylline formulations were less than satisfactory as many had inconsistent release rates resulting in variable plasma drug concentrations. Peak plasma concentrations could occur at any time between 1.5 and 4 hours and even the most reliable formulations tended to have a rapid dissolution rate, resulting in fast absorption and large swings in plasma theophylline concentrations between peak and trough levels, even when dosage intervals were as short as 6 hours. The rapid dissolution also caused a high incidence of gastric irritation.

Recent attempts have been made to overcome these problems by producing slow-release formulations of theophylline and this whole subject has been extensively reviewed (Merkus and Hendeles, 1983). Various techniques have been used to produce these slow-release formulations and they generally result in a decrease in the rate of disintegration and dissolution of the preparation. The aim is to allow a slow but constant rate of absorption to maintain plasma theophylline concentrations within a relatively narrow range (Weinberger and Hendeles, 1983). Peak plasma concentrations still show wide variation between subjects and can occur after 3 to 8 hours. There is no doubt that some of the slow-release preparations represent a major therapeutic advance on the previous formulations and many patients can be managed on twice-daily doses. However, although they perform very consistently *in vitro* some inconsistencies occur *in vivo;* there is considerable intersubject variation in both absorption and metabolism and the wide range of half-lives means that some patients, particularly smokers, still need 8-hourly therapy to maintain consistent plasma concentrations. Plasma drug monitoring remains essential to achieve optimal benefit from these preparations.

Apart from the formulation problems other factors can influence the absorption of theophylline. Absorption is slower at night than during the day so that morning trough concentrations are higher than evening troughs; a bonus for 'morning dippers'. Antacids and food interfere with absorption. In general, heavy meals with a high fat content delay absorption to a greater extent than light meals so that the time and height of the peak plasma concentration is reduced but the area under the curve remains the same. This delay in absorption is probably due to a combination of reduced contact with gastric juices and delayed gastric emptying (Thompson et al., 1983). However, individual variation is always greater than any effect of food and it is best to advise patients to take their tablets at the same time in relation to food every day rather than to suggest that it must be taken with or without food.

Rectal Route

Absorption from the rectal mucosa is less consistent than after oral administration but most of the drug escapes the portal venous system. Fairly high plasma concentrations are therefore achieved quite rapidly. However, the rectal route is not a popular one in Ango-Saxon communities and the use of suppositories is usually limited to a few patients who need maintenance therapy but for some reason cannot take or tolerate tablets.

Plasma Theophylline Concentrations and Bronchodilator Response

The clinical effectiveness of theophylline as a bronchodilator has been documented in many trials although its relative efficacy compared to the β_2-agonists is still debated. Interpretation of the trials is complicated by the different doses and different routes of administration used but an adequate dose of theophylline can produce much the same effect as inhaled β_2-agonists (Svedmyr et al., 1977).

The improvement in FEV_1 correlates closely with the plasma concentration of theophylline. The 'therapeutic range' is a narrow one, between 10 and 20 mg/L (55 to 110 μmol/L). Some bronchodilating effect can be seen at concentrations of 5 mg/L and there is a continuous increase in response up to 20 mg/L with no evidence of a plateau effect (Mitenko and Ogilvie, 1973). However, as will be discussed below, toxicity also correlates with plasma drug concentrations and many patients cannot tolerate levels higher than 20 mg/L. Therefore, in practice, the maximum bronchodilator effect is limited by side effects.

Side Effects

The most common side effects of oral treatment are anorexia, nausea, vomiting and mild central nervous system toxicity such as irritability or confusion. Nausea is usually associated with a plasma level of 15 mg/L, or greater, and is probably due to both a central effect and a local effect on the gastric mucosa. The problem appears to be increased with oral therapy. Acute abdominal pain, diarrhoea and, rarely, gastric bleeding have been reported. The slow-release preparations seem to be generally better tolerated. With increasing plasma concentrations, patients become 'nervous' and develop a tachycardia. There is a risk of arrhythmia and convulsions (see p.81). Nausea and vomiting do not necessarily develop when theophylline is given too rapidly by intravenous injection and a convulsion may be the first sign of toxicity (Svedmyr, 1979).

Methylxanthines are also diuretics and initial doses of theophylline tend to induce a diuresis and increase their own renal clearance. This effect is normally short-lived and does not influence the interpretation of steady-state plasma concentrations.

Therapeutic Drug Monitoring

Because of the narrow therapeutic range and the wide individual variation in kinetics, theophylline therapy should be monitored by measuring plasma drug concentrations (Ogilvie, 1981). For patients receiving aminophylline infusions assays should be carried out at 12 and 24 hours in order to adjust the infusion rate. It is essential to perform an assay before giving intravenous aminophylline in the emergency room if there is doubt about the patient's previous therapy. Plasma concentration monitoring during outpatient maintenance therapy is described in chapter V. 'Trough' plasma samples should be taken just before a dose is scheduled to indicate the lowest concentration achieved. Some authorities recommend taking a 'peak' sample but absorption is so variable that it is impossible to be certain when the peak will be and results can be misleading. This is especially true of slow-release preparations. However, if a patient complains of side effects for limited periods during the day it is then worth taking a sample to see if particularly high plasma levels coincide with the ill effects.

Combined Bronchodilator Therapy

There is at present a trend towards combining bronchodilator drugs of different types, both to increase efficacy and attempt to decrease side effects. Patients need combination therapy designed for their individual needs and thus fixed dose combinations have little or no place in a modern approach to treatment.

By working through different routes to the same final common pathway it is reasonable to expect an improved or increased

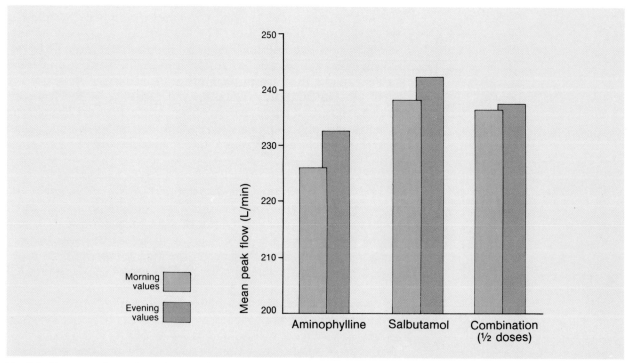

Fig. 2.8. Mean morning and evening peak flow during 28 days' treatment with oral aminophylline 200 to 550mg, oral salbutamol 3 to 9mg, or a combination of these drugs at half doses (after Blumenthal, 1980).

response with combinations of bronchodilators. If low concentrations of two drugs could produce the same response as a high concentration of one drug alone, there could theoretically be a useful reduction in those side effects not directly related to receptor stimulation although side effects with inhaled β_2-agonists at relatively high maintenance doses are negligible.

The combined effects of any two or more drugs may be additive or synergistic. In the first case their combined effects will equal the sum of the individual components whereas in the case of synergy or potentiation the combined effect exceeds the sum of the individual effects (Campbell et al., 1977; Paterson and Yellin, 1978).

In a clinical context, additive effects may also be of two types. It is possible by combining submaximal doses of two drugs to produce an increased effect compared with either alone in higher dose. It is also possible that having achieved maximal response with one drug, a second drug will produce further improvement.

All three types of interaction may be of therapeutic value and *in vitro* studies have indicated that they may occur.

Non-clinical Studies

Studies in guinea-pig trachea, using methacholine as a spasmogen and fenoterol and ipratropium bromide as bronchodilators, suggest that the combination of β-adrenoceptor agonists and anticholinergics does produce a synergistic effect (Offermeier, 1975). Studies have also been performed using combinations of β-adrenoceptor agonists and theophylline. This combination had a synergistic effect *in vitro* in the prevention of histamine release from sensitised cells (Lichtenstein and Margolis, 1968), and in causing relaxation of tracheobronchial smooth muscle (Lefcoe et al., 1975).

Of particular therapeutic interest is the observation that theophylline potentiates the bronchodilating effect of β-adrenoceptor stimulant drugs on human bronchial muscle *in vitro* much more in preparations from patients with obstructive airways disease than from those without such disease (Svedmyr, 1977).

In contrast, Trembath and Shaw (1978) found that in both normal subjects and asthmatics, the plasma cyclic AMP response to inhaled isoprenaline was enhanced by therapeutic doses of aminophylline but the effect was greater in the normal subjects.

Clinical Studies

The majority of studies have been of short term, single dose design thus having relevance to the treatment of an acute attack of asthma rather than to its long term treatment. A wide variety of different combinations has been investigated but the increased maximum bronchodilator effect has been less than additive. In the clinical situation, the important factor is whether a combination of two or more bronchodilators enhances the effect of one alone.

Problems in the Assessment of Bronchodilator Combinations

Table 2.5 lists a series of factors that need to be taken into account when considering clinical studies of bronchodilator combinations. Some of these relate to the general design of the studies, others to the particular drugs used.

Table 2.5. Important factors in the assessment of the response to more than one bronchodilator

Factor	
Diagnosis	Conclusions drawn from patients with asthma may not be applicable to those with bronchitis or emphysema
Object of using combination	Increase bronchodilatation • has full dose single therapy been tried? Decrease side effects • will half doses of both give comparable bronchodilatation with fewer side effects (fig. 2.8)?
Patient responsiveness	Patients should have been shown to be capable of a significant and reproducible response to bronchodilators
Administration route	Accurate comparisons cannot be made between routes; response varies with different routes because of: • different concentrations reaching the target organs • differences in metabolism • different receptor responsiveness
Order of administration	For anticholinergic/β-agonist combinations the order of administration may influence the response (Leahy et al., 1983)
Duration of study	Single dose studies are of limited use for predicting effect of long term combination therapy
Other drugs	In particular corticosteroids can alter the pattern of responsiveness
Specific drug effects	The dose of theophylline should be individually titrated before the study and plasma concentrations maintained within the optimum range; the bronchodilator response to theophylline depends on the plasma concentration

β₂-Adrenoceptor Agonist/
Methylxanthine
Combinations

Many studies have compared this combination of drugs. Whereas few of them fulfil all of the criteria for an ideal trial, they are unanimous in indicating an increased maximum bronchodilator effect which appears to be less than additive (see p.89). Those studies which were more prolonged also tended to show an extended duration of action with combination therapy compared with either drug alone.

Plasma Theophylline
Concentration

There are no published long term studies which compare the effects of adding a β-agonist in patients with either therapeutic or subtherapeutic plasma concentrations of theophylline. However, Svedmyr has data to suggest that some additional bronchodilatation can be achieved by the addition of an oral or inhaled $β_2$-agonist to doses of oral theophylline which produce plasma concentrations of 5 to 10 mg/L (Svedmyr, 1979). Some studies (which were not designed to show this effect) also lend support to the view that with combination therapy it is possible to have a lower 'therapeutic range' for theophylline (Lönnerholm et al., 1981).

Influence on Side Effects

In several studies low dose combinations caused fewer side effects than full doses of the β-adrenoceptor agonist (Eggleston et al., 1981; Svedmyr and Svedmyr, 1980; Wolfe et al., 1978). In contrast, oral theophylline plus oral terbutaline or salmefamol caused more tremor than the same dose of the $β_2$-agonist alone (Dyson and Campbell, 1977; Shapiro et al., 1981). In most cases, however, full dose combinations usually caused a similar number of side effects to the individual drugs given alone in both single dose and multiple dose studies. There is likely to be considerable intersubject variation in relation to this and it will also depend on whether the side effects of the two agents are similar, e.g. tremor, or different, e.g. nausea. On present information it would seem that the logical way to reduce side effects is to give the $β_2$-agonist by aerosol and attempt to keep theophylline plasma concentrations low in the therapeutic range.

β-Adrenoceptor Agonist/
Anticholinergic
Combinations

Many studies have combined β-adrenoceptor agonists with nebulised atropine methonitrate or aerosol ipratropium bromide. Studies conducted before 1978 often failed to detect any significant increase in maximum bronchodilatation from combined therapy, probably because of methodological factors (Shenfield, 1982). More recent studies and those with ipratropium bromide have generally noted a slightly increased maximum effect when salbutamol or fenoterol have been combined with the anticholinergic agent in patients with asthma and/or bronchitis (Lightbody et al., 1978). Diagnosis is probably a critical factor in any study involving anticholinergics because of the differential response between asthmatics and bronchitics (see p.195). Patient characteristics have not always been clearly defined or described but it has been noticed that the effects of the $β_2$-adrenoceptor agonists were relatively greater in atopic than in non-atopic asthmatics (Ruffin et al., 1977). In general, a combination which includes an anticholinergic agent is likely to be of more value in patients with bronchitis than in those with asthma.

The few studies that compared the effects of low doses of both drugs with a full dose of each component have noted similar effects with both regimens (Elwood and Abboud, 1982). A great majority of studies have observed the combined effects of full doses of both drugs and have generally reported a greater peak effect and occasionally an increased duration of effect relative to either drug alone. The high efficacy of the β_2-agonists make it unlikely that an anticholinergic agent will have much additional effect on maximal bronchodilatation and as both are usually given by aerosol, side effects are rarely a problem at full doses.

In summary, therefore, there is a theoretical basis for using combination therapy and considerable evidence from clinical trials that it is possible to improve ventilatory function to a limited degree by this means. In some cases, side effects can be reduced by giving half doses of two drugs rather than full doses of one drug alone, although patient compliance with prescribed regimens may be impaired by using multiple therapy. The place of combination therapy in the clinical management of asthma is discussed in chapters III and V.

References

Ahlquist, R.P.: A study of the adrenotropic receptors. American Journal of Physiology 153: 586 (1948).

Altounyan, R.: Variation of drug action on airway obstruction in man. Thorax 19: 406 (1964).

Andersson, K.E. and Persson, C.G.A.: Extrapulmonary effects of theophylline. European Journal of Respiratory Diseases 61 (Suppl. 109): 17-28 (1980).

Bateman, J.R.M.; Pavia, D.; Shearan, N.F.; Newman, S.P. and Clarke, S.W.: Effects of terbutaline sulphate aerosol on bronchodilator response and lung mucociliary clearance in patients with mild stable asthma. British Journal of Clinical Pharmacology 15: 695 (1983).

Bergstrand, H.: Phosphodiesterase inhibition of theophylline. European Journal of Respiratory Diseases 61 (Suppl. 109): 37 (1980).

Berkowitz, B.A. and Spector, S.: Effect of caffeine and theophylline on peripheral catecholamines. European Journal of Pharmacology 13: 193 (1971).

Blumenthal, I.: A comparative trial of slow-release aminophylline, salbutamol and a half dose combination in the prevention of childhood asthma. Journal of International Medical Research 8: 400 (1980).

Brown, P.J.; Dusci, L.J. and Shenfield, G.M.: Lack of dose dependent kinetics of theophylline. European Journal of Clinical Pharmacology 24: 525 (1983).

Campbell, I.A.; Middleton, W.G.; McHardy, G.J.R.; Sholter, M.V.; McKenzie, R. and Kay, A.B.: Interaction between isoprenaline and aminophylline in asthma. Thorax 32: 424 (1977).

Conolly, M.E.; Tashkin, D.P.; Hui, K.K.P.; Lither, M.R. and Wolfe, R.N.: Selective subsensitisation of beta-adrenergic receptors in central airways of asthmatics and normal subjects during long-term therapy with inhaled salbutamol. Journal of Allergy and Clinical Immunology 70: 423 (1982).

Crompton, G.K.: A comparison of responses to bronchodilator drugs in chronic bronchitis and chronic asthma. Thorax 23: 45 (1968).

Crompton, G.K.: Inhalation devices. European Journal of Respiratory Diseases 63: 489 (1982).

Cushley, M.J.; Lewis, R.A. and Tattersfield, A.E.: Comparison of three techniques of inhalation on the airway response to terbutaline. Thorax 38: 908 (1983).

Davies, D.S.: Pharmacokinetics of inhaled substances. Postgraduate Medical Journal 51 (Suppl. 17): 69 (1975).

Davis, C. and Conolly, M.E.: Tachyphylaxis to beta-adrenoceptor agonists in human bronchial smooth muscle: studied in vitro. British Journal of Clinical Pharmacology 10: 417 (1980).

Dyson, A.J. and Campbell, I.A.: Interaction between choline theophyllinate and salmefamol in patients with reversible airways obstruction. British Journal of Clinical Pharmacology 4: 677 (1977).

Eggleston, P.A.; Beasley, P.P. and Kindley, R.T.: The effects of oral doses of theophylline and fenoterol in exercise-induced asthma. Chest 79: 399 (1981).

Elwood, R.K. and Abboud, R.T.: The short-term bronchodilator effects of fenoterol and ipratropium in asthma. Journal of Allergy and Clinical Immunology 69: 467 (1982).

Engel, G.: Subclasses of beta-adrenoceptors – a quantitative estimate of beta$_1$- and beta$_2$-adrenoceptors in guinea pig and human lung. Postgraduate Medical Journal 57 (Suppl. 1): 77 (1981).

Engelhardt, A. and Klupp, H.: The pharmacology and toxicology of a new tropane alkaloid derivative. Postgraduate Medical Journal 51 (Suppl. 7): 82 (1975).

Foreman, J.C.; Mongar, J.L.; Gomperts, B.D. and Garland, L.G.: A possible role for cyclic AMP in the regulation of histamine secretion and the action of cromoglycate. Biochemical Pharmacology 24: 538 (1975).

Fredholm, B.B.: Theophylline actions on adenosine receptors. European Journal of Respiratory Disease 61 (Suppl. 109): 29 (1980).

Galant, S.P.; Duriseti, L.; Underwood, S. and Insel, P.A.: Decreased beta-adrenergic receptors on polymorphonuclear leucocytes after adrenergic therapy. New England Journal of Medicine 299: 933 (1978).

Gray, B.J.; Frame, M. and Costello, J.F.: A comparative double-blind study of the bronchodilator effects and side effects of inhaled fenoterol and terbutaline administered in equipotent doses. British Journal of Diseases of the Chest 76: 341 (1982).

Harper, T.B.; Gaumer, H.R.; Waring, W.; Brannon, R.B. and Salvaggio, J.E.: A comparison of cell-mediated immunity and suppressor T-cell function in asthmatic and normal children. Clinical Allergy 10: 655 (1980).

Hartley, J.P.R.; Nogrady, S.G. and Gibby, O.M.: Bronchodilator effects of dry salbutamol powder administered by Rotahaler. British Journal of Clinical Pharmacology 4: 673 (1977).

Hartzema, A.G.; Pancorbo, S. and Davis, S.: Personality traits and theophylline metabolism. Biopharmaceutics and Drug Disposition 3: 311 (1982).

Higbee, M.D.; Kumar, M. and Galant, S.P.: Stimulation of endogenous catecholamine release by theophylline: a proposed additional mechanism of action for theophylline effects. Journal of Allergy and Clinical Immunology 70: 377 (1982).

Horrobin, D.F.: Methylxanthine phosphodiesterase inhibitors behave as prostaglandin antagonists in a perfused rat mesenteric artery preparation. Prostaglandins 13: 33 (1977).

Hume, K.M. and Gandevia, B.: Forced expiratory volume before and after isoprenaline. Thorax 12: 276 (1957).

Iodice, F.; Rufolo, L.; Piscione, F. and De Michele, G.: Haemodynamic and ventilatory effects of intravenous salbutamol in patients affected by COLD. Respiration 40: 272 (1980).

Kennedy, M.C.S. and Simpson, W.T.: Human pharmacological and clinical studies on salbutamol: A specific β-adrenergic bronchodilator. British Journal of Diseases of the Chest 63: 160 (1969).

Koëter, G.H.; Jonkman, J.H.G.; de Vries, K.; Schoenmaker, R.; Greving, J.C. and Zeeuw, R.A.: Pharmacokinetics of sustained release theophylline in low and high multidose regimes. British Journal of Clinical Pharmacology 12: 647 (1981).

Kolbeck, R.C.; Speir, W.A.; Carrier, G.O. and Bransome, E.D.: Apparent irrelevance of cyclic nucleotides to the relaxation of tracheal smooth muscle induced by theophylline. Lung 156: 178 (1977).

Lands, A.M.; Arnold, A.; McAuliff, J.P.; Luduena, F.P. and Brown, T.G.: Differentiation of receptor systems activated by sympathomimetic amines. Nature 214: 597 (1967).

Larsson, S. and Svedmyr, N.: A comparison of two modes of administering stimulants in asthmatics: Tablets and metered aerosol. Scandinavian Journal of Respiratory Diseases 101 (Suppl.): 79 (1977).

Larsson, S.; Svedmyr, N. and Thiringer, G.: Lack of bronchial beta adrenoceptor resistance in asthmatics during long-term with terbutaline. Journal of Allergy and Clinical Immunology 59: 93 (1977).

Leahy, B.C.; Gonim, S.A. and Allen, S.C.: Comparison of nebulised salbutamol with nebulised ipratropium bromide in acute asthma. British Journal of Diseases of the Chest 77: 159 (1983).

Lefcoe, N.M.; Toogood, J.H. and Jones, T.R.: In vitro pharmacologic studies of bronchodilator compounds: Interactions and mechanisms. Journal of Allergy and Clinical Immunology 55: 94 (1975).

Lefkowitz, R.J.; De Lean, A.; Hoffman, B.B.; Stadel, J.M.; Kent, R.; Thomas, M. and Limbird, L.: Molecular pharmacology of adenylate cyclase coupled – and β-adrenergic receptors. Advances in Cyclic Nucleotide Research 14: 145 (1981).

Lesko, L.J.: Dose dependent elimination kinetics of theophylline. Clinical Pharmacokinetics 4: 449 (1979).

Lichtenstein, L.M. and Margolis, S.: Histamine release *in-vitro*: inhibition by catecholamines and methylxanthines. Science 161: 902 (1968).

Lightbody, I.M.; Ingram, C.G.; Legge, J.S. and Johnston, R.N.: Ipratropium bromide, salbutamol and prednisolone in bronchial asthma and chronic bronchitis. British Journal of Diseases of the Chest 72: 181 (1978).

Lonnerholm, G.; Foucard, T. and Lindstrom, B.: Combined treatment with sustained-release theophylline and beta 2-adrenoceptor-stimulating agents in chronic childhood asthma. British Medical Journal 282: 1029 (1981).

Lopez-Vidriero, M.T.; Das, I.; Smith, A.P.; Picot, R. and Reid, L.: Bronchial secretion from normal human airways after inhalation of prostaglandin $F_2\alpha$, acetylcholine, histamine and citric acid. Thorax 32: 734 (1977).

McElnay, J.C.; Smith, J.D. and Helling, D.: Guide to interactions involving theophylline kinetics. Drug Intelligence and Clinical Pharmacy 16: 533 (1982).

Merkus, R.W.H.M. and Hendeles, L. (Eds): Sustained Release Theophylline. A Biopharmaceutical Challenge to a Clinical Need (Excerpta Medica, Amsterdam 1983).

Middleton, E.: Antiasthmatic drug therapy and calcium ions: Review of pathogenesis and role of calcium. Journal of Pharmaceutical Sciences 69: 243 (1980).

Mitenko, P.A. and Ogilvie, R.I.: Rational intravenous doses of theophylline. New England Journal of Medicine 289: 600 (1973).

Offermeier, J.: Synergistic effects of SCH 1000 and beta-adrenergics on isolated organs. Postgraduate Medical Journal 51(Suppl.): 117 (1975).

Ogilvie, R.I.: Theophylline: clinical aspects; in Richens and Marks (Eds) Therapeutic Drug Monitoring, pp.434 (Churchill Livingstone, Edinburgh, Melbourne, New York 1981).

Pakes, G.E.; Brogden, R.N.; Heel, R.C.; Speight, T.M. and Avery, G.S.: Ipratropium bromide: A review of its pharmacological properties and therapeutic efficacy in asthma and chronic bronchitis. Drugs 20: 237 (1980).

Paterson, J.W. and Clark, T.: Aerosols in asthma. British Medical Journal 1: 557 (1971).

Paterson, J.W. and Shenfield, G.M.: Bronchodilators: Parts I and II. British Thoracic and Tuberculosis Association Review 4: 25 and 61 (1974).

Paterson, J.W. and Yellin, R.H.: Combined bronchodilators in severe outpatient asthma. Current Therapeutics 19 (No 10): 14 (October 1978).

Paterson, J.W.; Courtenay-Evans, R.J. and Prime, F.J.: Selectivity of bronchodilator action of salbutamol in asthmatic patients. British Journal of Diseases of the Chest 65: 21 (1971).

Paterson, J.W.; Woolcock, A.J. and Shenfield, G.M.: State of the art. Bronchodilator drugs. American Review of Respiratory Diseases 120: 1149 (1979).

Persson, C.G.A.: Xanthines for asthma – present status. Trends in Pharmacological Sciences 3: 312 (1982).

Petrie, G.R. and Palmer, K.N.V.: Comparison of aerosol ipratropium bromide and salbutamol in chronic bronchitis and asthma. British Medical Journal 1: 430 (1975).

Plit, M.; Goldman, H.I. and Cassel, M.L.: The bronchodilator action of fenoterol (Berotec) in asthma studied with selected pulmonary function texts. Medical Proceedings 18: 41 (1972).

Ruffin, R.E.; Fitzgerald, J.D. and Rebuck, A.S.: A comparison of the bronchodilator activity of SCH 1000 and salbutamol. Journal of Allergy and Clinical Immunology 59: 136 (1977).

Shapiro, G.G.; McPhillips, J.J.; Smith, K.; Furukawa, C.T.; Pierson, W.F. and Bierman, C.W.: Effectiveness of terbutaline and theophylline alone and in combination in exercise-induced bronchospasm. Pediatrics 67: 508 (1981).

Shenfield, G.M.: Combined bronchodilator therapy. Drugs 24: 414-439 (1982).

Shenfield, G.M.; Evans, M.E. and Paterson, J.W.: The effect of different nebulisers with and without intermittent positive pressure breathing on the absorption and metabolism of salbutamol. British Journal of Clinical Pharmacology 1: 295 (1974).

Shenfield, G.M.; Evans, M.E. and Paterson, J.W.: Absorption of drugs by the lung. British Journal of Clinical Pharmacology 8: 583 (1976).

Shohat, B.; Volovitz, B. and Varsano, I.: Induction of suppressor T cells in asthmatic children by theophylline treatment. Clinical Allergy 13: 487 (1983).

Simonsson, B.G.; Jacobs, F.M. and Nadel, J.A.: Role of autonomic nervous system and the cough reflex in the increased responsiveness of airways in patients with obstructive airways disease. Journal of Clinical Investigation 46: 1812 (1967).

Solis-Cohen, S.: The use of adrenal substance in the treatment of asthma. Journal of the American Medical Association 34: 1164 (1900).

Svedmyr, N.: Theophyllines today. Scandinavian Journal of Respiratory Diseases 101 (Suppl.): 125 (1977).

Svedmyr, N.: Terbutaline and terbutaline combined with theophylline in asthmatics. Acta Pharmacologica et Toxicologica 44 (Suppl.): 47 (1979).

Svedmyr, K.: Beta$_2$-adrenoceptor stimulants and theophylline in asthma therapy. European Journal of Respiratory Diseases 62 (Suppl. 116): 8 (1981).

Svedmyr, N. and Simonsson, B.G.: Drugs in the treatment of asthma. Pharmacology and Therapeutics 3: 397 (1978).

Svedmyr, K.; Mellstrand, T. and Svedmyr, N.: A comparison between effects of aminophylline, proxyphilline and terbutaline in asthmatics. Scandinavian Journal of Respiratory Diseases 101 (Suppl.): 139 (1977).

Sydbom, A. and Fredholm, B.B.: On the mechanism by which theophylline inhibits release of histamine from rat mast cells. Acta Physiologica Scandinavica 114: 243 (1982).

Tashkin, D.P.; Conolly, M.E.; Deutsch, R.I.; Hui, K.K.; Littner, M.; Scarpace, P. and Abrass, I.: Subsensitization of beta-adrenoceptors in airways and lymphocytes of healthy and asthmatic subjects. American Review of Respiratory Disease 125: 185 (1982).

Thompson, P.J.; Kemp, M.W.; McAllister, W. and Turner-Warwick, M.: The prescribing of slow release theophylline in patients with airways obstruction with particular reference to the effects of food on absorption. British Journal of Diseases of the Chest 77: 293 (1983).

Trembath, P.W. and Shaw, J.: Potentiation of isoprenaline-induced plasma cyclic AMP response by aminophylline in normal and asthmatic subjects. British Journal of Clinical Pharmacology 6: 499 (1978).

Ullah, M. and Saunders, K.B.: Influence of age on response to ipratropium bromide and salbutamol in asthmatic patients. Progress in Respiratory Research 14: 150 (1980).

Weinberger, M. and Hendeles, L.: Slow release theophylline rationale and basis for product selection. New England Journal of Medicine 308: 760 (1983).

Widdicombe, J.G.; Kent, D.C. and Nadel, J.A.: Mechanism of bronchoconstriction during inhalation of dust. Journal of Applied Physiology 17: 613 (1962).

Wolfe, J.D.; Tashkin, D.P.; Calvarese, B. and Simmons, M.: Bronchodilator effects of terbutaline and aminophylline alone and in combination with asthmatic patients. New England Journal of Medicine 298: 363 (1978).

Chapter III

The Role of Bronchodilators in the Management of Asthma: An Overview

The enormous growth in sales of bronchodilator drugs for treating asthma over the past 15 to 20 years prompts the question: Is this increased drug consumption really necessary? As this volume demonstrates, bronchodilator therapy is rarely unjustified and the present demand results from the contribution of a number of different factors.

Factors Contributing to the Increasing Use of Bronchodilators

Improvements in Diagnosis

Asthma is far from being overdiagnosed. In the past and still today it is underdiagnosed either because patients ignore their disability or because they are labelled and treated as having bronchitis. When 284 nine-year-old children with wheeze were surveyed it was found that only half of those most affected had been diagnosed as asthmatic (Anderson et al., 1981). Similarly, in a study of 179 seven-year-old Tyneside children who had experienced at least one episode of wheeze since commencing school, Speight and his colleagues found that the diagnosis of asthma had been offered to the parents of only 21 children, despite the fact that the great majority had visited a doctor for chest symptoms (Speight et al., 1983). Only 3 of 56 children experiencing a number of separate wheezy episodes a year had been labelled asthmatic.

Community surveys have reached similar conclusions. For example, one survey found that less than 50% of asthmatics were receiving appropriate bronchodilator therapy (McQueen et al., 1979). However, the growing realisation that many respiratory problems are, in fact, asthma, and that many asthmatics cough but rarely wheeze, has enhanced diagnostic accuracy and increasingly patients previously diagnosed as bronchitic are now being classified as asthmatic.

The changing criteria for hospital admissions for asthma has meant a substantial increase in the number of patients attending hospital, and receiving bronchodilator therapy. Stanhope and his colleagues reviewed hospital discharge rates for asthma and found that in most age groups there was a substantial rise between the late 1950s and the middle 1970s (Stanhope et al., 1979). This was largely due to changes in hospital admission procedure and increased utilisation of disease care facilities by lower socioeconomic groups. However, as the data from the Tyneside study (Speight et al., 1983) demonstrates, bronchodilator use is likely to continue to rise as it is increasingly appreciated that many patients with respiratory symptoms, particularly children, do in fact have asthma and not bronchitis.

Pharmacological Developments

In view of the significant side effects of adrenaline (epinephrine) and ephedrine, the reluctance of patients and physicians to use them is understandable. The development of selective β_2-agonist bronchodilators administered by metered dose aerosols revolutionised antiasthma therapy by avoiding most side effects while providing the patient with a convenient, portable device which would give rapid and predictable relief. These developments, and the greater reliability of the slow-release formulations of theophyllines have greatly improved patient compliance.

Patient-practitioner relationships have similarly benefited as the doctor can now ensure instant relief of wheezing.

Bronchodilators as Prophylactic Drugs

While Osler's adage that 'asthmatics pant into old age' was a comfort to patients of past generations, nowadays practitioners of modern medicine and the community expect more than mere survival with continued disability. Antiasthmatic therapy has emerged from the restrictions of 'on-demand' treatment to relieve respiratory distress and now has a positive prophylactic role in promoting a full, vigorous life free of dyspnoeic constraints.

The coincident development of sodium cromoglycate (cromolyn sodium) and inhaled corticosteroids supplied a versatile armamentarium for managing the chronicity of asthma. By a process of analysis, guesswork, trials and experience bronchodilators have become established in selected patients in their second role, as prophylactic agents administered regularly. While the optimal balance between the various prophylactic regimens may still have to be found, current practice has clearly established that regular bronchodilator therapy frees many patients from their recurrent symptoms. As lack of patient compliance is increasingly recognised as a major cause of treatment failure the value of using a single drug for both symptom relief and prophylaxis cannot be overestimated.

Geographical Differences

There is little doubt that asthma is more of a problem in some communities than others. Gregg (1977) summarised data from various prevalence studies and suggested asthma was least common in rural India (0.2%) and Scandinavia (0.7-2.0%); but more common in Australia and New Zealand (5.0-7.4%), but all such surveys are flawed by difficulties of diagnosis and definition. For example, when wheeze and wheezy bronchitis were included, up to 24.9% of people interviewed in one London survey had experienced some symptoms.

Environmental changes can adversely affect some people and the shift to urban living has been shown to increase the asthmatic incidence (Godfrey et al., 1975). Similarly, a major increase in the prevalence of asthma in Tokelauan islanders who shifted to an urban New Zealand environment was reported compared with those who remained in the islands (Waite et al., 1980).

While geographical differences in asthma prevalence and treatment fashions influence bronchodilator usage, the type of bronchodilator used can be much influenced by differences in drug regulatory body approval. Inhaled selective β-agonists, such as salbutamol (albuterol) have been enthusiastically adopted in the United Kingdom, Europe, and Australia since the late 1960s but have only recently been released in the United States where their level of use is still growing. In contrast, theophyllines have been widely used in the United States and the more recently developed slow-release formulations, having originated there are now being used more widely in other countries.

Table 3.1. The goals of asthma treatment

1. Reverse acute attacks
2. Decrease attack frequency and severity
3. Help patients live as normal a life as possible
4. Ensure that patients understand about their disease and the details and pitfalls of their treatment
5. Increase lung function towards normal
6. Limit the problems of drug therapy

Is Asthma on the Increase?

Until carefully designed long term studies are available, it is not possible to conclude whether asthma is increasing in prevalence or severity. However, there are suggestions that in some communities the disease is occurring more frequently. Hospital admission rates for asthma have been on the increase in many countries for at least 10 years. It is difficult to interpret these data, which may relate to changes in criteria for hospital admission (Stanhope et al., 1979). In New Zealand, where asthma fatality rates soared in the late 1970s (Wilson et al., 1981; Jackson et al., 1982), there is a strong impression that asthma severity is increasing. Whatever the explanation for increased asthma hospital admissions, or for any apparent increase in severity of asthma both circumstances are contributing to the increasing use of bronchodilator drugs.

Goals of Asthma Management

The aims of therapy should be clearly defined for each individual patient. A suggested approach is summarised in table 3.1. There are many philosophies of asthma management but increasingly a positive overall approach with a long term plan is advocated. Too often patients are provided only with bronchodilator treatment for symptom relief and little attention is paid to other therapeutic modalities, patient education or long term organisation.

Reverse Acute Attacks

The most obvious therapeutic requirement for any patient is relief of acute dyspnoea. Bronchodilating drugs are of proven efficacy in this situation and are now the first step in therapy for all patients, irrespective of whether the bronchodilator is administered by inhalation from a metered dose aerosol or as dry powder, orally, or, in an emergency by nebuliser or injection. It is imperative that patients should know what to do and be able to decide when to use their treatment.

Decrease Attack Frequency and Severity

The decision to change from bronchodilator therapy 'on-demand' to regular prophylactic treatment depends on the increasing frequency of attacks. As perception of the severity of their bronchospasm is often poor (Rubinfeld and Pain, 1976) the judgement of patients with chronic but apparently mild symptoms must be backed by objective air flow measurements to measure the severity of their obstruction.

Help the Patient Enjoy a Normal Life

One great reward from modern bronchodilator therapy with metered dose aerosols is that the patient is guaranteed freedom from unexpected attacks of asthma. With planned antiasthmatic management, most patients can participate fully in leisure activities and are rarely hindered by significant airflow obstruction. Without positive therapy, many patients have to restrict their activities, which at school designates them as nonparticipants, and at work as unreliable nuisances if much time is lost because of symptoms.

Identify and Control Trigger Factors

There are two reasons for identifying factors that precipitate asthmatic attacks in patients. Firstly, when patients are aware of trigger factors such as exercise, infection, anxiety and allergies, they can more readily cope with their disease by avoiding the avoidable or by anticipating attacks and using treatment prophylactically. As patients become aware of the pattern of their asthma they become less concerned; understanding the disease is an effective therapy for anxiety. Secondly, avoidance of some factors, particularly occupational triggers, can result in a complete loss of symptoms in some patients.

Limit the Problems of Drug Therapy

At best a drug treatment, particularly if regular, is inconvenient and occasionally accompanied by side effects. It is important to design a therapeutic regimen to be as unobtrusive and trouble-free as possible so that the patient's compliance can be maintained (chapter IV). The timing of doses, selection of administration routes and consideration of the patient's own preference is important. Inhaled therapy usually involves minimal side effects and so is increasingly preferred to oral administration.

Maintain Patient Compliance

In a recent study, the author's group followed 59 asthmatic patients considered by their general practitioners to be under good control, for a period of 6 months (Wilson et al., 1984). All patients were managed on a standard regimen of salbutamol and beclomethasone dipropionate 2 puffs 4 times daily. Although, for the majority, this was merely a continuation of their previous medication, more than two-thirds experienced a significant improvement, particularly in that they lost their nocturnal symptoms. This improvement was largely the result of better patient compliance. Each patient had to record his or her medication in a daily diary and whereas many had previously been irregular with their treatment, the discipline of the diary was sufficient to maintain adherence to the prescribed regimen. Treatment failure is more often attributable to noncompliance or failure to understand the treatment regimen than to longer term deterioration in the patient's asthma.

Components of Overall Asthma Management

Modern asthmatic treatment involves far more than just drug therapy but comprises a complex inter-relationship of education, symptom relief and prevention, and non-pharmacological treatments with both patients and physicians sharing the decision-making role (table 3.2). Later chapters in this book address the use of bronchodilators in specific clinical situations. The present chapter presents an overall perspective of asthma management.

Drugs

Bronchodilators constitute the first, and for many patients the only component of their pharmacological regimen. The large number of preparations available, together with the many prophylactic agents, present the doctor with a variety of drugs from which to

Table 3.2. The components of asthma therapy

1.	Drug therapy – which must be sufficient in dose and appropriate in action to reverse the different constituents of bronchial obstruction and to reduce reactivity of bronchi
2.	Patient education – relieves anxiety, enables patient to cope with treatment
3.	Crisis plan – what to do when usual therapy fails
4.	Allergic factors – identify and control. Their removal from the patient's environment may significantly improve asthma
5.	Exercise – a gradual increase in physical fitness is frequently accompanied by a reduction in symptomatic asthma
6.	Psychotherapy – some patients need help to cope with their anxieties from asthma or those which accentuate their asthma. Overprotective parents must be educated
7.	Physiotherapy – help in teaching patients inhalation therapy

choose. While β_2-agonist bronchodilators such as salbutamol, fenoterol* and terbutaline have a predictable action in the great majority of asthmatic patients, more careful consideration and even a therapeutic trial is necessary to determine the effectiveness in any individual patient of other drugs such as theophylline, sodium cromoglycate and even the inhaled steroids. Lack of response to a particular drug may result from non-compliance, incorrect use of the drug, too low a dose, or because the patient is a true non-responder. Some treatment schedules are discussed below.

Patient Education

In few other conditions is the prospect of therapy so long or the patient's role in manipulating therapy so important as in bronchial asthma. While compliance is easy to sustain when patients have symptoms, it is rather more difficult to maintain during asymptomatic periods unless patients have a clear idea of what their treatment is intended to achieve and how to use it. Patients must be able to recognise dangerous and severe attacks and to respond appropriately. Errors in drug administration arise largely because the patient either does not understand the instructions provided or has received no instructions. Chapter IV discusses in detail how best to educate a patient about his bronchodilator therapy.

Crisis Plan

Patients must have a crisis plan which clearly indicates what steps they must take if the usual medication fails to relieve their symptoms, or if their asthma is deteriorating rapidly. These instructions must be simple and direct and should cover:
1) Recognition of the crisis
2) Initiation of appropriate therapy
3) Seeking medical help to confirm action already taken and if rapid relief is not achieved despite having followed the instructions.

Control of Allergic Factors

In some patients, immediate IgE-mediated hypersensitivity reactions are a cardinal precipitating factor of frequent asthmatic attacks. Nonspecific bronchial hyper-reactivity is increased follow-

* For product availability in the USA, see appendix B.

ing an allergen-triggered asthmatic attack (Cockcroft, 1983). However, a prolonged period of avoidance of selected allergens can result in a reduction in bronchial hyper-reactivity with a resultant improvement in the patient's asthma (Platts-Mills, 1982). Thus, identification of allergic factors can be very important particularly when occupational asthma is associated with sensitivity to a single allergen (Pepys and Hutchcroft, 1975). When allergen sensitivity is only part of the total asthmatic picture, identification of the clinically relevant allergens can help patients avoid unnecessary attacks or plan their therapy by anticipating an attack. Occasional patients become symptom-free with the dispatch of a major allergen factor such as a domestic pet.

Immunotherapy

Desensitisation has been widely practiced in asthma patients with recognisable allergic sensitivities but is of only limited value. Before introducing immunotherapy it is important to consider the potential side effects and long term complication of treatment. Seasonal asthma associated with grass pollen can respond well to pollen immunotherapy, and evidence from one study suggests that the late reaction to dust mites can be reduced in some patients by this means (Warner, 1978). There are few data from controlled and objective studies to support the desensitisation of asthma patients when other allergic factors are present.

Exercise

Many patients notice that their asthma improves as their physical fitness increases. An objective reduction in bronchial hyper-reactivity has recently been demonstrated in patients during the course of an intensive fitness campaign (Bundgaard et al., 1983). Of course while improving fitness, patients commonly precipitate exercise-induced asthma and will need to use their bronchodilators to prevent this.

Physiotherapy

Although many patients are often referred to physiotherapists for various breathing exercises and instruction on sputum expulsion, only a few patients are helped by this practice. However, physiotherapists are the ideal paramedical group to educate patients about aerosol practice, use of nebulisers and expiratory flow measurement devices.

Psychotherapy

Occasional patients require psychiatric assistance to cope with their asthma or stress factors which may precipitate their asthma. A few appear to become fatalistic about recurrent life-threatening attacks and may require help to adjust to their dependence on medication.

Relationship Between General Practitioner and Specialist or Hospital Clinic

It is too easy for patients who have required hospital treatment to be tossed between their community doctor and the hospital clinic. It is important that one practitioner has the central role in their management to coordinate recommendations from different sources. While the resources of a hospital clinic can be invaluable in stages of assessment and diagnosis the general practitioner remains the person first called in times of emergency and so clearly should retain central control of the patient's management.

Treatment Schedules for Different Grades of Asthma

As asthma increases in severity, more complex patterns of management are required.

The schemes described below are a personal selection and guide within which many variations are possible, dictated by individual patient circumstance and practitioner preference. Inherent in this guide is the firm belief that positive approaches to treatment benefit the patient more in both the short and long term than more casual, 'on-demand', minimal treatment management.

Occasional Mild Asthmatic Attacks

Children Under the Age of Five Unable to Use Metered Dose Aerosols

- No therapy may be needed other than calming the anxiety of both child and parent
- Some children, although unable to use a metered aerosol β_2-agonist manage using a breath-activated system to inhale the drug as a powder. Salbutamol and fenoterol* are available in this form. Alternatively a spacer attachment with a metered dose aerosol can be successful (p.100)
- A β_2-agonist bronchodilator can be administered as an elixir or tablet
- Short-acting theophyllines can be taken similarly
- When a nebuliser unit is available, administration of nebulised bronchodilator respirator solution through a face mask will work satisfactorily, though it must be used under careful control by parents who are well acquainted with the advantages and disadvantages of this form of therapy. This practice is usually reserved for patients with more severe asthma and the complications of the system are discussed later in this chapter and in appendix C.

Older Children and Adults

- A β_2-agonist bronchodilator administered by metered dose inhaler
- Where the patient's coordination is poor, the inhaled powder form is a satisfactory substitute
- Oral bronchodilator medication can be considered for those who prefer it or where the clinician is concerned about an excessive zeal with an inhaled drug. Occasionally, children use the aerosol in a fashion similar to glue sniffing. It should be remembered that the effect of oral medication is slower in onset.

Occasional Severe Attacks

This group is reviewed at length in chapter X. It is important to remember that some patients in this group suffer intensive allergic reactions which are almost anaphylactic in nature (Broom and Fitzharris, 1983).

Chronic Asthma

There are two major reasons for initiating prophylactic therapy in asthma:

1) It may be possible by aggressive treatment to shift the patient's asthma from an active to a quiescent phase. There is some evidence that inhaled beclomethasone dipropionate and sodium cromoglycate depress bronchial hyper-reactivity (Crompton, 1983;

---

* Fenoterol as a dry powder for inhalation is not available in the United States or the United Kingdom.

Table 3.3. Guidelines for initiation of prophylactic therapy

1.	When occasional mild attacks convert to occasional severe or dangerous attacks
2.	When attack frequency increases to about 6 or more a year, each attack lasting more than 24 hours
3.	When patients' lives begin to be disrupted with time lost from school or work
4.	When patients become worried about themselves and their condition
5.	If complications of asthma, such as chest deformities, begin to appear
6.	If lung function test results indicate continuing moderate bronchoconstriction despite an absence of symptoms

Dickson and Cole, 1979). By adopting a positive therapeutic approach some patients can enter asymptomatic phases where they require little or no continuous medication.

2) When symptoms become too severe or too frequent, more regular therapy is required. Guidelines for introducing prophylactic medication are summarised in table 3.3.

Very Young Children Unable to Use an Inhaler

- An oral β_2-agonist bronchodilator can be administered as an elixir or tablets 3 times a day
- As an alternative, oral theophylline medication can be used. Children tolerate this drug well but blood levels must be checked after induction therapy is complete
- Regular treatment with bronchodilators and prophylactic drugs such as sodium cromoglycate and beclomethasone dipropionate can be achieved by using either dry powders for inhalation or nebulised respirator solutions. Some parents and patients find the latter too inconvenient to manage.

Older Children and Adults

- Long term bronchodilator therapy alone can be used as prophylactic antiasthma therapy. It has the advantage of supplying the patient with a drug for all purposes – immediate relief of symptoms and prevention. Many patients will use one medication on a long term basis where they will not reliably use two.

  If sodium cromoglycate or inhaled steroids are to be used, their effectiveness is increased when they are given on a background of bronchodilator therapy. The optimal approach for single drug management is a β_2-agonist given by a metered dose aerosol 3 or 4 times daily, irrespective of symptoms. Alternatives include the slow-release theophyllines which have the convenience of twice-daily dosage and the advantage of providing control of nocturnal asthma in most patients; however the dosage must be assessed by monitoring plasma theophylline concentrations (p.82). Ipratropium bromide may also be used as single drug therapy, by metered dose aerosol 3 or 4 times daily.
- Sodium cromoglycate is an ideal prophylactic, if it works, as it is safe and effective and protects many patients against exercise-induced asthma which responds poorly to oral theophylline therapy. However, as seen in chapter VII an inhaled β_2-agonist is even more effective against exercise-induced asthma. Administration of sodium cromoglycate as a dry pow-

der is easily achieved, even in poorly coordinated patients, but a therapeutic trial is necessary before concluding whether or not the drug is effective. While most patients using sodium cromoglycate do so against a background of regular bronchodilator therapy, a small group, usually children with nocturnal or exercise-induced cough, can be well controlled by cromoglycate alone. However, as with inhaled steroids, all patients on sodium cromoglycate therapy must also have a bronchodilator available, if not for regular therapy at least for 'on-demand' treatment of acute attacks.

● Inhaled steroids, such as beclomethasone dipropionate, are the most frequently successful prophylactic therapy for addition to bronchodilators. By doubling the dose, the frequency of administration can usually be reduced from 4 times daily to twice daily. High dose formulations are now available in some countries to control patients with more severe symptoms.

It is not always appreciated that with the addition of inhaled steroids to their regular β_2-agonist therapy nocturnal asthma can be abolished in many patients (see p.144). In a recent study by the author's group (Wilson et al., 1984) 25 patients whose symptoms of nocturnal asthma disappeared with the introduction of regular beclomethasone dipropionate and salbutamol found these symptoms returned when the inhaled steroid was stopped.

● The author finds that single bronchodilator therapy is usually satisfactory but when single drug therapy is inadequate prefers to add either beclomethasone dipropionate or sodium cromoglycate as the second step in management before opting for a second bronchodilator preparation. It must be remembered that medication with most bronchodilators is aimed primarily at the bronchial smooth muscle and they may not provide relief when other components of airways obstruction such as mucosal oedema or inflammatory changes predominate. Acute attacks may be very aggressive in the absence of inhaled and oral steroids.

Severe Acute Asthma

Management of severe acute asthma is discussed in detail in chapter X.

The Poorly Controlled Asthmatic

It is essential to recognise the signs that a patient's asthma is under inadequate control and further medication is necessary. The major warning signs are:
1) Frequent daily bronchodilator use
2) Increasing nocturnal asthma
3) Frequent early morning cough
4) More frequent acute attacks
5) Troublesome exercise-induced asthma and
6) Suboptimal ventilatory function.

Assessment of Progress

Reliance on a patient's symptoms alone as the index of progress is unsatisfactory, for this may correlate poorly with objective measurements of expiratory airflow. When regular therapy is used patients should measure their peak flow readings at home with a portable flow meter from time to time. During severe acute asthma a more extensive assessment of progress is needed as described in chapter X.

Objective measurements of airflow obstruction can:

- Determine the severity of airflow obstruction
- Identify day-to-day variations in respiratory function
- Assess the response to treatment
- Identify patients with very unstable asthma
- Record the severity of acute attacks

Home Nebulisers

There is a growing trend towards using nebuliser units for the delivery of antiasthmatic medication at home. Nebulisers are very efficient and effective at delivering a high dose of drug and in overcoming the difficulties of administering drugs to poorly co-ordinated, severely debilitated, or very young patients. Nebuliser therapy is unnecessary for most patients. There is a hazard in their use; when patients fail to respond to nebulised bronchodilator treatment their bronchial obstruction is likely to be more severe than if they had lost response to bronchodilator therapy by metered dose aerosol. Larsson (1979) has drawn attention to fatalities presumed to result from over reliance on the effectiveness of home nebulisers. If home nebulisers are required then daily air flow measurements are a mandatory safeguard.

References

Anderson, H.R.; Bailey, P.A.; Cooper, J.S. and Palmer, J.C.: Influence of morbidity, illness label and social, family and health service factors on drug treatment of childhood asthma. Lancet 2: 1030 (1981).

Broom, B.C. and Fitzharris, P.: Life-threatening inhalant allergy: Typical anaphylaxis induced by inhalational allergen challenge in patients with idiopathic recurrent anaphylaxis. Clinical Allergy 13: 169 (1983).

Bundgaard, A.; Ingemann-Hansen, T.; Halkjaer-Kristensen, J.; Schmidt, A.; Block, I. and Anderson, P.K.: Short-term physical training in bronchial asthma. British Journal of Diseases of the Chest 73: 147 (1983).

Cockcroft, D.W.: Hypothesis: Mechanism of perennial allergic asthma. Lancet 2: 253 (1983).

Crompton, G.K.: The use of inhaled steroids in the management of asthma; in Clark, T.J.H. (Ed) Steroids in Asthma: A Reappraisal in the Light of Inhalation Therapy, p. 166 (ADIS Press, Auckland 1983).

Dickson, W. and Cole, M.: Severe asthma in children – a 10 year follow up; in Pepys, J. and Edwards A.M. (Eds) The Mast Cell: Its Role in Health and Disease, p. 343 (Pitman Medical Publishers, London 1979).

Godfrey, R.C.: Asthma and IgE levels in rural and urban communities of the Gambia. Clinical Allergy 5: 201 (1975).

Gregg, I.: in Clark, T.J.H. (Ed) Asthma, 2nd Edition (Saunders, W.B. and Co., Philadelphia 1983).

Jackson, R.T.; Beaglehole, R.; Rea, H.H. and Sutherland, D.C.: Asthma mortality: A new epidemic in New Zealand. British Medical Journal 285: 771 (1982).

Larsson, S.: Problems of inhalation therapy. Scandinavian Journal of Respiratory Diseases 103 (Suppl.): 50 (1979).

McQueen, F.; Holdaway, M.D. and Sears, M.R.: A study of asthma in a Dunedin suburban area. New Zealand Medical Journal 89: 335 (1979).

Pepys, J. and Hutchcroft, B.J.: Bronchial provocation tests in etiological diagnosis and analysis of asthma. American Review of Respiratory Disease 112: 829 (1975).

Platts-Mills, T.A.E.; Mitchell, E.B.; Nock, P.; Tovey, E.R.; Moszoro, H. and Wilkins, S.R.: Reduction of bronchial hyperreactivity during prolonged allergen avoidance. Lancet 2: 675 (1982).

Speight, A.N.P.; Lee, D.A. and Hey, E.N.: Underdiagnosis and undertreatment of asthma in childhood. British Medical Journal 286: 1253 (1983).

Rubinfeld, A.R. and Pain, M.C.F.: Perception of asthma. Lancet 1: 882 (1976).

Stanhope, J.M.; Rees, R.O. and Mangan, A.J.: Asthma and wheeze in New Zealand adolescents. New Zealand Medical Journal 90: 279 (1979).

Waite, D.A.; Eyles, E.F.; Tonkin, S.L. and O'Donnell, T.V.: Asthma prevalence in the Tokelauan children in two environments. Clinical Allergy 10: 71 (1980).

Warner, J.O.: Mites and asthma in children. British Journal of Diseases of the Chest 72: 79 (1978).

Wilson, J.D.; Sutherland, D.C. and Thomas, A.C.: Has the change to beta-agonists combined with oral theophylline increased cases of fatal asthma? Lancet 1: 1235 (1981).

Wilson, J.D.; Reilly, H.; Sutherland, D.C. and Kolbe, J.: Ketotifen in adult asthma: Failure to find clinical response or steroid-sparing effect. In preparation (1984).

Chapter IV

Getting the Best Out of Bronchodilator Therapy

P. Sherwood Burge

If a diabetic patient was told that the control of her diabetes required at least three separate drugs, of which the dose of one needed to be controlled depending upon blood drug levels, the second according to the long term progress of the disease, and the third to be self-adjusted on a 4-hourly basis depending on symptoms, she would look at the doctor in disbelief. Yet this is exactly what we are asking many of our patients with moderate to severe asthma to do. Outpatient control of asthma is more complicated than any other disease for both the patient and the physician; thus it is not surprising that control is often suboptimal. Few patients readily adapt to complicated treatment regimens.

Most patients coming to their doctor with symptoms of reversible airways obstruction expect to be given a diagnosis, the cause of their disease, and a cure. It is important that the diagnosis of asthma is confirmed to both the doctor's and the patient's satisfaction. Only when the patient is convinced that a cure is unlikely and that many of the precipitating factors are unavoidable, will compliance with the more complicated maintenance regimens be a possibility.

Doctors have been slow to appreciate the need to educate asthmatic patients about their disease. Possibly this stems from the days when asthma was thought to be caused by stress and anxiety, implying that it was partly the patient's fault and that if only he would 'sort himself out' then his asthma would go away.

This chapter is based on the premise that asthma is a variable disease and therefore requires variable treatment. If the doctor were in constant communication with the patient it is likely that relatively frequent changes in both drug dosage and frequency might be advised. Since doctor-patient contact is limited the patient needs to be taught how to make these adjustments himself and to know when to call for help. What follows is a personal view of this education process and the drug regimens discussed may differ from the manufacturers' recommendations on dosage and frequency of administration.

Establishing the Doctor-Patient Relationship

Generally, asthma is a chronic disease, requiring long term care. In most cases, the asthmatic patient is managed entirely by the general practitioner and the success of any proposed treatment will depend on the doctor-patient relationship (see below). [When a hospital doctor is also involved, the relative roles of the general practitioner and the hospital doctor need to be defined.] All long term asthmatics should be seen regularly by their general practitioner since patient education is much easier and more effective when the patient is well and confident than during illness when treatment has failed.

When treatment fails it is very easy to blame the patient and undermine the doctor-patient relationship. Treatment failure may be caused by a number of factors including inadequate assessment of the severity of the disease, inappropriate instruction of the patient, or by the doctor failing to compromise between an optimal therapeutic regimen and one which is acceptable to the patient. (Bargaining is an important part of a good relationship!)

A system of contact must be established for emergencies when asthma gets out of control. The patient should know what to do if his condition deteriorates. Occasionally lives may be saved by asthmatics having direct access to hospital, but most emergencies can be adequately managed by the patient or his general practitioner.

Establishing Therapeutic Control of Asthma: Oral or Inhaled Drugs?

Targeting of drugs to the required site of action increases the effect and decreases the systemic toxicity. It is therefore better and safer to give drugs for asthma by inhalation rather than orally. The only exceptions to this are the the theophyllines, and systemic corticosteroids when they are required for severe acute asthma. There is no evidence that oral β_2-agonists given in addition to inhaled β_2-agonists increase the peak bronchodilating effect or the duration of action of the inhaled drug. There is a role for oral bronchodilating drugs at night, as the administration of slow-release formulations is only possible by the oral route. Taking drugs by inhalation is more complicated for the patient but the benefits in terms of speed of onset and reduced toxicity outweigh these disadvantages in the vast majority.

The Correct Use of Inhalers

There is considerable variation in instructions for use with different types of inhaler which is not backed by scientific evidence. Many of the advocated regimens are complicated and have theoretical advantages which have not been proved in practice. There should be a basic technique taught to everybody with a few optional extras for the experts. The technique needs to be taught and re-assessed regularly.

Pressurised Aerosol Inhalers

Although there are various designs of aerosol inhaler on the market they all have a common basic structure (see appendix C). Patients can find aerosol inhalers confusing and difficult to use; even the most simple instructions may cause problems.

For example, about 2% of patients do not remove the cap from the inhaler before use. If the patient is given an elementary description of the working of aerosol inhalers it should help him understand the importance of the basic instructions, e.g. shaking the aerosol before use (to ensure even distribution of the drug in the propellant gases); holding the aerosol upright before actuation (the metering chamber, which controls the volume released on actuation, will only fill correctly when upright); and allowing 20 seconds between actuations (evaporation of the gases after release causes cooling and contraction of the metering chamber; unless it is allowed to warm and expand, the dose released will be reduced).

The standard method of using a pressurised inhaler is described in appendix C. In addition to the usual instructions, the patient should also be advised (a) to hold his chin up as this makes a relatively straight passage between the inhaler and the lungs, and (b) that only one actuation per inhalation should be used.

Use of Multiple Doses: Commonly prescribed doses of bronchodilators involve the inhalation of 2 to 4 puffs several times a day. Fortunately, it is no longer recommended that a patient allows 2 minutes between inhalations of a bronchodilator or a 10-minute gap between using a bronchodilator and a prophylactic agent such as beclomethasone dipropionate. Studies which compared the effect of giving beclomethasone dipropionate before and after sal-butamol have shown no difference (Muers and Dawkins, 1983). However, it seems reasonable to take the bronchodilating drug first.

It is the author's practice to recommend that each puff be taken immediately after the one before, providing that inspiration is slow and the breath is held for at least 10 seconds (see p.216). This means that inhalations will be spaced about 15 to 20 seconds apart, which overcomes the problem of cooling of the metering chamber discussed above. Better compliance is likely when doses are given rapidly one after the other than when complicated timing regimens are advocated.

Advanced Inhalation Techniques: There is evidence that the proportion of the drug reaching the lungs can be increased by (a) holding the mouth wide open and placing the inhaler between the lips, thus enlarging the oral cavity, and (b) holding the inhaler a few centimetres away from the open mouth (appendix C, fig. 2). Although the latter route is probably better in theory, it needs to be practised in front of a mirror to ensure that the dose is delivered into the mouth rather than over the face. These two techniques should be used only by those patients who have mastered the standard technique.

Problems with the Use of Pressurised Aerosol Inhalers:

1) The most common problem is incorrect synchronisation of inhalation with actuation of the inhaler. Constant practice is needed to correct this.

2) When using the inhaler the patient should inspire only through the mouth. Closing the mouth round the inhaler often causes breathing in through the nose and when this happens a cloud of propellant can usually be seen coming out of the mouth on subsequent exhalation. Most of the drug will then be lost in the exhalation.

3) Sometimes the blast of cold propellant (freons) on the back of the mouth causes the patient to either stop inhalation completely or to inspire through the nose. Most patients can learn to overcome this 'cold freon' effect, particularly if the inhaler is held a little way from the mouth. If the problem persists a change to a powder inhaler, or a 'spacer' device will overcome it.

4) The act of inhalation may cause coughing, although when this occurs with a bronchodilator it is usually as a result of the loosening of sputum plugs. However, pressurised inhalers occasionally cause troublesome coughing and a change to a dry powder inhaler may overcome this.

5) Paradoxically, bronchodilators can cause wheezing and

increasing airways obstruction. Fortunately such problems are rare. Although β_2-agonists, ipratropium bromide* and corticosteroid inhalers have all been responsible for precipitating asthma occasionally, this is generally not drug-induced but is caused by either the freon propellants or by material leached from the valve mechanisms or in the case of ipratropium may be associated with the bromide moiety (see p.176). A switch to an alternative preparation or different formulation of the same drug usually solves this problem.

Dry Powder Inhalers ('Rotahalers')

The advantages and disadvantages of this type of inhaler are briefly described in appendix C. The optimal method of using these inhalers has not been established. Several studies have attempted to estimate the dose of dry powder salbutamol given by 'Rotahaler' which is equivalent in clinical response to $200\mu g$ (2 puffs) of salbutamol from an aerosol. The results have ranged from 200 to $400\mu g$. This variability may reflect the poor 'Rotahaler' administration technique used in some studies. Until a better method is described the best advice for the patient is to suck these inhalers as hard as possible (appendix C, fig. 6). The 'Rotahaler' system may not function properly in humid conditions because the powder tends to stick inside the capsule and the gelatin capsules are not always pulled apart when damp. The 'Rotahaler' is also affected by static which makes the powder stick inside the plastic chamber.

'Spacer' Devices

For patients with problems of coordination with pressurised inhalers an alternative to the use of dry powder inhalers is a 'spacer' attachment which acts as a reservoir for the drug after actuation of the aerosol. The 'tube spacer', a pocket-sized device, and the 'Nebuhaler' are the most commonly used devices (appendix C, figs. 4 and 5). Their use is discussed in appendix C and the value of improvised 'spacers' in children is described in chapter VI.

Nebulisers

Nebulisers, which produce an aerosol or vapour from a solution, are an efficient means of delivering drugs to the lung without requiring patient cooperation. Most β_2-agonists are available as respirator solutions for nebulisation. For details of the administration of bronchodilators by nebuliser see appendices B and C.

A Patient Education System

The aim of this system is to teach a patient to be able to adjust asthma treatment to the best possible advantage, to cope with emergencies, and to cope with unsolicited advice from neighbours about the best treatment for asthma. Thus there should be some discussion of treatments patients are *not* having, as well as the ones which they are. The simplest way to provide this information would be by a printed leaflet. Many such leaflets are available but all suffer from the problem of having to be general rather than tailored to the needs of an individual. It is very easy for a patient reading one of these booklets to find a section that clearly

---

* For product availability in the USA, see appendix B.

does not apply to him; having ignored such sections, the value of the information in other sections which do apply, is diminished.

The system described has been developed from one devised by Dr Alistair Brewis. The basic concept is that the information is hand written by the doctor for each individual patient. The process of hand writing is important since it has to be done slowly, giving the patient ample opportunity to raise questions as the education proceeds and for the educator to amend the instructions to those which are compatible with the life style of the patient. The eventual treatment agreed on after such an educational exercise is frequently different from that one would have prescribed without discussion with the patient.

The instructions are divided into three main sections – drugs for the relief of asthma, drugs for the prevention of asthma and instructions for emergency treatment. An instruction card ruled out in these three sections is used so the patient has a durable record which can be shown to other doctors who may have to treat him.

Drugs Which Provide Relief   <u>RELIEVERS</u>

BLUE

VENTOLIN
dose 2 puffs

Intermittent Therapy

An inhaled selective β_2-agonist is the safest, most effective and most convenient initial treatment for asthma. A number of β_2-agonists are available and there is little clinical difference between them (see p.26). It is not generally appreciated that these drugs have different tastes (reproterol, for example, has an unpleasant taste which is disguised with a strong peppermint flavour) and that this may influence the willingness of the patient to comply with the prescribed regimen.

Ipratropium bromide, an anticholinergic agent, has a different mechanism of action to the β_2-agonists and in an occasional patient produces a better response. When maximal doses of β_2-agonists do not provide adequate relief it is always worth trying ipratropium bromide either in addition to, or instead of, the β_2-agonist. Ipratropium bromide is administered in a similar way to the β_2-agonists but the onset of bronchodilatation is slower and patients should not expect an immediate response.

The patient can be confidently assured of the safety of β_2-adrenergic aerosols. It should be remembered that the total dose of β_2-agonist in a pressurised inhaler is relatively small [even assuming 100% absorption, the inhalation of the complete contents (200 metered doses) of a salbutamol canister would only be equivalent to an oral dose of five 4mg tablets], so that toxicity from the excessive use of an aerosol is unlikely.

The only important side effect which needs to be discussed with the patient is tremor. Fortunately, tachycardia is rarely seen with standard doses given by inhalation and generally is caused by the much higher systemic doses given in severe acute asthma (see p.176).

Temporary benefit only – lasts 2-4 hours

Patients who expect their β_2-agonist therapy to cure them need to be disillusioned. It is also important to ask them how long the relief from their inhalers lasts since it is often much less than the expected 2 to 4 hours duration. However, the duration of relief is in part dose-related and patients who have a reasonable response to the standard dose may have this response extended if the dose is doubled. If the relief obtained from one of the longer acting β_2-agonists lasts for less than one hour this indicates that either the inhaler has been used incorrectly, or that the asthma is very severe and requires much more aggressive treatment.

Can repeat dose every 3 hours if necessary

The shortest interval advocated is two hours for those few patients who have a very short duration of relief – most obtain a more sustained effect. It is worth reminding patients that inhalations can be used throughout the night, if they wake, as well as during the day.

Can use additional doses before exercise

β_2-agonists are very effective in preventing attacks of exercise-induced asthma (chapter VII). A pre-exercise dose, taken in addition to regular therapy, can be inhaled about 5 minutes before strenuous exercise.

Does not work for very severe attacks (call doctor)

It is essential that the patient understands the limitations of inhaled β_2-agonist therapy. Non-responsiveness to inhaled therapy indicates an attack of severe asthma which requires intensive treatment. To those who have never experienced an attack of this severity before it is simply stated that they should call their doctor at whatever time of the day or night this occurs. However, a patient who has had severe attacks before and knows from past experience that these do not begin with catastrophic suddenness, is told to start his emergency treatment (see below).

Many patients are worried that they will 'get used' to their inhaled β_2-agonist if it is used regularly. This possibility is discussed in chapter V and although it appears that tolerance is not a significant clinical problem, patients may fail to respond to their usual aerosol therapy during severe acute asthma, or may become 'resistant' because of mucus plugging or bronchial wall oedema. It is reasonable to advise patients that tolerance can occur but that when it does it is temporary and indicates a need for more intensive therapy and that full efficacy can be restored, usually following a course of corticosteroids.

Regular Therapy

Many asthmatic patients require regular bronchodilator medication in addition to their 'as needed' therapy. The main choices are:

a) Add a prophylactic drug such as an inhaled steroid or sodium cromoglycate (cromolyn sodium) and continue with 'on-demand' β_2-agonists. This is the preferred next step, as prophylactic drugs are capable of improving the underlying bronchial hyper-reactivity and often raise the level of lung function sufficiently to make periods of deterioration less significant.

b) Prescribe a β_2-agonist regularly, perhaps with 'on-demand' β_2-agonists as well. The main problems with this regimen is that none of the β_2-agonists has a useful half-life exceeding three hours in the majority of patients. It is is therefore often necessary to give the drugs three-hourly.

c) Add an oral theophylline to 'on-demand' β_2-agonists. In the author's view the other two regimens are safer with fewer side effects.

Additional relievers —
Phyllocontin OO dose 450mg night and morning
Too little has little benefit, too much causes nausea and vomiting
Best taken regularly

Oral theophyllines are particularly indicated for persisting nocturnal and early morning asthma in patients already on a prophylactic drug.

It is worth stressing the narrow therapeutic ratio of theophyllines and that for their optimal use plasma levels should be maintained between 10 to 20 mg/L. Some people develop nausea and vomiting at very low levels. This particularly occurs in those with oesophageal reflux in whom the drugs are rarely tolerated. About 20% of all asthmatics fail to tolerate even low doses of theophyllines.

Some patients develop insomnia and some children, enuresis. A few experience vivid dreams. These side effects are worth discussing. However, in the majority, slow-release preparations are well tolerated. Nausea and vomiting may not occur as a side effect before fits develop, when mortality is high. Thus it is important to measure plasma levels to ensure both efficacy and safety (see p.82). Theophyllines are the only standard drug for asthma for which drug monitoring is necessary. Plasma level measurement can be of great use in identifying patients whose asthma is uncontrolled due to non-compliance. Theophyllines are best taken regularly as it is difficult to achieve an adequate plasma concentration when the drugs are given intermittently.

Do not take extra doses if your asthma is bad

Patients must understand that theophylline is different from their other medicines as it cannot be used as 'on-demand' therapy and the dose should be neither increased nor decreased without the advice of their doctor.

AVOID AMINOPHYLLINE INJECTIONS

Bolus aminophylline injections in a patient already receiving oral theophyllines can give rise to potentially fatal toxicity and should be avoided (see p.178). In severe acute asthma, alternative therapy, such as nebulised, intravenous or subcutaneous injections of salbutamol or terbutaline should be used.

Prophylactic Therapy

There are a number of treatments which can be considered as 'preventers'. A detailed discussion of the use of sodium cromoglycate (cromolyn sodium), ketotifen or inhaled corticosteroids is not appropriate here, but using inhaled beclomethasone dipropionate as an example, patient education for the prophylactic agents is as follows:

PREVENTERS

No immediate effect

Must use regularly whether good or bad

The patient must understand that prophylactic medication acts to prevent the onset of a wheezing attack and must therefore be taken regularly and in the appropriate dosage. As discussed earlier, when inhaled corticosteroids are being taken in addition to β_2-agonists it is probably advisable to take the β_2-agonist first. The prophylactic agents have no immediate effect and will not act as 'relievers'. Unlike the β_2-agonists, the inhaled corticosteroids do not prevent exercise-induced asthma.

When given by inhalation corticosteroids are not associated with the same hazards as systemic therapy. One of the side effects which may be encountered is *Candida albicans* infection of the oral cavity and vocal cords, causing soreness of the mouth, and a hoarse voice. The infection may either resolve spontaneously or can be treated with nystatin mouthwashes or amphotericin lozenges. Deposition of corticosteroid on the vocal cord can cause hoarseness which it has been suggested is caused by myopathy of the laryngeal musculature. The use of a large 'spacer' device should reduce vocal cord deposition and may diminish this problem.

DOES NOT PREVENT SEVERE ATTACKS

Patients should understand that even with regular prophylactic treatment severe asthma might still develop. When this happens, more aggressive treatment will be required to re-establish control before returning to the basic prophylactic regimen.

DO NOT RUN OUT

About 20% of all hospital admissions for acute asthma occur because patients have run out of their regular treatment and control has been lost. It is pointless prescribing inhalers one at a time (any inhaler may fail to work at all for technical reasons) and at each consultation patients should be questioned about their supply of medication and reminded to always carry their inhalers with them.

Emergency Treatment

In discussing the management of the severe attacks of asthma patients may be considered in three groups:

1) Those who have never experienced severe acute asthma
2) Patients who have had previous attacks which were gradual in onset and often associated with respiratory tract infections
3) Those who develop sudden, catastrophic attacks.

The first group will not need any advice on the management of severe asthma and in addition to the instructions outlined above require only guidance on the use of antibiotics. Patients in the third group whose episodes of severe asthma develop suddenly should have ready access to parenteral medication, oxygen and nebuliser units. The instructions for emergency treatment outlined below are inappropriate for these patients who should be told always to call a doctor at the first sign of an attack.

However, many experience a slow deterioration of their condition and the instructions and advice needed by this group (group 2) are as follows:

EMERGENCY TREATMENT

PREDNISOLONE IS AN IMPORTANT RESERVE TREATMENT FOR SEVERE ASTHMA

Many patients are very wary of corticosteroids having often seen these drugs used inappropriately in the past. Patients' anxieties and worries need to be discussed frankly and the potential benefits and risks of this form of treatment explained.

Side effects?
Only with large doses for a long time (many months)

Many of the more severe side effects of corticosteroids are dose-dependent. Patients on not more than 7.5mg daily of prednisolone or its equivalent, are unlikely to develop any of the long term complications. With doses of 7.5 to 15mg daily they may put on weight and develop a Cushingoid appearance or some other long term side effect, the more serious of which (with the exception of weight gain and the 'moon face' which can develop rapidly) only arise over a period of months or years. Fortunately, long term high dose corticosteroids are very seldom necessary in asthma.

Short courses are (safe)

day 1	OOOOOO	6 x 5mg
day 2	OOOOO	5 x 5mg
day 3	OOOO	4 x 5mg
day 4	OOO	3 x 5mg
day 5	OO	2 x 5mg
day 6	O	1 x 5mg
day 7	STOP	

Take whole dose first thing each morning.

A common cause of hospital admission is failure of a six-day reducing course of corticosteroids to be effective. Patients should be told that if their condition deteriorates while taking the course of prednisolone they should start again with the highest doses and call for help. Therefore, it is advisable to ensure that an excess of tablets is available.

When to start a short course of prednisolone?

1. *Inhalers don't work*

2. *Terrible nights*

3. *Morning asthma lasts till lunchtime*

4. *Immobilised*

5. *Gradual deterioration so that 1-4 are inevitable*

6. *If you have an emergency injection for your asthma*

When an attack of wheezing is not relieved by the usual inhaler therapy a short course of oral corticosteroids should be started. There is evidence that steroids may restore responsiveness to the β_2-agonists (see p.169). Respiratory infections may cause a slow deterioration in asthma and often more benefit is achieved if prednisolone is started before the deterioration becomes severe. Patients who keep continuous records of their PEFR are frequently able to detect an early deterioration in function and initiate prednisolone treatment appropriately. Often an acute attack of asthma at home is treated with parenteral β_2-agonists or aminophylline. This provides short term relief while corticosteroid therapy takes effect.

Respiratory infections are an important cause of deteriorating asthma

Antibiotics – When Are They Indicated?

Many infections causing deterioration in asthma are viral and will not respond to antibiotics.

Antibiotics are rarely indicated

In a controlled trial of amoxycillin versus placebo in patients admitted to hospital with severe asthma (Graham et al., 1982) there was no difference detected between the response of the antibiotic-treated patients and that of the placebo group. While antibiotics are seldom harmful when given for acute asthmatic attacks it must be realised that it is the doctor who is being treated and not the patient.

Never sufficient on their own – always increase your preventers at the same time

As they do not relieve wheeze or prevent asthma, nor affect the viral infections which are often responsible for the deterioration, antibiotics should only be prescribed in addition to more aggressive antiasthma treatment, if they are used at all.

The Completed Patient Education Card

Examples of completed cards are shown in figures 4.1 and 4.2. At first sight a completed card can appear rather daunting. However, it is easily understood by the patient as it was compiled in stages during discussion with him. If a pre-printed form of this type were given to the patient there would be much less chance of its being read or understood. Figure 4.2 shows a simplified education form designed for a 9-year-old girl with intermittent asthma principally triggered by exercise and viral infection.

Assessment of the Response to Treatment

Accurate assessment of response can be difficult, partly because of the variable nature of the disease and partly because patients tend to be at their best during the day when seen in doc-

RELIEVERS

BLUE

VENTOLIN
dose 2 puffs

(Good) (Safe)

Temporary benefit only — lasts 2-4 hours

Take 2 puffs every 4 hours regularly. Can take an extra dose in between if your breathing is bad.

Maximum dose 24 puffs per 24 hours.

DOES NOT WORK FOR VERY SEVERE ATTACKS

Phyllocontin 450mg (OO) night and morning
Too little has no effect
Too much causes nausea and vomiting
Do not take extra doses when bad

(AVOID AMINOPHYLLINE INJECTIONS)

PREVENTERS

BROWN

BECOTIDE

Dose when well — 4 puffs night and morning

Dose when asthma worse — 8 puffs night and morning

(Good), (Safe)

DO NOT RUN OUT

No immediate benefit

Must use regularly whether good or bad.

Can cause sore mouth or hoarse voice.

DOES NOT PREVENT REALLY SEVERE ATTACKS

EMERGENCY TREATMENT

PREDNISOLONE important reserve treatment for severe attacks:

day 1   OOOOOO   6 x 5mg
day 2   OOOOO   5 x 5mg
day 3   OOOO   4 x 5mg
day 4   OOO   3 x 5mg
day 5   OO   2 x 5mg
day 6   O   1 x 5mg
day 7   STOP

Take whole dose first thing each morning.

SIDE EFFECTS?

Only with large doses for a long time

Short courses of prednisolone are (Safe)

When to start a short course?

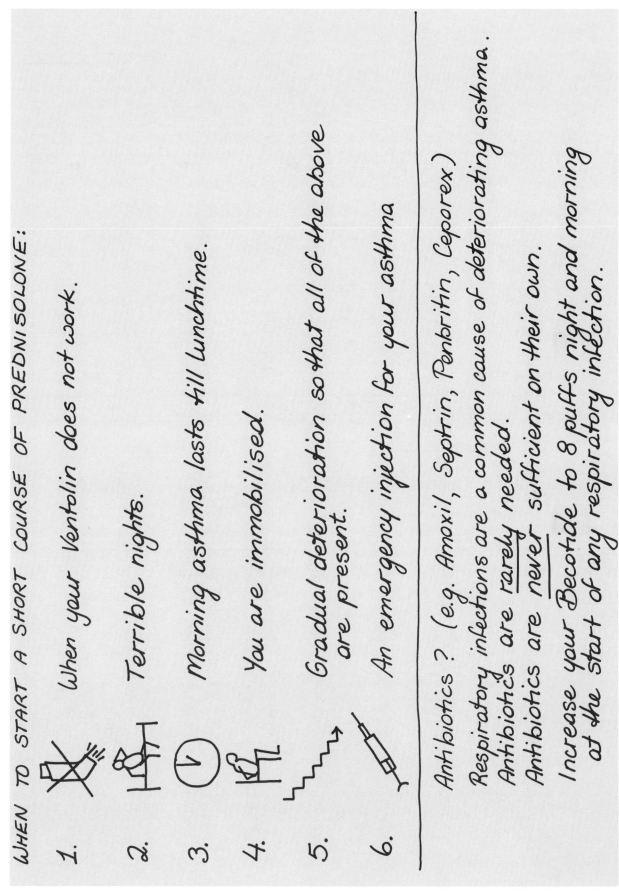

WHEN TO START A SHORT COURSE OF PREDNISOLONE:

1. When your Ventolin does not work.

2. Terrible nights.

3. Morning asthma lasts till lunchtime.

4. You are immobilised.

5. Gradual deterioration so that all of the above are present.

6. An emergency injection for your asthma

Antibiotics ? (e.g. Amoxil, Septrin, Penbritin, Ceporex)
Respiratory infections are a common cause of deteriorating asthma.
Antibiotics are rarely needed.
Antibiotics are never sufficient on their own.

Increase your Becotide to 8 puffs night and morning at the start of any respiratory infection.

Fig. 4.1. A completed patient education card for a severe asthmatic patient with regular morning 'dips' and in whom major asthma is precipitated by infection.

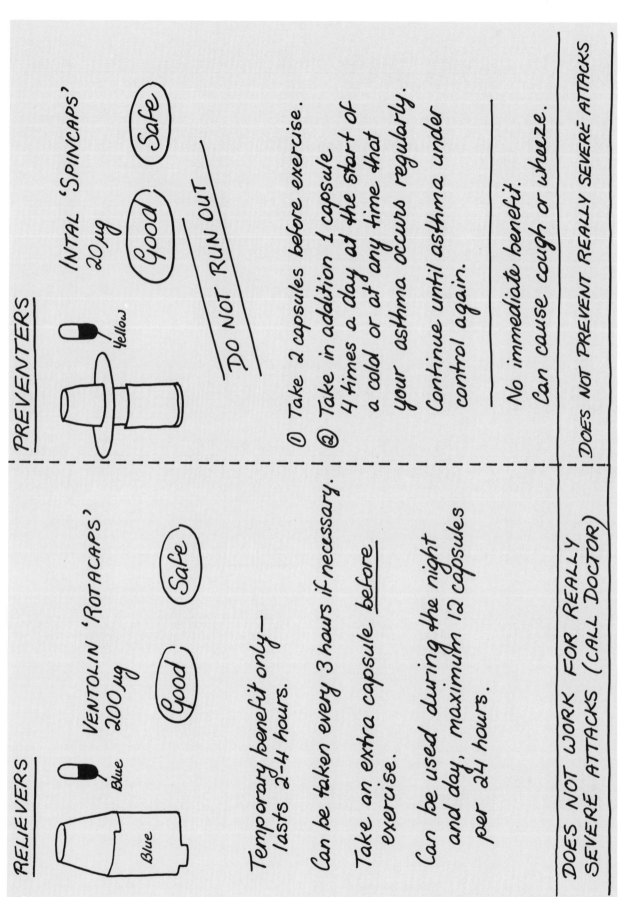

Fig. 4.2. A completed patient education card for a 9-year-old child whose asthma is mainly triggered by exercise and viral infection.

tors' surgeries and clinics. There is a normal diurnal variation in airways calibre which is increased in asthmatics (chapter VIII), and respiratory function is lowest in the latter part of the night and on waking. A patient with few symptoms in the middle of the day may tell his physician that he was so breathless during the night that he was unable to talk. It is very easy for the doctor not to be worried by this history because of the normal appearance of the patient during the consultation yet the patient may experience the same nocturnal distress that night. It is surprising how many doctors are unconcerned about these symptoms which if they were of equal severity in a patient with cardiac failure would almost always result in aggressive treatment.

Assessment in the Clinic

Unless specific questions are put to the patient the physician might easily miss quite severe morbidity. Patients may be away from school or work for weeks at a time because of their asthma without necessarily telling their physician about it. The following questions should be routinely asked:

● Have you woken up short of breath during the night?
● Are you short of breath on waking in the morning and if so, for how long?
● Are your activities limited by your asthma, in particular have you had any time off work or school?
● What treatment are you taking and what recent changes have been made?
● Have any of your treatments run out?
● Have you had any severe attacks of asthma?

Measurement of Lung Function

Some measurement of lung function (FEV_1, FVC or PEFR) should be made at every visit. Ideally measurements should be taken before and after using a bronchodilator; this also allows inhaler technique to be checked. The post-bronchodilator measurement can be particularly useful as a gradual decline – which may be unnoticed by the patient – is often an indication for increasing the prophylactic treatment.

Records Kept by the Patient

Records kept by the patient are fundamental to the management of the more severe asthmatic. With such records a physician seeing a patient intermittently can be much more help, rather than listening to a few anecdotes about how the patient has been in the last few days. Either records of peak flow or symptoms recorded on a diary card, or both can be used. Diary cards are used more frequently in children, and peak flow records in adults, although there is no clear reason for this. Each of these assessments measures something different – a diary card measures symptoms as perceived by the patient or his parents, whereas the peak flow is an objective measurement of lung function. Many of the more difficult asthmatics have a poor perception of changes in airway calibre. A few over-react to small changes in airway calibre. More critically, patients with more severe asthma frequently under-react to quite marked changes particularly when the onset is relatively gradual. For these, peak flow records are invaluable (Burdon et al., 1982).

Ideally, peak flow measurements should be recorded every 4 hours, before and after inhalation of a bronchodilator, although

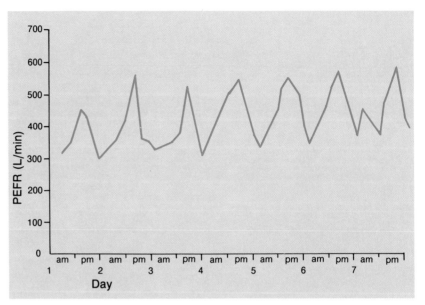

Fig. 4.3. The peak flow record of an untreated asthmatic patient showing the characteristic diurnal variability and the extent of nocturnal asthma. The diagnosis of asthma in this patient was confirmed by the peak flow record.

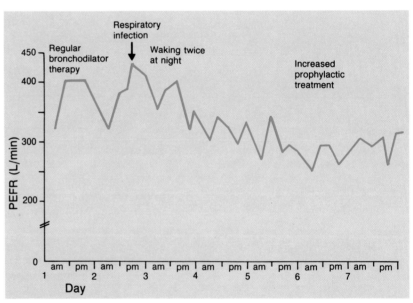

Fig. 4.4. A peak flow record showing the gradual deterioration in lung function following a viral respiratory infection in a patient on regular bronchodilator therapy.

this is impractical in most cases. Patients with severe acute asthma who required hospital admission should continue to record these measurements following discharge until their maintenance is well established. Selected patients with less severe asthma should also make regular measurements, at least 3 times a day. It is important that lung function is measured as soon as they get up in the morning, to estimate the 'morning dip', and again before going to bed at night. At least one reading in the middle of the day is also desirable. Figure 4.3 illustrates the value of PEFR records in diagnosing asthma in a patient who appeared normal on examination. The gradual deterioration in lung function associated with respiratory infection is clearly shown in figure 4.4.

Special Problems

The scheme for patient education described should ensure optimum therapy for the great majority of patients. However, there are a few special circumstances when alternative forms of treatment are needed.

An extreme example is provided by patients whose religion requires that they fast; Muslims may not take anything by mouth or by inhalation from dawn until sunset during the month of Ramadan each year. Special dispensation can sometimes be obtained but most patients prefer not to take treatment during the day. Unless the physician anticipates the situation and arranges alternative treatment before Ramadan many patients will stop their treatment and severe acute asthma may develop.

Every clinician has his share of 'impossible' patients and it is surprising that the incidence of severe asthma is not higher, considering the complicated regimens which they are expected to follow. It is only because the treatment is so effective that most patients are prepared to comply. For those who cannot a simpler regimen, preferably involving only twice-daily dosing is needed. The longer acting oral β_2-agonists, the slow-release theophyllines, and low doses of oral prednisolone are appropriate for these patients. It is probably better to compromise with a sub-optimal regimen than to insist on one with which the patient cannot comply.

Acknowledgements

The contributions of Doctors Roger Altouynan and Alistair Brewis in providing the majority of the original proposals in this chapter are acknowledged.

References

Burdon, J.G.W.; Juniper, E.F.; Killian, K.J.; Hargreave, F.E. and Campbell, E.J.M.: The perception of breathlessness in asthma. American Review of Respiratory Disease 126: 825 (1982).

Graham, V.A.L.; Milton, A.F.; Knowles, G.K. and Davies, R.J.: Routine antibiotics in hospital management of acute asthma. Lancet 1: 418 (1982).

Muers, M. and Dawkins, K.: Effect of timed interval between inhalation of beta agonist and corticosteroid aerosols on the control of chronic asthma. Thorax 38: 378 (1983).

Further Reading

Burge, P.S.: Trigger factors in asthma; in Clark (Ed.) Steroids in Asthma, chapter V, pp.61 (ADIS Press, Auckland 1983).

Newman, S.P.: The correct use of inhalers; in Clark (Ed.) Steroids in Asthma, appendix 1, pp.210 (ADIS Press, Auckland 1983).

Turner-Warwick, M.: Patterns of response in asthma as measured by serial peak flow readings. On observing patterns of airflow obstruction in chronic asthma. British Journal of Diseases of the Chest 71: 73 (1977).

Chapter V

Bronchodilators in the Prevention of Asthma

Anne E. Tattersfield

There can be little doubt that the major changes in asthma over the last 30 years have been the improvement in control of asthma symptoms and reduction in morbidity. These changes are largely attributable to the development and effective use of potent bronchodilator drugs, which modify and control the symptoms of asthma whilst not affecting the underlying abnormality. Unfortunately, the reduced morbidity has not been associated with a similar reduction in mortality from asthma.

There is considerable variation in severity of the clinical features of asthma: some patients suffer from unremitting cough and breathlessness while others experience only an occasional wheeze. Although many patients will require little treatment, a large number will need long term, regular therapy in order to lead a normal active life.

This chapter discusses the use and long term effects of the three main groups of bronchodilators in the prevention and suppression of the clinical manifestations of asthma.

Should Bronchodilator Treatment be Given Regularly or 'On-Demand'?

The decision to use bronchodilators intermittently is influenced by two factors:

● Whether patients are able to comply with 'on-demand' regimens; and
● Whether regular treatment has any long term benefits.

Studies in both children and adults have shown that patients taking regular β_2-agonists took slightly higher doses, resulting in slightly better PEFR and FEV_1 values than when treatment was taken as required (Lenney et al., 1979; Shepherd et al., 1981). There was no evidence to suggest that the patients were better clinically on regular treatment, or that regular treatment produced any long term benefit. Further information is needed on this important point, particularly in children.

Many patients with mild asthma prefer to take 'on-demand' treatment and often do so with an FEV_1 of less than the possible maximum. This approach appears to be satisfactory as long as the patient is largely asymptomatic. If the patient experiences more frequent wheezing or occasional episodes of more severe asthma, regular therapy should be given in addition to 'on-demand' treatment. This is particularly important in children who are less able to take 'on-demand' therapy. Treatment of severe nocturnal asthma usually requires high dose β_2-agonist by inhalation or orally, inhaled corticosteroid, or slow-release theophylline. In exercise-induced asthma, inhalation of a dose of β_2-agonist 5 minutes before exercise can prevent the onset of an attack. The 'on-demand' dose can be taken in combination with regular therapy (chapter VII).

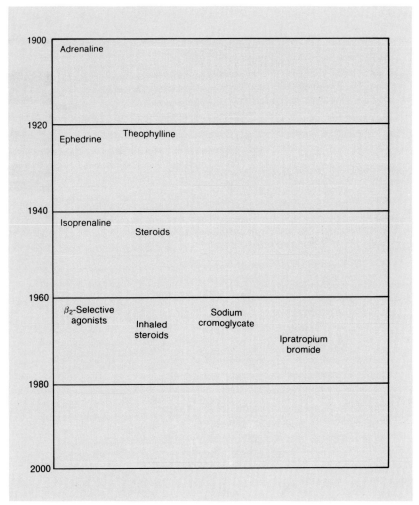

Fig. 5.1. Developments in therapy for asthma in the twentieth century.

Oral theophylline therapy should be given regularly and it must be made clear to the patient that the dose should not be increased without medical advice. The slow onset of action of the anticholinergic drugs makes them unsuitable for treatment 'on-demand'.

Most patients with other than mild asthma require regular bronchodilator treatment, preferably by inhalation, with additional 'on-demand' therapy to relieve breakthrough symptoms. Patients should understand the need and the indications for both forms of treatment (chapter IV).

Bronchodilators for Regular Therapy

When introducing regular bronchodilator therapy, treatment should be adapted for each individual. Ideally, a bronchodilator which is to be used long term should fulfil certain criteria:

- Effective bronchodilating action
- Satisfactory onset and duration of effect
- Convenient for patient to take
- Low toxicity
- Additive effect with other bronchodilators
- No development of tolerance.

Table 5.1. Adrenoceptors thought to be responsible for the main actions and side effects of sympathomimetic amines in clinical practice

Tissue	Receptors	Response
Airways	β_2	Bronchodilatation, reduction in mediator release from mast cells, increased mucus production and ciliary activity
	α	?Bronchoconstriction ?Increased mediator release from mast cells
Heart	β_1	Tachycardia, inotropic action
Blood vessels	β_2	Dilatation
	α	Constriction
Uterus	β_2	Relaxation
Muscle	β_2	Tremor
'Metabolic'	β_2	Increased glucose, insulin lactate, pyruvate, free fatty acids, glycerol and ketone bodies. Decreased potassium, phosphate and calcium.

Background

Until the beginning of the twentieth century, asthma was treated with a variety of substances including morphine, arsenic and extracts of plants containing atropine, hyoscyamine and hyoscine. Adrenaline (epinephrine) was isolated in 1901 and was used subsequently by inhalation for asthma. Ephedrine, introduced in the 1920s, was the first oral sympathomimetic agent for asthma. Although the bronchodilating effect of theophylline was identified as early as 1921, systematic investigation of the methylxanthines for asthma was delayed until the late 1930s. Coffee had been recommended earlier as 'one of the commonest and best reputed remedies of asthma', and recent investigations suggest that strong coffee may be an effective bronchodilator (Becker et al., 1984).

Thus, the bronchodilating activity of anticholinergic, sympathomimetic and methylxanthine compounds has been recognised for over 50 years (fig. 5.1). Since then, chemical modification of the original compounds and advances in formulation technology have resulted in compounds with a more selective therapeutic action, fewer unwanted effects, and in a wider range of formulations (see p.23; appendix A).

β-Adrenoceptor Agonists

Adrenoceptor agonists can be classified according to their adrenoceptor activity (p.22). The early drugs, adrenaline and ephedrine, stimulated both α- and β-adrenoceptors and were associated with a number of undesirable cardiovascular effects, and have no place in the regular treatment of asthma.

Receptor Activity

Table 5.1 outlines the type of adrenoceptor responsible for the main actions and side effects of the adrenoceptor agonist drugs. Isoprenaline was the first sympathomimetic compound with pure β-adrenoceptor activity and is usually the standard by which other drugs are assessed. The major limitation to its use is its equal activity at β_1- and β_2-receptors and consequent dose-related tachycardia.

Bronchodilatation with little cardiac effect should be achieved by an agent with only β_2-receptor activity. There are several adrenoceptor agonists with a more selective action at β_2-receptors than isoprenaline (see table 2.2, p.24).

Choice of a β₂-Agonist

There is no clinical evidence that any β_2-agonist will produce greater maximum bronchodilatation than another. The more selective drugs have obvious advantages over the older, non-selective agents and are now used in preference. Factors which should be considered in selecting a β_2-agonist for regular therapy are the duration of effect and the route by which it can be administered.

Duration of Effect

In general, the duration of response following inhalation of a β-agonist is 3 to 6 hours depending on the dose. Rimiterol* has a shorter duration of effect, 1 to 2 hours.

Side Effects

In general, the adverse reactions of each drug correspond to its receptor activity. Although tachycardia and palpitations occur less frequently with the β_2-agonists than with isoprenaline, tachycardia is associated with high dose β_2-agonist therapy, probably due to reflex vagal withdrawal rather than direct cardiac stimulation. Arrhythmias and angina can develop following the use of high dose β_2-agonists by nebuliser, particularly in patients with pre-existing heart disease (Neville et al., 1982; Tattersfield, 1983) and have rarely been reported with recommended doses orally and by metered dose inhaler (Adverse Drug Reactions Advisory Committee, 1979; Al-Hillawi et al., 1984; Banner et al., 1979).

Skeletal muscle tremor, a fall in arterial oxygen tension, increased blood glucose and hypokalaemia are all associated with β_2-receptor activity and consequently are seen with all drugs in this group. With the exception of mild muscle tremor, which may arise with standard oral and inhaled doses, the other effects are not a problem with regular treatment. Metabolic effects can occur with parenteral therapy.

Tolerance

The main concern about the long term use of β-agonists has been that patients may develop tolerance (tachyphylaxis, resistance) to their effect, as has been demonstrated *in vitro* and in animals (see p.31). Although in the 1960s two retrospective studies of patients taking very high doses of inhaled isoprenaline (up to one inhaler/day) suggested that tolerance can develop in some patients taking high doses regularly (Reisman, 1970; Van Metre, 1969), many patients have taken up to, or slightly more than the recommended doses of inhaled β-agonists regularly by metered dose inhaler for 14 years and the effectiveness of the drugs has been maintained. In general, β_2-agonists are less effective when asthma deteriorates, but responsiveness returns as the condition improves.

In addition, over 40 prospective studies have been conducted in which patients have been given high or maximum recommended doses of oral or inhaled β_2-agonists. Although individual studies may be criticised, on balance, the evidence suggests that tolerance does not normally develop in patients taking recommended doses of β_2-agonists either orally or by inhalation. These studies do not exclude the occasional possibility of a patient developing tolerance, although this would appear to be extremely rare. Studies conducted in the author's unit suggest that regular inhalation of high dose salbutamol may be associated with a de-

---

* For product availability in the USA, see appendix B.

Table 5.2. The main actions of theophylline

Respiratory system	Bronchodilatation Reduction in mediator release from mast cells Increased mucociliary clearance Respiratory stimulation Increased force of contraction of fatigued diaphragm (disputed)
Cardiovascular system	Direct chronotropic and inotropic effect Arrhythmias Venodilatation ⎫ Vasodilatation ⎭ postural hypotension Increased resistance of cerebral arterioles Stimulation of vagal and vasomotor centre
Central nervous system	Stimulant effect → insomnia, vomiting, fits, irritability, confusion and disorientation
Kidney	Diuresis
Skeletal muscle	Tremor

creased responsiveness to β-agonists, although no deterioration in FEV_1 or FVC was detected (Stainforth and Tattersfield, 1983).

Misunderstanding has arisen because tolerance has been shown to develop in the airways of normal subjects taking inhaled β-agonists (Harvey and Tattersfield, 1982; Holgate et al., 1977; Tashkin et al., 1982) and can easily be demonstrated *in vitro* (chapter II), and in tissues other than the airways in asthmatic patients (Larsson et al., 1977). The reason for the differences is not clear but the only findings of clinical relevance are those in the airways of asthmatic patients which have largely failed to show the development of tolerance. In long term use orally or by metered dose inhaler β_2-agonists maintain their therapeutic effect.

Methylxanthines

The large number of methylxanthine products marketed as bronchodilators consists of various formulations of theophylline base, theophylline salts (e.g. aminophylline) which dissociate to theophylline *in vivo*, and non-theophylline compounds (table 2.3, p.33). Enprophylline, a non-methylated xanthine is currently being evaluated. Theophylline salts and methylxanthines other than theophylline have no proven advantage over theophylline itself.

Theophylline compounds are available for oral, rectal and parenteral administration.

Slow-release Theophylline

Inter-individual variation in the degree and rate of absorption of oral theophyllines has resulted in the introduction of slow-release theophylline preparations, designed to give a continuous, graded release of a drug over 10 to 12 hours. The incidence of gastric irritation is lower with the sustained release products compared with other oral formulations.

Bronchodilatation and
Plasma Concentration

Both the therapeutic response to theophylline and the incidence of side effects are closely related to plasma concentrations of the drug (see p.38). With intravenous aminophylline, bronchodilatation was detected with plasma levels as low as 5 mg/L and increased progressively as plasma levels increased up to 20 mg/L

(Mitenko and Ogilvie, 1973). It has always been assumed that the same relationship would hold with oral theophylline. However, a recent study found that a small increase in FEV_1 occurred when mean theophylline plasma levels rose from 6 to 12 mg/L, but that no further increase in FEV_1 was achieved by increasing the plasma levels to 19 mg/L (Klein et al., 1983). Plasma levels of 10 to 20 mg/L are said to be optimal since they combine a reasonable amount of bronchodilatation with a relatively low incidence of side effects. In Europe, where oral theophylline is seldom the sole treatment for asthma, a more conservative therapeutic range of 7.5 to 15 mg/L is often used.

Side Effects

The main side effects of theophylline therapy are due to its effects on the cardiovascular and central nervous systems (table 5.2), although gastrointestinal irritation is also a prominent feature. Central nervous system toxicity often presents in children as fits or irritability, while elderly patients are more likely to complain of confusion and disorientation. The most common adverse reactions are nausea, vomiting and anorexia. Although some patients cannot tolerate even low doses of theophylline, the incidence of side effects and the development of toxicity are related to plasma concentrations (fig. 5.2).

In 8 patients with tonic-clonic convulsions the mean theophylline plasma concentration was 53 mg/L (Zwillich et al., 1975). Unfortunately, there are large individual differences and patients with theophylline levels > 100 mg/L have been asymptomatic (Snodgrass et al., 1980), while convulsions have occurred with levels as low as 25 mg/L (Zwillich et al., 1975).

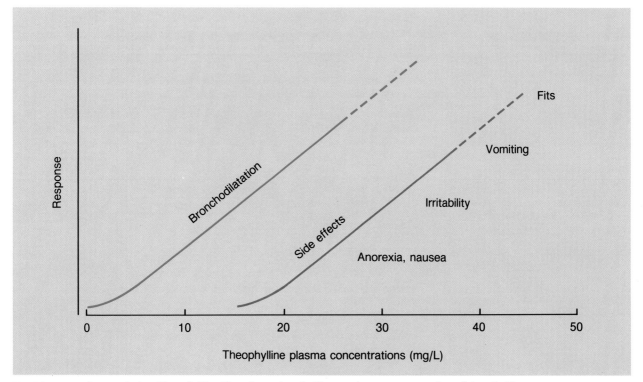

Fig. 5.2. Approximate relationships of side effects from theophylline to plasma concentration of theophylline.

The long term incidence of side effects with methylxanthines is difficult to assess. Most long term studies of methylxanthine treatment have been carried out in patients whose theophylline plasma levels were maintained in the optimum range (10 to 20 mg/L) and in these patients the incidence of adverse effects is very low. However, theophylline plasma level monitoring is standard practice neither in United Kingdom, nor elsewhere, and it is unlikely that most doctors are fully conversant with the large number of factors which might alter theophylline clearance. The prevalence of severe side effects and death in unmonitored theophylline-treated patients is unknown. Usually fairly low doses are prescribed so that the risk of toxicity is minimal. This is true for the majority of patients but some experience toxic side effects even with conservative dosage regimens, and these reactions may not be recognised as being drug induced (Woodcock et al., 1983). When plasma levels were measured in patients not routinely monitored, toxic levels were reported in 8 and 20% of patients, while the majority had subtherapeutic levels (< 10 mg/L) [Toennesen et al., 1981; Woodcock et al., 1983].

Two situations of particular risk are:

a) the use of intravenous aminophylline to treat severe acute attacks in a patient on regular long term therapy (see p.178); and

b) the patient who is taking two methylxanthine preparations concurrently.

The latter is more likely to occur when the patient receives a compound drug preparation containing theophylline.

Establishing Theophylline Maintenance Therapy

Weinberger and Hendeles (1983) have suggested a scheme for establishing optimal therapy in ambulatory patients. They recommend giving a small initial dose based on bodyweight followed by further increments after 3 and 6 days, if tolerated. Plasma theophylline levels are checked after a further 3 days, 4 hours after the last dose. Further adjustments are made if necessary to obtain a theophylline concentration in the therapeutic range. Having stabilised therapy, plasma levels should be monitored regularly every 6 to 12 months, or more frequently in children or in patients whose control is suboptimal. Most slow-release preparations if administered every 12 hours will usually provide fairly stable levels in non-smoking adults, but children and adults who smoke may require 8-hourly administration. As a standard precaution, patients should be told to halve their dose when they are febrile and not to take additional drug therapy without establishing the safety of the combination. Theophylline should be avoided in patients with epilepsy, peptic ulcer, abnormal liver function or heart failure (tables 5.3 and 5.4).

Anticholinergic Agents

Anticholingeric agents, which act as competitive antagonists at muscarinic cholinergic receptors, induce bronchodilatation by reducing vagal tone to bronchial smooth muscle (see p.18). Atropine sulphate and atropine methonitrate have been available by inhalation for many years and although side effects are uncommon with recommended doses, urinary retention and glaucoma can occur.

The introduction of ipratropium bromide provided a drug with bronchial selectivity and poor penetration into the central

Table 5.3. Factors affecting theophylline clearance[1]

Increased clearance	Decreased clearance

Enzyme-inducing drugs, e.g.
  ethanol
  phenobarbitone
  rifampicin
  sulphinpyrazone, etc.
Tobacco
Marihuana
Barbecued meat
High protein, low carbohydrate diet
Youth
Cystic fibrosis
	Enzyme-inhibiting drugs, e.g.
	  cimetidine
	  oral contraceptives
	  β-blockers
	  erythromycin compounds
	  troleandomycin
	Caffeine
	High carbohydrate diet
	Age
	Obesity
	Antiviral vaccines

	Factors altering hepatic blood flow and/
	or oxygenation, e.g.
	  cirrhosis
	  congestive cardiac failure
	  pulmonary oedema
	  chronic obstructive airways disease
	  cor pulmonale
	  fever
	  viral infection

1 – Antacids may alter the rate of absorption of theophylline from slow-release preparations by increasing gastric pH.

Table 5.4. Variation of theophylline half-life with age, smoking and disease

Situation of patient	Approximate theophylline half-life (h)
Neonates	30
Children < 1 year	20
Children 1-6 years	3
Children 6-17 years	4
Healthy non-smoking adults	7-8
Healthy smoking adults	4-5
Heart failure	23
Alcoholic cirrhosis	26

nervous system. The drug is not administered orally or parenterally, but is available as an aerosol and nebuliser solution for inhalation. Ipratropium bromide causes fewer side effects than atropine but untreated narrow angle glaucoma is a contraindication to its use. Studies of ipratropium bromide by metered dose inhaler have found no evidence of reduced mucociliary clearance in patients with reversible airways obstruction (Pavia et al., 1979). Paradoxically, ipratropium has occasionally caused bronchoconstriction. Although this has occurred more frequently with nebulised therapy it has also been reported following use of the metered dose inhaler. The explanation for this reaction is not yet known.

In asthma, the bronchodilating effect of ipratropium bromide is generally less than that achieved by β_2-agonists (Ruffin et al., 1977) although in bronchitic patients it has an effect at least equal to that of the β_2-agonists (see p.32).

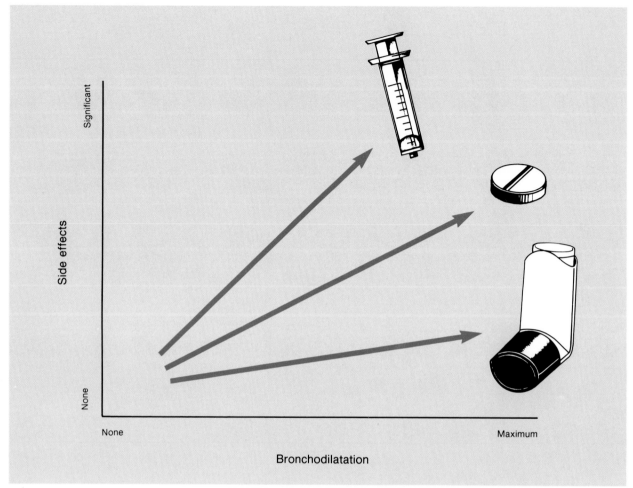

Fig. 5.3. Diagram of the relationship between adverse and beneficial effects with different routes of administration.

Choice of Administration Route for Regular Therapy

The route of administration is an important determinant of the balance of beneficial and adverse effects from bronchodilators (fig. 5.3).

Inhalation

Inhalation is the route of choice whenever possible since it produces equivalent bronchodilatation at lower doses and with fewer side effects than the oral or intravenous route (Hetzel and Clark, 1976; Larsson and Svedmyr, 1977). In the United Kingdom, β-agonists are most frequently administered by inhalation. Although some bronchodilatation is achieved by prolonged inhalation of theophylline, the small response and unpleasant taste make this route impractical.

The Metered Dose Inhaler

The metered dose inhaler is the most convenient method of administration for most patients and is suitable for both regular and 'on-demand' treatment. As described in appendix C, the inhaler canister contains 200-400 doses of drug combined with freon propellants. Studies of deliberate overdose show that the risks from the propellant are minimal, unless the inhaler is grossly overused (Dollery et al., 1970). Patients should be instructed on the use of a metered dose aerosol inhaler, and inhaler technique should be checked frequently (chapter IV; appendix C).

Only 10% of the dose from a metered dose inhaler enters the lungs but this is enough to produce near maximal response in most patients. A large proportion of the dose (80%) is swallowed but the therapeutic effect of this swallowed fraction is small since only $80\mu g$ of salbutamol will be swallowed from 1 puff of inhaled salbutamol whereas an effective oral dose is 2 to 4mg.

The 'Rotahaler'

Alternative methods of inhalation include the 'Rotahaler', aerosol inhalers with automatic triggering mechanisms, 'spacer' devices and nebulisers. These are all described in appendix C. The 'Rotahaler' appears to be as effective in producing bronchodilatation as the metered dose inhaler and it is especially useful for young children and in adults unable to use a metered dose inhaler. Some patients find inhalation of a dry powder slightly irritant.

'Spacers'

'Spacer' devices are designed to attach to aerosol inhalers. The efficacy of a 'spacer' device will depend on its shape and size; large devices are more effective but also more clumsy. 'Spacers' reduce the amount of drug which is lost by impaction in the mouth and oropharynx and also have the advantage that aerosol actuation and inhalation do not need to be coordinated. Consequently, improved bronchodilatation may be achieved (Cushley et al., 1983).

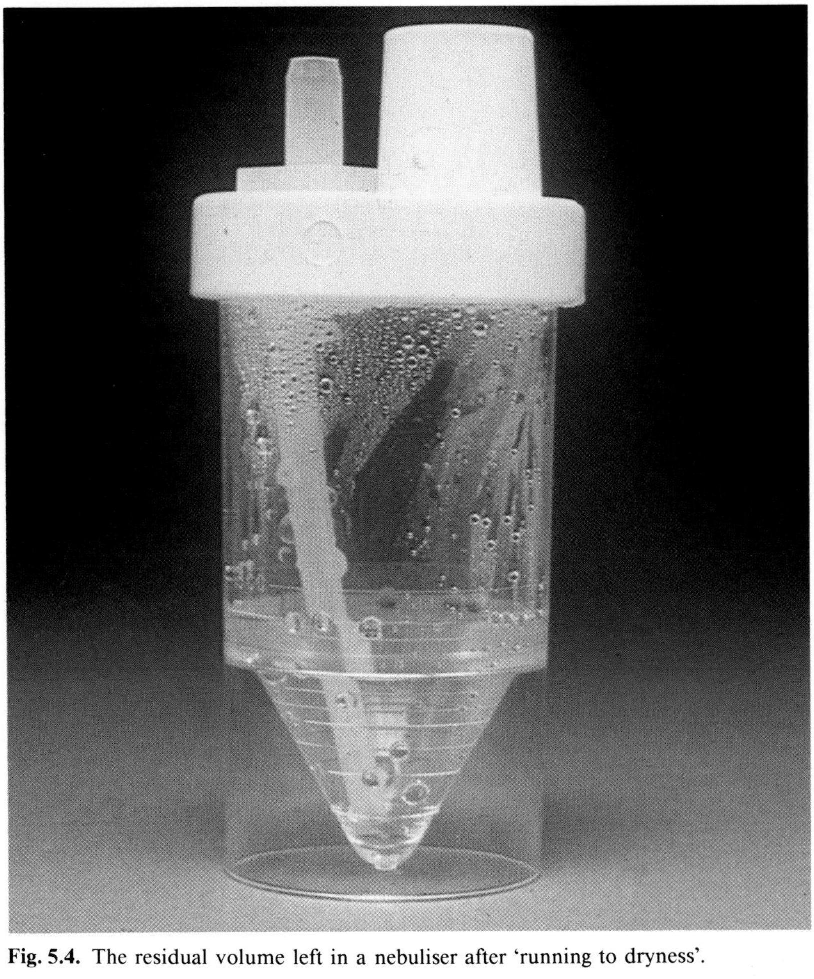

Fig. 5.4. The residual volume left in a nebuliser after 'running to dryness'.

As described in appendix C, different forms of 'spacer' device are available.

Nebulisers

Ipratropium bromide and most β_2-agonists are available as respirator solutions. The mechanism by which nebulisation of these these solutions is achieved and the different types of nebuliser available are described in appendix C.

The amount of drug inhaled by a patient from a nebuliser is influenced by the residual volume of the nebuliser (fig. 5.4), the flow rate, which alters the particle size, and the volume of nebuliser solution used (fig. 5.5). Studies with radiolabelled markers (Lewis et al., 1982) suggest that the proportion of the dose inhaled from a nebuliser is similar to that inhaled from the metered dose inhaler (Newman et al., 1981), with approximately 10% of the nebulised dose entering the lungs. The main difference between the two techniques is that with the metered dose inhaler most of the drug is ingested after impaction in the mouth and oropharynx, while with nebulisation, most of the drug not entering the lungs is lost in the apparatus, or exhaled to the atmosphere (fig. 5.6).

Oral Administration

The disadvantages of oral therapy in terms of increased side effects and delayed onset of effect compared with inhalation are described elsewhere (see p.29). The inhaled route is preferable for β_2-agonists but inhalers of any type may occasionally be inappropriate because of poor understanding or physical disability, or for very young children. Tablet or syrup formulations of β_2-agonists are, therefore, a convenient alternative. The bronchodilator syrups marketed in the United Kingdom are all sugar free.

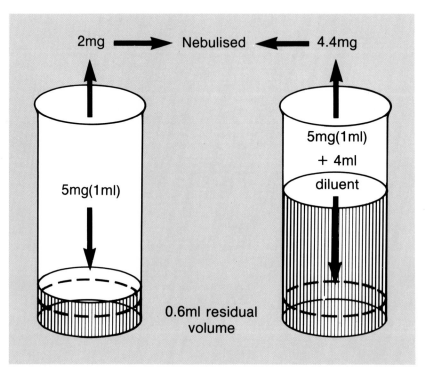

Fig. 5.5. Effect of variation in diluent volume on the amount of drug leaving a nebuliser, assuming a residual volume of 0.6ml. In practice, the residual volume is often greater.

Which Bronchodilator for Regular Therapy

Theophylline or β₂-Agonist?

There are important international differences in the choice of first-line therapy in asthma (see p.18). In the United States, regular oral theophylline is the usual first-line maintenance therapy, while in Britain, Australasia and most European countries, initial treatment is more likely to be an inhaled β_2-agonist. Long term comparisons of the effects of the two forms of treatment have not been carried out; in short term comparisons inhaled β_2-agonists were either equally effective or marginally more effective than oral theophylline when plasma theophylline levels were maintained in the optimum range. The comparative convenience, side effects and risks of each therapy will determine the choice of initial treatment.

In support of theophylline therapy, it is argued that many patients, particularly children, find tablets less conspicuous and more convenient to take than inhaled medication. Also, the incidence of side effects is very low when theophylline plasma levels are monitored and the dosage is titrated appropriately. However, many patients will not tolerate theophylline, it cannot be used 'on-demand', and the process of monitoring plasma levels is expensive, time-consuming and invasive.

In contrast, long term β_2-agonists by metered dose aerosol inhaler and even orally, are associated with maintained effectiveness and a low incidence of minor side effects, whilst severe toxicity is negligible. Estimates of plasma concentrations are unnecessary and with appropriate instruction the patient can often adjust his or her own therapy (chapter IV).

The risk of serious side effects from theophylline is inversely related to the time and trouble taken to control therapy. In a retrospective study at the Brompton Hospital 3 of 28 patients (8% of

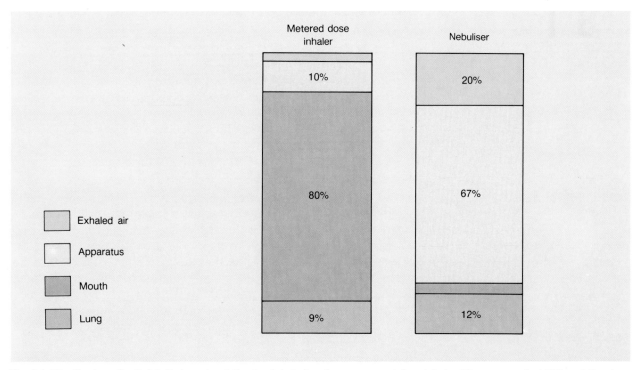

Fig. 5.6. Distribution of radiolabelled marker following inhalation from a metered dose inhaler (Newman et al., 1981) and 'Inspiron mini-neb' jet nebuliser (Lewis et al., 1982).

those assayed) with theophylline levels in the toxic range, developed convulsions and 2 patients died. This study suggests that theophylline toxicity accounts for considerable hidden morbidity in the United Kingdom.

When plasma levels are monitored and both the patient and the doctor appreciate the complexity of theophylline clearance, the risk with theophylline therapy is probably similar to that with β_2-agonists; however this situation is seldom achieved. Theophylline then has no clear cut advantage over β_2-agonists as initial treatment for asthma and it presents a greater potential hazard.

Dosage of β_2-Agonists

Optimal maintenance dosage can be determined easily for β-agonists. Bronchodilatation is easily demonstrated and if airways function (FEV_1 or PEFR) is measured before and after inhalation of a dose of β_2-agonist, a quantitative response can be shown. Regular assessment of respiratory function in a patient taking a β_2-agonist provides the physician with an assessment of the response to the prescribed dose and confirmation that responsiveness is maintained.

In practice, there is little interpatient variation in the dose of a β_2-agonist which produces satisfactory bronchodilatation in patients with mild or moderate asthma and the recommended maintenance dosage of e.g. salbutamol by aerosol – 2 puffs 3 to 4 times daily, is effective in the majority of patients. In those whose response is inadequate, it is safe to increase this dose but a recommended maximum should be given to each patient with instructions to return if this is exceeded. For most patients the daily maximum dose will be 12 to 16 inhalations. The dose of orally administered β_2-agonists is limited by side effects which are less likely to occur with inhaled doses. Oral and inhaled doses of some of the available β_2-agonists are given in table 5.5 and 5.6 (for more detailed dosage information, see appendix B).

Combination Treatment

When to Use Combined Therapy

If a patient is symptomatic on treatment with a single drug the physician should confirm that the prescribed dose is being taken in the correct manner. The next step is either to increase the dose of that drug or add another drug. Higher doses of any drug are associated with an increased incidence and greater risk of severe side effects. If patients are not controlled on 12 to 16 puffs of a β_2-agonist daily, additional treatment should be instituted.

Choice of Combined Therapy

β_2-Agonist + Prophylactic

The second drug of choice is usually an inhaled prophylactic agent because of their low incidence of side effects. Overall, inhaled steroids are most useful (Morrison Smith, 1983). Corticosteroids have been shown to restore the airway responsiveness to β_2-agonists in resistant asthmatic patients (Ellul-Micallef and Fenech, 1975; Holgate et al., 1977), but studies in more conventional patients with stable asthma have only shown an additive effect between corticosteroids and β_2-agonists and not the synergistic effect one would expect if corticosteroids increased receptor responsiveness (Dahl and Johansson, 1982; Harrison and MacKay, 1980). Sodium cromoglycate (cromolyn sodium) can be very effective in certain patients, particularly atopic children and adolescents.

If symptoms persist despite maximal doses of β_2-agonist and

Table 5.5. Doses of β_2-agonists administered by inhalation

Approved name	Form	Strength	Manufacturers' recommended doses for long term therapy
Fenoterol hydrobromide	Aerosol	200 µg/puff	200-400µg 3-4 times daily
Orciprenaline sulphate	Aerosol	750 µg/puff	750-1500µg 4-6 times daily
Pirbuterol hydrochloride	Aerosol	200 µg/puff	200-400µg 3-4 times daily
Reproterol hydrochloride	Aerosol	500 µg/puff	1000µg 3 times daily
Salbutamol	Aerosol	100 µg/puff	200µg 3-4 times daily
	'Rotacaps'	200, 400 µg/capsule	400µg 3-4 times daily
Terbutaline sulphate	Aerosol	250 µg/puff	250-500µg 3-4 times daily

Table 5.6. Doses of selective β_2-agonists administered orally

Approved name	Form	Strength (mg)	Manufacturers' recommended doses for long term therapy
Isoetharine hydrochloride	Tablet	10	10-20mg 3-4 times daily
Orciprenaline sulphate[1]	Tablet	20	20mg 4 times daily
Pirbuterol hydrochloride[1]	Tablet	10, 15	10-15mg 3-4 times daily
Reproterol hydrochloride[1]	Tablet	20	10-20mg 3 times daily
Salbutamol[1]	Tablet	2, 4	2-4mg 3-4 times daily
	Tablet (slow-release)	8	8mg at night or twice daily
Terbutaline sulphate[1]	Tablet	5	5mg 2-3 times daily
	Tablet (slow-release)	7.5	7.5mg at night or twice daily

1 – Available as elixir, suitable for paediatric use.

a prophylactic drug, the addition of a second bronchodilator, either oral theophylline or inhaled ipratropium bromide, should be considered.

β_2-Agonist + Theophylline

Although a synergistic effect was originally anticipated, the effect of combining a β_2-agonist and theophylline is usually less than additive (Handslip et al., 1981). Studies investigating the addition of oral theophylline to inhaled β_2-agonists in patients with chronic asthma have consistently found only a small further increase of 5 to 10% in FEV_1, or PEFR measurements compared with inhaled therapy alone. The incidence of side effects associated with the combined therapy shows wide interstudy variation (0-50%) despite similar theophylline plasma concentrations. This must reflect differences in the way that side effects are elicited and illustrates the difficulties of comparing different drugs from the literature.

Theophyllines should only be continued in a patient who achieves useful bronchodilatation without a significant increase in side effects.

β_2-Agonist + Ipratropium Bromide

The addition of ipratropium bromide to conventional doses of a β_2-agonist has also usually produced slightly greater bronchodilatation than either drug alone. In chronic asthma this combination resulted in a 5 to 10% increase in FEV_1 or PEFR, although the effect was less marked in patients on larger doses of salbutamol (Ullah et al., 1981). In children, the addition of ipratropium to their regular β_2-agonist therapy for 4 weeks was associated with a reduction in symptoms and an increase in PEFR (Mann and Hillier, 1982).

For Consideration When Contemplating Combination Therapy

When single drug therapy alone is inadequate and combination therapy is considered, the following general points can be made:

● There is no good clinical evidence of a synergistic action between two different bronchodilators; the benefit is at best likely to be an additive effect. The combined effect of β_2-agonists and inhaled corticosteroids is also additive.

● When a large dose of one bronchodilator is used the effect of a second is likely to be much less than additive, suggesting that there is a 'ceiling' effect for response. The point at which the patient is better served by using two drugs rather than increasing the dose of the first depends on the side effects and potential toxicity of the first.

● It is very difficult to assess the importance of side effects from published studies of combined therapy, particularly with theophyllines.

● Patient compliance may be impaired with multiple drug regimens.

In Summary

Although many patients with asthma require minimal treatment, a large number will need long term, regular therapy in order to lead a normal active life.

Inhaled β-agonists are very successful as first-line maintenance treatment for asthma, with minimal side effects and continued effectiveness long term. At present the risks of unmonitored theophylline therapy are unknown, but are almost certainly higher than previously estimated. Facilities for measuring theophylline plasma levels should be more widely available, although the low therapeutic index will continue to limit its usefulness in clinical practice.

When a second drug is required for maintenance, most patients will respond to an inhaled corticosteroid; in selected patients, especially atopic children and adolescents, sodium cromoglycate is very effective.

Further long term studies comparing inhaled β-agonists and theophylline, singly and in combination, are needed.

References

Adverse Drug Reactions Advisory Committee: Fenoterol. Medical Journal of Australia 2: 92 (1979).

Al-Hillawi, A.H.; Hayward, R. and Johnson, N.M.: Incidence of cardiac arrhythmias in patients taking slow release salbutamol and slow release terbutaline for asthma. British Medical Journal 288: 367 (1984).

Banner, A.S.; Sunderrajan, E.V.; Agarwal, M.K. and Addington, W.W.: Arrhythmogenic effects of orally administered bronchodilators. Archives of Internal Medicine 139: 434 (1979).

Becker, A.B.; Simons, K.J.; Gillespie, C.A. and Simons, F.E.R.: The bronchodilator effects and pharmacokinetics of caffeine in asthma. New England Journal of Medicine 310: 743 (1984).

Cushley, M.J.; Lewis, R.A. and Tattersfield, A.E.: Comparison of three techniques of inhalation on the airway response to terbutaline. Thorax 38: 908 (1983).

Dahl, R. and Johansson, S.A.: Effect on lung function of budesonide by inhalation, terbutaline s.c. and placebo given simultaneously or as single treatments. European Journal of Respiratory Diseases (Suppl. 122): 132 (1982).

Dollery, C.T.; Draffan, G.H.; Davies, D.S.; Williams, F.M. and Conolly, M.E.: Blood concentrations in man of fluorinated hydrocarbons after inhalation of pressurised aerosols. Lancet 2: 1164 (1970).

Ellul-Micallef, R. and Fenech, F.F.: Effect of intravenous prednisolone in asthmatics with diminished adrenergic responsiveness. Lancet 2: 1269 (1975).

Handslip, P.D.J.; Dart, A.M. and Davies, B.H.: Intravenous salbutamol and aminophylline in asthma: A search for synergy. Thorax 36: 741 (1981).

Harrison, R.N. and MacKay, A.D.: Hydrocortisone and bronchial beta-adrenergic responsiveness. Thorax 35: 238 (1980).

Harvey, J.E. and Tattersfield, A.E.: Airway response to salbutamol: Effect of regular salbutamol inhalations in normal, atopic and asthmatic subjects. Thorax 37: 280 (1982).

Hetzel, M.R. and Clark, T.J.: Comparison of intravenous and aerosol salbutamol. British Medical Journal 2: 919 (1976).

Holgate, S.T.; Baldwin, C.J. and Tattersfield, A.E.: Beta-adrenergic agonist resistance in normal human airways. Lancet 2: 375 (1977).

Klein, J.J.; Leftowitz, M.S.; Spector, S.L. and Cherniak, R.M.: Relationship between serum theophylline levels and pulmonary function before and after inhaled beta-agonists in 'stable' asthma. American Review of Respiratory Disease 127: 413 (1983).

Larsson, S. and Svedmyr, N.: Bronchodilating effect and side-effects of beta$_2$-adrenoceptor stimulants by different modes of administration (tablets, metered aerosol and combinations thereof). American Review of Respiratory Disease 116: 861 (1977).

Larsson, S.; Svedmyr, N. and Thiringer, G.: Lack of bronchial beta-adrenoceptor resistance in asthmatics during long-term treatment with terbutaline. Journal of Allergy and Clinical Immunology 59: 93 (1977).

Lenney, W.; Milner, A.D. and Hillier, E.J.: Continuous and intermittent salbutamol tablet administration in asthmatic children. British Journal of Diseases of the Chest 73: 277 (1979).

Lewis, R.A.; Cushley, M.J.; Fleming, J.S. and Tattersfield, A.E.: Is a nebuliser less efficient than a metered dose inhaler and do pear-shaped extension tubes work? American Review of Respiratory Disease 25: 94 (1982).

Mann, W.P. and Hillier, E.J.: Ipratropium bromide in children with asthma. Thorax 37: 72 (1982).

Mitenko, P.A. and Ogilvie, R.I.: Rational intravenous doses of theophylline. New England Journal of Medicine 289: 600 (1973).

Morrison Smith, J.: Inhaled steroids in the mangement of childhood asthma: including data from long term follow-up of a large personal series; in Clark (Ed.) Steroids in Asthma, p.193 (ADIS Press, Auckland 1983).

Newman, S.P.; Pavia, D.; Moren, F.; Sheahan, N.F. and Clarke, S.W.: Deposition of pressurised aerosols in the human respiratory tract. Thorax 36: 52 (1981).

Neville, E.; Corris, P.A.; Vivian, J.; Nariman, S. and Gibson, G.J.: Nebulised salbutamol and angina. British Medical Journal 285: 796 (1982).

Pavia, D.; Bateman, J.R.M.; Sheahan, N.F. and Clarke, S.W.: Effect of ipratropium bromide on mucociliary clearance and pulmonary function in reversible airways obstruction. Thorax 34: 501 (1979).

Reisman, R.E.: Asthma induced by adrenergic aerosols. Journal of Allergy 46: 162 (1970).

Ruffin, R.E.; Fitzgerald, J.D. and Rebuck, A.S.: A comparison of the bronchodilator effect of Sch 1000 and salbutamol. Journal of Allergy and Clinical Immunology 59: 136 (1977).

Shepherd, G.L.; Hetzel, M.R. and Clark, T.J.H.: Regular venous symptomatic aerosol bronchodilator treatment of asthma. British Journal of Diseases of the Chest 75: 215 (1981).

Snodgrass, W.; Sawyer, D.; Conner, C.S.; Rumbock, B.H.; Peterson, R.G. and Sullivan, J.: Asymptomatic theophylline overdose. Drug Intelligence and Clinical Pharmacy 14: 783 (1980).

Stainforth, J.N. and Tattersfield, A.E.: Airway responsiveness to high dose nebulised salbutamol in chronic asthma. Clinical Science 64: 13 (1983).

Tashkin, D.P.; Conolly, M.E.; Deutsch, R.I.; Hui, K.K.; Littner, M.; Scarpace, P. and Abrass, I.: Subsensitization of beta-adrenoceptors in airways and lymphocytes of healthy and asthmatic subjects. American Review of Respiratory Disease 125: 185 (1982).

Tattersfield, A.E.: Autonomic bronchodilators; in Clark, T.J.H. (Ed.) Asthma, 2nd Ed., pp. 301 (Saunders, Philadelphia 1983).

Toennesen, J.; Lowry, R. and Lambert, P.M.: Oral theophylline and fatal asthma. Lancet 2: 200 (1981).

Ullah, M.I.; Newman, G.B. and Saunders, K.B.: Influence of age on response to ipratropium and salbutamol in asthma. Thorax 36: 523 (1981).

Van Metre, T.E.: Adverse effects of inhalation of excessive amounts of nebulised isoproterenol in status asthmaticus. Journal of Allergy 43: 101 (1969).

Weinberger, M. and Hendeles, L.: Slow release theophylline. Rationale and basis for product selection. New England Journal of Medicine 308: 760 (1983).

Woodcock, A.A.; Johnson, M.A. and Geddes, D.M.: Theophylline prescribing, serum concentrations and toxicity. Lancet 2: 610 (1983).

Zwillich, C.D.; Sutton, F.D.; Neff, T.A.; Cohn, W.M.; Mattay, R.A. and Weinberger, M.M.: Theophylline induced seizures in adults. Annals of Internal Medicine 82: 784 (1975).

Chapter VI

Bronchodilators in Childhood Asthma

A.D. Milner

Asthma is most common in childhood. Recent epidemiological studies in Newcastle (Speight et al., 1983) and Croydon (Anderson et al., 1981) have found that at the ages of 7 and 8 years, respectively, more than 11% of all children have recurrent wheezing attacks. Using histamine and exercise challenge tests in a very well designed trial, the Newcastle group showed that these wheezy children had abnormal airway lability, confirming their asthma (table 6.1). Many children have symptoms which are sufficiently severe to keep them away from school, often for as much as 6 weeks each year, and to prevent them from taking part in normal play activities. Additionally, many are either misdiagnosed or inappropriately treated by their medical practitioners. Much of this unnecessary distress could be avoided if doctors would follow the maxim that in childhood all recurrent wheezing is due to asthma until proved otherwise, and that recurrent coughing associated with asthma almost always responds dramatically to appropriate treatment, a feature strikingly absent when the coughing results from other causes.

Patterns of Childhood Asthma

The clinical picture of asthma in childhood is, to a large extent, determined by the age of the child.

The First Two Years of Life

Although some parents state that symptoms start in the first 2 to 3 weeks of life, most children have their first coughing and wheezing attacks at 3 to 6 months of age, symptoms arising within

Table 6.1. Data on North Tyneside children (from Speight et al., 1982)

Total number of questionnaires	2700
Wheezing in previous two years	11%
Wheezing (asthma) in previous year	9.3%
Diagnosed as asthmatic	1.2%
Bronchodilator therapy with <4 wheezing episodes per year	18%
Bronchodilator therapy with >12 wheezing episodes per year	68%

Table 6.2. Causes of recurrent wheezing and coughing in the first 2 years of life

Common	Uncommon	Rare
Asthma	Cystic fibrosis	Chronic obstructive airways disease
	Recurrent aspiration – reflux	Immune deficiency states
	Foreign body	Immotile cilia syndrome
		Fibrosing alveolitis

Table 6.3. Sequential information on 21 children followed for 4 years after an initial attack of acute severe bronchiolitis (Henry, 1983)

	First year only	Second year only	Third or fourth years	Any time
Wheeze	13 (62%)	12 (57%)	13 (62%)	17 (81%)
Episode of cough or wheeze lasting > 2 weeks	7 (33%)	7 (33%)	12 (57%)	14 (67%)
Admission to hospital	2 (10%)	0 (0%)	0 (0%)	2 (10%)

Status at 3½-year follow-up:
  Improving (or well) (14)
  Same   (6)
  Getting worse   (1)

1 to 2 days of an upper respiratory tract infection. The children are usually afebrile, are often not particularly distressed, and yet have obvious wheezing on examination. Usually, they will be described as having 'wheezy bronchitis' and will be prescribed antibiotics. The symptoms then resolve within 3 to 5 days. There is no evidence whatsoever that antibiotics in any way modify the natural history of these attacks. This pattern, with or without breathlessness, is repeated following subsequent upper respiratory tract infections. Coughing is sometimes the predominant symptom, particularly at night, and may be the only manifestation of asthma. Some babies have persistent symptoms and these require close assessment to exclude conditions such as cystic fibrosis, recurrent aspiration and congenital conditions (e.g. lobar emphysema) [table 6.2]. It is claimed that persistent symptoms can be caused by intolerance to dietary factors, particularly milk and egg, although in clinical practice the number of babies who benefit from changing to less allergenic milk, such as that from goats and soy, seems very small.

Some children may also have eczema but concurrent hay fever and obvious onset of symptoms after contact with animals are relatively rare, indicating that allergic factors are not usually of much consequence at this age.

Children Aged 2 to 5 Years

Between the ages of 2 and 5, many attacks of wheezing and coughing are again causally related to upper respiratory tract infections but symptoms lasting a few minutes can also be brought on by exercise, particularly by running in cold weather. By the age of 3 or 4 years, attacks can also be induced by emotional factors, not infrequently leading to wheezing on Christmas Eve, before going out to a party or when departing on holiday. A history of cough and wheeze after contact with animals, pollens or house dust, emerges more often, although this is still uncommon. Persistent coughing, sometimes misdiagnosed as whooping cough, remains a common factor, often keeping the child and family awake night after night. Dyspnoea occurs more frequently in children of this age, occasionally requiring admission to hospital.

The School Child

After the age of 5 years, the pattern depends largely on the severity of the condition. Most asthmatic children have occasional, but distressing wheezing and coughing, lasting for days and usually associated with a cold or contact with allergens. Exercise-induced bronchoconstriction is very common but may occur only at times when the asthma is proving troublesome or the weather very cold (chapter VII). Those with more severe problems (less than 2% of the population) have either frequent, severe attacks or chronic symptoms of varying severity.

There are two other distinct patterns of childhood asthma:

Wheezing After Acute Bronchiolitis

More than 80% of children who have acute bronchiolitis in infancy will have recurrent attacks of coughing and wheezing in the next few years (table 6.3). These symptoms are certainly due to an abnormal airway lability. Many children seem to grow out of their tendency to wheeze and cough by the age of 5 or 6 years. Other distinguishing features are that skin tests are often negative and there is rarely a history of allergy or wheezing in the family, suggesting that the symptoms are secondary to damage caused by the bronchiolitis rather than the bronchiolitis being the first manifestations of a genetically determined disorder (table 6.4).

Massive Lobar/Lung Collapse/Consolidation

A small number of children have several episodes in which, after a brief period of coughing and breathlessness, they become acutely unwell with cyanosis and rapid, feeble pulse. On examination and radiographically, the findings are those of extensive uni- or multilobar pneumonia (fig. 6.1). The children are almost always given systemic corticosteroids and intravenous antibiotics and are dramatically better within 12 to 48 hours, with almost total clearance of their chest x-ray findings. Between these episodes, overt asthmatic symptoms may develop with coughing and wheezing on exercise or in response to mild upper respiratory tract infections. Most grow out of this tendency by the age of 3 or 4 years. Occasionally a lobe fails to re-expand leading to fibrosis and/or bronchiectasis.

The most important aspect of childhood asthma is that, with the exception of those under 18 months of age, response to appropriate therapy is usually dramatic.

Response to and Tolerability of Bronchodilators

Response to bronchodilators is more rapid, and often more complete, in childhood than in adult life, so bronchodilators form the first line of therapy for all asthmatic children, whether they have only very occasional attacks or severe, chronic symptoms. This rapidity of response is accompanied by a remarkably low incidence of side effects compared to adults, indicating a high level

Table 6.4. Clinical features of children 10 years after respiratory syncytial virus (RSV) infection (predominantly bronchiolitis) in infancy (from Pullan and Hey, 1982)

	RSV	Control
Number of children	130	111
Ever wheezed	42%	19%
Wheezed in last 2 years	22%	13%
Wheezy sibs or parents	17%	16%
Abnormal airway lability (exercise or histamine)	25%	7%
Positive skin test	19%	30%

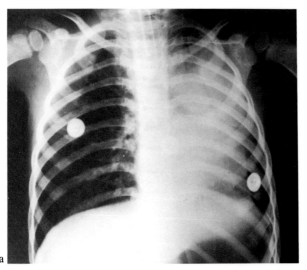
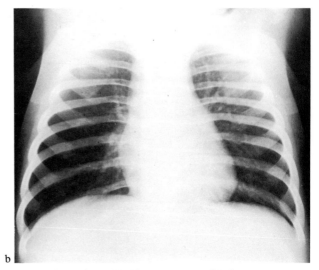

a   b

Fig. 6.1. Chest x-ray of a 2-year-old asthmatic child on admission (a) and 48 hours later (b). The dense consolidation responded to systemic corticosteroids and nebulised salbutamol and represents mucus retention and not pneumonia.

of tolerability. Thus, with the exception of the methylxanthine derivatives, a 2-year-old child can safely be given at least 25% of the adult dose, a 5-year-old 50% of the dose, and over the age of 10 to 12 years, standard adult therapy can be used.

Oral Therapy

Most of the β_2-adrenoceptor agonist drugs are available in both liquid and tablet form. Dosage guidelines for oral therapy are given in table 6.5. The time to onset of action (15-20 minutes) and to full effect (45-60 minutes) seems to be very similar with both dosage forms. In the United Kingdom bronchodilator syrup formulations are sugar-free. There is some evidence, based on laboratory tests, that terbutaline has a relatively longer half-life than the other drugs in the group (Ardal et al., 1978) but no controlled studies have suggested that any one product is superior.

Table 6.5. Dosage guidelines for oral β_2-agonists

Name (trade name)	Formulation	Unit dose (mg)	Unit doses/day[1]		
			1-3 years	3-7 years	7-15 years
Orciprenaline (metaproterenol) ('Alupent')	Syrup (5ml)	10	½ × 3	½-1 × 3	1 × 4 or 2 × 3
	Tablets	20			1 × 3
Reproterol ('Bronchodil')	Syrup (5ml)	10	½ × 3	½-1 × 3	1-2 × 3
	Tablets	20			½-1 × 3
Salbutamol (albuterol) ('Ventolin')	Syrup (5ml)	2	1 × 3	1 × 3	1-2 × 3
	Tablets	2		1 × 3	1-2 × 3
	Tablets	4			1 × 3
	Slow-release tablets	8		½ at night	1 at night
Terbutaline ('Bricanyl')	Syrup (5ml)	1.5	½ × 3	½-1 × 3	1-2 × 3
	Tablets	5			½-1 × 3
	Slow-release tablets	7.5			1 at night

1 – Doses are those used in the author's unit and may differ from manufacturers' recommendations.

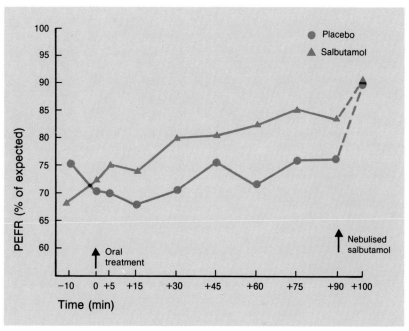

Fig. 6.2. Peak flow measurements before and after salbutamol (2mg) and placebo syrup in 12 young asthmatic children. Response is relatively slow and undramatic compared to the improvement after inhalation of nebulised salbutamol (2.5mg in 2ml water).

Many doctors commence the treatment of children with asthmatic symptoms with continuous oral β_2-agonist therapy. However, continuous salbutamol (albuterol) tablet therapy had no apparent advantage over intermittent administration in a group of children with moderate asthma (Lenney et al., 1979).

Although the oral route is highly convenient and can be used by even the youngest child, the relatively slow onset of action and incomplete relief of bronchoconstriction obtained limit its use to children with relatively mild and intermittent symptoms (fig. 6.2). The slow-release tablets (salbutamol and terbutaline)* can sometimes be useful in the management of nocturnal symptoms (see p.142) but cannot be swallowed by children under 6 or 7 years.

Inhalation Therapy
(table 6.6)

Aerosol Inhalers

Few children under the age of 8 years can coordinate breathing and aerosol activation sufficiently well to justify the use of an aerosol. For those who can, the administration of β_2-agonists by this type of device provides relief in 1 to 2 minutes with a peak effect occurring within 15 to 20 minutes. Although mild tachycardia may occur, tremor is far less apparent than in adults, even after 2 to 3 inhalations. Inhalations of β_2-agonists immediately prior to exercise have proved by far the most effective way of preventing exercise-induced bronchoconstriction (see p.126). The dose delivered is small, a salbutamol aerosol delivers only one-fortieth of the standard oral 4mg dose, so it is extremely unlikely that even excessive use will produce worrying side effects. However, the use

* For product availability in the USA, see appendix B.

Table 6.6. Inhaler preparations of β_2-agonists

Name (trade name)	Formulation	Unit dose (mg)	Maximum daily dose[1] (unit doses/day)	
			3-7 years	7-15 years
Fenoterol ('Berotec')	Aerosol	0.2		1-2 × 4
Orciprenaline ('Alupent')	Aerosol	0.75		1 × 8
Rimiterol ('Pulmadil')	Aerosol	0.2		1-2 × 6
Reproterol ('Bronchodil')	Aerosol	0.5		1 × 6
Salbutamol ('Ventolin')	Aerosol 'Rotacaps' 'Rotacaps'	0.1 0.2 0.4	1 × 6	1-2 × 8 1 × 8 1 × 6
Terbutaline ('Bricanyl')	Aerosol	0.25		1-2 × 4

1 – Doses are those used in the author's unit and may differ from manufacturers' recommendations.

of increasingly high doses usually indicates that the child's asthma is getting out of control and that changes in therapy are urgently required.

Powder Inhalations

For children who are unable to use the pressurised aerosol device, salbutamol powder delivered by the 'Rotahaler' system provides a very useful alternative. Although not quite as convenient as the aerosol, it has been used in children as young as 3 years (Lenney et al., 1978). The speed of onset of drug action with the 'Rotahaler' compares favourably with the aerosol delivery systems and it seems equally effective in blocking exercise-induced bronchoconstriction.

Respirator Solution (fig. 6.3)

Although the 'Rotahaler' and aerosol devices are effective in most situations, when bronchoconstriction becomes severe and the ability to generate adequate inspiratory flow declines, progressively less of the active substance reaches the required delivery site. The use of a β_2-agonist respirator solution (table 6.7), administered by a nebuliser and compressor, overcomes this problem, producing conditions whereby the child breathes in air or oxygen containing the nebulised drug over a 5- to 10-minute period. This ensures good penetration deep into the lungs. There is no evidence that the use of a positive pressure ventilator triggered by the child's breath is necessary or that breathing through a mouthpiece rather than a face mask produces a better clinical response, although on theoretical grounds, the 'drop out' of drug in the upper respiratory tract will be less with the positive pressure ventilator. The dose used in the nebuliser (table 6.7) is relatively large compared to the aerosol and powder inhaler devices, but at least 80% will not penetrate the airways. A mild increase in heart rate of 2 to 6 beats per

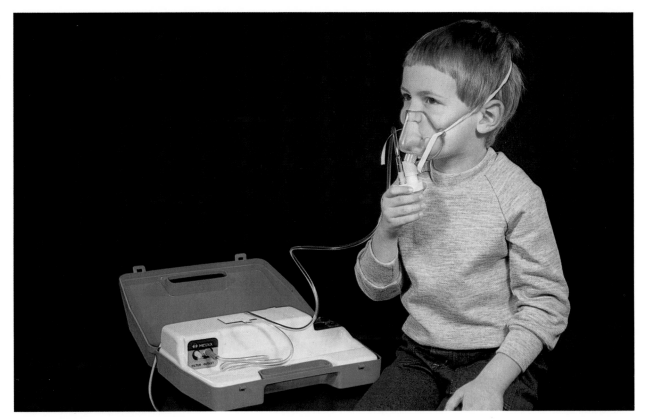

Fig. 6.3. Child inhaling a bronchodilator drug using a nebuliser/compressor system.

minute is common (Milner and Ingram, 1971) and transient tremor is sometimes seen, particularly in the older child. The doses can be repeated at 3- to 4-hourly intervals. A poor response to therapy, or an improvement which lasts for only 1 to 2 hours, are indications that the asthma is still not under control and that additional treatment, possibly systemic corticosteroids, is urgently required (chapter X).

Table 6.7. β_2-Agonists for nebulisation

Name (trade name)	Formulation	Dose/ml	Maximum doses/day[1]		
			1-3 years	3-7 years	7-15 years
Fenoterol ('Berotec')	Respirator solution Bottle (20ml)	5mg			0.2ml × 3
Rimiterol ('Pulmadil')	Respirator solution 'Nebcaps' (12.5mg)	5mg			2.5ml × 4
Salbutamol ('Ventolin')	Respirator solution Bottle (20ml) 'Nebules' (2.5ml)	5mg 1mg	0.5ml × 4 2.5ml × 4	0.5ml × 4 2.5ml × 4	0.5-1ml × 4 2.5ml × 4
Terbutaline ('Bricanyl')	Respirator solution Bottle (20ml) Ampoule (2ml)	10mg 2.5mg	0.25ml × 4 1ml × 4	0.5ml × 4 1-2ml × 4	0.5ml × 4 2ml × 4

1 – Doses are those used in the author's unit and may differ from manufacturers' recommendations.

Fig. 6.4. Young asthmatic child receiving salbutamol from an aerosol with the help of a disposable polystyrene coffee cup.

Nebuliser systems have proved extremely useful in the management of asthma in children under the age of 5 and many paediatric units now provide home nebulisers for preschool children who have been admitted to hospital with asthma on at least two occasions. Thus, in the author's unit some children receive regular inhalations of sodium cromoglycate (cromolyn sodium) respirator solution and a β_2-agonist, such as salbutamol, is used in addition when symptoms are present.

Spacer Devices

Although highly effective, the nebulisers are cumbersome, slow and relatively expensive. For this reason, a number of aerosol 'interface' devices ('spacers') have been devised which overcome the coordination problems to varying degrees (appendix C).

The 'tube spacer', a box-like extension, has been the least effective device, as the dose is lost if the child breathes out before commencing inspiration. This has been no better than the standard aerosol device in young children. At the other extreme is the aerodynamically designed 'Nebuhaler', which has a 750ml capacity and is the shape of a rugby football and which incorporates a one-way valve (see appendix C, fig. 5). This may have a place in the treatment of the severe acute attack in some children. A rather less sophisticated approach is the 'coffee cup system' in which a standard aerosol is inserted into a hole in the bottom of a polystyrene coffee cup (fig. 6.4). The cup is held loosely over the child's face and the aerosol fired 10 times (Henry et al., 1983). This method of delivery seems to equal the efficacy of the nebuliser in acute asthma (fig. 6.5). It has proved extremely useful in the management of the severe acute attack outside hospital. The dose the child will receive is again unlikely to exceed one-tenth of the standard oral dose and can be repeated after 3 to 4 hours.

Intravenous and Intramuscular Routes

Although many of the β_2-agonists are available for intravenous or intramuscular use (table 6.8) there is no firm evidence that these routes offer any benefit over inhalation (see p.174). Combined therapy with β_2-agonists and aminophylline is more likely to produce tachycardia when the former are given by IM or IV injection (Edmunds and Godfrey, 1981). The injectable preparations are, nevertheless, effective and can be safely used in domiciliary practice. The intravenous injections can be given either intermittently or by continuous infusion (appendix B, table 3).

The Role of Bronchodilators in Childhood Asthma

In many children with intermittent symptoms, inhaled bronchodilator drugs taken at the onset of coughing and wheezing are sufficient to control the asthma to an extent which allows an entirely normal life. It is crucial to stress to the parents that β_2-agonists are most effective when taken early in the attack, before the airways have filled with secretions and cellular debris. Many are reluctant to start therapy early, feeling that too frequent use will reduce its efficacy leaving them helpless 'when treatment is really needed'. It is most important to stress repeatedly that tol-

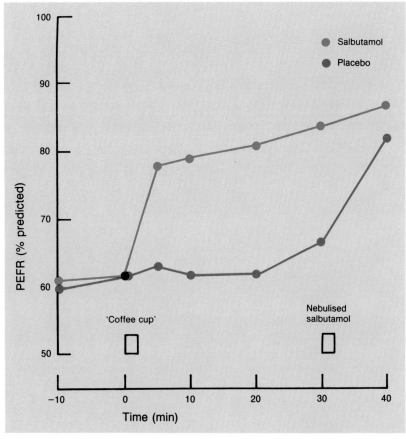

Fig. 6.5. Peak flow before and after the inhalation of 10 puffs of salbutamol or placebo using a coffee cup in young asthmatic children. Inhalation of nebulised salbutamol respirator solution had little additional effect.

erance does not occur in childhood, that inhaled bronchodilator drugs are in themselves safe, and that it is preferable to start therapy early rather than wait until the attack has progressed to the stage where systemic corticosteroids, or even hospital admission, are necessary.

In children whose symptoms cannot be adequately controlled by maximal doses of either oral or inhaled β_2-agonists alone additional drug therapy may be required.

Oral and Inhaled β_2-Agonist Therapy

A recent report (Grimwood et al., 1983) has suggested that regular therapy with both oral and inhaled β_2-agonists, such as salbutamol, is likely to benefit the asthmatic child by combining the rapid action and greater efficacy of the inhaled preparation with the sustained action of the oral form (fig. 6.6). There may be a number of asthmatic children for whom this approach would be beneficial.

β_2-Agonists and Inhaled Corticosteroids

The introduction of corticosteroids by inhalation has had a major impact on the management of children with asthma whose symptoms cannot be controlled by regular β_2-agonist therapy. Inhaled corticosteroids are essential for the management of all children who require regular or intermittent systemic steroids, and for those who have been admitted to hospital more than once in the previous 12 months. There is a strong case for considering their use in all children who, despite adequate treatment with mast cell stabilisers and regular β_2-agonists, continue to have significant symptoms which prevent them from enoying a normal active life.

Inhaled corticosteroids may cause side effects: oral thrush (although this seems to be less of a problem in children than in adults) and hoarseness. If used in large doses (equivalent to at least 1200μg beclomethasone dipropionate per day) they will have a measurable effect on adrenal function and can even produce fluid retention (Milner, 1982). There is, however, no evidence that children come to any long term harm from any of these and suspicion that long term therapy might produce changes in the mucosa of the airways has not been substantiated in any way.

Many authorities recommend that β_2-agonists should be given regularly to all children receiving inhaled corticosteroids. These

Table 6.8. β_2-Agonists for parenteral administration

Name	Formulation	Unit dose (mg/ml)	Route	Maximum dose/day[1]		
				1-3 years	3-7 years	7-15 years
Orciprenaline ('Alupent')	Ampoules (1ml)	0.5	IM	0.25ml	0.5ml	1.0ml
Salbutamol ('Ventolin')	Ampoules (5ml) (1ml)	0.05 0.5	IV	0.006 mg/kg bodyweight × 4		
Terbutaline ('Bricanyl')	Ampoules (1ml)	0.5	IV/IM/SC	0.010 mg/kg bodyweight × 4		

1 – Doses are those used in the author's unit and may differ from manufacturers' recommendations.

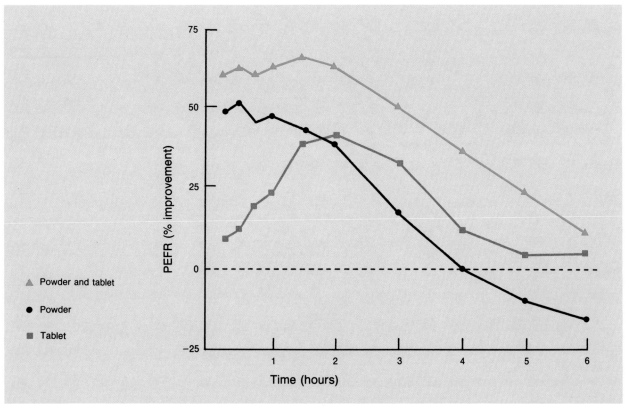

Fig. 6.6. Peak flow measurements (PEFR) after salbutamol tablets, powder or both in combination in school children with asthma. The combination provides the rapid response of the powder with the sustained action of the tablet formulation (after Grimwood et al., 1983).

should be given by the inhaled route, preferably before the inhaled corticosteroid. The steroid can then be inhaled as an aerosol or, in the case of beclomethasone dipropionate, as a powder using the 'Rotahaler' device. Additional doses of β_2-agonists can be taken for coughing and wheezing.

There are, however, some children who respond so well to a small dose of inhaled corticosteroid, e.g. beclomethasone dipropionate 100μg twice daily, that it may be acceptable to give β_2-agonists purely to treat breakthrough symptoms rather than regularly.

β_2-Agonists and Sodium Cromoglycate

In some children with frequent symptoms, in whom adequate control of their condition cannot be achieved with appropriate doses of oral and inhaled β_2-agonists, and who continue to miss school regularly and are unable to join in with normal physical activities, regular therapy with sodium cromoglycate 3 to 4 times a day is worth a trial. Children over the age of 8 years can often use the aerosol preparation, but most school children will need to rely on the 'Spinhaler' delivery system. Although some children obtain dramatic improvement with this treatment, even they will have attacks of coughing and wheezing which occur at times when environmental factors are particularly adverse. They will then require β_2-agonist therapy, preferably by inhalation using either an aerosol or 'Rotahaler' device.

Table 6.9. Slow-release theophylline preparations (available in the United Kingdom)

Product name	Formulation	Unit dose	Unit doses/day[1]		
			1-3 years	3-7 years	7-15 years
'Nuelin-SA'	Tablet	175mg theophylline			1 × 2
'Nuelin-SA' 250	Tablet	250mg theophylline			1 × 2
'Phyllocontin Paediatric'	Tablet	100mg aminophylline (equiv. to 80mg theophylline)		1 × 2	1-2 × 2
'Slo-Phyllin'	Capsules		1 × 2		
	White pellets	60mg theophylline		1-2 × 2	
	Brown/clear pellets	125mg theophylline		1 × 2	1-2 × 2
	Blue/white pellets	250mg theophylline			1 × 2
'Theo-Dur'	Tablets	200mg theophylline		½ × 2	1 × 2

1 – Approximate doses only, individual doses should be calculated on body weight and adjusted according to plasma levels.

β₂-Agonists and Methylxanthines

The group of children who benefit most from sodium cromoglycate are also likely to get considerable relief from regular therapy with oral theophyllines. Theophyllines may be particularly useful for those children aged 2 to 5 years who find the use of any form of inhaler difficult. Fortunately, they seem to be well tolerated by this age group and moderate prophylaxis may be obtained by lower therapeutic levels (5 to 8 mg/L) than is usual in adults. The appropriate dose should be estimated for each child and adjusted according to therapeutic response and plasma concentrations. There are now a number of slow-release preparations (table 6.9) which need to be given only twice a day. One formulation is marketed as slow-release granules inside a clear capsule. These granules can be tipped out on to a teaspoon and given to children as young as 2 years of age.

A possible association between theophylline therapy and learning and behaviour problems in children has recently been identified (Furakawa et al., 1984). If confirmed, this may have implications for the long term use of theophyllines in children. The main disadvantage of theophylline is the relatively high incidence of gastrointestinal symptoms and the worry that IV aminophylline given in an emergency situation to a child who is already on high dose oral therapy may produce a severe toxic reaction, with convulsions and possibly even death. When coughing, wheezing and breathlessness become evident, inhaled β₂-agonists will still be required. When given concurrently with β₂-agonists the use of theophyllines results in only a modest additive effect (p.89).

β₂-Agonists and Ketotifen

Ketotifen, an antihistamine with mast cell stabilising properties, has no obvious role in childhood asthma.

β₂-Agonists and Ipratropium Bromide

Ipratropium bromide is another drug the role of which in childhood asthma is still very much under review. It is a cholinergic blocking agent and its main action is to antagonise the bronchoconstrictor effect of the parasympathetic system (chapter II).

As ipratropium acts by an entirely different mechanism to the β-agonists, it is possible that it will have a role in childhood asthma either on its own or in combination. It is available in the United Kingdom as an aerosol, either on its own or in combination with fenoterol, and as a respirator solution which may have a place in the management of the severe acute asthmatic attack (see p.180). Further work is needed to assess whether ipratropium bromide given in combination with a β_2-agonist really does constitute a significant advance in the management of childhood asthma (Mann and Hiller, 1981).

β_2-Agonists and Systemic Corticosteroids

When children require regular systemic corticosteroids either orally or as tetracosactrin ('Synacthen') injection, maximal bronchodilator therapy should be given so that the dose of corticosteroids can be kept as small as possible. These children, who represent less than 1 in 10,000 of the childhood population, should be issued with nebulisers and compressors so that they can receive this form of β_2-agonist therapy at least each morning and night. The midday doses of bronchodilator drugs can then be taken using either an aerosol or a 'Rotahaler' device.

Bronchodilators in the First Two Years of Life

β_2-Adrenoceptor Agonists

It has been known for some years that wheezy children in the first year of life get little, if any, benefit from bronchodilator drugs. Phelan and Williams failed to find any response to nebulised isoprenaline (isoproterenol) when airways resistance was measured by a total body plethysmograph (Phelan and Williams, 1969). Similarly, nebulised salbutamol failed to produce a response in a small group of wheezy babies (Radford, 1975). Rutter and his colleagues, using the forced oscillation technique to measure total respiratory resistance in 23 babies, found no bronchodilator response to either nebulised salbutamol or isoprenaline (Rutter et al., 1975) [fig. 6.7], even though there was a detectable increase in heart rate, indicating that adequate drug penetration had occurred. The same technique was used to study nebulised adrenaline and phenylephrine, a drug with predominantly α-adrenoceptor activity, but virtually identical results were found, with no child showing a significant improvement (Lenney and Milner, 1978).

In a further study, nebulised salbutamol (2.5mg) was given to wheezy children between the ages of 5 and 43 months, and the response was recorded using both the forced oscillation technique and the total body plethysmograph (Lenney et al., 1978). All those over the age of 20 months obtained useful improvement in lung function and a reduction, or total abolition, of wheezing on auscultation. However, no child under the age of 18 months obtained useful improvement (fig. 6.8) and indeed most showed a small deterioration, possibly related to the acidity of the salbutamol respirator solution (pH 3.5).

Occasionally wheezy children under the age of 18 months do get relief. The youngest child in whom we have been able to demonstrate relief was 10 months old, but results of clinical examination and respiratory function testing suggest that very few children benefit under the age of 15 months, while all children 18 to 20 months, or more, respond in a similar manner to the older asthmatic child.

These findings have been challenged by workers who consider

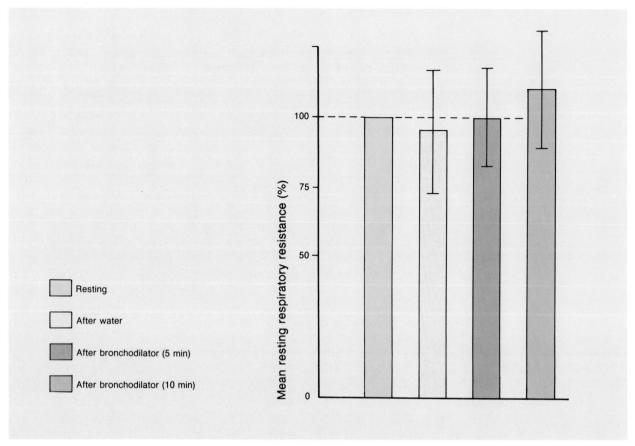

Fig. 6.7. Total respiratory resistance before and after nebulised water and either isoprenaline or salbutamol in 23 wheezy infants, expressed as a percentage of initial result. No child showed a useful improvement (after Rutter et al., 1975).

that nebulised β_2-agonists are often useful during the first 15 months of life. They state that wheezing attacks in many babies resolve within 24 to 48 hours of commencing nebulised therapy. They suggest that in our earlier studies (Lenney et al., 1978; Lenney and Milner, 1978), measurements were made on babies who were sedated and were therefore convalescent rather than critically ill, and so our findings are not representative of acute severe attacks. To answer these criticisms, we have devised a system to measure the total work of breathing which does not depend on heavy sedation and can, therefore, be used in situations where the babies are acutely distressed. Using this, we have found no baby under the age of 18 months obtaining a clinically useful improvement from nebulised β_2-agonist, even though the nebulised dose produces a significant increase in heart rate, indicating that penetration into the lungs has occurred.

Anticholinergic Agents and Corticosteroids

Nebulised ipratropium bromide (250μg in 2ml) produces bronchodilatation in approximately 40% of babies in the first 18 months of life (Hodges et al., 1981). This response is not age-related (fig. 6.9) and babies seem to improve with relief of coughing and wheezing within 10 to 20 minutes of therapy. Why babies should fail to respond to β_2-agonists in the first 18 months of life remains a mystery. Smooth muscle, although not as abundant as

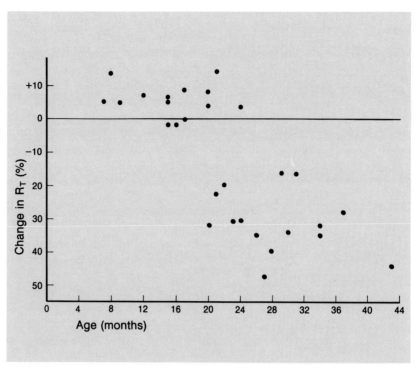

Fig. 6.8. Percentage change in total respiratory resistance (R_T) after nebulised salbutamol in wheezy babies and toddlers. No baby under 18 months showed an improvement (fall), while this was a consistent finding in children over 20 months of age (after Lenney and Milner, 1978).

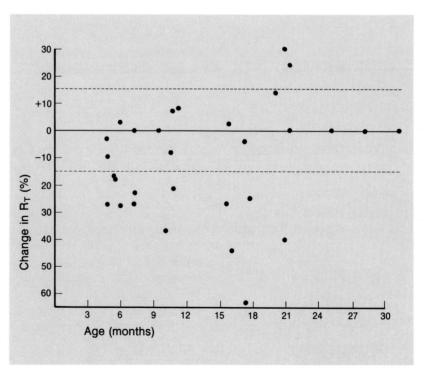

Fig. 6.9. Percentage change in total respiratory resistance (R_T) after nebulised ipratropium bromide in wheezy babies and toddlers. Approximately 40% showed a useful improvement (fall) which was not age-related (after Hodges et al., 1981).

in later life, is certainly present. β_2-Receptors are active in fetal life and are present in babies, although in smaller numbers than in the second and third year of life. The response to ipratropium bromide makes it unlikely that the lack of improvement with β_2-agonist therapy is related to structural factors in the lungs, i.e. it is unlikely that the airway diameter is so critical that mucosal changes alone produce bronchoconstriction.

Sodium cromoglycate also seems of limited use in the first year of life (Henry et al., 1984) and there is no evidence that nebulised β_2-agonists and sodium cromoglycate in combination confer any additional benefit.

The response to systemic corticosteroids is also unpredictable in infancy, many infants having attacks which appear to be uninfluenced by therapy, but a recent publication (Tal et al., 1983) has suggested that salbutamol given in combination with systemic corticosteroids does significantly shorten the course of wheezing attacks, even at this very young age. However, the typical bronchodilator response seen in later life, with the relief of coughing and wheezing within 2 to 5 minutes, did not seem to occur.

Recently an aqueous suspension of beclomethasone dipropionate for use with a respirator or nebuliser has been developed. Preliminary data suggest that in doses of $100\mu g$ 3 or 4 times daily, this preparation may be beneficial in children over one year of age (Brogden, 1983).

The author now recommends that any baby who has wheezing and is at least 10 months of age, be given a β_2-agonist as first-line therapy, preferably as a nebulised solution. If the child fails to improve, or is under the age of 10 months, the most appropriate management is nebulised ipratropium bromide ($250\mu g$ in 2ml) every 4 to 6 hours. Nebulised sodium cromoglycate is unlikely to be successful in children under the age of 1 year but may be in those in the second year of life. In severe acute wheezing attacks, systemic corticosteroids are justified, particularly if the baby is very distressed and not feeding. A trial of a β_2-agonist, which can be repeated for subsequent attacks, is worthwhile and the parents can be assured that eventually this will be a highly effective form of therapy.

Methylxanthines

There is little information on the use of theophylline preparations, but anecdotal experience suggests that these have nothing to offer to the wheezy baby in the first year of life.

Advice to Parents on the Use of β_2-Agonist Therapy

An essential part of the management of childhood asthma is ensuring that parents and, when sufficiently mature, the child, are fully aware of what is meant by the diagnosis of asthma, how the condition is likely to affect the child and how therapy can be used to ensure that he leads as normal a life as possible. A significant part of this educational process is a discussion of β_2-agonists, as these are the first line of therapy for all wheezy attacks in children over the age of 15 months. The parents must be entirely familiar with the various modes of administration. If a 'Rotahaler' or aerosol device is in use, the technique must be checked on each attendance at the surgery or clinic, since even after faultless teaching, a pattern of coordination is easily lost, depriving the child of the full therapeutic benefit. It is very important that lung function (peak

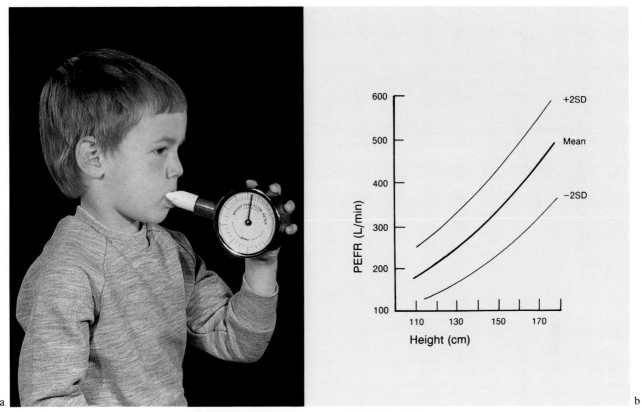

a   b

Fig. 6.10. a) Child blowing a peak flow meter; and b) normal values of PEFR in children.

flow) is checked before and after therapy (fig. 6.10). This will provide a useful record of the severity of the bronchoconstriction when the child attended the clinic, and also documents the degree of relief which can be obtained by the β_2-agonist. If the initial peak flow is low, and response to therapy is poor despite adequate technique, further therapy, possibly in the form of inhaled or even systemic steroids is indicated (fig. 6.11). The demonstration of an improvement in peak flow can also be used to convince parents of the diagnosis of asthma when children are coughing rather than wheezing.

Many parents are understandably conservative in their use of β_2-agonists for their child's asthma and it is essential that time is spent explaining that these drugs are safe and, if used early, will produce rapid relief of coughing and wheezing. If they are withheld, the attack may progress, leading to gross hyperinflation secondary to mucosal oedema and intraluminal secretions in addition to the smooth muscle constriction. At this stage, a β_2-agonist is unlikely to be totally effective and further therapy and even admission to hospital may become inevitable. The parent must, therefore, be entirely clear about when the β_2-agonist should be given, whether this is part of regular therapy, or indicated only at the onset of coughing and wheezing or just before vigorous exercise. The parents and, where applicable, the child, should also fully understand what doses are prescribed and how frequently they can be repeated. There is probably little point in repeating oral therapy more often than every 6 hours but aerosols and 'Rotahalers' can

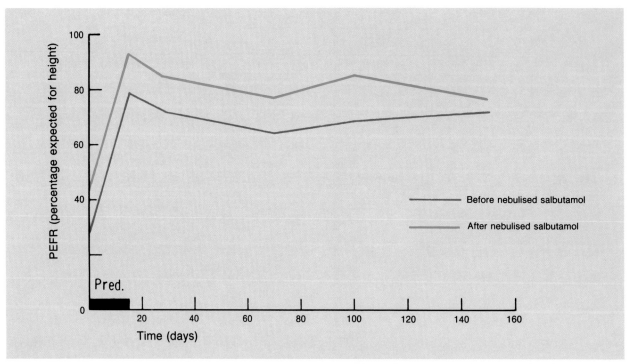

Fig. 6.11. Peak flow before and after nebulised salbutamol in a group of children with severe chronic asthma. Virtually normal lung function is achieved by a 2-week course of systemic corticosteroids.

be used as often as every 3 hours without fear of side effects because, as shown earlier, the dose by inhalation is relatively very small.

The response to inhaled β_2-agonists can also be used to provide very useful information on further management. If the child responds with complete relief of coughing, wheezing, and breathlessness for at least 4 hours, it is entirely safe and reasonable for him to continue on his established therapy. If response is only partial, or lasts only 1 to 2 hours, the asthma is slipping out of control and further therapy is urgently required. In some situations, the parents will be advised to take their child up to the local Accident and Emergency Department, or to the general practice surgery or clinic, to receive nebulised β_2-agonist therapy. If this becomes a frequent requirement it is worth instructing the family in the 'coffee cup system' (see above) as this often works in situations where the child is unable to generate a high enough inspiratory flow to obtain relief from the aerosol or 'Rotahaler'. Again, it is essential to stress that the parents must seek immediate advice if the child fails to obtain relief lasting at least 2 hours.

In Summary

β_2-Agonists form the first-line therapy for all children with asthma. When used appropriately they can often ensure that the asthmatic child is able to lead an entirely normal life with only minimal symptoms. They are also essential in the management of more severe asthma, where they can produce rapid relief of breakthrough symptoms and allow the doses of more toxic substances to be kept to a minimum.

References

Anderson, H.R.; Bailey, P.A.; Cooper, J.S. and Palmer, J.C.: Influence and morbidity, illness label, and social, family, and health service factors on drug treatment of childhood asthma. Lancet 2: 1030 (1981).

Ardal, B.; Beaudry, P. and Eisen A.H.: Terbutaline in asthmatic children: a dose-response study. Journal of Pediatrics 93: 305 (1978).

Brogden, R.N.: Inhaled steroids: Studies in adult and childhood asthma; in Clark (Ed.) Steroids in Asthma, p.135 (ADIS Press, Auckland 1983)

Edmunds, A.T. and Godfrey, S.: Cardiovascular response during severe acute asthma and its treatment in childhood. Thorax 36: 534 (1981).

Furakawa, C.T.; Shapiro, G.G.; Du Hamel, T.; Weimer, L.; Pierson, W.E. and Bierman, C.W.: Learning and behaviour problems associated with theophylline therapy. Lancet 1: 621 (1984).

Grimwood, K.; Fergusson, D.M. and Dawson, K.P.: Combination of salbutamol inhalational powder and tablets in asthma. Archives of Disease in Childhood 58: 283 (1983).

Henry, R.L.: Personal communication (1983).

Henry, R.L.; Milner, A.D. and Davies, J.G.: Simple drug delivery system for use by young asthmatics. British Medical Journal 286: 2021 (1983).

Henry, R.L.; Hiller, E.J.; Milner, A.D.; Hodges, I.G.C. and Stokes, G.M.: Nebulised ipratropium bromide and sodium cromoglycate in the first two years of life. Archives of Disease in Childhood. 59: 54 (1984).

Hodges, I.G.C.; Groggins, R.C.; Milner, A.D. and Stokes, G.M.: Bronchodilator effect of inhaled ipratropium bromide in wheezy toddlers. Archives of Disease in Childhood 56: 729 (1981).

Lenney, W. and Milner, A.D.: At what age do bronchodilator drugs work? Archives of Disease in Childhood 53: 707 (1978).

Lenney, W.; Milner, A.D. and Hiller, E.J. The use of salbutamol powder in childhood asthma. Archives of Disease in Childhood 53: 958 (1978).

Lenney, W.; Milner, A.D. and Hiller, E.J. Continuous and intermittent salbutamol tablet administration in asthmatic children. British Journal of Diseases of the Chest 73: 277 (1979).

Mann, N.P. and Hiller, E.J.: Ipratropium bromide in children with asthma. Thorax 36: 72 (1981).

Milner, A.D. and Ingram, D.: Bronchodilator and cardiac effects of isoprenaline, orciprenaline and salbutamol aerosols in asthma. Archives of Disease in Childhood 46: 502 (1971).

Milner, A.D.: Steroids and asthma. Pharmacology and Therapeutics 17: 229 (1982).

Phelan, P.D. and Williams, H.E.: Studies of respiratory function in infants with recurrent asthmatic bronchitis. Australian Paediatric Journal 5: 187 (1969).

Pullan, C.R. and Hey, E.N.: Wheezing asthma and pulmonary dysfunction 10 years after infection with respiratory syncytial virus in infancy. British Medical Journal 284: 1665 (1982).

Radford, M.: Effect of salbutamol in infants with wheezy bronchitis. Archives of Disease in Childhood 50: 535 (1975).

Rutter, N.; Milner, A.D. and Hiller, E.J.: Effect of bronchodilators on respiratory resistance in infants and young children with bronchiolitis and wheezy bronchitis. Archives of Disease in Childhood 50: 719 (1975).

Speight, A.N.P.; Lee, D.A. and Hey, E.N.: Underdiagnosis and undertreatment of asthma in childhood. British Medical Journal 286: 1253 (1983).

Tal, A.; Bavilski, C.; Yohai, D.; Bearman, J.E.; Gorodischer, R. and Moses, S.W.: Dexamethasone and salbutamol in the treatment of acute wheezing in infancy. Pediatrics 71: 13 (1983).

Chapter VII   Bronchodilators in Exercise-induced Asthma

S. Godfrey

It has been known for almost 300 years that exercise can cause an attack of asthma in a susceptible subject (Floyer, 1698). This exercise-induced asthma (EIA) can be a major source of inconvenience to the otherwise asymptomatic patient. This is particularly true of younger, more athletically active patients, but EIA occurs at all ages. Occasionally, EIA may be virtually the only symptom of the disease and this has sometimes led to the erroneous impression that EIA is a disease in its own right. In fact, careful investigation shows that such subjects have other evidence of bronchial hyper-reactivity and exercise is merely one of the various mechanisms by which an attack of asthma can be precipitated (Godfrey, 1982). As we shall see, there are many similarities between EIA and hyperventilation-induced asthma (HIA) but spontaneous hyperventilation is not normally encountered to any large degree.

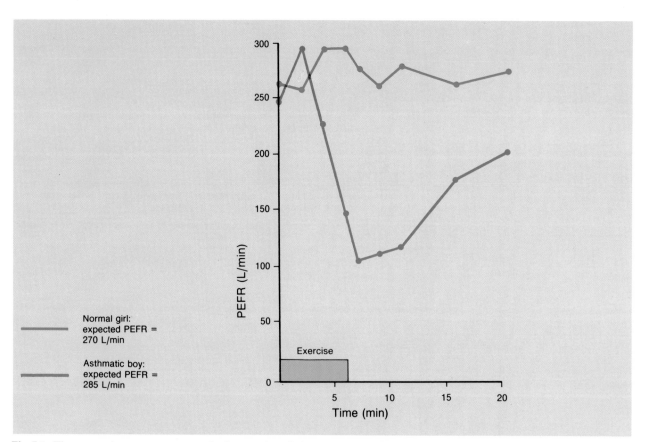

Fig. 7.1. The contrasting responses to exercise in an asthmatic boy and a healthy girl who both began exercise with their lung function close to their predicted normal values. The boy developed a typical attack of exercise-induced asthma (after Godfrey, 1974).

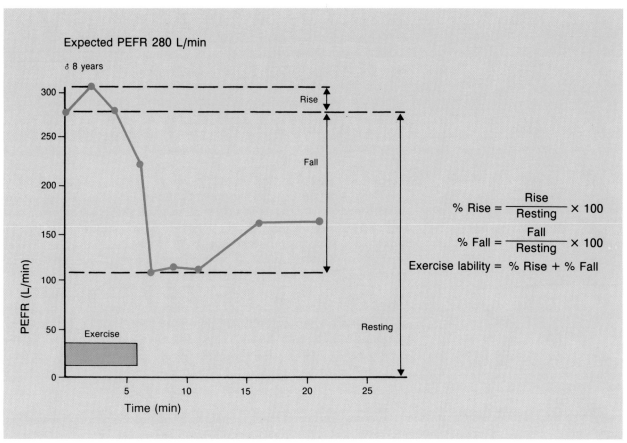

Expected PEFR 280 L/min

♂ 8 years

% Rise = $\dfrac{\text{Rise}}{\text{Resting}} \times 100$

% Fall = $\dfrac{\text{Fall}}{\text{Resting}} \times 100$

Exercise lability = % Rise + % Fall

Fig. 7.2. Typical changes in peak expiratory flow rate (PEFR) in an attack of exercise-induced asthma, showing the conventional indices used to quantitate the response (after Godfrey et al., 1973).

The Pattern of EIA

The pattern of the response of the asthmatic patient to an adequate exercise stimulus is quite consistent, as is illustrated in figure 7.1. In this case, the exercise consisted of 6 minutes of hard treadmill running. The initial resting lung function was good and for the first 2 to 4 minutes there was actually some improvement. By the sixth minute, however, lung function had begun to deteriorate and the fall in lung function continued for another 3 to 5 minutes after stopping exercise. Thereafter lung function began to recover, returning to the baseline level 20 to 30 minutes after the end of exercise. This pattern of response is typical of EIA in both children and adults, although the maximum post-exercise fall may be reached a little later in adults (5-7 minutes) compared with children (3-5 minutes). It should be noted that although the asthma is induced by the exercise, the attack reaches its climax some minutes after the exercise has stopped. Experience with testing for EIA suggests that in the patients with the most marked response, lung function begins to fall earlier in exercise and may even necessitate aborting the test, but this has never been formally investigated.

The quantitation of EIA is important, especially when considering the effects of various medications which can, themselves, alter lung function. The nomenclature preferred by the author is illustrated in figure 7.2. This separates the rise in lung function during exercise from the fall after exercise. Since we are concerned with the induced asthma, it is the post-exercise fall, expressed as a percentage of the pre-exercise baseline lung function, which indicates the response. This index is identical to the $\Delta FEV_1\%$ ('percent fall index') used in many recent publications.

A problem arises when considering the response to exercise following medication which alters baseline lung function. This is illustrated schematically in figure 7.3. If baseline function improves, an identical absolute post-exercise fall will result in a smaller percent fall index, or $\Delta FEV_1\%$. Likewise, the absolute post-exercise FEV_1 may be higher than in the control test, even though a significant fall has occurred from the drug-induced elevated baseline level. Even when the change in baseline induced by a drug is apparently quite small, it is not certain that the change in airway calibre is small because of the 'fourth power' law, relating the diameter of a tube to the resistance to airflow. Thus, a similar change in diameter has a much more profound effect when airways are narrowed than when they are dilated. All this means that in the absence of an absolute measure of airway calibre, it is safest to express the effects of exercise and pharmacological agents in absolute terms when comparisons are being made. The minimal requirement for objectivity is to give the baseline level as well as the $\Delta FEV_1\%$.

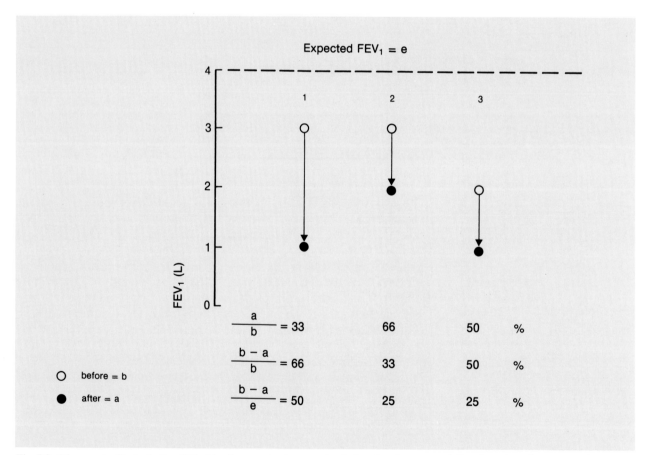

Fig. 7.3. Diagram to illustrate the difficulties in quantitating exercise-induced asthma, especially when there is a change in baseline lung function. While it matters little which index is used when comparing tests 1 and 2, any comparisons between these tests and test 3 become a question of semantics.

The Functional Changes in EIA

There is general agreement that in asthmatics, exercise results in obstruction of the airways over a wide region of the bronchial tree and this obstruction is reflected by a decrease in all the common indices of lung function. Although claims are made from time to time that one or other test is more 'sensitive' in detecting change, those who have formally studied this subject have concluded that it matters little which test is used (McNeill et al., 1966; Saunders and Rudolf, 1978). As illustrated in figure 7.1, the early part of exercise results in bronchodilatation and this has been studied in some detail using the non-effort-dependent forced oscillatory technique (Mansfield et al., 1979). An initial fall in resistance was recorded which persisted throughout exercise in asthmatic children only to give way to a rise in resistance (EIA) on stopping exercise. Interestingly, the fall in resistance during exercise was rather less marked in asthmatic children than in control non-asthmatic subjects.

After exercise, when the attack of EIA develops there is generalised airways obstruction with hyperinflation, as reflected in the forced expiratory flow-volume loop. By using a mixture of 80% helium and 20% oxygen (He/O_2) instead of air, some investigators have attempted to partition the airways obstruction between the larger and smaller airways (Benatar and Konig, 1974; McFadden et al., 1977). These studies have shown considerable variation between subjects, although it is interesting that the 'large airway' group of McFadden and co-workers had their EIA attenuated by an anticholinergic agent, in comparison to the 'small airway' group, whose EIA was more affected by stored chemical mediator release (McFadden et al. 1977). Recent studies however, have cast very serious doubt on the simplistic interpretation of He/O_2 studies in terms of large and small airway function (Knudson and Schroter, 1983).

Using static pressure-volume curves together with forced expiratory flow volume curves, some workers concluded that EIA was accompanied by widespread airway closure, and that in some subjects an increase in total lung capacity occurred (Freedman et al., 1975). This may have been caused by a temporary loss of elastic recoil, which would have also contributed to the reduction in forced expiratory flow rates at low lung volume.

The precise mechanism accounting for the airways obstruction in EIA is uncertain. The speed of onset and recovery (fig. 7.1) strongly suggest a rapidly reversible process and it is natural to suppose that this is contraction and relaxation of bronchial smooth muscle. This idea has been challenged by McFadden and his colleagues, who related higher basal histamine levels to more active asthma with a more peripheral site of airways obstruction, and suggested that a state of inflammation of the airways may determine the responses to exercise (McFadden et al., 1980). It is nonetheless difficult to see how inflammatory changes could appear and disappear in a few minutes. Until very recently it was generally accepted that the response to exercise was the type of early reaction illustrated in figure 7.1. However, a recent study found that 33% of children and adults developed a second, late reaction, 4 to 10 hours after the exercise (Lee et al., 1983). This late response bears similarities to the late response to allergen, and is much more likely to be caused by inflammatory changes than bronchospasm. However, for practical purposes, EIA in the large majority of subjects consists of a simple early attack of what appears to be bronchospasm.

Who Gets EIA?

As implied earlier, EIA is not a disease in its own right and exercise appears to be just one of the several mechanisms that can provoke an attack in a patient with asthma. Clinical experience suggests that the large majority of asthmatic patients develop EIA when they exercise hard enough under the appropriate conditions. However, many patients, especially very young children and adults, never exercise hard enough to produce symptoms of EIA, and others exercise, as we shall see later, in a fashion which is not very effective in inducing asthma (low asthmagenicity).

Defining EIA

Before discussing the incidence of EIA, it is very important to define what is meant by an abnormal response to exercise. Curiously, most investigators have been content to fix arbitrary criteria, such as a fall in FEV_1 greater than 15%. This is clearly scientifically unacceptable. The only valid method is to define the response of the normal population by statistical parameters. Such an investigation was carried out on 548 children aged 12 years who had no personal or family history of asthma or allergic diseases (Burr et al., 1974). They found the lung function response to exercise in these children was normally distributed, with a mean postexercise value of 97.5% of the resting pre-exercise value, the standard deviation being 6.1%. This means that about 97% of normal children will have a post-exercise fall in lung function which does not reach less than 85.3% of the resting pre-exercise value, i.e. the upper limit of the percent fall of peak expiratory flow rate (PEFR) in normal 12-year-olds is, indeed, 15%. In another study in children, Mellis and his colleagues reported the upper limit of normal ΔFEV_1 to be 10% and for PEFR to be 12.5% (Mellis et al., 1978). Our own studies in both children and adults suggested an upper limit for the percent fall index of about 10% (Anderson et al., 1975b).

Incidence of EIA

Using the criteria of a 10 to 15% fall in post-exercise lung function as indicative of a positive response, various studies are reasonably in agreement as to the incidence of EIA in the population of asthmatics. One study of 97 unselected asthmatic children (Godfrey, 1974) gave an incidence of positive tests of 70 to 86%. Similarly, Kattan and co-workers found an incidence of 83 to 84% in children (Kattan et al., 1978), while Eggleston and Guerrant (1976) found an incidence of 71% in children. Studies in adults (Haynes et al., 1976) recorded an incidence of EIA of 82 to 87%. One of the problems in defining the population incidence of EIA is the rather large variation in the response of the individual to repeat testing. Even with careful standardisation of test procedure, one group of workers found the coefficient of variation in percent fall index to repeat testing within one week to be 21%, and even higher for repeated testing on the same day (Silverman and Anderson, 1972). Similarly high coefficients of variation for repeated testing over periods of several months were found in other studies (Eggleston and Guerrant, 1976), although the reproducibility was a little better in those subjects with more marked EIA. It is likely that this variability has a biological, rather than an experimental cause (see below).

Exercise Lability

The next question to be considered is whether or not EIA is specific for asthma or whether it also occurs in patients with other disorders. Here again a certain amount of confusion has arisen because of the use of different criteria for judging bronchial reactivity and for defining population groups. As shown in figure 7.2, the bronchial response to exercise includes an initial bronchodilatation followed, after stopping exercise, by bronchoconstriction. The total bronchial response to exercise can be quantitated by the sum of the percent rise and the percent fall, and this is termed the exercise lability. Various studies have reported an increase in exercise lability in children who were well but had wheezed as infants, in relatives of children with asthma and wheezy bronchitis and in children with cystic fibrosis (Konig et al., 1972; Konig and Godfrey 1973a,b; Levison and Godfrey, 1976). However, in all these groups, the increased bronchial responsiveness was predominantly caused by the bronchodilatation during exercise and they did not develop a significant post-exercise fall in lung function, i.e. they did not have EIA.

Relationship of EIA to Asthma

A particular problem has been the apparent increase in exercise-induced changes in lung function in patients with atopic diseases other than asthma, e.g. hay fever (Kawabori et al., 1976). However, careful inspection of the data reveals that these atopic subjects did have histories of wheezing at some time and were almost certainly mild asthmatics. In a study of hyperventilation-induced asthma, it was clearly shown that there was almost no overlap in response between subjects with asthma and hay fever, but considerable overlap between the hay fever patients and the normal control subjects (Deal et al., 1980). It seems fair to conclude that true EIA occurs only in patients with asthma, although the disease need not be clinically troublesome at the time of study.

This raises the question as to the relationship, if any, of EIA to the general severity of the asthma. Many studies have demonstrated that it is possible to produce marked EIA in a patient whose lung function is normal before the exercise. Furthermore, 2 studies found no correlation between the resting lung function and the severity of the EIA (Sly, 1970; Silverman and Anderson, 1972) but another study (Mellis et al., 1978) found a lower incidence of EIA in children with better resting lung function. Various studies have shown EIA to occur in mild and severe asthma and in intrinsic as well as extrinsic asthma (Silverman and Turner-Warwick, 1972). In a study of several years' duration, a group of children with chronic perennial asthma, who were treated with various medications, were studied as they passed through puberty. The children undertook exercise tests at regular intervals, and the results are summarised in figure 7.4. It can be seen that there was no correlation between the severity of EIA and the clinical severity of their asthma, as judged by their need for medication. Even following puberty and the associated improvement, EIA persisted for several months. These facts, as well as others concerning the effect of drugs on EIA, emphasise the care needed before equating EIA with clinical asthma.

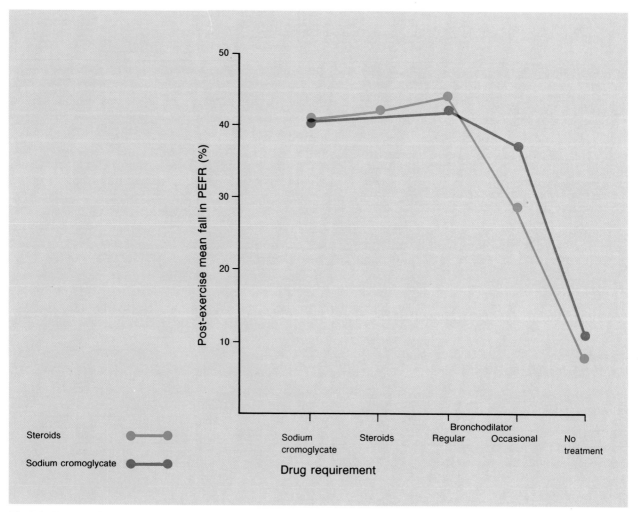

Fig. 7.4. Post-exercise fall in peak expiratory flow rate (PEFR) related to the stage of asthma during the long term follow-up of groups of children who either never required more than sodium cromoglycate to control their symptoms or who required continuous steroids at some stage. As they recovered, both groups progressed through stages in which they required regular, occasional and finally no bronchodilators. In all but the last stage, there was no significant change in the severity of exercise-induced asthma in either group (after Balfour-Lynn et al., 1980).

Conditions Needed to Produce EIA

One of the reasons for the variable incidence of EIA in population studies and for the relatively poor reproducibility of EIA is that very specific conditions are required to provoke an attack. It has been known since the time of Sir John Floyer (1698) that different types of exercise have differing asthmagenicity and swimming, in particular, is much less likely to provoke asthma than running (Fitch and Morton, 1971). In a series of studies, it was shown that the severity of EIA depended upon the duration of exercise and the severity of the work (Anderson et al., 1975b). Thus, EIA was more marked as duration of exercise increased to between 6 and 8 minutes. More prolonged exercise did not have any greater effect and indeed some subjects 'ran through' their EIA with prolonged exercise, without developing an attack when they stopped. The severity of EIA also increased with the severity of the task, up to a work rate of about two-thirds of the maximum oxygen consumption – a level resulting in a heart rate of about 170 to 180/min in children and 140 to 150/min in adults. Finally, intermittent work, e.g. running short sprints with a rest between runs, does not cause EIA (Schnall and Landau, 1980). Many older studies used unsuitable exercise protocols, such as prolonged or intermittent exercise (running up and down stairs), and as a result were unreliable.

In the past 5 years, a much greater understanding has been achieved of the influence of environmental conditions on EIA and the pathways involved in the induction of the bronchospasm, so that some of the findings concerning asthmagenicity can now be explained. A number of investigators have shown that EIA is more marked when the patient breathes cold, dry air than warm, humid air and that the severity of EIA can be correlated with the degree of cooling of the airways that occurs during exercise (Bar-Or et al., 1977; Chen and Horton, 1977; Deal et al., 1979a,b; Strauss et al., 1977; Weinstein et al., 1976). This goes some way to explain the low asthmagenicity of swimming, in which humid air is normally breathed, but in a study which arranged for children to swim and breathe dry air (Bar-Yishay et al., 1982), the occurrence of EIA was much lower (39%) than following running. Recent studies have shown that the level of ionisation of the inspired air can have a small but significant effect on the severity of EIA (Ben-Dov et al., 1983), and there is also a distinct possibility that, as with histamine challenge (Cockcroft et al., 1977), the severity of EIA depends upon the level of allergic stimulation to which the patient is exposed. This can help explain some of the variability in EIA which is to be expected if exercise tests are performed under varying environmental conditions.

Pathways Involved in EIA

For a long time it has been known that an attack of EIA can render the patient relatively refractory to a subsequent attack (McNeill et al., 1966). The diminishing effect on EIA of repeated exercise tests of identical severity is clearly seen in figure 7.5. The extent of this refractory period following EIA was defined by having patients undertake pairs of exercise tests of equal intensity but with differing intervals between the tests in each pair (Edmunds et al., 1978). The refractoriness wore off with a half-life of about 1 hour, so that by 3 to 4 hours after the initial test the subject was again fully responsive.

The most logical explanation for the existence of a refractory period following EIA is that some metabolic process is involved which requires resynthesis of effector agents. Alternative hypotheses, such as the persistence of adrenergic drive (Stearns et al., 1981) seem barely credible given the observed rapid decline of adrenaline (epinephrine) and noradrenaline (norepinephrine) levels after exercise (Larsson et al., 1982; Zielinski et al., 1980) and the fact that this supposed adrenergic drive does not prevent the initial attack of EIA when the levels of catecholamines would be the greatest. It has recently been shown that at least one chemical mediator, neutrophil chemotactic factor (NCF), is released from mast cells during the exercise period preceding EIA (Lee et al., 1982). The nature and magnitude of the NCF released resembled that released during antigen-induced asthma (AIA) and both the release of NCF and the EIA could be prevented by administering sodium cromoglycate (cromolyn sodium) before exercise. Several years ago, Silverman and Andrea (1972) showed that sodium cromoglycate prevented EIA if given immediately after exercise but before the attack of EIA is fully developed. All these findings strongly suggest that EIA is due to the effect of mediators liberated during the exercise period. A second rise of NCF has been documented in those patients with a late response to exercise (Lee et al., 1983), thus further emphasising the similarity of EIA and AIA.

Quite apart from any controversy about the role of the mediator, there still exists a vigorous argument as to the mechanism by which EIA is triggered. One school of thought maintains that EIA is but one manifestation of hyperventilation-induced asthma (HIA) and that both are triggered by cooling of the airways (Deal et al., 1979b). There are, however, a number of objections to this unifying hypothesis. In particular, exercise performed while breathing warm humid air (which prevents airway cooling and EIA), nevertheless induced a refractory period, suggesting that exercise *per se* and not cooling is responsible for mediator release (Ben-Dov et al., 1982; Henriksen et al., 1981). In parallel experiments, hyperventilation breathing warm humid air, did not induce a refractory period to HIA, suggesting that exercise and hyperventilation are different stimuli (Bar-Yishay et al., 1983a,b). It seems only fair to conclude that, at present, the trigger site for EIA is uncertain but whatever the trigger mechanism might be, mediator release is involved in the process.

Effect of Drugs on EIA

Interpretation of Drug Effects on EIA

Because EIA has so many features resembling spontaneous asthma it has naturally received considerable attention from those interested in the pharmacological treatment of asthma. Since exercise is a naturally occurring stimulus to asthma there would seem

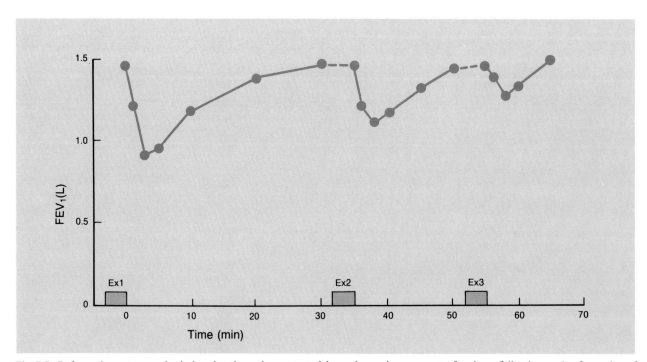

Fig. 7.5. Refractoriness to exercise-induced asthma demonstrated by a decreasing amount of asthma following each of a series of equally severe exercise tests (after Godfrey, 1983a).

Table 7.1. Potential problems of interpretation of an exercise challenge in the evaluation of a drug to be used to treat asthma

---

Methodological problems
    Effect of drug on baseline lung function
    Effect of type, severity and duration of exercise
    Effect of environmental temperature, humidity and ionisation

Problems inherent in EIA
    Variability of EIA even under standard conditions
    Refractory period following EIA

Problems inherent in the drug
    Prolonged action may prejudice randomisation

Problems related to the nature of clinical asthma
    Stopping other medication may precipitate an attack
    Level of antigenic stimulation can alter reactivity
    Severity of EIA unrelated to clinical severity
    Poor correlation between effect on EIA and clinical asthma

---

to be an *a priori* advantage for using EIA as a model, rather than asthma induced by other pharmacological agents, such as histamine or methacholine. Although this is broadly correct, very considerable care is needed in the interpretation of drug effects on EIA. The reasons for this are summarised in table 7.1 and discussed below.

Methodological Problems

The chief methodological problem involved in the evaluation of drugs in EIA has already been noted when considering quantitation of EIA. If a drug has no detectable effect on basal lung function (e.g. sodium cromoglycate or steroids), then any effect on EIA is readily obvious. When, however, the drug is a bronchodilator (e.g. β-adrenoceptor agonists or an anticholinergic) the interpretation of the effect is complicated by the largely unknown change in the initial airway calibre. Apart from this problem of interpretation it is obviously very important to pay careful attention to the various factors discussed above which can alter the severity of EIA, notably the type, duration and severity of exercise and the environmental conditions under which the test is performed.

Problems Inherent in EIA

Even under the most standardised conditions, EIA has a very significant variability which can render comparisons between drugs and placebo, or between different drugs, very difficult. Ideally, tests should be performed at short intervals but, as we have seen, the phenomenon of the refractory period complicates matters. In practice, it is essential to leave 2 to 3 hours between tests and to randomise the order of drug administration to avoid problems of refractoriness. There is very considerable doubt as to the validity of tests performed at intervals greater than a day or two, in view of the major changes that can occur in the responsiveness to exercise – possibly resulting from antigenic or environmental changes. The only acceptable method must be to use an adequate double-blind technique for the drugs and placebo, which are studied as close together as possible.

Problems Inherent in Drugs

Most drugs active against EIA have a duration of action which can be quite prolonged depending on the drug and the route of administration. This creates major problems for the randomisation of controlled studies, since the administration of the active drug before the placebo will invalidate the placebo test unless it is delayed long enough for the drug effect to have worn off. This prolonged delay (for example until the next day) may create problems in terms of reproducibility as discussed above. The failure to use a randomised order could prejudice the results in subjects with a marked refractory period who were always given the placebo first.

Problems Related to Clinical Asthma

There are a number of difficulties arising from the nature of 'natural' or 'spontaneous' clinical asthma. A relatively common problem arises when current medication has to be stopped in order to undertake exercise challenge tests. The clinical condition of the patient may deteriorate, so that the exercise tests cannot be performed, or the changing clinical state may invalidate any comparative studies between drugs and placebo. As previously discussed, the level of allergic stimulation may profoundly affect EIA and this is often difficult to control in patients sensitive to common perennial allergens, such as the house dust mite. A further problem is the fact that the severity of EIA is not directly related to the severity of clinical asthma (and hence to the type of drugs needed for its control). Finally, as will be discussed below, for reasons not yet understood, there may be no relationship between the efficacy of a drug in EIA and its efficacy in clinical asthma.

Sympathomimetic Bronchodilators and EIA

From the very first of the modern studies of EIA (Jones et al., 1962, 1963; McNeill et al., 1966) it was known that adrenaline or isoprenaline (isoproterenol) could inhibit EIA if given before exercise. Such drugs are stimulants of several types of autonomic receptor (chapter II) but the inhibition of EIA is seen equally well with selective β_2-agonists such as salbutamol (albuterol), terbutaline or fenoterol*. The selective agents are all powerful bronchodilators and they can inhibit EIA, even when the resting level of lung function is close to normal, as shown in figure 7.6. In terms of potency, there seems to be little to choose between the modern selective β_2-adrenoceptor agonists as far as the inhibition of EIA is concerned.

The mode of action of β-agonists in EIA is not entirely clear and a number of interesting studies have cast doubt on the simplistic concept that they act directly on the bronchial smooth muscle to prevent its contraction when stimulated by a mediator. Anderson and her colleagues were the first to report that while aerosolised fenoterol (400μg) blocked EIA in most subjects for up to 4 hours, oral terbutaline (5mg), despite causing bronchodilatation did not have much effect on the EIA (Anderson et al., 1975a). They repeated the study with aerosolised (200μg) and oral (0.1 mg/kg) salbutamol (Anderson et al., 1976) and came to the same conclu-

---

* For product availability in the USA, see appendix B.

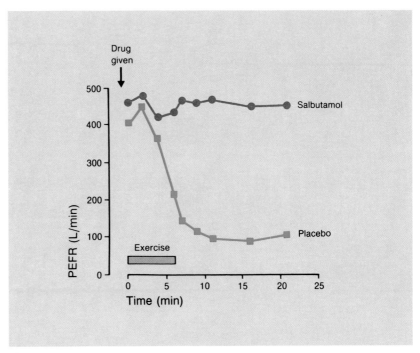

Fig. 7.6. Inhibition of exercise-induced asthma by pretreatment with salbutamol aerosol (after Godfrey, 1975).

sions. When oral terbutaline (5mg) and orciprenaline (metaproterenol) [20mg] were compared with placebo, it was found that they gave little protection from EIA after 90 minutes, but that some benefit was seen, particularly with terbutaline, 3 hours after administration of the drug (Morse et al., 1976). In contrast to these studies, Francis and co-workers found oral salbutamol (0.15 mg/kg) just as effective as aerosolised salbutamol (200µg) in suppressing EIA in asthmatic children and they suggested that failure of oral therapy to prevent EIA in earlier studies was due to the low doses used (Francis et al., 1980). The oral drug blocked EIA for up to 6 hours. Similarly, in a more recent study, oral terbutaline 2.5mg was effective in blocking EIA in adolescents (Shapiro et al., 1981). At present there is no definite explanation for these conflicting results although dosage may be an important factor.

In an attempt further to elucidate the mode of action of β-adrenoceptor agonists in EIA, 11 subjects were given isoetharine or isoprenaline and then exercised after the bronchodilator effect had worn off (Hetzel et al., 1977). The magnitude of the protection from EIA was unrelated to the magnitude of the previous bronchodilator response. Additionally, 3 subjects were still protected against EIA at a time when the bronchodilator effect had worn off, suggesting that β-adrenoceptor agonists may have more than one mode of action, possibly including the inhibition of mediator release (Tattersfield, 1983).

Finally, for those who believe that hyperventilation-induced asthma is synonymous with EIA, Rossing and his colleagues have shown a shift to the right in the dose response curve for cold thermal stress after giving orciprenaline (Rossing et al., 1982), though this could, of course, merely be due to an effect on the target organ.

Methylxanthines and EIA

Methylxanthine derivatives, such as theophylline and aminophylline, have been used for many years in the treatment of asthma. For a long time it was thought that they acted simply as bronchodilator agents by virtue of their antagonism to phosphodiesterase, which caused an elevation of cyclic AMP in the bronchial smooth muscle cell with resultant relaxation. More recently, other suggestions have been made concerning their action (see p.20), indicating that these drugs may have a prophylactic role in therapy (Weinberger and Hendeles, 1983). There is no doubt that theophylline has an effect on EIA (Jones et al., 1963) but the evaluation of this type of agent is complicated by the fact that the initial baseline lung function is elevated. Even so, a graded inhibition of EIA, dependent upon the plasma theophylline level at the time of the exercise, has been convincingly demonstrated (Pollock et al., 1977). More recently, Phillips and co-workers investigated the efficacy of a slow-release aminophylline preparation on EIA in 9 adult subjects with plasma theophylline levels of about 11 mg/L (Phillips et al., 1981). The baseline peak flow rate in the treatment studies was only some 6% higher than in the control tests, but exercise caused only a 13 to 19% fall in lung function with aminophylline compared with a 29 to 30% fall in the control tests.

Sodium Cromoglycate (Cromolyn Sodium)

Of considerable practical and theoretical interest were the observations that sodium cromoglycate could inhibit EIA (Davies, 1968) and that this inhibition occurred only if the drug was given before exercise and not if it was given at the end of exercise but before the onset of the asthma (Silverman and Andrea, 1972). These, coupled with the recent studies showing that sodium cromoglycate inhibited neutrophil chemotactic factor release by exercise (Lee et al., 1982) gives support to the idea that EIA involves mediator release during exercise. Sodium cromoglycate has never been convincingly shown to be a bronchodilator and other suggested modes of action could be explained by the inhibition of mediator release. The efficacy of sodium cromoglycate in preventing EIA is not in doubt, since it has no detectable effect on baseline lung function. The magnitude of the protection is not as great as that for the adrenoceptor agonists, and the protection wears off over about 6 hours (fig. 7.7). Usually there is 50% protection a few minutes after the drug is inhaled and this protection is halved after about 3.5 hours (Godfrey, 1983b). There are different methods of inhaling sodium cromoglycate, but in children experience suggests that the original powdered form of the drug is more effective in preventing EIA than its administration by pressure-packed aerosol (Bar-Yishay et al., 1983c).

Atropine

Atropine and other anticholinergic agents, e.g. ipratropium bromide, are powerful bronchodilator drugs, the former having considerable side effects when given in large doses. There is at present an active argument between those who feel that these drugs inhibit EIA (Sheppard et al., 1983) and those who feel that they have little effect on either exercise- or hyperventilation-induced asthma (Borut et al., 1977; Griffin et al., 1982). Part of the problem may arise from the interpretation of results with a drug which markedly alters baseline bronchial tone. In view of the circumstantial evidence that airway tone determines the response to lib-

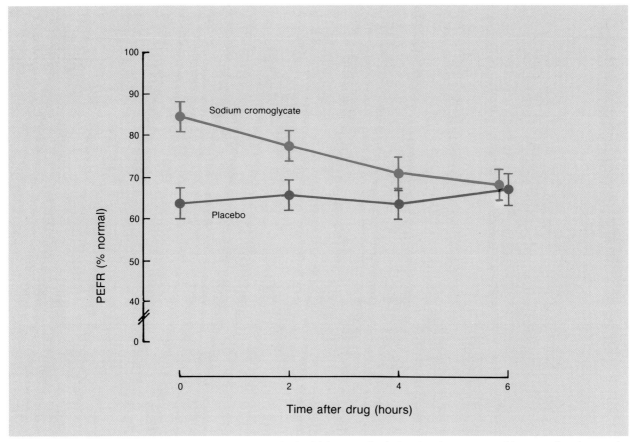

Fig. 7.7. The duration of action of sodium cromoglycate in inhibiting exercise-induced asthma measured by repeating the exercise test every 2 hours after the patient had received either placebo or active drug (after Anderson et al., 1975b).

erated mediator in EIA (Ben-Dov et al., 1982), it would seem likely that atropine would reduce the response to exercise, but the extent of its effect is still uncertain.

Corticosteroids

Perhaps most disappointing of all has been the general finding that corticosteroids, by whatever route of administration have little or no inhibitory effect on EIA (Jaffe et al., 1973; McNeill et al., 1966). This is perhaps not so surprising because they also have a minimal effect on the immediate response to antigen inhalation, which is similar in many ways to EIA. The lack of efficacy of corticosteroids in EIA presents particular problems for the asthmatic patients with more troublesome asthma, in whom corticosteroids will help their general condition but will leave them susceptible to exercise-induced attacks. Such patients have to take additional medication especially to cope with the problem of EIA. One ray of hope, however, comes from a recent study in which there was some diminution in EIA following regular use of inhaled budesonide (Henriksen and Dahl, 1983).

Other Drugs

Various other agents have been investigated to determine their efficacy in EIA. Of greatest significance, at least theoretically, has been the demonstration of the inhibition of EIA by the calcium gate-blocking drug, nifedipine (Barnes et al., 1981). This effect could be due to the inhibition of mediator release but this has not yet been determined. Various other so called 'anti-allergic' agents have either failed to demonstrate any inhibitory effect on EIA in properly controlled trials, e.g. ketotifen (Kennedy et al., 1980), or have not been found to be clinically acceptable.

Relative Efficacy of Drugs in EIA

In an attempt to determine the relative efficacy of different agents known to affect EIA, a group of children who received these drugs on different occasions before exercise were studied (Godfrey and Konig, 1976). The results are summarised in figure 7.8 which shows that salbutamol was clearly the most effective agent, while sodium cromoglycate, theophylline, and atropine were rather less protective, although the interpretation of the effects of atropine and theophylline depends upon the evaluation of the shift in baseline lung function. A direct comparison between oral terbutaline and theophylline suggested that they were equally effective in preventing EIA (Shapiro et al., 1981), while another comparison between sodium cromoglycate and theophylline suggested that greater improvement was seen with the latter (Pollock et al., 1977).

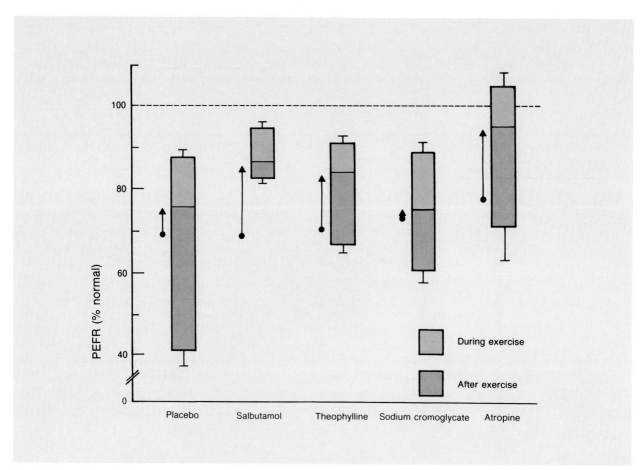

Fig. 7.8. The effect of different drugs on exercise-induced asthma in a group of 15 children, with lung function expressed as a percentage of predicted, to emphasise absolute changes. The arrows indicate the change from the resting lung function (if any) following the administration of the drug at rest before the start of exercise. The bars indicate SEM (after Godfrey and Konig, 1976).

Practical Management of EIA

For older children and young adults who are active, EIA can be a major problem. It is clearly undesirable that they should be prevented from taking part in sports and other strenuous physical activities, and it is therefore the responsibility of the physician to provide adequate treatment for the problem. From what has been said above, there is little doubt that for most patients the inhalation of 2 puffs of a selective β_2-adrenoceptor agonist from a pressurised canister inhaler is the most practical treatment. It is essential that the inhalation technique is perfect and that the drug is inhaled about 5 minutes before the type of exercise which the patient knows from previous experience is likely to cause wheezing. Usually this is fairly hard, continuous exercise, e.g. running for 5 minutes, and it is less common with the intermittent type of exercise that occurs in many team games. For reasons discussed earlier, swimming rarely causes much EIA. The protection afforded by the inhaled sympathomimetic will last about 4 hours. If exercise is prolonged, e.g. a hiking trip, it may be necessary to repeat the dose.

For the patient unable to use a pressurised canister inhaler properly, an alternative would be the powder inhaler form of salbutamol ('Rotahaler') which is easier to use, or wet nebulised salbutamol, which if used just for preventing EIA, is very inconvenient. There is evidence to suggest that oral β-agonists may not be very effective.

Patients who are regularly taking sodium cromoglycate or theophylline should be reasonably well protected against EIA, but because these drugs are not powerful protectors, additional medication may be needed before strenuous exercise. Once again, the most effective agent would be an inhaled β_2-agonist. It is difficult to see the place for either sodium cromoglycate or theophylline in the prevention of EIA in a patient not taking them regularly for prophylaxis of chronic asthma. It is true that sodium cromoglycate, having no detectable cardiovascular effects, is theoretically the safest drug to use, but in practice there is no evidence that sympathomimetics are harmful during exercise. The efficacy of theophylline in EIA is less than that of the β-agonists and is critically dose-dependent. Since the therapeutic blood level is achieved only for a relatively short time after a single dose when a short-acting preparation is used, and adequate blood levels are reached only after several hours with a long-acting preparation, there seems to be no logical basis for using theophylline just to prevent EIA on an 'as needed' basis.

If the patient has not received adequate medication to prevent EIA and an attack occurs, it will normally pass without treatment in about 30 minutes. If available, a wet nebulised adrenoceptor agonist will reverse the bronchospasm almost immediately. A pressure-packed canister inhaler can be tried but its efficacy will depend on the ability of the patient to inhale the drug while suffering an attack of EIA.

In Summary

Exercise-induced asthma presents a fascinating opportunity to study the basic physiological and pharmacological pathways involved in asthma. Studying the therapeutic effects of various medications has shed light both on the mechanism of asthma and the action of drugs. Exercise-induced asthma can readily be prevented by the inhalation of a selective β_2-adrenoceptor agonist shortly before exercise.

References

Anderson, S.D.; Rozea, P.J.; Dolton, R. and Lindsay, D.A.: Inhaled and oral bronchodilator therapy in exercise induced asthma. Australian and New Zealand Journal of Medicine 5: 544 (1975a).

Anderson, S.D.; Silverman, M.; Konig, P. and Godfrey, S.: Exercise induced asthma. British Journal of Diseases of the Chest 69: 1 (1975b).

Anderson, S.D.; Searle, J.P.; Rozea, P.; Bandler, L.; Theobald, G. and Lindsay, D.A.: Inhaled and oral salbutamol in exercise-induced asthma. American Review of Respiratory Disease 114: 493 (1976).

Balfour-Lynn, L.; Tooley, M. and Godfrey, S.: Relationship of exercise induced asthma to clinical asthma in childhood. Archives of Disease in Childhood 56: 450 (1980).

Bar-Yishay, E.; Gur, I.; Inbar, O.; Neuman, I.; Diln, R.A. and Godfrey, S.: Differences between running and swimming as stimuli for exercise induced asthma. European Journal of Applied Physiology 48: 387 (1982).

Bar-Yishay, E.; Ben-Dov, I. and Godfrey, S.: Refractory period following hyperventilation-induced asthma. American Review of Respiratory Disease 127: 572 (1983a).

Bar-Yishay, E.; Gur, I.; Levy, M.; Volozni, D. and Godfrey, S.: Refractory period following induced asthma: Comparative contribution of exercise and isocapnic hyperventilation. Thorax 38: 849 (1983b).

Bar-Yishay, E.; Gur, I.; Levy, M.; Volozni, D. and Godfrey, S.: Duration of action of sodium cromoglycate on exercise-induced asthma: comparison of two formulations. Archives of Disease in Childhood 58: 624 (1983c).

Barnes, P.J.; Wilson, N.M. and Brown, M.J.: A calcium antagonist, nifedipine, modifies exercise induced asthma. Thorax 36: 726 (1981).

Bar-Or, O.; Neuman, I. and Dotan, R.: Effects of dry and humid climates on exercise-induced asthma in children and adults. Journal of Allergy and Clinical Immunology 60: 163 (1977).

Benatar, S.R. and Konig, P.: Maximal expiratory flow and lung volume changes associated with exercise induced asthma in children and the effect of breathing a low-density gas mixture. Clinical Science and Molecular Medicine 46: 317 (1974).

Ben-Dov, I.; Bar-Yishay, E. and Godfrey, S.: Exercise induced asthma without respiratory heat loss. Thorax 37: 630 (1982).

Ben-Dov, I.; Amirav, I.; Shochina, M.; Amitai, I.; Bar-Yishay, E. and Godfrey, S.: The effect of negative ionisation of inspired air on the response of asthmatic children to exercise or histamine challenge. Thorax 38: 584 (1983).

Borut, T.C.; Tashkin, D.P.; Fischer, T.J.; Katz, R.; Rachelefsky, G.; Siegel, S.C.; Lee, E. and Harper, C.: Comparison of aerosolized atropine sulphate and SCH 1000 on exercise-induced bronchospasm in children. Journal of Allergy and Clinical Immunology 60: 127 (1977).

Burr, M.L.; Eldridge, B.A. and Borysiewicz, L.K.: Peak expiratory flow rates before and after exercise in school children. Archives of Disease in Childhood 49: 923 (1974).

Chen, W.Y. and Horton, D.G.: Heat and water loss from the airways and exercise-induced asthma. Respiration 34: 305 (1977).

Cockcroft, D.W.; Ruffin, R.E.; Dolovich, J. and Hargreave, F.E.: Allergen-induced increase in non-allergic bronchial reactivity. Clinical Allergy 7: 503 (1977).

Davies, S.E.: The effect of disodium cromoglycate on exercise-induced asthma. British Medical Journal 3: 593 (1968).

Deal, E.C.; McFadden, E.R.; Ingram, R.H.; Breslin, F.J. and Jaeger, J.J.: Airway responsiveness to cold air and hyperpnea in normal subjects and those with hay fever and asthma. American Review of Respiratory Disease 121: 621 (1980).

Deal, E.C.; McFadden, E.R.; Ingram, R.H. and Jaeger, J.J.: Hyperpnea and heat flux: initial reaction sequence in exercise-induced asthma. Journal of Applied Physiology 46: 476 (1979a).

Deal, E.C.; McFadden, E.R.; Ingram, R.H.; Strauss, R.H. and Jaeger, J.J.: Role of respiratory heat exchange in production of exercise-induced asthma. Journal of Applied Physiology 46: 467 (1979b).

Edmunds, A.T.; Tooley, M. and Godfrey, S.: The refractory period after exercise induced asthma, its duration and relation to severity of exercise. American Review of Respiratory Disease 117: 247 (1978).

Eggleston, P.A. and Guerrant, J.L.: A standardised method of evaluating exercise-induced asthma. Journal of Allergy and Clinical Immunology 58: 414 (1976).

Fitch, K.D. and Morton, A.R.: Specificity of exercise-induced asthma. British Medical Journal 4: 577 (1971).

Floyer, Sir John: A Treatise of the Asthma, 1st Ed. (Wilkin and Innis, London 1698).

Francis, P.W.J.; Krastins, I.R.B. and Levinson, H.: Oral and inhaled salbutamol in the prevention of exercise induced bronchospasm. Pediatrics 66: 103 (1980).

Freedman, S.; Tattersfield, A.E. and Pride, N.B.: Changes in lung mechanics during asthma induced by exercise. Journal of Applied Physiology 38: 974 (1975).

Godfrey, S.: Exercise induced asthma; in Clark and Godfrey (Eds) Asthma, 2nd Ed. (Chapman and Hall, London 1983a).

Godfrey, S.: Anti-allergic agents; in Clark and Godfrey (Eds) Asthma, 2nd Ed. (Chapman and Hall, London 1983b).

Godfrey, S.: Problems peculiar to the diagnosis and management of childhood asthma. British Thoracic and Tuberculosis Association Review 4: 1 (1974).

Godfrey, S.: Stimuli to bronchostriction – basic mechanisms. Israel Journal of Medical Science 18: 297 (1982).

Godfrey, S.: Exercise induced asthma; clinical, physiological and therapeutic implications. Journal of Allergy and Clinical Immunology 56: 1 (1975).

Godfrey, S.; Silverman, M. and Anderson, S.: Problems of interpreting exercise induced asthma. Journal of Allergy and Clinical Immunology 52: 199 (1973).

Godfrey, S. and Konig, P.: Inhibition of exercise induced asthma by different pharmacological pathways. Thorax 31: 137 (1976).

Griffin, M.P.; Fong, K.F.; Ingram, R.H. and McFadden, E.R.: Dose-response effects of atropine on thermal stimulus-response relationships in asthma. Journal of Applied Physiology 53: 1576 (1982).

Haynes, R.L.; Ingram, R.H. and McFadden, E.R.: An assessment of the pulmonary response to exercise in asthma and an analysis of the factors influencing it. American Review of Respiratory Disease 114: 739 (1976).

Henriksen, J.M.; Dahl, R. and Lundqvist, G.R.: Influence of relative humidity and repeated exercise on exercise-induced bronchoconstriction. Allergy 36: 463-470 (1981).

Henriksen, J.M. and Dahl, R.: Effects of inhaled budesonide alone and in combination with low dose terbutaline in children with exercise induced asthma. American Review of Respiratory Disease 128: 993 (1983).

Hetzel, M.R.; Batten, J.C. and Clark, T.J.H.: Do sympathomimetic amines prevent exercise-induced asthma by bronchodilatation alone? British Journal of Diseases of the Chest 71: 109 (1977).

Jaffe, P.; Konig, P.; Ijaduola, O.; Walker, S. and Godfrey, S.: Relationship between plasma cortisol and peak expiratory flow rate in exercise induced asthma and the effect of sodium cromoglycate. Clinical Science and Molecular Medicine 45: 533 (1973).

Jones, R.S.; Buston, M.H. and Wharton, M.J.: The effect of exercise on ventilatory function in the child with asthma. British Journal of Diseases of the Chest 56: 78 (1962).

Jones, R.S.; Wharton, M.J. and Buston, M.H.: The place of physical exercise and bronchodilator drugs in the assessment of the asthmatic child. Archives of Disease in Childhood 38: 539 (1963).

Kattan, M.; Keens, T.G.; Mellis, C.M. and Levison, H.: The response to exercise in normal and asthmatic children. Journal of Pediatrics 92: 718 (1978).

Kawabori, I.; Pierson, W.E.; Conquest, L.L. and Bierman, C.W.: Incidence of exercise-induced asthma in children. Journal of Allergy and Clinical Immunology 58: 447 (1976).

Kennedy, J.D.; Hasham, F.; Clay, M.J.D. and Jones, R.S.: Comparison of action of disodium cromoglycate and ketotifen on exercise-induced bronchospasm in childhood asthma. British Medical Journal 281: 145 (1980).

Knudsen, R.J. and Schroter, R.C.: A consideration of density dependence of maximum expiratory flow. Respiratory Physiology 52: 125 (1983).

Konig, P.; Godfrey, S. and Abrahamov, A.: Exercise induced bronchial lability in children with a history of wheezy bronchitis. Archives of Disease in Childhood 47: 578 (1972).

Konig, P. and Godfrey, S.: The prevalence of exercise induced bronchial lability in families of children with asthma. Archives of Disease in Childhood 48: 513 (1973a).

Konig, P. and Godfrey, S.: Exercise induced bronchial lability and atopic status of families with wheezy bronchitis. Archives of Disease in Childhood 48: 942 (1973b).

Larsson, K.; Hjemdahl, P. and Martinson, A.: Sympathoadrenal reactivity in exercise-induced asthma. Chest 82: 560 (1982).

Lee, T.H.; Brown, M.H.; Nagy, L.; Causon, R.; Walport, M.J. and Kay, A.B.: Exercise induced release of histamine and neutrophil chemotactic factor in atopic asthmatics. Journal of Allergy and Clinical Immunology 70: 73 (1982).

Lee, T.H.; Toshikazu, N.; Papageorgiou, N.; Ikura, Y. and Kay, A.B.: Exercise induced late asthmatic reactions with neutrophil chemotactic activity. New England Journal of Medicine 308: 1502 (1983).

Levison, H. and Godfrey, S.: Pulmonary aspects of cystic fibrosis; in Mangos and Talamo (Eds) Cystic Fibrosis – a projection into the future (Stratton Intercontinental Medical Book Corp., New York 1976).

Mansfield, L.; McDonnell, J.; Morgan, W. and Souhrada, J.F.: Airway response in asthmatic children during and after exercise. Respiration 38: 135 (1979).

McFadden, E.R.; Ingram, R.H.; Haynes, R.L. and Wellman, J.J.: Predominant site of flow limitation and mechanisms of post exertional asthma. Journal of Applied Physiology 42: 746 (1977).

McFadden, E.R.; Soter, N.A. and Ingram, R.H.: Magnitude and site of airway response to exercise in asthmatics in relation to arterial histamine levels. Journal of Allergy and Clinical Immunology 66: 472 (1980).

McNeill, R.S.; Nairn, J.R.; Millar, J.S. and Ingram, C.G.: Exercise induced asthma. Quarterly Journal of Medicine 35: 55 (1966).

Mellis, C.M.; Kattan, M.; Keens, T.G. and Levison, H.: Comparative study of histamine and exercise challenges in asthmatic children. American Review of Respiratory Disease 117: 911 (1978).

Morse, J.L.C.; Jones, N.L.J. and Anderson, G.D.: The effect of terbutaline on exercise induced asthma. American Review of Respiratory Disease 113: 89 (1976).

Phillips, M.J.; Ollier, S.; Trembath, P.W. and Davies, R.J.: The effect of sustained-release aminophylline on exercise-induced asthma. British Journal of Diseases of the Chest 75: 181 (1981).

Pollock, J.; Kiechel, F.; Cooper, D. and Weinberger, M.: Relationship of serum theophylline concentration to inhibition of exercise-induced bronchospasm and comparison with cromolyn. Pediatrics 60: 840 (1977).

Rossing, T.H.; Weiss, J.W.; Breslin, F.J.; Ingram, R.H. and McFadden, E.R.: Effects of inhaled sympathomimetics on obstructive response to respiratory heat loss. Journal of Applied Physiology 52: 1119 (1982).

Saunders, K.B. and Rudolf, M.: The interpretation of different measurements of airways obstruction in the presence of lung volume changes in bronchial asthma. Clinical Science of Molecular Medicine 54: 313 (1978).

Schnall, R.P. and Landau, L.I.: The protective effects of short sprints in exercise induced asthma. Thorax 35: 828 (1980).

Shapiro, G.; Phillips, J.J.; Smith, K.; Furukawa, C.T.; Pierson, W.E. and Bierman, C.W.: Effectiveness of terbutaline and theophylline alone and in combination in exercise-induced bronchospasm. Pediatrics 67: 508 (1981).

Sheppard, D.; Epstein, J.; Holtzman, M.J.; Nadel, J.A. and Boushey, H.A.: Effect of route of atropine delivery on bronchospasm from cold air and methacholine. Journal of Applied Physiology 54: 130 (1983).

Silverman, M. and Anderson, S.D.: Standardization of exercise tests in asthmatic children. Archives of Disease in Childhood 47: 887 (1972).

Silverman, M. and Andrea, T.: Time course of effect of disodium cromoglycate on exercise-induced asthma. Archives of Disease in Childhood 47: 419 (1972).

Silverman, M. and Turner-Warwick, M.: Exercise-induced asthma: response to disodium cromoglycate in skin-test positive and skin-test negative subjects. Clinical Allergy 2: 137 (1972).

Sly, R.M.: Exercise related changes in airyway obstruction: frequency and clinical correlates in asthmatic children. Annals of Allergy 28: 1 (1970).

Stearns, D.R.; McFadden, E.R.; Breslin, R.J. and Ingram, J.R.: Reanalysis of the refractory period in exertional asthma. Journal of Applied Physiology 50: 503 (1981).

Strauss, R.H.; McFadden, E.R.; Ingram, R.H. and Jaeger, J.J.: Enhancement of exercise-induced asthma by cold air. New England Journal of Medicine 297: 743 (1977).

Tattersfield, A.: Autonomic Bronchodilators; in Clark and Godfrey (Eds) Asthma, 2nd Ed. (Chapman and Hall, London 1983).

Weinberger, M. and Hendeles, L.: Use of Theophylline for Asthma; in Clark and Godfrey (Eds) Asthma, 2nd Ed. (Chapman and Hall, London 1983).

Weinstein, R.E.; Anderson, J.A.; Kvale, P. and Sweet, L.C.: Effects of humidification on exercise-induced asthma (EIA). Journal of Allergy and Clinical Immunology 57: 250 (1976).

Zielinski, J.; Chodosowska, E.; Radomyski, A.; Arajzkiewicz, Z. and Kozlowski, S.: Plasma catacholamines during exercise induced bronchoconstriction in bronchial asthma. Thorax 35: 823 (1980).

Chapter VIII

Bronchodilators in the Prevention of Nocturnal Asthma

M.R. Hetzel

Nocturnal asthma presents a particular therapeutic problem. While most clinicians interested in this phenomenon would agree that bronchodilator drugs are the most valuable treatment, the present management of the condition is far from satisfactory. This problem is at least partly attributable to our incomplete knowledge of the mechanisms underlying nocturnal asthma. Before considering the practicalities of bronchodilator therapy, the significance to the clinician of nocturnal wheezing and present views on the pathophysiology will be discussed.

Characteristics of Nocturnal Asthma

Historical Background

The observation that asthma patients are often most wheezy at night or in the early morning is far from new. The phenomenon was noted by Moses Maimonides (1192), Body Physician to the asthmatic son of Saladin, who observed that 'sleep in this disease is rather harmful'. Thomas Willis (1679), who first suggested that bronchial smooth muscle constriction was the cause of asthma attacks, observed that they often occurred at night and attributed this to overheating of the body at night by bedclothes which caused 'a more plentiful sucking in of air'. Subsequently, several other physicians described nocturnal asthma, including Floyer (1698) and Trousseau (1868), who were themselves asthmatic, and who gave accounts of persistent nocturnal wheezing over many years. Laennec, with the introduction of his stethoscope (1827), described wheezes on auscultation and noted that some asthma patients could be observed to wheeze during their sleep.

Clinical Implications of Nocturnal Asthma

Although described in medical textbooks for centuries, nocturnal asthma has attracted research interest only in the last 10 years or so. This is probably because the severity of nocturnal asthma in some patients was not appreciated until objective measurement became common with the regular recording of peak expiratory flow rate (PEFR), both in hospital and by patients at home. My own interest in the potential importance of nocturnal asthma was provoked by a study of all asthma admissions to Brompton Hospital, London, between 1974 and 1976, in which an attempt was made to identify those patients at greatest risk of sudden death (Hetzel et al., 1977a). In 1169 asthma admissions there were 10 episodes when patients suddenly sustained a respiratory arrest and in 3 cases resuscitation was not successful. Nine of these episodes, all of which occurred a few days after admission, were in patients whose attacks were not considered to be severe since they lacked 'risk' factors, e.g. tachycardia or pulsus paradoxus (see p.172) at the time of admission. However, patients had marked nocturnal wheezing before respiratory arrest, as evidenced by wide variation

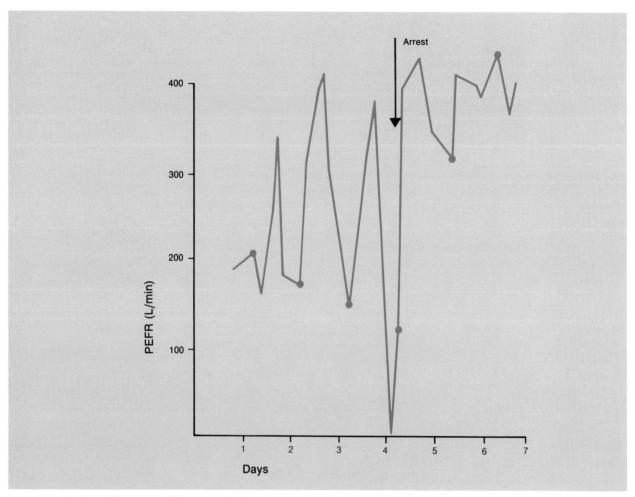

Fig. 8.1. PEFR chart of a patient with nocturnal asthma who sustained a ventilatory arrest in hospital. Days are marked at midnight. Early morning readings at 6am are shown as solid circles (after Hetzel et al., 1977a).

in their PEFR measurements, taken 4-hourly throughout the day. The records showed that readings at 6am had fallen by over 50% of the highest daily reading. Eight of the 9 arrests occurred between midnight and 6am. An example is illustrated in figure 8.1.

These observations suggest that nocturnal asthma, with a marked diurnal variation in PEFR, may be associated with an increased risk of sudden death. However, as asthma deaths are relatively uncommon and mostly occur outside hospital, it is not yet known what proportion of sudden asthma deaths might be associated with this phenomenon. Evidence in favour of this hypothesis is that asthma deaths are apparently more common at night. By pooling the results of four separate studies of asthma deaths (Editorial, 1983) it was shown that 93 of a total 219 deaths occurred between midnight and 8am. This represents a 28% increased liability of death from asthma at night. Although deaths from all causes are somewhat more common at night, with an increased frequency of 5%, the nocturnal preponderance of asthma deaths is highly significant. However, confirmation will be possible only if the practice of recording PEFR at home becomes more widespread, providing objective evidence from patients dying outside hospital. The sudden death of two young asthmatics, in whom PEFR measurements which were recorded at home shortly before death showed large amplitude variation in PEFR, have already been described (Bateman and Clarke, 1979).

Incidence and Severity of Nocturnal Asthma

There are no data on the true incidence of nocturnal asthma since virtually all studies have been carried out in hospitalised patients. From these, it appears that nocturnal asthma may persist for long periods of time (fig. 8.2), but the patients studied were severe asthmatics and therefore a highly selected population. It should be remembered, however, that a high proportion of asthma deaths are known to occur in patients who have never been admitted to hospital. For example, in a series of 90 deaths in Cardiff, 33% of cases had no record of hospital admission, and in all these cases death occurred outside hospital (MacDonald et al., 1976). Data from hospital studies suggest that nocturnal asthma, in which the PEFR may fall by more than 50% from the highest daytime reading, may occur in as many as 30% of asthmatic patients (Hetzel et al., 1977a).

Experience with paediatric asthmatic patients confirms that children also experience nocturnal asthma, but as in adults, there is little data available. However, one important study has been

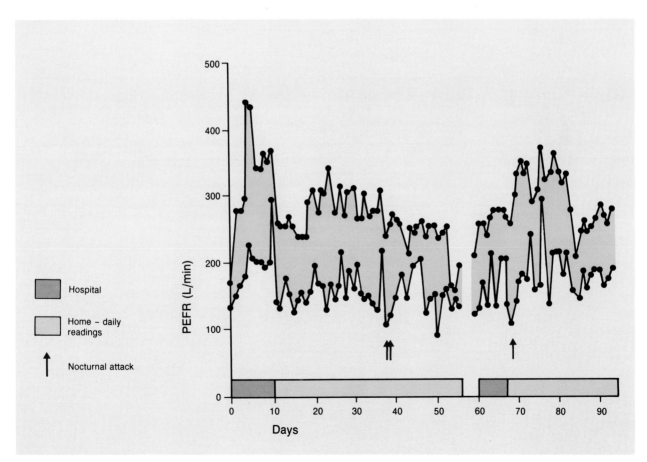

Fig. 8.2. Pattern of PEFR rhythm amplitude in a patient with chronic nocturnal asthma. The darker blue area indicates the difference between highest and lowest daily peak flow readings on initial recruitment during admission to hospital with acute asthma, and subsequent home monitoring of PEFR by the patient himself. Note the persistence of the amplitude in PEFR (after Hetzel, 1979).

carried out in the community and it showed interesting contrasts with previous work. The investigators recruited asthmatic children on the basis of a previous history of wheezing (Johnston et al., 1983). Peak flow monitoring in 63 children, who satisfied the authors' criteria for asthma, suggested a much lower incidence of nocturnal asthma, since the mean amplitude of their PEFR rhythm was only 12% of their average daily reading. This contrasts with results of studies in adults which suggest that asthmatics are likely to display amplitudes of over 20% (Hetzel and Clark, 1980). Either there may be some real differences in nocturnal asthma in adults and children, or, more probably, the discrepant values reported reflect different degrees of disease severity in the populations studied.

The Circadian Rhythm in Airway Calibre

A number of studies have established beyond all reasonable doubt that nocturnal asthma relates to a circadian rhythm in airway calibre (Editorial, 1981). This rhythm is also present in normal subjects and in other types of chronic airflow limitation, but, in these instances, the rhythm shows a much lower amplitude. At one time it was generally believed that nocturnal asthma resulted from exposure to the house dust mite, feathers or other allergens in bedding. However, as nocturnal asthma is equally common in asthmatics with negative skin tests to inhaled allergens as in atopic asthmatics with positive skin tests and histories suggesting hypersensitivity to these allergens, this is clearly not the explanation. Nocturnal falls in PEFR have been shown to persist in asthmatics with house dust mite sensitivity during study periods in environments with filtration systems designed to exclude these allergens, although the overall level of PEFR did improve (Reinberg et al., 1970).

A circadian rhythm in airway calibre in normal subjects can be demonstrated by measuring PEFR at regular intervals and using computer methods to detect rhythmicity in the data. Using this approach in a study of 221 healthy controls who recorded PEFR 4 times daily for 7 days, a significant rhythm was detected in 66% of subjects (Hetzel and Clark, 1980). The mean amplitude (peak to trough measurement) was, however, only 8% of the individual mean value. A similar study in asthmatics showed rhythms with a very similar phase to the normal (i.e. the highest readings, or acrophase, were recorded between 2 and 4pm in most cases) but the amplitude was much greater, with all peak to trough changes more than 25%. The only difference between the rhythm of airway calibre in asthmatics and normal subjects is in the magnitude of the PEFR rhythm.

The amplitude of PEFR rhythm appears to reflect the degree of bronchial lability. Thus, large amplitudes are frequently seen in asthma patients as they recover from acute attacks in hospital (fig. 8.3). With improvement towards their usual PEFR, the amplitude usually decreases. It is within this period of very high amplitude, in the first few days of treatment, that the risk of sudden death is apparently greatest (Hetzel et al., 1977a).

This same relationship between PEFR amplitude and bronchial lability can be demonstrated by bronchial challenge. Davies and his colleagues showed that in patients with asthma induced by grain dust, challenge when their PEFR was stable could result

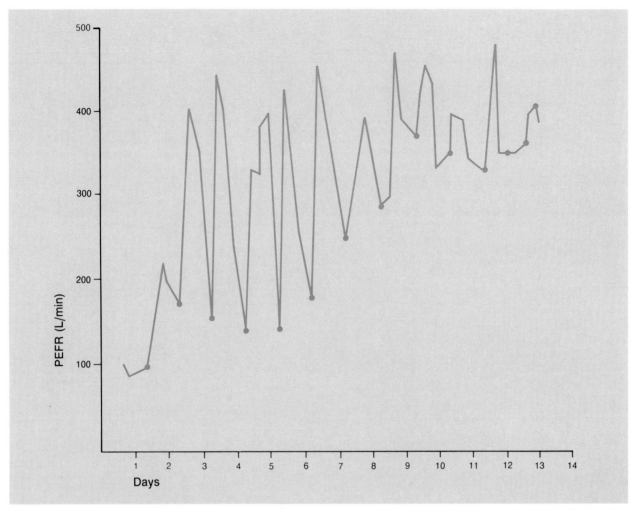

Fig. 8.3. Pattern of recovery in PEFR after admission for acute asthma. Days are marked at midnight, solid circles indicating 6am readings. As PEFR improves, large amplitude swings in PEFR are seen from the third to ninth days. During this period, bronchial lability increases and amplifies the stimulus of the normal circadian rhythm in airway calibre (after Hetzel, 1979).

in recurrent nocturnal wheezing for several days, with large swings in PEFR (Davies et al., 1976). Thus, it appears that bronchial lability is increased by immunological or other mechanisms in the naturally occurring or post-challenge attack and this amplifies the constant stimulus of the underlying normal circadian rhythm to produce nocturnal asthma. A similar phenomenon is common in pollen asthma where patients often notice 'hay fever', perhaps with mild wheezing, immediately after exposure and then develop more severe wheezing at night. Recent work has further demonstrated this relationship (Ryan et al., 1982). The bronchial response to histamine challenge as PC_{20} (histamine concentration required to cause a fall of > 20% in FEV_1) in normal subjects and asthmatics, was compared with the amplitude of PEFR records (Ryan et al., 1982). It was found that the lower the PC_{20} (greater bronchial lability), the lower the morning reading of PEFR and the greater the amplitude in the PEFR rhythm. Moreover, the response to inhaled salbutamol (albuterol) also correlated inversely with the morning fall in PEFR and the PC_{20}. Results for asymptomatic asthmatics

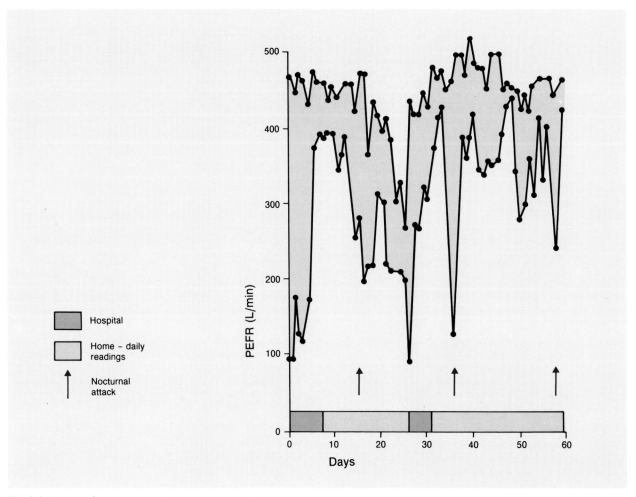

Fig. 8.4. Pattern of PEFR monitoring in another patient studied as in fig. 8.2. In this patient, large amplitudes in PEFR are associated only with acute asthma attacks and, at other times at home, her PEFR is near normal with minimal falls in PEFR at night. This type of patient may possibly be at greatest risk of sudden death from asthma since bronchial lability can fluctuate so widely and rapidly (after Hetzel, 1979).

were found to be intermediate between normal subjects (low lability, high PC_{20}, low amplitude in PEFR) and symptomatic asthmatics (high lability, low PC_{20}, high amplitude).

Patients commonly maintain a large amplitude in PEFR for prolonged periods (fig 8.2). A study of home monitoring after discharge, in asthmatics who showed morning falls in PEFR of more than 25% while in hospital, demonstrated that most patients had a persistent high amplitude for up to 2 years. However, a minority show large amplitudes for only short periods, associated with acute attacks (fig. 8.4). While it is not possible to make valid conclusions from these small numbers of patients, it would appear that it may be only those patients in this latter category who are at risk of sudden death.

Mechanisms of Circadian Rhythm in Airway Calibre

No 'biological clock' has yet been satisfactorily identified, although many circadian rhythms, such as body temperature and electrolyte excretion, are known to exist. Normally, these various rhythms show close synchronisation with each other and many show their lowest point (bathyphase) during the night. Many workers believe that a 'master clock', possibly in the hypothalamus, drives these rhythms, or at least keeps them internally synchronised. This master clock is in turn synchronised by external factors, particularly the cycle of light and darkness. When these synchronisers are removed and the rhythms are allowed to 'free run', as in studies in caves or bunkers, the natural circadian period, usually of slightly longer than 24 hours emerges (hence circadian-*circa diem*). The PEFR rhythm behaves similarly and responds to changes in working hours like other circadian rhythms. Studies of asthmatics on shift work (Clark and Hetzel, 1977) show that a change of shift reduces amplitude and, if maintained for several days, the rhythm re-establishes itself with a large amplitude: the lowest readings in PEFR being on waking, irrespective of the actual time of day (fig. 8.5).

Figure 8.6 summarises some of the mechanisms which have been studied as possible controllers of the PEFR rhythm. An early theory was that PEFR was influenced by plasma cortisol, since the nocturnal fall in cortisol precedes the fall in PEFR by a few hours. However, if continuous cortisol infusions are given to asthmatics so as to completely obliterate the normal rise and fall of cortisol the PEFR rhythm continues unchanged (Soutar et al., 1975).

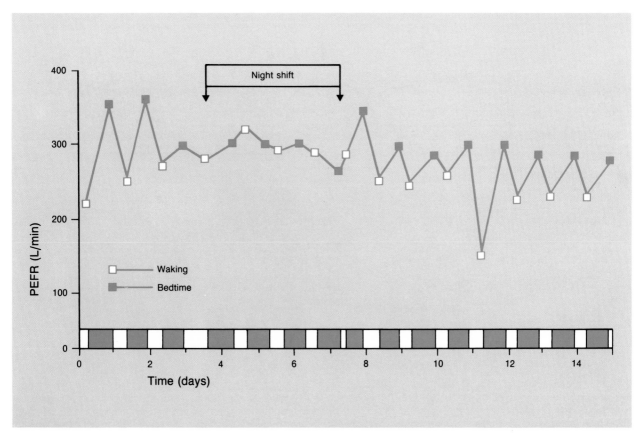

Fig. 8.5. Effect of shift work on the circadian rhythm in PEFR. When this asthmatic patient goes onto a night shift, the amplitude of the PEFR rhythm, measured by waking and bedtime readings only, decreases, and the phase of the rhythm is also disturbed so that the waking reading is occasionally higher than at bedtime. 'Scrambling' of the biological clock by shift work can, therefore, have some beneficial effect on nocturnal asthma. At the base of the figure, open squares indicate awake periods. Days are marked at midnight (after Hetzel, 1979).

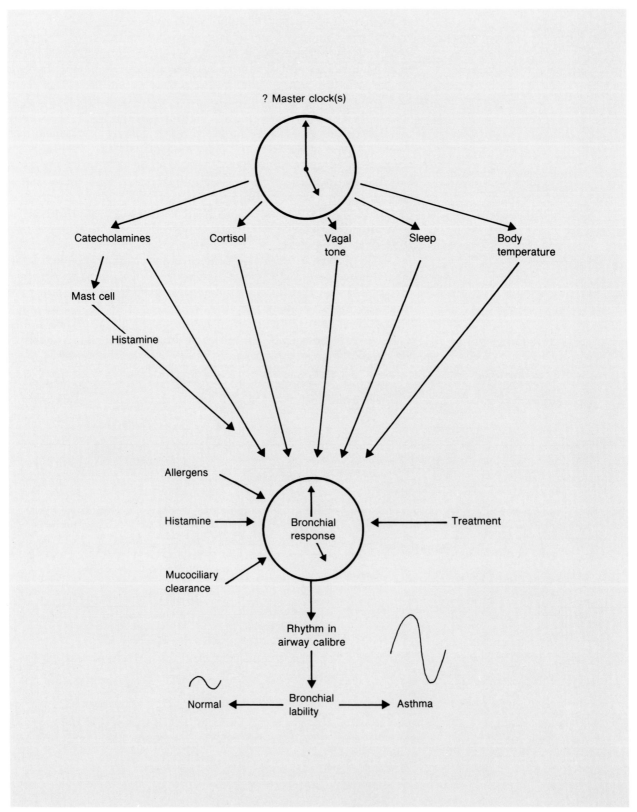

Fig. 8.6. Hypothesis of mechanisms underlying circadian rhythm in airway calibre. A master clock may drive the airway rhythm through the influence of mediators, such as the rhythm in circulating catecholamines. These may have an indirect effect by permitting increased release of mediators from mast cells at night. Further local circadian response in the mast cell and bronchial smooth muscle may also be involved. The sum total of these effects produces the rhythm in airway calibre. Bronchial lability then amplifies this rhythm. Low lability in normal subjects results in an asymptomatic, low amplitude in PEFR; marked lability in unstable asthmatics produces a large amplitude rhythm and nocturnal symptoms.

Sleep

Another suggestion was that sleep may be responsible and relationships of nocturnal asthma to the EEG have been studied. Kales and his colleagues found no relationship to sleep phase in adults analysing the EEG pattern just before patients woke with asthma, but did find that attacks were apparently prevented by deep phase IV sleep in children (Kales et al., 1968, 1970). However, a more recent study documented 26 nocturnal attacks in 8 patients with a mean fall in PEFR of 52% of pre-sleep values. The majority of attacks (85%) occurred in the last one-third of the night when REM sleep was most common (Malo et al., 1980). Ear oximetry showed falls in oxygen saturation of 5 to 15% and episodes of sleep apnoea were recorded in 4 cases.

Sleep monitoring without waking the patient is difficult to achieve, and this, of course, complicates the interpretation of these studies. Catterall and his colleagues studied patients with stable asthma and found that in comparison with normal controls, asthmatics slept less well and had more frequent periods of irregular breathing and falls in oxygen saturation (Catterall et al., 1982).

Most of these episodes occurred during REM sleep and were related to hypopnoea or apnoea. The severity of nocturnal hypoxaemia was related to the level of oxygen saturation when the subjects were awake, but did not correlate with the overnight fall in FEV_1. However, the fall was small in these asymptomatic patients. These workers also studied the effects of waking asthmatics from periods of REM and non-REM sleep on different nights. In the patients, but not in the controls, FEV_1 and PEFR fell significantly more when they were awoken from REM sleep. Animal studies have suggested a greater variability in airway tone during REM sleep.

It is not clear whether REM sleep represents a cause or an effect of nocturnal asthma. If REM sleep is a causal factor, this has not yet led to the development of an effective treatment. Attempts to prevent nocturnal asthma by sleep deprivation (Hetzel and Clark, 1979) produced inconsistent results. Some patients did not develop a nocturnal fall in PEFR when they were kept awake, but others did. Most probably, therefore, all these observations simply result from the fact that the fall in PEFR at night roughly coincides with the sleep-wakefulness rhythm, but is not caused by it.

Body Temperature

There is an interestingly close relationship between the rhythms in PEFR and body temperature (fig. 8.7). Again, this is probably just a further example of independent rhythms which are closely synchronised. However, in view of recent observations on the contribution of heat flux in the lung to the causation of exercise-induced asthma, it has been suggested that the small nocturnal fall in body temperature (approximately 0.5°C) could cause sufficient lung cooling to produce bronchoconstriction (Chen and Chai, 1982). The investigators were able to reduce the nocturnal fall in PEFR by giving asthmatic patients warm, humidified air through the night, achieving a greater benefit when this was combined with bronchodilator therapy. Since body temperature itself was probably not raised significantly by this manoeuvre, it is questionable whether the effect of this treatment was not simply to achieve some reduction in bronchial lability.

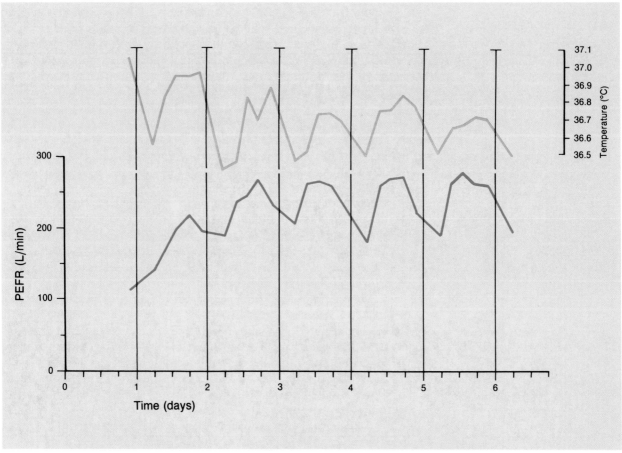

Fig. 8.7. Comparison of PEFR and oral temperature rhythms. Pooled data from a group of asthmatics in hospital shows the close relationship in phase between these two circadian rhythms. This does not, however, prove that the temperature rhythm is driving the rhythm in PEFR (after Hetzel, 1979).

Catecholamines

At present the most plausible mediator of the PEFR rhythm appears to be the fluctuating level of circulating catecholamines. Measurements of urinary adrenaline (epinephrine) and noradrenaline (norepinephrine) in asthmatics showed some correlation between the nocturnal falls in PEFR and urinary catecholamine excretion (Soutar et al., 1977). It was also shown that in a few patients, increased vagal tone at night contributed to PEFR changes. Subsequently, Barnes and his colleagues were able to measure plasma adrenaline, cyclic AMP and histamine levels and relate these to PEFR in normal controls and asthmatics (Barnes et al., 1980). The nocturnal fall in the PEFR correlated with falls in plasma adrenaline and cyclic AMP. The circadian variation in plasma adrenaline levels was similar in both normal and asthmatic subjects. In asthmatics, but not in the controls, a nocturnal rise in plasma histamine was also seen. Low dose infusions of adrenaline at night reduced the fall in PEFR. The investigators concluded that the catecholamine cycle influences the rhythm in airways calibre by a 'permissive' action on mast cells, so that increased release of histamine, and presumably other mediators, occurs at night. The much greater release of histamine in asthmatics might be attributed to their less stable, 'leaky' mast cells.

Although attractive, this theory does not explain the clinical observation that even intravenous infusions of β_2-agonists or methylxanthines will not necessarily prevent nocturnal asthma. Moreover, there is a fascinating paradox that although these drugs, given as overnight infusions or slow-release oral preparations may not prevent nocturnal asthma once it has developed, a small dose of aerosol bronchodilator usually produces a dramatic and rapid improvement (Hetzel et al., 1977b; Fairfax et al., 1980). This suggests that there might be a local circadian rhythm in β_2-adrenoceptor responsiveness to sympathomimetic drugs but Barnes and his colleagues consider this unlikely since they found close relationships between the rhythmic values for adrenaline and cyclic AMP in their study (Barnes et al., 1980). Some other rhythmic factors may be important. There is evidence of a circadian rhythm in bronchial reactivity, independent of resting levels of airway tone. Bronchial challenge studies with histamine, acetylcholine or allergens in sensitised asthmatics all show increased sensitivity in the night and early morning. Similar observations have also been made for reactions to allergens in skin tests. This is more evidence in support of the concept of local biological clocks in the mast cells and bronchial smooth muscle. Studies have shown that the mucociliary clearance of radio-labelled polystyrene particles given by aerosol is slowed by sleep, but this may not represent a true circadian rhythm (Bateman et al., 1977).

Thus, as seen in figure 8.6, control of the PEFR rhythm is almost certainly a composite of several different rhythms, possibly mediated by one master clock. The master clock may have a second level of effect, through catecholamines and other chemical messengers, by actions on subsidiary clocks present in mast cells and bronchial smooth muscle. Although most of this figure is hypothesis, and even if only a little of it is relevant, it is clearly unlikely that any single drug will be totally successful in abolishing the rhythm in PEFR. Thus, while bronchodilators are of value, the considerable difficulty experienced in trying to achieve effective treatment of nocturnal asthma in some patients would imply that other mechanisms, as yet undiscovered, are also involved.

Bronchodilator Therapy in Nocturnal Asthma

When attempts are made to treat nocturnal asthma with bronchodilators or other drugs, a whole spectrum of response is seen. At one extreme, minimal regular treatment may be very effective in some asthmatics and at the other, patients are almost totally refractory to all available treatments, displaying nocturnal symptoms over long periods of time.

Nocturnal asthma may be a prominent presenting feature, even in mild asthmatics. An erroneous diagnosis of, for example, cardiac disease may be made. These patients usually have good symptomatic response to bronchodilator aerosol therapy during attacks and this helps confirm the diagnosis. As with asthmatics with other patterns of disease, they are best treated with regular inhaled bronchodilator therapy throughout the day, e.g. salbutamol 200μg 4 times a day. The principle of treatment here is that bronchial lability is reduced with regular treatment. This works well in mild cases, providing patients can accept the concept that treatment during their waking hours will prevent nocturnal symptoms. The PEFR rhythm is never abolished by such treatment but the amplitude is reduced to near normal levels in those who respond to treatment. However, even after treatment, the stimulus from the biological clock remains unchanged. In addition, factors such as allergen challenge may still contribute to nocturnal asthma by altering the ambient level of bronchial lability.

More refractory cases do not respond to regular inhaled bronchodilator therapy alone. Symptoms may be under excellent control during the day, with near normal PEFR, but severe nocturnal symptoms and falls in PEFR persist. The conventional approach is then to add additional treatment through the night, but it is important to continue regular daytime treatment as 'background' control. Three therapeutic approaches are worthy of consideration:

1) Slow-release oral β_2-agonist at night
2) Slow-release oral methylxanthine at night
3) High dose β_2-agonist by metered dose inhaler at bedtime.

Some patients may eventually need treatment by more than one method, require inhaled or even oral corticosteroids, or may fail to respond to any therapy. The relative merits of these drugs will now be considered.

Slow-release Oral β_2-Agonists

These preparations were initially developed as an alternative to conventional tablets in an attempt to obtain a sustained bronchodilator effect while minimising the usual side effects of oral therapy. Unfortunately, side effects are still fairly common with therapeutic doses. Tremor and restlessness are most troublesome and, even if treatment is effective, many patients find that they wake frequently though they may not be wheezy. Salbutamol and terbutaline* are available as slow-release preparations in the United Kingdom. There is little to choose between them, but it may be worth trying another if the first proves unsatisfactory, particularly if nocturnal asthma is controlled but side effects occur.

One study has shown that a dose of 16mg of slow-release salbutamol, given regularly at midnight, in a group of 14 asthmatics, achieved average blood levels of 3.7 ng/ml at midnight and 17.3 ng/ml at 6am (Fairfax et al., 1980). This was compared with the effects of continuous intravenous infusion of salbutamol at a rate of 8 μg/kg/hour, which achieved mean plateau blood levels of 20.3 ng/ml. Thus, the oral preparation was capable of sustaining therapeutic blood levels overnight almost as effectively as an intravenous infusion. Unfortunately, the effect on nocturnal asthma was slight. The mean overnight fall in PEFR on placebo was 25.5% and this was reduced to only 20.9% by salbutamol 'Spandets'. Nevertheless, when inhaled salbutamol 200μg was given at 6am, PEFR improved to levels similar to the best readings during the day. If, as already discussed, this difference in response is not due to a rhythmic change in β_2-adrenoceptor sensitivity to bronchodilator drugs, it could be because the receptors are more accessible to inhaled drugs.

---

* For product availability in the USA, see appendix B.

Slow-release Oral
Methylxanthines

These are now the most popular drugs for the treatment of nocturnal asthma in the United Kingdom. They are, however, the most difficult of the 3 modes of nocturnal bronchodilator therapy to use because of the wide variation in individual pharmacokinetics, low therapeutic index and frequent side effects (chapter II). Measurement of plasma levels is highly desirable but at present this service is not readily available to many clinicians in the United Kingdom.

Most slow-release theophylline preparations are intended for use twice-daily. Peak plasma levels of theophylline at 4 to 6 hours should be below 20 mg/L and trough levels at 10 to 12 hours should be above 10 mg/L. In practice, a wide range of doses may be required to achieve this. For example, one study, conducted in a group of 24 asthmatics, found that the total daily dose of one aminophylline preparation required to maintain therapeutic blood levels ranged from 450 to 2250mg (Greening et al., 1981). Unfortunately, the doses of theophyllines which provide clinical benefit in nocturnal asthma, are associated with a high incidence of side effects.

Barnes and his colleagues have suggested that twice-daily treatment is unnecessary for the management of nocturnal asthma and that, if given only at night, side effects are better tolerated as the patient is asleep (Barnes et al., 1982). They titrated the nocturnal dose of slow-release aminophylline in 12 patients to that which gave a plasma theophylline concentration of about 10 mg/L ten hours after treatment. Using the appropriate dose in individual patients, they were then able to reduce the mean variation between morning and evening PEFR from 22% to 5%. The doses given ranged from 550 to 775mg (considerably in excess of the manufacturers' standard recommended dose). These patients did not have particularly severe nocturnal asthma; the mean morning PEFR was 283 L/min before treatment and 332 L/min on aminophylline, and significant reversibility in morning PEFR, with a mean rise to 400 L/min, was noted after aerosol salbutamol.

If slow-release theophyllines are to be used effectively in nocturnal asthma one must progressively titrate the dose until the therapeutic range is achieved or until side effects prohibit a further increase. Unfortunately, side effects do not necessarily indicate toxic, or even therapeutic blood levels (see p.81). One suggestion is that a dose of 16 mg/kg/day is reasonable for most patients, and that side effects are unlikely to be seen before plasma levels in excess of 25 mg/L are achieved (Greening et al., 1981). However, a large survey of patients at Brompton Hospital (Woodcock et al., 1983) showed that, although side effects were most common with plasma levels higher than 20 mg/L (62% of their cases), they were almost equally seen in patients with levels in the therapeutic range (24%) and in those with subtherapeutic blood levels of less than 10 mg/L (26%). It is therefore possible to induce side effects while giving a dose unlikely to provide much clinical benefit.

More recently, preparations for once-daily treatment have been introduced. It is claimed that by giving these in the evening, good nocturnal blood levels are attained and that a low therapeutic level, with less side effects, is also maintained during the following day. One study showed that by giving the total daily dose of a slow-release theophylline as a single dose in the evening at 9pm, fairly satisfactory plasma levels were maintained through the following 24 hours (Thompson et al., 1981). However, this and subsequent studies have also shown that the pharmacokinetics of theophylline differ between night and day. The half-life is prolonged at night, which, although it may improve control of nocturnal asthma, also increases the risk of toxicity. A recent study, in which patients received doses which gave therapeutic plasma levels within 5 to 12 hours of morning doses, compared the effect of giving anhydrous theophylline at 10am and 10pm (Primrose, 1983). Peak levels were achieved within a mean of 8.3 hours after night doses compared with 5.3 hours with morning treatment. Also Jonkman and his colleagues, who studied the effects of both slow-release oral and IV aminophylline, showed that trough levels after 12 hours were higher after nocturnal administration. Thus, nocturnal administration of aminophylline should favour control of early morning wheezing (Jonkman and Vander Boon, 1983). Other studies have shown that the toxicity of theophyllines may be influenced by posture, with better drug tolerance achieved when the patient is supine during sleep.

High Dose Inhaled β_2-Agonists

The high incidence of side effects and relatively poor response seen with oral bronchodilator preparations, together with the frequent observation of a dramatic response of nocturnal and early morning wheeze to small doses of inhaled β_2-agonist would imply that aerosol therapy might be the treatment of choice. However, following inhalation of presently available β_2-agonists, bronchodilatation will last for only about 3 hours and the success of this treatment depends on the extent to which the duration of action can be increased by using larger bedtime doses.

As discussed in other chapters, it is clear that the very low toxicity of β_2-agonist inhalers will permit considerable increase in dosage and this approach has achieved some success in patients with poor reversibility to standard treatment. When terbutaline was given in a dose of 4mg 4 times a day, either by nebuliser or by aerosol with a 'tube spacer' attachment and using special canisters which delivered 1mg per actuation (4 times the usual dose), both were equally effective in improving symptoms and PEFR (Prior et al., 1982). A significant improvement, particularly in morning PEFR, was seen. Similarly, salbutamol given by nebuliser or a specially prepared high dose pressurised aerosol, produced equally good bronchodilatation at a dose of 4.8mg (Anderson et al., 1982). Thus, high dose inhalation at bedtime may be useful, but it probably does not matter what form of inhaler is used. If a nebuliser is not available, administration of high doses with conventional pressurised aerosols is tedious because of the number of puffs required. A useful alternative is to use the salbutamol 'Rotahaler' system as a fairly large dose can be easily given if the 400μg capsules are used.

Using salbutamol 800μg 4 times a day, together with beclomethasone dipropionate 400μg 4 times a day by 'Rotahaler', improvement in 8 of 14 cases of nocturnal asthma has been achieved (Horn et al., 1984) . Even more aggressive inhalation therapy has been attempted using continuous nebulisation of bronchodilators through a mask worn during sleep, but this system is poorly tolerated (Cochrane, unpublished data). During severe attacks, patients are more likely to obtain relief from a nebuliser than an aerosol if respiratory distress impairs their inhalation technique. Thus, the severe and refractory nocturnal asthmatic may benefit from the provision of a home nebuliser for use at night, although the 'Rotahaler' or a 'spacer' device may be cheaper alternatives. It is interesting to note that continuous subcutaneous infusion of high dose terbutaline has recently been reported as useful in two patients with severe early morning dipping (Ayres et al., 1984).

Which is Best?

Some studies have attempted to compare these different approaches to bronchodilator therapy in nocturnal asthma. In a double-blind study, 16mg of oral, slow-release salbutamol and 450mg of slow-release aminophylline were given at midnight. In 14 patients with nocturnal asthma, a mean overnight fall in PEFR of 25.5% with placebo improved to only 20.9% with salbutamol and 21.5% with aminophylline (Fairfax et al., 1980). Penketh and her colleagues, compared 400μg of salbutamol by 'Rotahaler' with 225mg of oral aminophylline, and salbutamol 800μg by 'Rotahaler' with 450mg of aminophylline, in a double-blind placebo-controlled study (Penketh et al., 1981). Both treatments were given twice daily to 12 patients. With the lower dosages of both drugs there was no significant improvement compared with placebo in overnight fall in PEFR, although aminophylline did reduce requirements for extra doses of aerosol salbutamol. With the higher doses, the overnight fall in PEFR improved to 21.4% with aminophylline and 21.5% with salbutamol, compared with a placebo response of 27.9%.

It is noteworthy that in both studies discussed above, therapeutic blood levels of theophylline (10-20 mg/L) were seldom achieved. Aminophylline, at a dose of 450mg, gave an average level of only 7 mg/L, indicating that any therapeutic response recorded was probably sub-optimal. The implications of these studies are that the dose of bronchodilator used may be more important than the choice of drug and that dosage must be tailored to the individual patient's needs. A really reliable comparative study would, therefore, require preliminary titration of doses of each preparation to find the maximum tolerated dose in individual patients and then a double-blind study to compare the effects of these predetermined doses. Not surprisingly, such a complex study has yet to be successfully conducted.

Another important point which has emerged, is that individual patients tend to respond better to one preparation than to another. This means that caution is advised when interpreting drug trials which compare mean results. It also implies that one should be prepared to try each mode of bronchodilator therapy in the maximum possible dose, before trying the next drug, if control is inadequate. If necessary, combinations of drugs may eventually be required either to achieve control when one drug alone fails, or to reduce the side effects induced by high dose, single drug treatment (see p.42). The order in which these are selected is perhaps a matter of personal preference, but it is convenient to try high dose inhaled β_2-agonist therapy first, since this is least likely to cause side effects, and then, if necessary, move on to oral treatment. Figure 8.8 outlines one possible approach to treatment.

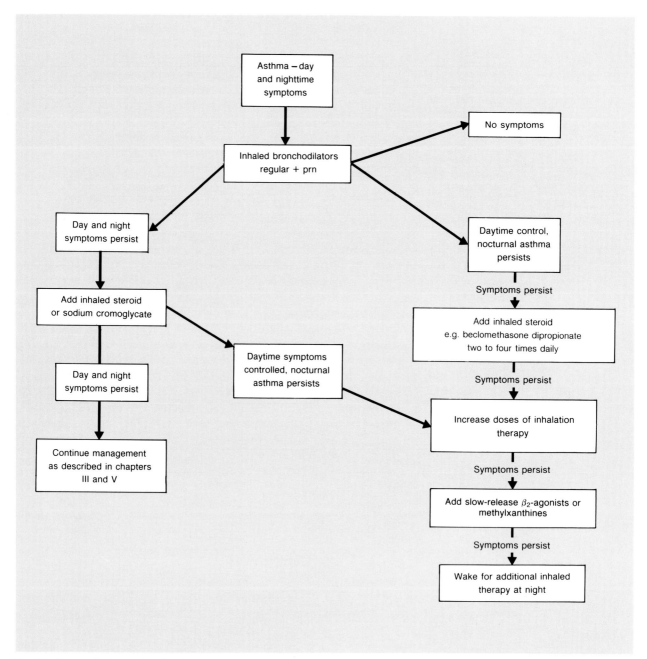

Fig. 8.8. Proposed scheme for the drug treatment of troublesome nocturnal asthma. Each mode of therapy should be used in the maximum possible dose before trying the next. Treatments associated with a poor response and unacceptable side effects should be discontinued. Ipratropium bromide has not been included because at present there is little evidence of its value in nocturnal asthma.

Treatment of Nocturnal Asthma in Children

Similar rules would seem to apply to treatment of nocturnal asthma in children. In the author's paediatric asthma clinic, nocturnal symptoms are a common presentation in the untreated asthmatic child but, as in adults, milder cases will respond well to inhaled bronchodilator therapy. From the age of about 3 years upwards this can conveniently be given by 'Rotahaler' as salbutamol 'Rotacaps' and many children quickly learn to assemble the inhaler themselves.

Regular bronchodilator therapy 2 to 4 times a day is often effective. More severe cases may respond to the addition of sodium cromoglycate (cromolyn sodium) or an inhaled corticosteroid which can also be conveniently given to younger children by the 'Rotahaler' system. Parents are often reluctant to accept the need for continuous regular therapy, particularly with inhaled steroids, but one must assume that the hazards of uncontrolled nocturnal asthma in children are the same as in adults.

If inhaled therapy is inadequate, oral theophyllines are probably more effective than oral slow-release β_2-agonists. These drugs may also have to be used in young children who cannot manage to use inhalers. Although some paediatric studies report side effects in up to 30% of patients, children are generally more tolerant of theophyllines than adults and it is somewhat easier to attain therapeutic blood levels. When 22 children with nocturnal asthma were studied, a mean theophylline dose of 11.3 mg/kg was needed to achieve therapeutic levels and assessment by peak flow measurement and symptom scores revealed improvement in over 70% (Evans et al., 1981). However, these claims of a favourable response have been criticised and the results of longer term studies of slow-release theophyllines in children suggest that these preparations are helpful only in milder cases (Wilson and Silverman, 1982).

A home nebuliser may be useful for younger children as an alternative to oral therapy or for administration of sodium cromoglycate, which may achieve control in milder cases. An important point to remember is that metabolism of theophyllines becomes less efficient at puberty and dosage must be reviewed at this time. The measurement of salivary theophylline concentration, if available, is often a more acceptable alternative to plasma level determination, especially for young children.

Timing of Bronchodilator Therapy in Nocturnal Asthma

It is simplest to give extra prophylactic bronchodilator therapy at bedtime. In theory, however, this may not always be the ideal time because one wishes to exert the maximal bronchodilator effect at the time of the bathyphase (lowest point) of the PEFR rhythm. In the case of inhalation therapy, maximum bronchodilatation would be expected to occur within 30 minutes of inhalation. Since nocturnal asthma attacks rarely occur within the first few hours of sleep, it is unlikely that the response to inhalation therapy will be maximal at the time of the nocturnal attack.

With slow-release oral preparations maximum plasma levels may be seen at any time from 4 to 8 hours after dosing. As theophylline half-life may be increased at night, some consideration should be given to the timing of the nocturnal dose. For example, a patient who usually wakes with attacks at 2am and goes to bed at midnight might achieve better control by treatment at 9pm than by taking his tablets at bedtime. In practice, however, such an approach is laborious and the resultant benefits are likely to be small. It would be necessary to establish, by PEFR monitoring through the night, the usual pattern of the rhythm to identify the time of maximum bronchoconstriction (most patients seem to vary in the time of their attacks from night to night). Then a nocturnal profile of plasma levels would be required to determine the pharmacokinetic pattern in the individual patient, as great intersubject variation exists. This would require admission to hospital and inves-

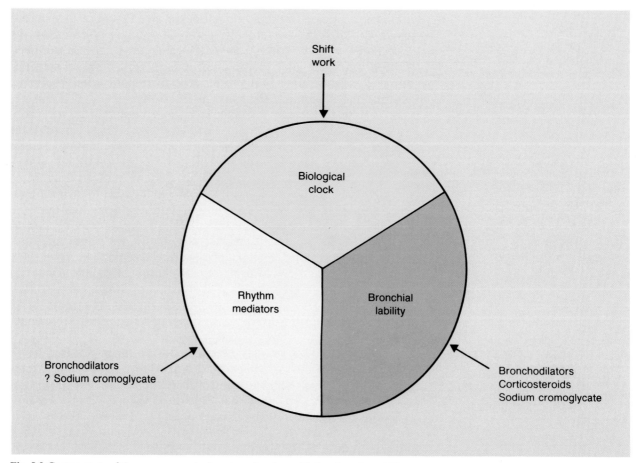

Fig. 8.9 Components of the management of nocturnal asthma. Little other than shift work can be tried to disrupt the biological clock, but bronchodilators are more versatile than other agents in that they can both reduce bronchial lability and protect against the effects of the nocturnal fall in catecholamines.

tigations conducted over several nights. Such a complex and time consuming assessment would be justified only in refractory cases.

For most routine clinical practice, it would therefore seem sensible to give all additional bronchodilator therapy at bedtime, unless there is a very clear pattern of attacks in the early part of the night. In patients on maximum possible bedtime therapy who continue to have nocturnal attacks, it may be worth considering arranging for the patient to be woken by an alarm clock during the night, before his worst asthma has developed, so that additional prophylactic therapy can be given by aerosol.

Other Drugs in Nocturnal Asthma

The addition of inhaled corticosteroids to regular inhaled bronchodilator therapy can improve control of nocturnal asthma (Horn et al., 1984). The role of oral corticosteroids is difficult to define but they are undoubtedly indicated when severe asthma is also present during the day.

Inhaled anticholinergic drugs may be useful but they have no clear advantages over β_2-agonists.

If the hypothesis is correct that the mechanism of nocturnal asthma is a 'permissive' effect of low catecholamine levels on mediator release from mast cells (Barnes et al., 1980), then sodium cromoglycate might be expected to be effective. This assumes that the mechanism of action of cromoglycate really is to prevent mediator release. In addition, the low toxicity of cromoglycate makes it an attractive proposition for high dose inhalation therapy. In a current investigation by the author, a dose of 280mg of nebulised cromoglycate per day is showing a small benefit, but nebulisation of these high doses is difficult and very time-consuming for patients.

Occasionally patients who are taking antihistamines for other reasons report improvement in their nocturnal asthma. This is most probably a result of their sedative effect. There is no doubt that patients can sleep through nocturnal asthma but the dangers of sedation in this condition should be obvious.

In Summary

It has been seen that nocturnal asthma represents the combined effect of a biological clock stimulating a variable degree of bronchial lability. Figure 8.9 illustrates the 3 major components involved in the hypotheses that have been considered. At present, bronchodilator drugs are clearly the most versatile agents for treatment of this phenomenon, which seems to involve several different mechanisms. The main limitation to their use, is the difficulty of giving them in sufficient doses in difficult cases. However, high dose inhalation therapy appears to hold some promise for the future.

An alternative approach is to 'stop the clock' but this is very difficult when its location is unknown. Very few agents have yet been identified which influence circadian rhythms. This can be done by 'scrambling the rhythm' with frequent changes in shift work, but this is obviously unacceptable to most patients.

References

Anderson, P.B.; Goude, A. and Peake, M.: Comparison of salbutamol given by IPPB and pressure packed aerosol in chronic asthma. Thorax 37: 612 (1982).

Ayres, J.; Fish, D.R.; Wheeler, D.C.; Wiggins, J.; Cochrane, G.M. and Skinner, C.: Subcutaneous terbutaline and control of brittle or appreciable morning dipping. British Medical Journal 288: 1715 (1984).

Barnes, P.; Fitzgerald, G.; Brown, M. and Dollery, C.: Nocturnal asthma and changes in circulating epinephrine, histamine and cortisol. New England Journal of Medicine 303: 263 (1980).

Barnes, P.; Neville, L.; Greening, A.P.; Timms, J. and Poole, G.N.: Single dose slow release aminophylline at night prevents nocturnal asthma. Lancet 1: 299 (1982).

Bateman, J.R.M.; Pavia, D. and Clarke, S.W.: Mucociliary clearance during sleep in healthy subjects. Thorax 32: 644 (1977).

Bateman, J.R.M. and Clarke, S.W.: Sudden death in asthma. Thorax 34: 40 (1979).

Catterall, J.R.; Calverley, P.M.A.; Breizinova, V.; Douglas, N.J.; Brash, H.M.; Shapiro, C.M. and Flenley, D.C.: Irregular breathing and hypoxaemia during sleep in chronic stable asthma. Lancet 1: 301 (1982).

Chen, W.Y. and Chai, H.: Airway cooling and nocturnal asthma. Chest 81: 675 (1982).

Clark, T.J.H. and Hetzel, M.R.: Diurnal variation of asthma. British Journal of Diseases of the Chest 71: 87 (1977).

Davies, R.J.; Green, M. and Schofield, N.M.: Recurrent nocturnal asthma after exposure to grain dust. American Review of Respiratory Disease 114: 1011 (1976).

Editorial: Asthma at night. Lancet 1: 220 (1983).

Editorial: The pulmonary clock. Thorax 36:481 (1981).

Evans, P.W.G.; Craven, I. and Evans, N.: Nocturnal wheezing in children: management with controlled release aminophylline. British Medical Journal 283: 18 (1981).

Fairfax, A.J.; McNabb, W.R.; Davies, H.J. and Spiro, S.G.: Slow release oral salbutamol and aminophylline in nocturnal asthma. Thorax 35: 526 (1980).

Greening, A.P.; Baillie, E.; Gribbin, H.R. and Pride, N.B.: Sustained release oral theophylline in patients with airflow obstruction. Thorax 36: 303 (1981).

Hetzel, M.R.: Observations on 24 hour periodicity in asthma. MD Thesis, University of London (1979).

Hetzel, M.R.; Clark, T.J.H. and Branthwaite, M.A.: Asthma: analysis of sudden deaths and ventilatory arrests in hospital. British Medical Journal 1: 808 (1977a).

Hetzel, M.R.; Clark, T.J.H. and Houston, K.: Physiological patterns in early morning asthma. Thorax 32: 418 (1977b).

Hetzel, M.R. and Clark, T.J.H.: Does sleep cause nocturnal asthma? Thorax 34: 749 (1979).

Hetzel, M.R. and Clark, T.J.H.: Comparison of normal and asthmatic circadian rhythms in peak expiratory flow rate. Thorax 35: 732 (1980).

Horn, C.R.; Clark, T.J.H. and Cochrane, G.M.: Inhaled therapy reduces morning dips in asthma. Lancet 1: 1143 (1984).

Johnston, I.D.A.; Anderson, H.R. and Patel, S.: Peak flow patterns in wheezy children. Thorax 38: 230 (1983).

Jonkman, J.H.G. and Vander Boon, W.J.V.: Nocturnal theophylline plasma concentration. Lancet 1: 1278 (1983).

Kales, A.; Beall, G.N.; Bajor, G.F.; Jacobson, A. and Kales, J.D.: Sleep studies in asthmatic adults: relationship of attacks to sleep stage and time of night. Journal of Allergy 41: 164 (1968).

Kales, A.; Kales, J.D.; Sly, R.M.; Scharf, M.D.; Tam, T.L. and Preston, T.A.: Sleep patterns of asthmatic children. All night EEG studies. Journal of Allergy 46: 300 (1970).

MacDonald, J.B.; MacDonald, E.T. and Seaton, A.: Asthma deaths in Cardiff 1963-74: 90 deaths outside hospital. British Medical Journal 2: 721 (1976).

Malo, J.L.; Walsh, J. and Montplaisir, J.: Sleep analysis of asthmatic subjects affected with nocturnal attacks. American Review of Respiratory Disease 121 (Suppl): 162 (1980).

Penketh, A.R.L.; Johnson, D.; Hetzel, M.R.; Clark, T.J.H.; Bellamy, D. and Cochrane, G.M.: Aerosol salbutamol versus slow release aminophylline in the treatment of nocturnal asthma. Thorax 36: 715 (1981).

Primrose, W.R.: Asthma at night. Lancet 1: 927 (1983).

Prior, J.G.; Nowell, R.V. and Cochrane, G.M.: High dose inhaled terbutaline in the management of chronic severe asthma. Thorax 37: 300 (1982).

Reinberg, A.; Gervais, P.; Franbourg, J.C.; Abulker, C.; Vignaud, D. and Dupont, J.: Rhythmes circadiens de fonctions respiratoires et de la temperature d'asthmatiques sejournant en millieu hypoallergenique. Presse Medicale 78: 1817 (1970).

Ryan, G.; Latimer, K.M.; Dolovich, J. and Hargreaves, F.E.: Bronchial responsiveness to histamine; relationship to diurnal variation of peak flow rate, improvement after bronchodilator and airway calibre. Thorax 37: 423 (1982).

Soutar, C.A.; Costello, J.; Ijaduola, O. and Turner-Warwick, M.: Nocturnal and morning asthma. Relationship to plasma corticosteroids and response to cortisol infusion. Thorax 30: 436 (1975).

Soutar, C.A.; Carruthers, M. and Pickering, C.A.: Nocturnal asthma and urinary adrenaline and noradrenaline secretion. Thorax 32: 677 (1977).

Thompson, P.J.; Butcher, M.A.; Frazer, L.A. and Marlin, G.E.: Pharmacokinetics of a single evening dose of slow release theophylline in patients with chronic lung disease. British Journal of Clinical Pharmacology 12: 443 (1981).

Wilson, N. and Silverman, M.: Controlled trial of slow release aminophylline in childhood asthma: are short term trials valid? British Medical Journal 284: 863 (1982).

Woodcock, A.A.; Johnson, M.A. and Geddes, D.M.: Theophylline prescribing, serum levels and toxicity. Thorax 38: 240 (1983).

Chapter IX

Bronchodilator Therapy in the Elderly

J.E. Stark and R.G. Dent

In common bureaucratic and medical terminology, one is deemed to be 'elderly' after the age of 65 years. This convenient classification is clinically unrealistic and unhelpful, concealing the fact that factors other than age alone are of more importance in medical care.

In the context of airflow obstruction and its treatment we can identify 4 main groups of patients.

1) 'Elderly and fit.' This group comprises the great majority of patients, at least in the first decade after 65 years. If respiratory symptoms develop the approach to diagnosis and management needs to differ little, if at all, from that which applies to those 10, 20 or 30 years younger. Nevertheless, pathological, physiological and metabolic changes of ageing will have occurred and may be important in some aspects of diagnosis and treatment.

2) 'Healthy for their age.' Patients in this group are without any specific illness but have one or more of the 'usual' or 'expected' disabilities of ageing, such as forgetfulness, loss of agility or altered sleep pattern, which may be of great importance in managing respiratory disease.

3) 'With one or more degenerative disease.' These are patients with a pathological disorder which limits or complicates the management of airflow obstruction. Arthritic hands, severe tremor or poor vision may hamper treatment of airway obstruction, particularly with inhaled drugs.

4) 'Elderly and ill.' These patients have, in addition to airflow obstruction, other respiratory or non-respiratory conditions which may complicate diagnosis, investigation or management. Thus, cardiac, digestive, metabolic or neurological illnesses may have an important bearing on the management of airflow obstruction.

Prevalence and Nature of Airflow Obstruction in the Elderly

Statistics on mortality and hospital admissions, published annually in many countries, are bedevilled by difficulties of definition and classification of different clinical diagnoses within the general heading of 'chronic airways disease'. The widely used Medical Research Council epidemiological definition of chronic bronchitis ('chronic or recurrent increase in the volume of mucoid bronchial secretion sufficient to cause expectoration') is applicable to many patients who on clinical criteria have typical asthma, as expectoration of sputum is a common feature of asthma, particularly in the older age groups. It is likely that as the incidence of cigarette smoking, and hence chronic bronchitis, declines, and the age of the population rises, an increasing proportion of those reported as having 'chronic bronchitis' or 'generalised airways obstruction' will, in clinical terms, be suffering from asthma.

Prevalence of Asthma in the Elderly

Until recently there was little awareness of asthma as a problem in the elderly. Indeed, there is no mention at all of asthma in a recent standard text book of geriatric medicine (Brocklehurst, 1978). In 1974, in a discussion of the general practitioner's view of common diseases, the statement is made that 'onset in later life of true asthma is unusual' (Fry, 1979).

Elderly Asthmatic or Chronic Bronchitic?

In the USA

Recently, Dodge and Burrows conducted a survey among a random sample of households in Tucson, Arizona (Dodge and Burrows, 1980). 3860 subjects completed questionnaires which incorporated the questions, 'Have you ever suffered from asthma?', 'Have you seen a doctor for this?', and similar inquiries about chronic bronchitis or emphysema, and shortness of breath or wheezing. They found that only a minority of the large number of subjects who had experienced wheezing had symptoms 'that were severe enough or characteristic enough to lead to a diagnosis of asthma by a physician'. The label attached by doctors to symptoms depended greatly on their diagnostic bias. For example, attacks of shortness of breath with wheeze were much more likely to be diagnosed as asthma if the subject had a history of childhood respiratory illness, positive allergy skin tests and had never smoked. It was also noted that the label 'asthma' was more likely to be applied to women than to men with identical symptoms. Attacks of shortness of breath with wheeze were more often diagnosed as chronic bronchitis than asthma, especially in older men. Of men over the age of 50 years, in whom a diagnosis of asthma had been made by a physician, 75% had a concomitant diagnosis of chronic bronchitis and/or emphysema. Many of the older subjects with recently diagnosed asthma had previously had their symptoms ascribed to chronic bronchitis and were only later labelled as asthmatic. In this study, the prevalence of 'acute asthma' was 6.3% in men, and 6.4% in women aged 60 to 69 years; and 7.9% in men, and 6.4% in women over 70 years of age (fig. 9.1). However, this investigation has been criticised on the grounds that there is an artificially high prevalence of asthma in Tucson due to immigration of asthmatic patients who erroneously believed that the climate would be good for them, and the large variety of highly allergenic trees and shrubs in the locality.

In Britain

In a smaller but more detailed investigation, 418 elderly people (1 in 8 of the population aged over 70 years) in a South Wales town were studied (Burr et al., 1979). Subjects were asked about respiratory symptoms, their lung function was tested and they had skin 'prick' tests to common allergens. Those who reported current asthma, nocturnal dyspnoea, wheezing or breathlessness, or whose FEV_1 improved after inhalation of a bronchodilator, were referred to a hospital chest clinic. Of the 12 subjects (2.9%) who were identified as having 'current asthma', 1 in 4 were receiving no appropriate treatment since they had not previously been diagnosed as asthmatic and one-third were receiving treatment but were unaware of the diagnosis. Another 3.6% had a history of asthma, giving an overall prevalence of 6.5% of any history of asthma.

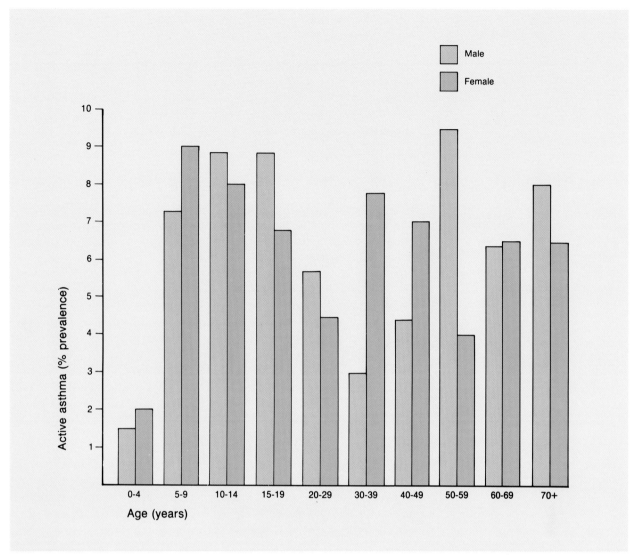

Fig. 9.1. Prevalence rate (%) of active asthma by age and sex, from a random sample of 3860 subjects in Tucson, Arizona, USA (data from Dodge and Burrows, 1980).

General

Asthma first appearing in old age is more common than is widely realised. The American study demonstrated that although the rate of new attacks of breathlessness with wheeze was equal for men and women, the diagnosis of asthma was confined almost entirely to women. Of the elderly subjects diagnosed as asthmatic in South Wales, 37% had first developed symptoms after the age of 55 years and 22% had their first symptoms after the age of 65 (Burr et al., 1979).

These and other studies have established that asthma is not uncommon in old age, and may even start at an advanced age, but it is frequently underdiagnosed or misdiagnosed. In the past, such diagnostic laxity probably had little impact on the patient's management, as effective and appropriate treatment for asthma was not available. However, with the development of potent and specific treatment regimens for the asthmatic patient, accurate diagnosis and therapy is essential.

Clinical Features of Asthma in the Elderly

Asthma may persist from youth into old age or may occur for the first time at an advanced age.

Age at Onset

Sex

It is often stated that asthma in the elderly is more common in women than in men but, as discussed above, this may merely reflect the greater tendency of doctors to ascribe symptoms in old men to chronic bronchitis. Some studies based on individual assessment of a sample of elderly population have actually revealed a higher prevalence in men.

Family History

In the study by Burr and his colleagues, a family history of asthma or hay fever in a first degree relative was found in 45% of elderly asthmatics compared to 16% of non-asthmatics of similar age. Such a family history was no more common in those with early onset of asthma than in those whose asthma first occurred at an older age.

Previous History

Often elderly patients with a recent diagnosis of asthma will recall earlier recurrent respiratory symptoms. It seems likely that these were associated with mild, undiagnosed asthma. A tendency to develop a prolonged cough after upper respiratory infections or repeated attacks of 'bronchitis' in a non-smoker are frequent antecedents of a later diagnosis of asthma and are now recognised as common features of the disease. Previous allergic disorders do not appear to predispose to asthma, and in one study a history of hay fever was only slightly more common in elderly asthmatics than in non-asthmatic old people (Burr et al., 1979).

Symptoms

Breathlessness, wheeze and cough are the characteristic symptoms of asthma at any age. There have been no detailed analyses of symptomatology in various age groups, but it is our impression that asthmatic symptoms in the elderly may differ in several respects from those of 'classical' asthma.

Breathlessness

Intermittent breathlessness is often nocturnal with the result that, having been described as 'paroxysmal nocturnal dyspnoea', an erroneous diagnosis of left ventricular heart failure is all too often made. Twelve of the 15 elderly asthmatic patients described by Lee and Stretton had paroxysmal nocturnal dyspnoea as a major symptom (Lee and Stretton, 1972).

Persistent breathlessness is not uncommon and reflects the tendency for the airflow obstruction of the elderly asthmatic to show less spontaneous variation than is characteristically seen at younger ages (Petheram et al., 1982). However, with careful questioning of the patient, or on serial measurement of airflow obstruction, the 'morning dip' associated with worsening symptoms and increased obstruction in the early morning hours can often be recognised. This is of great diagnostic value as it is not a usual feature of chronic bronchitis, chronic heart failure or other common causes of dyspnoea in the elderly.

Wheezing

The elderly asthmatic may often not describe wheezing spontaneously. A spouse or companion may sometimes find the patient's noisy breathing more disconcerting or worrying than the patient does.

Cough

This is a common and too little recognised symptom of asthma, which may overshadow wheeze or breathlessness, especially in children or the elderly. Sudden paroxysms of uncontrollable night cough can waken the patient and may cause great distress. Wheezing may not be noticed and breathlessness is often attributed to the stresses of coughing. A small amount of sticky or 'stringy' white sputum may eventually be produced. Nocturnal coughing of this type is not common in chronic bronchitis but may occur, often with wheezing, in patients with gastro-oesophageal reflux or oesophageal obstruction who inhale food while recumbent at night.

Investigations

Eosinophilia

When present in blood and sputum, eosinophilia may on occasions be a useful aid to the diagnosis of asthma in the elderly. Dodge and Burrows found that adults over the age of 40 years who subsequently developed asthma had significantly higher previous blood eosinophil counts than those who did not develop asthma (Dodge and Burrows, 1980). Eosinophilia however, is neither invariably nor even usually present and, in the Welsh survey, a blood eosinophilia was identified in 15% of elderly asthmatics compared with 7% of non-asthmatics. When detected, blood eosinophilia underlines the need to search hard for evidence of asthma as a treatable cause of airflow obstruction, even if everything else points to a less treatable cause, e.g. emphysema. Sputum eosinophilia has been considered for many years to be a valuable predictor of response to corticosteroids in patients with airflow obstruction (Brown, 1958). More recently, however, an excess of eosinophils has been demonstrated in the sputum of a high proportion of patients with chronic bronchitis (Turnbull et al., 1977). Burr and his colleagues found eosinophils in the sputum of 45% of elderly asthmatics but also in 25% of elderly non-asthmatics. We do not believe that routine examination of the sputum for eosinophils is a valuable investigation in airflow obstruction, and the technique is not always available. However, demonstration of large numbers of eosinophils in sputum may sometimes be helpful in drawing attention to the need to conduct a prolonged trial of oral corticosteroids if bronchodilator therapy alone does not produce an improvement.

Skin Tests

Asthma in the elderly is usually of the 'intrinsic' variety in which no external allergic cause can be found and subjects are not atopic. In a group of 330 patients whose asthma started after the age of 60 years, 88% were categorised as intrinsic (Ford, 1969). A very different result was found by Burr and co-workers who obtained positive skin prick tests in 26% of elderly asthmatics but nearly all of these had developed asthma before the age of 40 and were probably still suffering extrinsic asthma into old age.

How Does the Problem of Airflow Obstruction Differ in the Elderly?

The Diseases

As in younger adults the major causes of chronic or recurrent airways obstruction are chronic bronchitis, emphysema, and asthma (extensive and severe bronchiectasis now being rare). These conditions are fundamentally the same in old age but what does seem to differ is the degree of diligence with which physicians seek a precise diagnosis for their elderly patients. With increasing recognition that asthma is a common and treatable cause of airflow obstruction in old age clinicians are obliged to think more carefully than in the past about their elderly breathless patients.

Although the airflow obstruction of chronic bronchitis and emphysema is sometimes partially reversible with bronchodilators the improvement in exercise tolerance is usually slight (see chapter XI), whereas in asthma appropriate bronchodilator and, if necessary, corticosteroid therapy can lead to the complete remission of symptoms.

Problems of Clinical Recognition of Airflow Obstruction in the Elderly

Usually the initial complaint is of breathlessness, often associated with wheezing. However, respiratory noise may originate in the upper respiratory tract, especially in those who are ill (often slumped forward in bed or in a chair) or who have neurological problems such as stroke or bulbar weakness. Breathlessness from a different cause may then be wrongly attributed to airflow obstruction.

The very common kyphosis of ageing and the associated increase in anterior-posterior diameter of the thorax superficially resembles the 'barrel chest' of severe emphysema and in a patient with noisy breathing can lead to diagnostic confusion.

The monophonic and often mainly inspiratory wheeze of air passing a localised, usually malignant, narrowing of the trachea or main bronchus is very different from the polyphonic and widespread wheeze of generalised airways obstruction but is all too often not distinguished from the latter and in the cigarette smoker with lung cancer is frequently confused with worsening of chronic bronchitis.

The relationship between the severity of airflow obstruction and the findings on clinical examination is poor in the elderly, even in an episode of severe airflow obstruction. Measures that are helpful in the younger patient, such as a rising heart rate and the presence of pulsus paradoxus (see p.172) are less common in the elderly (Cooke et al., 1979; Petheram et al., 1982). This may be partly because the cardiovascular responses to hypoxaemia diminish with age (Kronenberg and Drage, 1973).

Problems of Measuring Airflow Obstruction in the Elderly

Many elderly people can perform spirometry adequately but as age increases and other diseases supervene, spirometric measurements may become difficult, unreliable or impossible. Some of the difficulties, such as incomprehension or lack of coordination, can be overcome with careful explanations and encouragement. In some patients common sense suggestions such as removing loose dentures can help, but in others conditions such as facial weakness after a stroke may make spirometry impossible. Peak expiratory flow measurements are usually easier to perform than formal spirometry.

A practical problem is the inaccessibility of normal reference values for any of these tests in the elderly. Few of the standard sources of normal values quote figures for subjects over the age of 65 although this information is available (Milne and Williamson, 1972). With the increasing age of the population, respiratory function data on older subjects should be included in tables and nomograms of normal physiological values (tables 9.1, 9.2; figs 9.2, 9.3). Even some experienced physicians will be surprised to see that an FEV_1 of 800ml is normal for some of their elderly patients.

Table 9.1. Approximate values for FEV_1 in normal elderly women and normal elderly men (data adapted from Milne and Williamson, 1972)

Age (years)	Height (cm)				
	140	150	160	170	180
Female					
60	1400	1600	1850	2050	
70	1200	1400	1650	1900	
80	1000	1200	1400	1600	
90	800	1000	1200	1400	
Male					
60		1700	2050	2450	2600
70		1550	1900	2500	2700
80		1400	1800	2200	2550
90		1300	1650	2000	2400

Table 9.2. Approximate values for FVC in normal elderly women and normal elderly men (data adapted from Milne and Williamson, 1972)

Age (years)	Height (cm)				
	140	150	160	170	180
Female					
60	1700	1950	2250	2500	
70	1500	1750	2100	2350	
80	1250	1500	1850	2100	
90	1000	1350	1600	1900	
Male					
60		2250	2850	3400	4000
70		2150	2700	3250	3850
80		2000	2550	3100	3700
90		1750	2400	2950	3550

A little used but clinically useful test of airflow obstruction, which can be easily applied to the elderly, is measurement of forced expiratory time (FET) [Lal et al., 1964]. A stethoscope is placed over the trachea in the neck and the duration of sound heard during a forced exhalation through the open mouth is measured on a stop watch or a wrist watch. An FET greater than 5 seconds is a fairly reliable indication of airflow obstruction.

Problems of Assessing Reversibility of Airflow Obstruction in the Elderly

The difficulties of measuring airflow obstruction obviously lead to similar difficulties of measuring reversibility. However, most elderly people who are in reasonable physical and mental health can perform one or other of the manoeuvres needed to measure obstruction, and serial measurements may be a valuable guide to reversibility. Purely clinical assessment is fraught with errors which may either deprive the patient of effective treatment or commit him to unnecessary therapy. Loss of wheeze and breathlessness after a single administration of a bronchodilator is uncommon in the elderly, even in those with asthma, and reliance on such a clinical assessment alone may lead to erroneous rejection of a diagnosis of asthma. Lesser degrees of improvement which are not

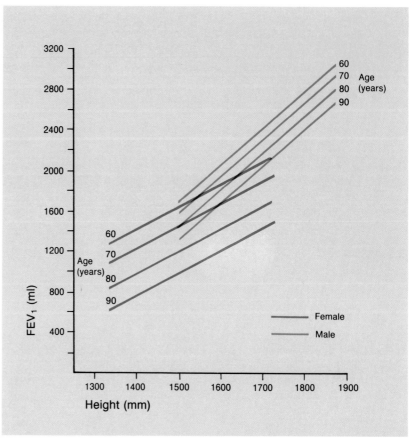

Fig. 9.2. Normal values of FEV$_1$ in elderly men and women based on height and age (after Milne and Williamson, 1972).

clinically evident may be detected by measurement before and after bronchodilator therapy, but failure to show such an improvement does not necessarily preclude a useful response to a longer course of therapy. Once again, reliance on clinical assessment during such a course of bronchodilator therapy can be misleading because of the difficulty elderly patients have in recalling symptoms from day to day, and the variability of subjective assessment of airflow obstruction (Rubinfeld and Pain, 1976). Occasional measurements of airflow obstruction are notoriously unreliable because the results may be influenced by a number of variables, including the patient's mood and situation, the time of the day and the equipment used. Important therapeutic decisions should, if possible, be based on regular measurements.

Self-monitoring

We ask our patients to record peak flow 3 times daily for 1 to 2 weeks without bronchodilator therapy to establish a baseline. It is, of course, an essential preliminary to watch the patient performing a peak flow manoeuvre and to ensure that he or she can read and record the result. The results can be displayed graphically on a chart provided for this purpose or in tabular form. Elderly patients may have difficulty displaying the results of peak flow measurements graphically and often record more accurately by tabulating the results (Hetzel et al., 1979). After these initial recordings, a bronchodilator is prescribed (and efforts are made to ensure that it is taken correctly and regularly) and peak flow records are continued as before. Even allowing for some vagaries of recording at this age, objective evidence of any response can usually be obtained.

As with younger patients, an improvement in symptoms is sometimes claimed despite no change in measured peak flow. In these cases other tests may suggest a mechanism for the response. The relaxed or slow vital capacity, for instance, may rise at a time when the PEFR or FEV$_1$ are not changing, and in these cases the improvement in symptoms may reflect a reduction of hyperinflation and of the work of breathing.

The same principle of attempting to measure changes in airflow obstruction applies particularly to trials of corticosteroid therapy as a decision to continue oral or inhaled steroids may depend on these results.

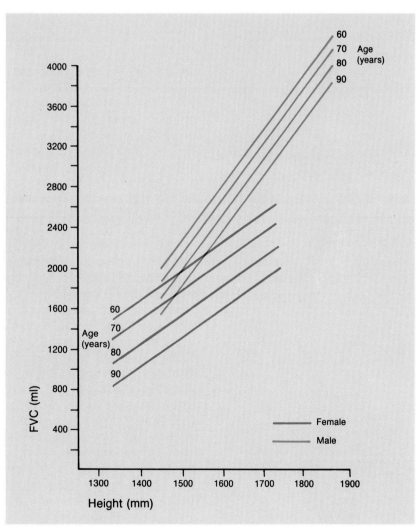

Fig. 9.3. Normal FVC values in elderly men and women based on height and age (after Milne and Williamson, 1972).

Special Aspects of Management in the Elderly

Less Clearcut Response to Bronchodilators

The agents available for the treatment of airflow obstruction in the elderly are those used in younger patients and most of the principles of management remain the same. The increased prevalence of coexisting chronic bronchitis and emphysema in the elderly (Manners, 1974) may lead to a less impressive absolute response to bronchodilator treatment (see p.192). Even in those with pure asthma there is a tendency for elderly patients to have persistent daily symptoms which may be less responsive to standard bronchodilator therapy alone and more often require corticosteroids as well (Petheram et al., 1982). Age alone may be associated with a diminished responsiveness to inhaled β_2-agonists in asthmatics (Ullah and Saunders, 1980) and it has been suggested that this may reflect a reduced β-adrenoceptor response, as is seen in human renal and cardiac tissue.

Drug Dosage and Adverse Effects

Age-related changes in the metabolic handling of drugs and the effects of coexisting non-respiratory disease on drug tolerance must be considered when prescribing for the elderly. Drug interactions may assume greater importance because of a larger number of drugs taken by patients at this age. The 3 major groups of drugs used in the therapy of airflow obstruction are discussed below:

β_2-Agonists

As with younger patients, β_2-agonists provide the most effective therapy for bronchospasm in the elderly and are the treatment of choice for airflow obstruction, whether related to pure asthma or to chronic bronchitis and emphysema. Side effects are uncommon with inhaled therapy and the newer, more selective agents are less likely to cause tachycardia or changes in blood pressure than the first generation of drugs which were less selective (chapter II). Side effects, especially tremor, are much more common with oral therapy. There are still many elderly patients taking oral β_2-agonist therapy regularly in doses which are too low to provide clinically useful bronchodilatation because conventional doses produced unpleasant side effects or are otherwise inappropriately maintained on oral bronchodilator drugs. Molloy and Hyland, for instance, were able to show that 20 consecutive elderly patients with chronic bronchitis, 16 of whom were maintained on oral salbutamol therapy (6-16 mg/day), showed no deterioration symptomatically or on measurement of airflow obstruction when their therapy was discontinued (Molloy and Hyland, 1980).

The use of ephedrine and non-selective β-agonists by mouth for the treatment of airflow obstruction should now be considered obsolete for any age group. In the elderly they may lead to urinary retention in patients with prostatism and are more likely to precipitate glaucoma or angina than are inhaled selective β_2-agonists. They may also produce troublesome stimulation of the CNS with anxiety, apprehension and insomnia. Combined tablets (often containing a methylxanthine and a barbiturate as well as ephedrine) should no longer be used. Many patients at present receiving oral β_2-agonist therapy would be better managed using the same drugs by the inhaled route (see p.29). There are no important intrinsic advantages of one selective β_2-agonist over another but the response to each preparation, the optimum dose and the susceptibility to side effects vary between patients. Individual preferences should be considered when trying to find the best drug and the most appropriate dosage regimen for each individual.

Although side effects of inhaled β_2-agonists are few, tremor and palpitation may, rarely, limit dosage in the elderly. In patients with coexisting ischaemic heart disease, angina can be precipitated by very large doses of inhaled β_2-agonists given by nebulisation and these patients should not usually be given high doses unless careful observation is possible (see p.79). An additional potential hazard for elderly patients with ischaemic heart disease who are receiving digoxin, is the tendency for β_2-agonists in high dosage to cause hypokalaemia. Although this reaction is more common when the drugs are given intravenously, it has also been reported after administration of large doses by nebuliser (Smith and Kendall, 1983). Hypokalaemia is more likely to occur in patients on concurrent diuretic therapy. Fortunately, none of these problems seems to apply to conventional low dosages of β_2-agonist drugs given by inhalation.

Anticholinergic Agents

Inhaled anticholinergic agents (e.g. ipratropium bromide* or atropine methonitrate) are well tolerated by elderly patients. There are many studies attesting to the effectiveness of inhaled atropine derivatives in relieving bronchospasm in patients with asthma and chronic bronchitis (see p.195) [Chamberlain et al., 1962] and many doctors have formed a clinical impression that this group of drugs may be particularly useful in the elderly. This may relate to the slightly diminished response to β_2-agonists in the elderly discussed above or may also reflect the greater incidence of coexisting chronic bronchitis, in which anticholinergic agents may be particularly useful (chapter XI) [Douglas et al., 1979]. Despite this, β_2-agonists are probably still the first choice for inhalation therapy in the elderly patient with airflow obstruction.

Side effects are rare following inhaled anticholinergics. Dry mouth is an uncommon complaint and the drying of bronchial secretions appears to be more of a theoretical problem than a practical one. However, these drugs should be avoided in patients with untreated closed-angle glaucoma. Although it has been shown that oral atropine derivatives can reduce sputum production in patients with chronic bronchitis (see p.22) they have little effect on bronchoconstriction and carry a high risk of precipitating urinary retention or difficulty with micturition, especially in the elderly (McNicol and Bruyns, 1964); thus, they are not recommended.

Methylxanthines

Oral theophylline derivatives are widely used in the treatment of airflow obstruction, especially in the United States (see p.18). Their clinical usefulness has been demonstrated in many trials but their relative efficacy compared to inhaled β_2-agonists and anticholinergics is still debated. Careful adjustment of the dose to produce optimum bronchodilatation, yet avoid unpleasant side effects, is difficult to achieve, making this group of drugs a less attractive first-line treatment than the safer inhaled drugs. However, long acting, slow-release theophylline preparations are useful

---

* For product availability in the USA, see appendix B

in those patients who have persistent early morning symptoms despite optimal inhaled therapy (Barnes et al., 1982).

Theophylline compounds are well absorbed at all ages but have a very variable half-life (3 to 10 hours). Hepatic metabolism is decreased in the elderly (but less so in smokers), especially in those over 75 years (Talseth et al., 1981), but this effect is not consistent enough to enable accurate adjustment of dosage on the basis of age alone (Blouin et al., 1981). This is partly because of the many other factors which can affect theophylline metabolism in the liver (see p.34), such as smoking, hepatic cirrhosis, congestive cardiac failure, pneumonia and severe airways obstruction itself (Powell et al., 1978). Elderly patients are probably more likely to be taking drugs which may alter theophylline disposition (see p.34). In practice, there is no alternative to repeated careful adjustment of the dosage to produce maximum therapeutic benefit with minimal side effects. When facilities permit, monitoring of plasma levels may prove useful in allowing fine adjustment of dose in the elderly patient in whom theophyllines are proving of particular therapeutic benefit.

Most of the side effects of excessive theophylline therapy are gastrointestinal, e.g. nausea, vomiting and abdominal pain. Tremor and tachycardia may occur but more serious side effects, e.g. cardiac arrhythmias, hypotension and convulsions have also been reported, especially in the elderly (Jacobs et al., 1976). Theophyllines should be used with care in patients with symptoms of prostatism since urinary retention may be precipitated, especially with the intravenous preparations used in severe asthma (Owens and Tannenbaum, 1981).

A potential problem, seen with increasing frequency, is acute toxicity from intravenous theophyllines given to patients with acute exacerbations of airflow obstruction who, unbeknown to the physician, are already taking oral theophyllines (see p.178). The intravenous loading dose should always be halved in patients who are taking oral theophylline preparations.

Delivery of Inhaled Drugs

Both β_2-agonists and anticholinergic agents are best given by the inhaled route in order to achieve maximum bronchodilatation with minimum systemic side effects. The most commonly used device for delivery is the pressurised aerosol. For maximal effect it is necessary to coordinate the actuation of the aerosol with inhalation and even in the young and fit this may prove difficult. Many elderly patients have difficulty with pressurised aerosols, usually because of poor coordination or severe arthritis and, whatever the patient claims, inhaler technique should be checked regularly.

In those who find coordination difficult, delivery can sometimes be greatly improved by the insertion of a reservoir or 'spacer' device between the aerosol and the mouth (Godden and Crompton, 1981; O'Reilly et al., 1983) [appendix C]. This allows the patient to actuate the aerosol once or several times to produce a cloud of drug particles in the reservoir which can be inhaled slowly, either in one inhalation, as from the 'tube' spacer (Godden and Crompton, 1981), or in several breaths from a larger pear-shaped chamber (O'Reilly et al., 1983). The larger reservoir 'pear' chambers ('Nebuhaler') are very effective and allow a much larger dose

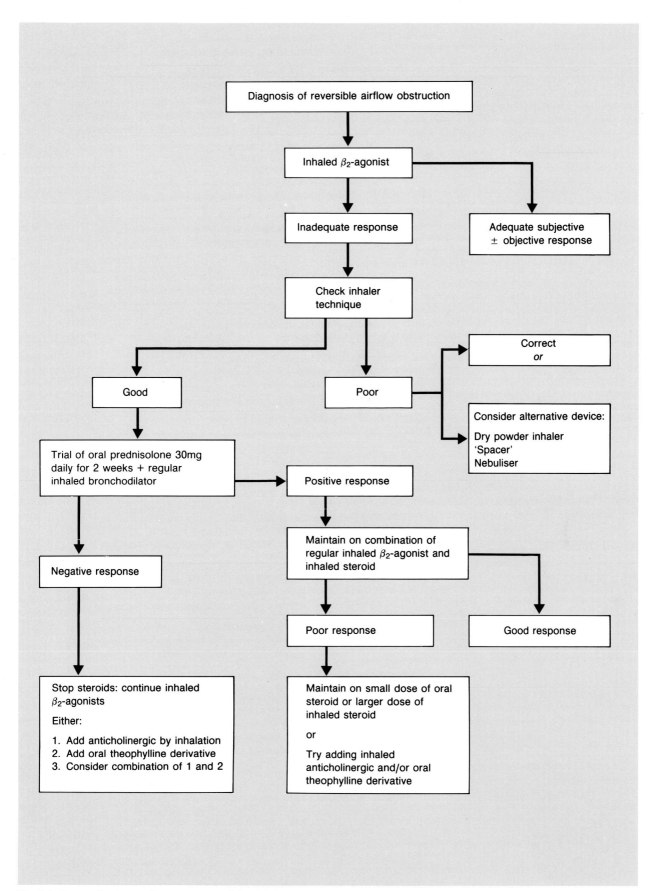

Fig. 9.4. Proposed scheme of management of the elderly asthmatic.

to be inhaled but are cumbersome for most patients to use outside the home. At present, not all the available β_2-agonist aerosols will fit the marketed 'spacers' or reservoirs.

Elderly people who have difficulty using pressurised aerosols may get better results from dry powder inhalers (Duncan et al., 1977). These devices overcome the difficulties of coordinating inhalation and actuation but they do require some manual dexterity as they have to be charged with a gelatin capsule, which contains the powdered drug, before each inhalation. This limits their usefulness for patients with arthritic hands or failing eyesight but, on the whole, the apparatus is convenient and portable. There is occasionally a problem of softening of the gelatin capsules in warm and damp conditions which may lead to clogging of the powder or the capsule failing to break open. Patients should be advised to store capsules in a cool, dry place.

Nebulisers are used quite extensively in hospitals to treat severe bronchospasm and are available for home use. The dose of drug administered is higher, with a correspondingly higher incidence of side effects. In our experience, few elderly patients require this equipment at home and it is important to avoid using it as an impressive (and expensive) placebo because of the potential problems of overdosage, infection from contaminated nebulisers and possible electrical risks.

The place of the larger pear-shaped reservoirs has not yet been established (see p.220) but they may provide a simple and effective means of delivering higher doses of inhaled bronchodilators, both as regular treatment and for use in exacerbations (see p.179).

The Practical Management of Reversible Airflow Obstruction in the Elderly

The approach to the management of the elderly asthmatic patient which is used in the authors' clinic is outlined in figure 9.4. Table 9.3 lists the distinguishing features between asthma and bronchitis which may be useful in confirming the diagnosis in the elderly patient.

In Summary

It is extremely important that an accurate diagnosis is made when an elderly patient presents with symptoms of airways obstruction. The possibility of the patient being asthmatic should always be considered and using established criteria it should be possible to differentiate between the elderly asthmatic and the elderly bronchitic patient. Inhaled β_2-agonists are the most appropriate initial treatment for most elderly asthmatics but the clinician must ensure that the dosage is adequate, and that the patient fully understands his treatment and can operate the inhaler device. Many elderly patients cannot use an aerosol inhaler correctly and an aerosol with a 'spacer' attachment, or a 'Rotahaler' device may be more appropriate. Compliance with the prescribed regimen should be confirmed and inhaler technique should be checked at regular intervals.

If a diagnosis of asthma has been established and additional treatment is required, the best approach is to introduce corticosteroids either regularly by inhalation, or as a short course orally. The dose of the corticosteroid should be reviewed frequently to ensure the maximum benefit to the patient. If the combination of a β_2-agonist and corticosteroid is still inadequate, additional treatment, either as inhaled ipratropium bromide or slow-release oral

Table 9.3. Distinguishing features of chronic asthma and chronic bronchitis

Chronic asthma	Chronic bronchitis
History	
Childhood respiratory illnesses	
Never smoked, or smoked very little	Heavy smoker
Onset of symptoms after stopping smoking	
Atopic symptoms	
Sudden (datable) onset of dyspnoea	Insidious onset of dyspnoea (undatable)
Rapid worsening of dyspnoea	Slowly worsening dyspnoea
Variable or intermittent dyspnoea (days free of dyspnoea)	Little variation – never free of dyspnoea
Little or no sputum	Frequent sputum (especially if purulent or mucopurulent)
Bouts of dyspnoea at rest	Dyspnoea on exertion
Paroxysmal unproductive cough	Cough productive of sputum
Night disturbed by symptoms	Nights good
Dyspnoea ± cough, worse on waking	Cough with sputum on waking or on getting out of bed
Examination	
Examination of the chest gives no guide	
Tests	
Blood eosinophilia	
Marked sputum eosinophilia	Little variation of peak flow
Marked variation of peak flow especially with morning dip	

theophylline, or both, should be considered. The use of theophyllines in the elderly patient can be particularly hazardous because of their potential toxicity and the number of factors (more likely to be present in an elderly person) which may influence their pharmacokinetics.

Thus, although the management of elderly asthmatic patients presents an especial challenge, with prior consideration of the possible complications, and with careful monitoring and instruction adequate control can be achieved.

References

Barnes, P.J.; Greening, A.P.; Neville, L.; Timmers, J.L. and Poole, G.W.: Single dose slow-release aminophylline at night prevents nocturnal asthma. Lancet 1: 299 (1982).

Blouin, A.; Erwin, W.G.; Foster, T.S. and Scott, S.: Pharmacokinetics of theophylline in young and elderly subjects. Gerontology 28: 323 (1981).

Brocklehurst, J.C.: Textbook of Geriatric Medicine and Gerontology, 2nd ed. (Churchill Livingstone, Edinburgh 1978).

Brown, H.M.: Treatment of chronic asthma with prednisolone. Significance of eosinophils in the sputum. Lancet 2: 1245 (1958).

Burr, M.L.; Charles, T.J.; Roy, K. and Seaton, A.: Asthma in the elderly: an epidemiological survey. British Medical Journal 1: 1041 (1979).

Chamberlain, D.A.; Muir, D.C.S. and Kennedy, K.P.: Atropine methylnitrate and isoprenaline in bronchial asthma. Lancet 2: 1019 (1962).

Cooke, N.J.; Crompton, G.K. and Grant, I.W.B.: Observations on the management of acute bronchial asthma. British Journal of Diseases of the Chest 73: 157 (1979).

Dodge, R.R. and Burrows, B.: The prevalence and incidence of asthma and asthma like symptoms in a general population sample. American Review of Respiratory Disease 122: 567 (1980).

Douglas, N.J.; Davidson, I.; Sudlow, M.R. and Flenley, D.C.: Bronchodilation and the site of airway resistance in severe chronic bronchitis. Thorax 34: 51 (1979).

Duncan, D.; Paterson, I.C.; Harris, D. and Crompton, G.K.: Comparison of the bronchodilator effects of salbutamol inhaled as a dry powder and by conventional aerosol. British Journal of Clinical Pharmacology 4: 669 (1977).

Ford, R.M.: Aetiology of asthma: a review of 11,551 cases (1958-1968). Medical Journal of Australia 1: 628 (1969).

Fry, J.: Common Diseases: Their Nature, Incidence and Care, 2nd ed., (MTP Press, Lancaster, 1979).

Godden, D.J. and Crompton, G.K.: An objective assessment of the tube spacer in patients unable to use a conventional pressurized aerosol efficiently. British Journal of Diseases of the Chest 75: 165 (1981).

Hetzel, M.R.; Williams, I.P. and Shakespeare, R.M.: Can patients keep their own peak flow records reliably. Lancet 1: 597 (1979).

Jacobs, M.H.; Senior, R.M. and Kessler, G.: Relationships between dosage, serum concentrations and toxicity. Journal of the American Medical Association 235: 1983 (1976).

Kronenberg, R.S. and Drage, C.W.: Alteration of the ventilatory and heart rate response to hypoxia and hypercapnia with ageing in normal men. Journal of Clinical Investigation 52: 1812 (1973).

Lal, S.; Ferguson, A.D. and Campbell, E.J.M.: Forced expiratory time: a simple test for airways obstruction. British Medical Journal 1: 814 (1964).

Lee, H.Y. and Stretton, T.B.: Asthma in the elderly. British Medical Journal 4: 93 (1972).

McNicol, M.W. and Bruyns, C.: Dibenaheptropine citrate (Brontina) – a double blind trial in chronic chest disease. British Journal of Diseases of the Chest 58: 135 (1964).

Manners, B.T.B.: Lung disease in a general practice with special reference to asthma, chronic bronchitis and eosinophilia. Journal of the Royal College of General Practitioners 24: 167 (1974).

Milne, J.S. and Williamson, J.: Respiratory function tests in older people. Clinical Science 42: 371 (1972).

Molloy, W. and Hyland, M.: Maintenance salbutamol in chronic bronchitis in the elderly. Age and Ageing 9: 272 (1980).

O'Reilly, J.F.; Buchanan, D.R. and Sudlow, M.F.: Pressurized aerosol with tube spacer is an effective alternative to nebulizer in chronic stable asthma. British Medical Journal 286: 1548 (1983).

Owens, G.R. and Tannenbaum, R.: Theophylline induced urinary retention. Annals of Internal Medicine 94: 212 (1981).

Petheram, I.S.; Jones, D.A. and Collins, J.V.: Assessment and management of acute asthma in the elderly: a comparison with younger asthmatics. Postgraduate Medical Journal 58: 149 (1982).

Powell, J.R.; Vozeh, S.; Hopewell, P.; Costello, J.; Scheiner, L.B. and Riegelman, S.: Theophylline disposition in acutely ill hospitalised patients. American Review of Respiratory Disease 118: 229 (1978).

Rubinfeld, A.R. and Pain, M.C.F.: Perception of asthma. Lancet 1: 882 (1976).

Smith, S.R. and Kendall, M.J.: Inhaled bronchodilators and hypokalaemia. Lancet 2: 218 (1983).

Talseth, T.; Kornstad, S.; Boye, N.P. and Bredesen, J.E.: Individualisation of oral theophylline dosage in elderly patients. Acta Medica Scandinavica 210: 489 (1981).

Turnbull, L.S.; Turnbull, L.W.; Leitch, A.G. and Crofton, J.W.: Mediators of immediate type hypersensitivity in sputum from patients with chronic bronchitis and asthma. Lancet 2: 526 (1977).

Ullah, M. and Saunders, K.B.: Influence of age on response to ipratropium bromide and salbutamol in asthmatic patients. Progress in Respiratory Research 14: 150 (1980).

Chapter X	# The Role of Bronchodilators in Severe Acute Asthma
	G.M. Cochrane

Death from asthma is rarely seen in the working life of many clinicians. However, severe acute asthma remains a common and lethal disease (British Thoracic Association, 1982), despite the introduction over the last 10 years of supposedly safer bronchodilator and prophylactic therapies. When assessed as standardised mortality rates, death rates associated with asthma have shown no significant improvement since the introduction of adrenaline (epinephrine) in the late 1890s, or ephedrine in 1926. In fact, the mortality rate, especially for the 5- to 34-year-olds increased dramatically shortly after the introduction of isoprenaline (isoproterenol) delivered from pressurised aerosols (Inman and Adelstein, 1969). Fortunately, this epidemic of deaths from asthma waned during the 1970s, but recently a study from New Zealand (Wilson et al., 1981) reported that the mortality rate there has again risen. Once more, the use of bronchodilator drugs has been implicated as a probable cause for the increase in deaths. In this latest epidemic, the combination of high dose nebulised β_2-agonist and slow-release preparations containing methylxanthines has been considered as a possible cause.

For the last 80 years, bronchodilators have been the standard therapy used by clinicians for patients suffering from severe asthma. Hence, there seems to be a paradox between the use of bronchodilators for acute asthma, and the possibility that these same drugs can lead to death during an acute attack.

Causes of Death from Asthma

Those who die from asthma are severely hypoxaemic, and death is a result of a cardiac arrest, frequently asystolic but occasionally in ventricular fibrillation. At post-mortem these patients almost invariably have mucosal oedema and gross mucous plugging of the airways. These findings suggest that they not only died from hypoxia associated with these airway abnormalities, but also that the terminal attack of asthma was prolonged over days rather than hours.

During the last few years, a number of studies have investigated the possible factors which have led to death from asthma (a) in hospital (Cochrane and Clark, 1975); (b) at home (Macdonald et al., 1976) and (c) overall asthma deaths in two separate parts of England (British Thoracic Association, 1982). The overall impression from these studies is that death from asthma was sudden and unexpected. More detailed analysis of the results has suggested possible causes for the 'apparent' catastrophic nature of asthma deaths (table 10.1).

Table 10.1. Factors associated with a fatal outcome from severe acute asthma

Why patients die from acute asthma

Failure of diagnosis
Speed of onset of the terminal attack
Inadequate perception by the patient of the severity of the attack
Inadequate assessment by the doctor of the severity of the attack
Therapy – too much, too little or the wrong combination

Failure of Diagnosis

A possible reason for asthma deaths is that the first attack is fatal. In fact, a number of deaths have occurred in patients previously not considered to be asthmatic. Certainly these patients have been unfortunate in that their first severe acute attack was overwhelming; but it is likely that many had been asthmatic but that this had not been appreciated. A survey in Newcastle upon Tyne of 7-year-old children suggested that nearly 11% had suffered significant asthma, but this had been diagnosed and suitably treated in only a small minority (Lee et al., 1983). Similarly, many adults tend to be labelled as 'chronic bronchitics' and therefore receive neither adequate prophylactic therapy nor suitable antiasthma therapy during an attack of wheezing. Although it is difficult to be emphatic that failure of diagnosis leads to asthma deaths, there is no doubt that this failure of diagnosis in those suffering from asthma deprives them of access to therapy which can improve their lifestyle dramatically (Speight et al., 1983). There is also a tendency for doctors to manage an acute illness according to previous diagnoses and thus a patient labelled as 'bronchitic' will be treated for bronchitis rather than for asthma.

Speed of Onset

The time course of fatal asthma attacks has been studied and it appears that there are varying intervals between the onset of the attack and death. One study showed that most severe attacks requiring attendance at a London casualty department were slowly progressive and had developed over a period of days (Bellamy and Collins, 1979). Other studies, however, which included patients who referred themselves to either a hospital department or their family practitioner, suggested that 50% of them sought medical advice within 24 hours of the onset of an attack (Arnold et al., 1982).

Catastrophic rapid attacks can and do occur, frequently with a fatal outcome, the time from the start of an attack to death being a matter of minutes. Fortunately, these are rare, but if such patients are identified they require instant self-medication. (The author has two such patients who carry a pre-packed syringe with 0.25mg of terbutaline for immediate subcutaneous injection, and have so far survived such episodes).

Lack of Patient Awareness of the Severity of Attacks

Another possible reason for death is that the patient is unaware of the severity of the asthma attack. The majority of asthmatics are acutely aware of worsening symptoms but, unfortunately, about 25% are unable to recognise the severity of an attack (Rubinfield and Pain, 1976). This failure of perception may be associated with poor compliance with prophylactic therapy (James et al., 1982). It is possible that the increase in airways resistance develops so slowly over a matter of weeks that the patient almost forgets what being 'well' is like (Burdon et al., 1982). This type of asthmatic is at risk of dying suddenly because only a minor increase in airways resistance may lead to a catastrophic fall in oxygen saturation (since the patient is already hypoxic and at the critical point on the oxygen haemoglobin dissociation curve) [Palmer and Flenley, 1976]. However, the study of Burdon and his colleagues also suggests that asthmatics with marked bronchial reactivity who suffer from rapid changes in airways resistance can negate the sensation of breathlessness (Burdon et al., 1982). Thus, those with a marked early morning dip in their PEFR are also at risk of dying from an attack of asthma.

Lack of Doctor Awareness of the Severity of an Attack

Most patients are far more accurate in assessing the severity of their airways obstruction than are their doctors (Shim and Williams, 1980), and many doctors still fail to appreciate the potentially fatal nature of an attack of asthma (Cochrane and Clark, 1975). This failure on the part of doctors has, in the past, led to errors in the assessment of how ill a patient may be during an attack of asthma. There is a risk that at least 1% of patients arriving at hospital with asthma attacks may die. Even when the doctor appreciates this risk, he or she is still unable to identify which patient will die. However, as will be discussed later, a more thorough clinical and physiological assessment may lead to a more positive therapeutic approach in treating each individual attack of asthma. This implies that there is effective and safe therapy for the treatment of severe asthma.

Therapy – Too Much, Too Little, or the Wrong Combination

Too Much β-Agonist

The epidemic of deaths which occurred after the introduction of pressurised isoprenaline aerosol therapy is still frequently cited as an example of the dangers of bronchodilator therapy. The fall in standardised mortality rates from asthma in the early 1970s, although paralleled by the reduction in sales of isoprenaline aerosols, is not reflected in the total sales of bronchodilator aerosols. In fact, sales of the more selective β_2-agonist aerosols have risen dramatically. At the same time as the above-mentioned decline in asthma death rates, there was increased prescribing of oral corticosteroids for acute asthma. Many doctors now believe that it was probably not the isoprenaline itself that led to the increase in deaths from asthma, but a number of factors. Doctors and patients were inadequately educated to understand the implications of self-administered isoprenaline therapy, with its effective, but short, duration of action. The concept that an increase in drug usage suggested a deterioration in asthma control and that this deterioration required additional therapy, such as a course of corticosteroids, was poorly recognised (Editorial, 1981).

Too Little Corticosteroid

The belief that corticosteroids help to prevent the development of severe acute asthma is now almost universally accepted, although some authors question their efficacy once the attack is established (Luksza, 1982a). Despite this acceptance, there are few incontrovertible studies to support the use of corticosteroids in any aspect of the treatment of asthma [this problem is well reviewed by Luksza (1982b) and Grant (1982)]. A prospective study of present therapeutic practice in the management of severe acute asthma in Oxfordshire (Arnold et al., 1983a) noted that if intravenous hydrocortisone was given in conjunction with an increase in bronchodilator therapy, patients were far less likely to require hospital admission. This is an important study, as it confirms the impression that the combination of corticosteroids and bronchodilators, given early, may prevent the progression of deteriorating asthma to severe life threatening asthma.

Combination Therapy

In New Zealand, there has been a recent increase in mortality which cannot be explained by changes in the classification of deaths from asthma or inaccuracies in death certification (Jackson et al., 1982). One suggestion is that this increase in asthma deaths was associated with the introduction of slow-release methylxanthine preparations (Wilson et al., 1981). However, this cannot be the only explanation, as slow-release methylxanthines were introduced some years after the initial increase in asthma mortality. Some deaths could have been associated with theophylline toxicity in patients already receiving slow-release methylxanthines and who were given an additional intravenous bolus of aminophylline during an acute exacerbation of their asthma. Another possible explanation is that there was a synergistic action of combining inhaled β-agonists with oral methylxanthine preparations, which increased the chance of death from asthma (Wilson et al., 1981).

In an independent assessment of the increase in deaths from asthma in New Zealand, Grant highlighted three other possible explanations (Grant, 1983). A number of patients had not received corticosteroids for their asthma during the exacerbation, a finding very similar to the United Kingdom studies, and virtually none had received oxygen therapy. Although these facts alone did not account for the deaths, the administration of corticosteroids and oxygen certainly may have prevented some. Another observation was that until very recently, respirator solutions of β_2-agonists for use in a nebuliser could be, and were, purchased without medical prescription. In 2 years, 6000 nebulisers had been purchased in New Zealand and Grant suggested that in the majority of cases physicians were unaware that their patients were using the nebulisers to deliver β_2-agonist drugs. Although the use of home nebulisers may be more widespread in New Zealand than elsewhere, it would appear that nebuliser solutions have rarely been supplied without prescription (Rea and Sutherland, 1983).

Not everyone agrees with Grant's conclusions or even that high doses of inhaled β_2-agonists are dangerous, but the New Zealand experience is chastening.

Table 10.2. Clinical assessment of the severity of an attack of asthma (after Jones, 1980)

Grade I	Able to carry out housework or job with difficulty
Grade II	Confined to a chair or bed but able to get up with moderate difficulty (IIa) or with great difficulty (IIb)
Grade III	Totally confined to a chair or bed
Grade IV	Moribund

Table 10.3. Assessment of severity of asthma[1]

Symptoms and signs	Scoring system	
	0	1
Loss of exercise tolerance (see table 10.2)	I-IIa	IIb or more
Using accessory muscles, tracheal tug and intercostal recession	Absent	Present
Wheezing	Absent	Present
Respiratory rate/minute	< 25/min (adult)	> 25/min
	< 30/min (child)	> 30/min
Pulse rate	< 110/min (adult)	> 110/min
	< 120/min (child)	> 120/min
Palpable pulsus paradoxus	Absent	Present
Peak expiratory flow rate L/min	> 100	< 100

1 — A system for scoring the severity of an attack of severe acute asthma. A total of 4, or more, suggests severe asthma requiring urgent treatment. Cyanosis occurs very late in an attack of severe acute asthma, and as it suggests imminent death it has been deliberately omitted from this assessment.

Assessment of Severity

Clinical Assessment

Although a few patients underestimate the severity of their symptoms, the majority with deteriorating asthma seek advice because of symptoms. Usually the complaint is of increasing shortness of breath on exertion, or even at rest. The assessment can be helped by determining the clinical severity of this loss of exercise tolerance. Jones suggested a grading for exercise tolerance (table 10.2) and pointed out that those whose asthma has reduced their exercise potential to grade IIb (confined to a chair or bed but able to get up with great difficulty), or worse, are more at risk of death (Jones, 1980).

Some do not have a striking loss of exercise tolerance during the day but are woken during the night with a paroxysmal attack of breathlessness. An increase in the number of attacks of nocturnal wakening with wheezing in the early hours of the morning is associated with deteriorating asthma. Increased frequency of the use of β-agonist aerosols is also an excellent guide to the severity of the attack. Observing the patient undressing for a physical examination often helps the clinician to appreciate how severely exercise tolerance is impaired.

Clinical signs indicating the severity of an attack of asthma are listed in table 10.3. There is no single predictive indicator of the severity of an attack, but the totalling up of several signs may give a guide to how ill the patient is.

Respiratory Signs

Cyanosis occurs very late in asthma and suggests impending death. During the development of an asthma attack the work of breathing is greatest during inspiration, and most patients complain of difficulty in breathing in. This is clearly seen by the use of the accessory muscles, with intercostal recession and tracheal tug. During the recovery phase of a severe attack PEFR may not change initially but accessory muscle work, tracheal tug and intercostal recession decrease. Wheezing, although usually very obvious and indicative of severe airflow obstruction, may be absent, and the situation is then more worrying, as the patient's asthma is so severe that it is impossible to generate adequate airflow to produce wheeze.

The respiratory rate is rarely measured by doctors, but a respiratory rate > 30/minute in a child or > 25/minute in an adult is associated with severe asthma. Pneumothorax or mediastinal emphysema are associated with a poor prognosis.

Cardiovascular Signs

Heart rate is an important indicator of asthma severity, with a rate of > 110/minute in an adult and > 120/minute in a child suggesting severe asthma. The use (or abuse) of β_2-agonists or methylxanthines should not be assumed to be a contributory factor to a rapid pulse. Appropriate treatment of the attack of asthma, with additional bronchodilators and corticosteroids, usually leads to a fall in heart rate. A low heart rate in patients over 55 years of age can lead to a false sense of security since, with increasing age, a sinus tachycardia does not always occur in response to the stress of asthma. Bradycardia is also found in severely hypoxaemic patients of any age.

Pulsus paradoxus (a respiratory systolic pressure difference), if easily felt at the wrist, indicates severe asthma. A survey in the author's unit demonstrated that by palpation of the pulse, most clinicians could detect a difference in pressure of 15mm Hg between inspiration and expiration, a value close to that suggesting severe asthma (Knowles and Clark, 1973). The mechanism for pulsus paradoxus is obscure, but explanations include cardiac tamponade secondary to hyperinflation and diaphragmatic flattening, and diminished venous return associated with high intrathoracic pressures and, much less likely, dehydration.

Respiratory Function

PEFR should be measured at home as well as in hospital, with values below 100 litres/minute indicating severe airflow obstruction. In hospital the forced expired volume in one second (FEV_1) can also be measured; a value of less than a litre, or below 30% of predicted normal, is considered by some to be the best single indication for hospital admission and treatment.

Facilities for measuring arterial blood gases are seldom available to the primary physician but arterial blood gas analysis should be performed in all patients referred to hospital. Patients are often severely hypoxaemic and hyperventilate, with a $PaCO_2$ less than the usually accepted normal. Alveolar hyperventilation is a common response to the hypoxaemia of asthma (Cochrane et al., 1980). In the presence of a PaO_2 below 60mm Hg, any value of $PaCO_2$ above 35mm Hg is a sign of severe disease.

Assessment of the severity of an attack is important in establishing what therapy should be given and how alert the clinician should be. Although severity scoring may seem complicated, when using the signs outlined in table 10.3, a score of 4 or more is associated with severe asthma and requires urgent action. A score of 4, one hour after initial treatment at home, or in the casualty department, suggests the patient requires hospital admission and further therapy (Fischl et al., 1981), although a recent report has suggested that such a system is not completely specific or sensitive in identifying the patients most at risk (Rose et al., 1984).

Bronchodilator Therapy in Severe Acute Asthma

Bronchodilator therapy is still considered one of the most important aspects of treatment of severe acute asthma, and it is therefore surprising that an indicator of worsening asthma is the increased usage of a β_2-agonist aerosol, with diminished response to its action. Tachyphylaxis has been fully discussed earlier (chapters II and V) but appears not to be a major cause of failed aerosol therapy.

Reasons for Failure of Aerosol Bronchodilators

Why do patients feel their pressurised aerosols of β_2-agonists are no longer effective? There is little data to answer this question, but one possibility is that the bronchoconstriction is so severe that higher doses of inhaled β_2-agonists are required to relieve it.This idea is supported by the difference between the magnitude of the dose delivered from 2 puffs of β_2-agonist aerosol and that delivered via nebuliser systems, the standard hospital treatment for asthma in the United Kingdom. Even when the loss of drug from the nebuliser system has been taken into account (fig. 10.1) the speculative dose reaching the airway below the larynx is frequently 20 times greater than that delivered from the aerosol.

In a survey from Sweden (Boe et al., 1983), plasma levels of β-agonists in asthmatics on inhaler therapy, measured on arrival in hospital, were high in only 4 of 45 patients. The remainder, despite high aerosol use, had low plasma levels.

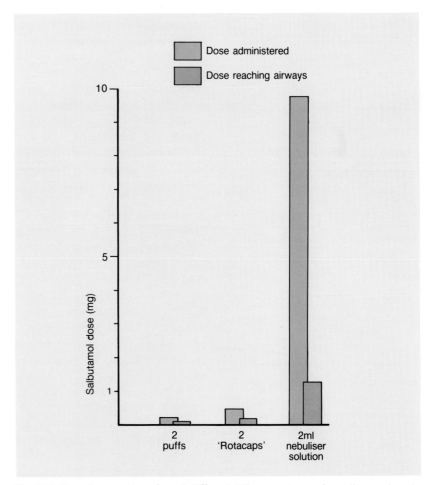

Fig. 10.1. Drug dosages given from 3 different delivery systems using salbutamol as the β_2-agonist, and the comparative dose of drug reaching the airway below the larynx.

Another possible reason is that it is difficult to inhale effectively from pressurised aerosols when asthma is severe. Certainly, breathless patients are far less able to hold their breath for 10 seconds to allow maximum sedimentation of the drug in the smaller airways. Similarly, dry powder delivery systems are less effective with falling peak inspiratory flow rates (PIFR falls in a similar fashion to PEFR during an attack of asthma but is infrequently measured because it is less repeatable and more subject cooperation is required).

Thus, during an attack of asthma, the patient who is normally able to deliver 20 to 30μg of β_2-adrenoceptor agonist to the lung from an initial 200μg [dose as for salbutamol (albuterol) pressurised aerosol] may be getting as little as 5μg to the airway. This minute dose may well account for the reduced length of action of inhaled β_2-agonist therapy in severe asthma.

During an attack of severe acute asthma, little of the inhaled drug reaching the airway will reach the most severely affected parts of the lung because of mucus plugging. Thus, more effective bronchodilatation may be achieved by the use of systemic bronchodilators, given orally or by injection. The drug will then be distributed throughout the whole lung via the pulmonary circulation.

Oral and Parenteral Administration of Bronchodilators in Severe Acute Asthma

Many studies have compared oral/parenteral, oral/inhaled, and parenteral/inhaled bronchodilators in the treatment of acute asthma. Unfortunately, there are virtually no comparable studies. This is due partly to the variable nature of the disease, and partly to the differences in drug availability and accepted usage of the emergency treatments for asthma in different areas of the world. A study of 3 groups of patients attending the emergency room with severe acute asthma compared intravenous aminophylline, subcutaneous adrenaline and inhaled isoprenaline (Rossing et al., 1980). Intravenous aminophylline was given in a dosage designed to obtain therapeutic blood levels at 1 hour, adrenaline as 0.3mg by subcutaneous injection, 3 times in 1 hour, and inhaled isoprenaline as 2.5mg, 3 times in 1 hour (equivalent to 75 puffs of a standard isoprenaline inhaler). Although there was no significant difference between groups at the onset of therapy, the mean improvement in bronchodilatation at the end of 1 hour was significantly greater for the adrenaline and isoprenaline groups. A further study by the same authors (Fanta et al., 1982) showed that in patients with severe asthma a solution of oral aminophylline raised plasma concentrations of theophylline as rapidly as the intravenous infusion.

There is a relative dearth of literature comparing the more selective β_2-agonists given subcutaneously or intramuscularly with subcutaneous adrenaline. However, Pang and his colleagues showed the efficacy of subcutaneous terbutaline in the treatment of acute asthma, but failed to compare it with similar doses of inhaled β_2-agonists (Pang et al., 1977). In the United Kingdom, most physicians in family practice and in hospital tend to use the more selective β_2-agonists, which are readily available, to avoid the cardiovascular problems associated with adrenaline or isoprenaline. Despite the argument that oral or parenteral administration should be more effective than inhaled therapy in severe acute asthma, studies have failed to show that intravenous salbutamol was more effective than inhaled therapy (Hetzel and Clark, 1976; Lawford et al., 1978; Nogrady et al., 1977; Spiro et al., 1975).

Aminophylline, intravenously or orally, seems to be a weak bronchodilator when compared with high doses of subcutaneous adrenaline or inhaled isoprenaline, and inhaled salbutamol seems as effective as intravenous salbutamol. Unfortunately, the issue is confused by a study which showed that intravenous aminophylline was more effective in both its speed of onset and bronchodilator effect than intravenous salbutamol, but salbutamol was given in a comparatively low dose (Evans et al., 1980). The dose of intravenous salbutamol in this study was shown to be inadequate by an American study of emergency room treatment of asthma (Fanta et al., 1982). These authors also showed no additional bronchodilator effect with the addition of aminophylline, in a dosage which gave therapeutic blood levels, in a group of patients given 7.5mg of inhaled isoprenaline over 1 hour, compared with a group given isoprenaline alone. Here it appeared that if maximum doses of a non-selective β-agonist drug were used there was no therapeutic advantage in also using methylxanthines. These patients were not given corticosteroids, which may increase responsiveness to bronchodilators, especially to the selective β_2-agonists (Shenfield et al., 1975).

Inhaled Selective
β_2-Agonists

Aminophylline is a potentially toxic drug (Hendeles and Weinberger, 1980; Woodcock et al., 1983), and in the United Kingdom, the standard emergency treatment for severe acute asthma is inhaled β_2-agonists given via a nebulisation system at a dose equivalent to 2.5 to 5mg of salbutamol. Nebulisation may be carried out by passive inhalation or with the addition of intermittent positive pressure breathing (IPPB) apparatus. The value of IPPB has been disputed and the conclusion of a trial which used comparative doses of inhaled salbutamol was that there was no advantage in using IPPB (Fergusson et al., 1983). Passive inhalation alone appears to be all that is needed in most cases.

Comparative trials with equipotent doses of selective β_2-agonists delivered by various inhalation devices have suggested that nebulisation is superior in the most severe attacks of asthma (PEFR below 100 L/min), although in about 60% of patients, dry powder administered by 'Rotahaler' is effective (Webber et al., 1982).

Morgan and his colleagues compared the response to 4mg of terbutaline delivered either by nebuliser or from a pressure-packed aerosol using a pear 'spacer' ('Nebuhaler') attachment, in severe asthma (Morgan et al., 1982). The pear 'spacer' attachment (appendix C) is a plastic cone with a one-way valve and is designed to contain the shape of the aerosol cloud, thus increasing airway deposition of the drug and obviating the need for inspiration coordination. In this study, there was no significant difference in either the degree or speed of onset of bronchodilatation between the aerosol attachment and the nebuliser system of drug delivery.

Anticholinergic
Bronchodilators

Atropine was previously suggested as a useful bronchodilator in severe acute asthma, but whether given intravenously or by inhalation, adequate bronchodilatation occurred only with high doses. Such high doses lead to an intolerable incidence of side effects and the possibility of increased sputum viscosity. Ipratropium bromide*, a quaternary ammonium compound (chapter II), does not have such untoward effects, and has recently been shown to be effective in severe acute asthma (Ward et al., 1981). Ipratropium bromide (0.5-1mg nebulised) appears to be as effective in producing initial bronchodilatation as salbutamol (5mg nebulised). It has recently been demonstrated that salbutamol (5mg nebulised) produced additional bronchodilatation at the end of 1 hour when given after ipratropium bromide, but this did not occur when ipratropium bromide was given after salbutamol (Leahy et al., 1983). Ipratropium bromide, although an effective bronchodilator in many patients, may lead to bronchoconstriction in the occasional patient (Patel and Tullett, 1983) and, therefore, could be dangerous as first line treatment of severe acute asthma. The mechanism for this bronchoconstriction is not known, but is considered to be related to the bromide, as bronchoconstriction has not been reported with inhaled atropine or atropine methonitrate. Bronchoconstriction may be precipitated by hypo- or hypertonic nebulised solutions (Schoeffel et al., 1981) and bronchodilator solutions should be diluted in isotonic saline (Patel and Tullett, 1983).

Complications of Bronchodilator Therapy In Severe Acute Asthma

Complications of bronchodilator therapy have been discussed in chapters II and V. In severe acute asthma where high doses are usually employed, side effects are frequently encountered. β_2-agonists rarely add to the tachycardia associated with the acute attack, but during the recovery phase, when absorption from the lung is higher, muscle cramps and muscle tremor may be noticed. Tenseness and headache, often associated with hot flushes, are also frequently reported. Angina pectoris has been reported in the elderly. Pre-existing hypokalaemia may be exacerbated by β_2-agonists. Increased hypoxaemia following the administration of parenteral bronchodilators may occur, but this has not been confirmed with the more selective β_2-agonists given by inhalation. Nausea and gastrointestinal disturbances are associated with high therapeutic levels of methylxanthines and, in cases of severe toxicity, cardiac arrhythmias, convulsions and death have been reported. Headache and tachycardia may occur with comparatively low theophylline blood levels. Ipratropium may lead to a dry mouth, visual side effects and, occasionally, prostatic symptoms.

Summary of the Use of Bronchodilators in Severe Asthma

There is no concord as to the most effective, rapid and safe bronchodilator to use in severe acute asthma. Many of the studies are conflicting, do not lend themselves to direct comparison and are not universally applicable because of the availability of different drugs in different countries. However, the majority opinion tends to favour using high doses of selective β_2-agonists delivered directly to the airway. Intravenous aminophylline still appears to have a role, but toxicity is a problem. Subcutaneous adrenaline in all but the most severe anaphylactoid type of reaction is rarely advocated in the United Kingdom although parenteral selective

---

* For product availability in the USA, see appendix B.

β_2-agonists are used. Ipratropium bromide is now identified as a useful additional inhaled therapy. However, the management of severe acute asthma should not rely solely on bronchodilators. Oxygen therapy, corticosteroids and supportive therapy are essential in order to prevent a fatal outcome from an attack of asthma.

Management of Severe Acute Asthma

There is no simple formula for the management of severe acute asthma, and the clinician must always assess the response to therapy and watch for any associated dangers. As stated earlier, severe asthma only rarely develops rapidly over minutes, and, therefore, the clinician may have time to prevent the development of such a bad attack. However, if appropriate action fails to prevent severe asthma developing or the patient does not seek advice early, the clinician may have to treat the attack in the home, during transfer to hospital, or in hospital.

Although ideal management differs little in the home or the hospital, there are real practical problems to be overcome in home management of severe asthma.

Deteriorating Asthma

Patients who complain of worsening symptoms, increasing bronchodilator aerosol usage or a falling PEFR, may not be severely ill (scoring less than 4 in table 10.3), but they still require some alteration of therapy. Where possible any particular cause for the increased symptoms should be identified and, in the presence of a pyrexia and increased sputum production, antibiotics are probably indicated. An increase in bronchodilator therapy is almost always required, but this should be in association with the use of corticosteroids. The increase may be achieved by increasing the frequency of β_2-agonist aerosol usage or the number of puffs taken on each occasion. Inhaler systems using higher drug concentrations may be tried. Some authors have advocated the addition of oral methylxanthines if they are not already being taken. Dosage should be given in accordance with the manufacturer's instructions, usually starting with a low dose and increasing after 3 days, to prevent initial accumulation and toxicity. Recently, high dose β_2-agonists from nebulisers have been used at home, especially in children (chapter VI). If home nebulisation of bronchodilators and/or prophylactic therapy are used, careful supervision is required daily to assess the response to therapy. Any deterioration in the patient's condition suggests that admission to hospital should be considered.

Two basic regimens for oral corticosteroids have been suggested: a 7-day course of oral prednisolone 40 mg/day for an adult (or 0.5 mg/kg bodyweight/day in children) and then stopping abruptly; or a similar dosage initially but reducing, either by 5mg per day or every other day, until the steroids are withdrawn. Whichever regimen is used, it is essential to monitor response to therapy. When the patient is reviewed, therapy may be continued, intensified or stopped, depending on exercise tolerance, symptoms and respiratory function. Measurement of PEFR at home 3 times a day allows an objective assessment of improvement or deterioration. Fortunately, many attacks do not progress to severe asthma and increased therapy may be slowly adjusted back to the original treatment. If the cause for the acute attack was inadequate prophylactic treatment, a modified regimen should be introduced.

Severe Acute Asthma
in the Home

Although emergency night calls are less common than in the past, family practitioners are still often called out at night for severe asthma. The circadian nature of airflow obstruction (chapter VIII) obviously accounts for the incidence of night referrals.

Treatment at home requires an adequate assessment of the severity of the attack and, if the patient is very severely ill, some treatment should be instituted before transfer to hospital. Apart from the assessment outlined above, the doctor should try and determine what has actually been taken over the previous few hours as this is frequently different from the prescribed therapy. With increasing symptoms from asthma, many patients tend to increase their bronchodilator therapy (James et al., 1982). Before aminophylline is given intravenously it is essential to know whether slow-release methylxanthine preparations have been taken (Woodcock et al., 1983), since patients also frequently increase the dose of these during an exacerbation of asthma (Stewart et al., 1984). Proprietary preparations which contain ephedrine, barbiturate, caffeine or theophylline may have been taken, and although the unit doses of these drugs are low, more than the recommended dose is often used.

Methylxanthines

Intravenous aminophylline has for many years been the mainstay of emergency bronchodilator therapy in the home, and the problems associated with methylxanthines have been discussed earlier. In general practice, where nebulisers are frequently unavailable for delivering selective β_2-agonists, aminophylline has to be given even though it is not ideal. The recommended initial doses of aminophylline have been too high in the past; the present recommended dose is 5.6 mg/kg given over 20 to 30 minutes. (This type of recommendation leads to considerable amusement in general practice as the family practitioner is now obliged to add a weighing scale and stop watch to his already cluttered bag.)

In practice, intravenous aminophylline given as a bolus of 250mg over 5 to 10 minutes is unlikely to produce toxic effects in most adults unless they are very thin. In obese patients, an additional 250mg given 20 to 30 minutes later, if they have not improved following the initial bolus, is unlikely to lead to toxic side effects. In children, half this dose is usually recommended. Slow intravenous injection is essential even if the 20 to 30 minutes recommended is obviously unreasonable. Unfortunately, concurrent medication with oral theophyllines can make intravenous aminophylline dangerous. In these circumstances, if the attack of asthma is life-threatening and other medication is not available, halving the dose of intravenous aminophylline is usually recommended.

Inhaled Selective β_2-Agonists

Many family practitioners now carry small, electrical air compressor units for driving nebuliser systems, but these are useless if the electrical fittings are not standard or there is no electricity supply. A simple light plastic foot pump has been developed as a driving system for the nebulisation of drugs, but the doctor needs to be fit! Nebulisers may be driven by compressed air or oxygen cylinders, but usually need high flow rates (8 L/min) to deliver the correct particle size of inhaled mist.

Nebulised β_2-agonist is usually given in a dose equivalent to

2.5 to 5mg of salbutamol (0.5-1ml of nebuliser solution) in 3 to 4ml of normal saline to obtain the most efficient delivery of the drug to the lung. Recently some selective β_2-agonists have become available as ready-mixed solutions to make home nebulisation simpler (appendix B).

Other Delivery Systems for Inhaled Bronchodilators

When increasing the frequency of use of pressurised aerosol β_2-agonist bronchodilators has failed and nebulisation is unavailable, what can the family practitioner do? In moderately severe asthma, dry powder delivery systems have been shown to be useful if the dose and frequency of inhalation are increased, but in the most severe cases the powder is often deposited only in the mouth. Recently, Morgan and his colleagues have shown that inhalation of 4mg of terbutaline (8 times the usual aerosol dose), delivered via a pear 'spacer' ('Nebuhaler'; see appendix C) was as effective in treating severe acute asthma as 4mg of terbutaline delivered via a nebuliser system (Morgan et al., 1982). The family practitioner is thus able to deliver a high dose of a β_2-agonist by using the standard terbutaline aerosol (250 μg/puff) and a 'Nebuhaler'.

Parenteral β_2-Agonists

Subcutaneous or intramuscular preparations of selective β_2-agonists are available, although there is no evidence that they are more effective than high dose inhaled therapy. If no other route of administration is available, subcutaneous terbutaline (0.5mg) or subcutaneous or intramuscular salbutamol (0.5mg) may be used. However, if the patient is severely ill with cardiovascular collapse, the drug may be poorly absorbed from these sites. In the United Kingdom, the use of subcutaneous adrenaline for severe acute asthma has become almost obsolete because of its cardiovascular side effects.

Corticosteroids in Severe Acute Asthma in the Home

In severe acute asthma, most physicians still believe corticosteroids should be given parenterally. Hydrocortisone should be given intravenously in a dose which is at least equivalent to that which can be obtained by maximal stimulation of the adrenal cortex. The usual recommended dose is 100mg for a child and 200mg for an adult, irrespective of body size and should be given over a few minutes. This dose will maintain cortisol levels in the region of 100 μg/L for 2 to 4 hours, but if the patient is not transferred to hospital, it will need to be repeated every 4 hours or oral corticosteroids given.

Oxygen Therapy

As discussed earlier, a possible cause of asthma fatalities is the combination of hypoxia with high dose β-agonists and theophyllines. As the mainstay of therapy in severe asthma is the delivery of higher doses of a bronchodilator, it seems logical that oxygen therapy should also be given, even in the home. Most asthmatics do not require long term oxygen therapy and therefore do not have oxygen at home. An increasing number of family practitioners carry oxygen cylinders around with them, but unfortunately, small portable cylinders contain only approximately 100 litres, which is delivered at only 2 or 4 L/minute. The ideal arrangement of using a portable oxygen cylinder to drive a nebuliser system for selective β_2-agonist inhalation has yet to be achieved, as nebulisers need high flow rates and the small oxygen cylinders would last only 10 to 15 minutes. Oxygen therapy may be administered at the same time as nebulised therapy is given from a portable air compressor if the oxygen is delivered at 2 to 4 L/minute via nasal prongs.

In Summary

Ideally, the patient should be treated with inhaled nebulised β_2-agonists, oxygen therapy (inspired oxygen 35-40%) and intravenous hydrocortisone. If a rapid response does not ensue, intravenous aminophylline can be given slowly, the dose being adjusted in the presence of concurrent methylxanthine medication. If nebuliser therapy for β_2-agonists is not available, more frequent inhalation from a pressurised aerosol may be tried, especially with a spacer attachment.

Deaths due to asthma could possibly be reduced if a kit for the management of severe asthma, consisting of a portable oxygen cylinder with a low flow rate nebuliser system for inhaled β_2-agonists, and syringes for intravenous hydrocortisone and aminophylline administration was available to family practitioners.

Transfer to Hospital

There are few known guidelines to help decide which patients should be transferred to hospital. A survey in Oxfordshire (Arnold et al., 1983b) showed that the majority of children with severe acute asthma were likely to be admitted to hospital. Fewer adults were admitted and usually were those who had high pulse rates and very low peak flows. Most family practitioners who are within easy reach of hospital will transfer patients who score 4 or more, using the scoring system shown in table 10.3. Transfer to hospital is itself associated with mortality and therefore most authorities suggest initial treatment as outlined above, and then during transfer oxygen should be given. If further β_2-agonists are required then 2 puffs of an aerosol may be given every 5 minutes during transfer. Intramuscular or subcutaneous β_2-agonists may also be used at this stage.

Treatment of Severe Acute Asthma in Hospital

Treatment of severe acute asthma in hospital is very similar to emergency treatment in the home, but is usually a lot easier from a practical point of view. Assessment of severity usually includes arterial blood gas, analysis, ECG, chest radiograph, FEV_1 and measurement of serum electrolytes, especially potassium.

Bronchodilator Therapy

Initial management in hospital is to give a selective β_2-agonist by nebuliser, usually in a dose of 2.5 to 5mg of salbutamol, or its equivalent, every 2 to 4 hours. Nebulised therapy requires a driving source for nebulisation and in hospital oxygen is preferred. Although a flow rate of 8 L/min is used for most nebuliser systems, this is not usually associated with an inspired oxygen concentration greater than 50%. Recently, nebulised ipratropium bromide has been used in the treatment of severe acute asthma in hospital (0.5-1mg, 4- to 6-hourly, diluted with normal saline). The efficacy of ipratropium bromide in acute asthma is established, but there is still some doubt about its efficacy compared with inhaled β_2-agonists, and therefore it should not be used as first-line therapy. Additional bronchodilatation may possibly be achieved by the combination of ipratropium and a β_2-agonist (see p.89) and thus side effects from both drugs may be lessened by reducing both doses and giving 2-hourly alternate inhalations. The author uses 1mg of ipratropium bromide 4-hourly in severely ill asthmatics, although this is greater than the recommended dose.

Selective β_2-agonists are occasionally given intravenously for practical reasons, usually because the patient requires ventilation or does not tolerate a face mask or nasal prongs. The dose of intravenous β_2-agonist varies, and the manufacturer's instructions should be followed (see appendix B). Salbutamol is usually given as an infusion of 5mg in 500ml of normal saline or dextrose (100 μg/ml) and the infusion rate is from 3 to 20 μg/min. For profoundly ill patients, or for those who have not responded to the initial bronchodilator therapy (or bronchodilator plus steroid) after 1 hour, intravenous aminophylline may be useful.

Methylxanthines

The present recommended dose for adults is 5.6 mg/kg bodyweight over 20 to 30 minutes followed by 0.5 mg/kg bodyweight per hour, with a plasma level estimation after 24 hours (see appendix B). These doses should be halved in the presence of liver disease or heart failure. If methylxanthines have been given before reaching hospital a blood sample for theophylline level estimation should be taken on arrival, and the result may well be available at the end of the hour, allowing adjustment of the aminophylline dosage. If the patient is severely ill and is already receiving oral theophylline maintenance treatment but the theophylline plasma level is not known, then aminophylline 3 mg/kg body weight should be given as a slow intravenous bolus followed by an infusion of 0.25 mg/kg bodyweight per hour. Every attempt should be made to obtain theophylline plasma level estimations in all cases as too low a level will be associated with a less than optimal therapeutic effect and a toxic level may be lethal. Ideally, blood levels should be measured 8- to 12-hourly in the first 24 hours, but if such a service is not available, a theophylline plasma level estimation 24 hours after starting therapy should prevent major catastrophes. Toxic levels are usually maximal at 24 hours, even when a patient has received previous oral theophylline medication.

Corticosteroid Therapy in Severe Acute Asthma

Corticosteroid dosage in severe acute asthma is still debated, but most authors recommend a plasma level of hydrocortisone of between 100 to 150μg/100ml. This is equivalent to a dose of 3 to 4 mg/kg bodyweight given every 6 hours. The author's practice is to give (if not already given before admission) 200mg hydrocortisone as a bolus. The hydrocortisone levels are then maintained by 6-hourly infusions of 4 mg/kg bodyweight for the next 24 hours (usually 200-300mg hydrocortisone 6-hourly). The dose is usually reduced to 3 mg/kg bodyweight 6-hourly as an infusion over the next 24 hours if there has been an improvement in the clinical indices outlined in table 10.3. Prednisolone 40 to 60mg orally is started during the second 24 hours. If the clinical improvement is maintained, treatment is changed to oral prednisolone 40 to 60mg daily during the phase of recovery.

Additional Therapy and Supportive Measures in Acute Asthma

The use of oxygen therapy has already been stressed and it should be given continuously at 2 to 4 L/min by nasal prongs (Flenley, 1983) or face mask. Patients should be adequately rehydrated and potassium supplements should be given when ne-

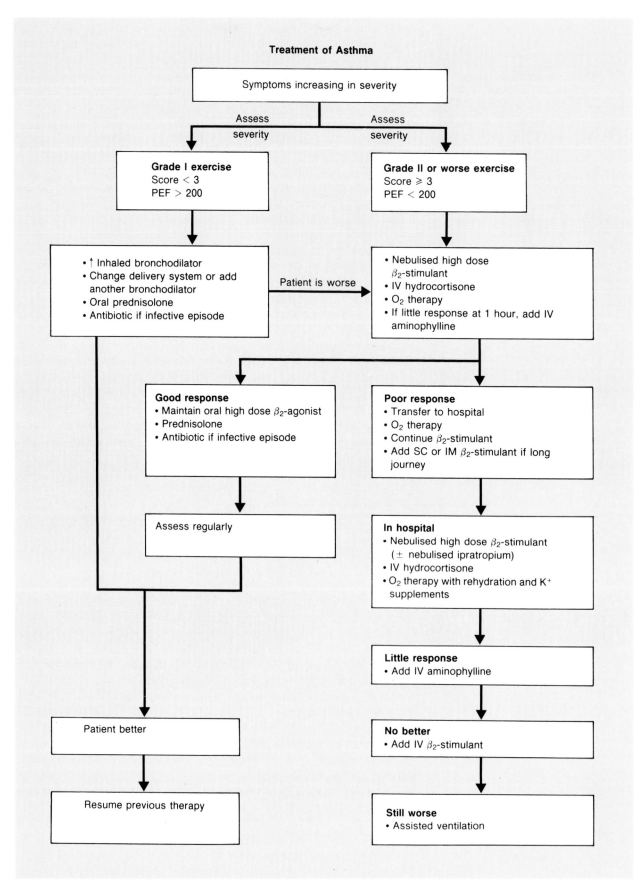

Fig. 10.2. A simplified outline of the treatment of severe acute asthma.

cessary, since acute asthma is associated with hypokalaemia, and treatment with corticosteroids and parenteral β-agonists can further increase potassium loss. Antibiotics are given in the majority of cases despite the low incidence of proven respiratory tract infection in acute asthma. In children there is more evidence to support their use. However, antibiotics are reasonably safe, and it is therefore probably better to err on the side of caution. Patients whose asthma is not responding to maximal therapy and who are developing carbon dioxide retention should be ventilated.

In Summary

Inhaled high dose β_2-agonists should be given via a nebuliser system with controlled oxygen therapy. Hydrocortisone should be given intravenously and inhaled ipratropium bromide, which may produce useful additional bronchodilatation, may be given also. In severely ill patients, if these measures have failed, or if ipratropium bromide is not available, intravenous aminophylline should then be given, with a full understanding of the risk of theophylline toxicity. Hypoxia, dehydration and hypokalaemia should be corrected. If such measures fail, supportive ventilation should be considered early rather than late. Intravenous β_2-agonists may occasionally be required. Patients should be regularly assessed to see that they are responding to therapy (fig. 10.2).

Bronchodilators in the Recovery Phase of Acute Asthma

Many asthmatics respond rapidly to therapy and because of this doctors may be tempted to discharge them early from hospital. Unfortunately, the patient is well only because of the high dose of β_2-agonist, and other therapy given while in hospital. Early discharge associated with a rapid reduction in therapy frequently leads to recurrence of asthma. The dose of β_2-agonist drug recommended for hospital treatment is 25 times greater than that recommended for therapy at home (2 puffs of aerosol inhaler 4 times a day).

Exchange of Nebulised β-Agonist for Aerosol Therapy

During the recovery phase, the dose of inhaled β_2-agonist should be reduced, aiming to reach the dosage level at which control was previously achieved. Regular assessment of recovery is essential; the patient should be monitored for any signs of relapse, the pulse rate should be frequently checked and PEFR measurements made 4 times a day. Side effects can often be used as an indicator of improvement, and when a patient on 5mg of nebulised salbutamol 4-hourly, or its equivalent, complains of tremor or cramps, the dose may be halved and still produce equivalent bronchodilatation but no systemic side effects. Further reduction of the quantity of inhaled β_2-agonist (usually reducing the frequency from 6 to 4 times a day) should follow before discharge. A different delivery system may be used, effecting a reduction in drug dosage at the same time. The dose of salbutamol by 'Rotahaler' can be up to 4 times (400μg) that in one puff of the aerosol (100μg) and salbutamol 'Rotacaps' 800μg, four to five times a day, may be appropriate therapy before re-introducing the previous aerosol regimen. This treatment, however, is expensive. Alternatively a higher dose of β_2-agonist may be delivered by a 'Nebuhaler' attachment with a terbutaline aerosol, with the patient taking 4 to 8 puffs via the 'Nebuhaler' 4 to 5 times daily.

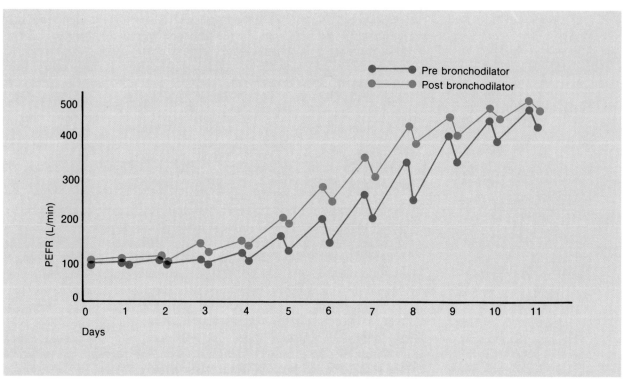

Fig. 10.3. Pattern of peak expiratory flow rate (PEFR) in a patient recovering from severe acute asthma showing the development of morning dips and increased reversibility.

Oral Bronchodilators

Frequently severe nocturnal dips in peak expiratory flow rate develop during the recovery phase (fig. 10.3) and this is associated with an increased risk of death from asthma at night (Hetzel et al., 1977) [chapter VIII]. Oral theophylline may be added to try to diminish the severity of these nocturnal dips in PEFR. For patients already receiving aminophylline, intravenous administration should be changed carefully to oral administration. Blood level estimations should be made with suitable adjustments to dose. A low plasma level of theophylline associated with a stable PEFR in a patient who is well suggests that an increase in theophylline dose is not required. In this situation, theophylline therapy may be stopped.

Oral slow-release β_2-agonists are available but do not seem to be very effective in preventing the nocturnal fall in PEFR and are associated with a significant incidence of side effects. Increasing the evening dose of inhaled nebulised β_2-agonist may reduce the nocturnal dip in PEFR but side effects may occur.

Additional Therapy

Inhaled ipratropium bromide is usually reduced, and may be stopped before discharge as the nebulised dose is high compared with that by pressurised aerosol and few patients regularly use this preparation at home. Oral corticosteroids are usually continued in hospital but are either reduced or stopped after discharge or inhaled corticosteroids reintroduced. If inhaled corticosteroids are used, these should be started a few days before oral therapy is stopped as they may take a few days to achieve their maximal effect.

The high demand for acute hospital beds does not always allow time for full re-establishment of the previous antiasthma drug regimen; but it is important not to discharge patients so abruptly that their therapy may be altered from 20mg of nebulised salbutamol, or its equivalent, to 800µg per day, with similar dramatic falls in the doses of ipratropium bromide, theophylline and corticosteroids.

Discharge from Hospital

While the acute attack of asthma which necessitated hospital admission may have been unavoidable, the factors which might have precipitated this attack should be considered. Was the previous prophylactic regimen adequate and if so, was the treatment being taken? A survey at the author's hospital of patients attending casualty with an attack of asthma, has shown that most did not know what therapy had been prescribed and were frequently taking medication randomly.

It is important that, if possible, a prophylactic regimen should be agreed with the patient before discharge. Each should then be given *written instructions* (see chapter IV). Discharge from hospital is also a good time to check inhaler use, teach patients good inhaler technique and remind them that regular prophylactic therapy will often prevent acute attacks and subsequent hospital admissions.

Patients who have been poorly controlled should, in addition to written instructions concerning drug therapy, always be given a peak flow meter to assess any relapse of their asthma despite regular therapy (chapter IV). An early follow-up appointment should be made.

Further Management

Further management should be carried out in conjunction with the family practitioner. In parts of the United Kingdom, self-referral systems for treatment of acute attacks of asthma have been shown to be very effective (Crompton et al., 1979) whereas in others they have not been associated with an obvious improvement in either morbidity or mortality rates from asthma (Anderson et al., 1980). Self-referral systems seem to be most successful where the patient, family practitioner and hospital doctor work as a team to get the best out of the very effective therapy available for asthma.

References

Anderson, H.R.; Bailey, P. and West, S.: Trends in the hospital care of acute childhood asthma 1970-8: a regional study. British Medical Journal 281: 1191 (1980).

Arnold, A.G.; Lane, D.J. and Zapata, E.: The speed of onset and severity of acute severe asthma. British Journal of Diseases of the Chest 76: 157 (1982).

Arnold, A.G.; Lane, D.J. and Zapata, E.: Acute severe asthma: factors that influence hospital referral by the general practitioner and self referral by the patient. British Journal of Diseases of the Chest 77: 51 (1983a).

Arnold, A.G.; Lane, D.J. and Zapata, E.: Current therapeutic practice in the management of acute severe asthma. British Journal of Diseases of the Chest 77: 123 (1983b).

Bellamy, D. and Collins, J.V.: 'Acute' asthma in adults. Thorax 34: 36 (1979).

Boe, J.; Carlsson, L.G.; Melta, L. and Karlson, B. Ljungholm: Acute asthma - drug intake, plasma levels, and effect of terbutaline i.v. injection. S.E.P. Conference, Edinburgh, September 1983 (to be published).

British Thoracic Association: Death from asthma in two regions of England. British Medical Journal 285: 1251 (1982).

Burdon, J.G.W.; Junifer, E.G.; Killian, K.J.; Hargreave, F.E. and Campbell, E.J.H.: The perception of breathlessness in asthma. American Review of Respiratory Disease 126: 825 (1982).

Cochrane, G.M. and Clark, T.J.H.: A survey of asthma mortality in patients between the ages of 35 and 64 in the Greater London Hospitals in 1971. Thorax 30: 300 (1975).

Cochrane, G.M.; Prior, J.G. and Wolff, C.B.: Chronic stable asthma and the normal arterial pressure of carbon dioxide in hypoxia. British Medical Journal 281: 705 (1980).

Crompton, G.K.; Grant, I.W.B. and Bloomfield, P.: Edinburgh emergency asthma admission service: report on 10 years' experience. British Medical Journal 2: 1199 (1979).

Editorial: Acute severe asthma. Lancet 1: 313 (1981).

Evans, W.V.; Monie, R.D.H.; Crimmins, J. and Seaton, A.: Aminophylline, salbutamol and combined intravenous infusion in acute severe asthma. British Journal of Diseases of the Chest 74: 385 (1980).

Fanta, C.H.; Rossing, T.H. and McFadden, E.R.: Emergency room treatment of asthma. American Journal of Medicine 72: 416 (1982).

Fergusson, R.J.; Carmichael, J.; Rafferty, P.; Willey, R.F.; Crompton, G.K. and Grant, I.W.B.: Nebulised salbutamol in life-threatening asthma; is IPPB necessary? British Journal of Diseases of the Chest 77: 255 (1983).

Fischl, M.A.; Pitchenik, A. and Gardner, L.B.: An index predicting relapse and need for hospitalisation in patients with acute bronchial asthma. New England Journal of Medicine 305: 783 (1981).

Flenley, D.C.: New drugs in respiratory disorders. British Medical Journal 286: 871 (1983).

Grant, I.W.B.: Are corticosteroids necessary in the treatment of severe acute asthma? British Journal of Diseases of the Chest 76: 125 (1982).

Grant, I.W.B.: Asthma in New Zealand. British Medical Journal 286: 374 (1983).

Hendeles, L. and Weinberger, M.M.: Poisoning patients with intravenous theophylline. American Journal of Hospital Pharmacy 37: 49 (1980).

Hetzel, M.R. and Clark, T.J.H.: Comparison of intravenous and aerosol salbutamol. British Medical Journal 2 (6041): 919 (1976).

Hetzel, M.R.; Clark, T.J.H. and Branthwaite, M.H.: Asthma: analysis of sudden deaths and ventilatory arrests in hospital. British Medical Journal 1 (6064): 808 (1977).

Inman, W.H.W. and Adelstein, A.M.: Rise and fall of asthma mortality in England and Wales in relation to use of pressurised aerosols. Lancet 2: 279 (1969).

Jackson, R.T.; Beaglehole, R.; Rea, H.H. and Sutherland, D.C.: Mortality from asthma: a new epidemic in New Zealand. British Medical Journal 285: 771 (1982).

James, P.; Henry, J. and Cochrane, G.M.: Compliance with therapy in patients with chronic airflow obstruction. Thorax 37: 778 (1982).

Jones, E.S.: The recognition and management of acute severe asthma: in A.J. Bellingham (Ed.) Advanced Medicine (vol. 16), p.9 (Pitman Medical, London 1980).

Knowles, G.K. and Clark, T.J.H.: Pulsus paradoxus as a valuable sign indicating severity of asthma. Lancet 2: 1356 (1973).

Lawford, P.; Jones, B.J.M. and Milledge, J.S.: Comparison of intravenous and nebulised salbutamol in initial treatment of severe asthma. British Medical Journal 1 (6105): 84 (1978).

Leahy, B.C.; Gomm, S.A. and Allen, S.C.: Comparison of nebulised salbutamol with nebulised ipratropium bromide in acute asthma. British Journal of Diseases of the Chest 77: 159 (1983).

Lee, D.A.; Winslow, N.R.; Speight, A.W.P. and Hey, E.N.: Prevalence and spectrum of asthma in childhood. British Medical Journal 286: 1256 (1983).

Luksza, A.R.: A new look at adult asthma. British Journal of Diseases of the Chest 76: 11 (1982a).

Luksza, A.R.: Acute severe asthma treated without steroids. British Journal of Diseases of the Chest 76: 15 (1982b).

Macdonald, J.B.; Seaton, A. and Williams, D.A.: Asthma deaths in Cardiff 1963-74: 90 deaths outside hospital. British Medical Journal 1 (6024): 1493 (1976).

Morgan, M.D.L.; Singh, B.V.; Frame, M.H. and Williams, S.J.: Terbutaline aerosol given through pear spacer in acute severe asthma. British Medical Journal 285: 849 (1982).

Nogrady, S.D.; Hartley, J.P.R. and Seaton, A.: Metabolic effects of intravenous salbutamol in the course of acute severe asthma. Thorax 32: 559 (1977).

Palmer, K.N.V. and Flenley, D.C.: Pathophysiology of gas exchange and arterial blood gas and pH in asthma: in Weiss and Segal (Eds) Bronchial Asthma; Mechanisms and Therapeutics, p.317 (Little, Brown and Co., Boston 1976).

Pang, L.M.; Rodriguez, Martinez.; Davis, W.J. and Mellins, R.B.: Terbutaline in the treatment of status asthmaticus. Chest 72: 469 (1977).

Patel, K.R. and Tullett, W.M.: Bronchoconstriction in response to ipratropium bromide. British Medical Journal 286: 1318 (1983).

Rea, H.H. and Sutherland, D.C.: Asthma in New Zealand. New Zealand Medical Journal 96: 312-313 (1983).

Rose, C.C.; Murphy, J.G. and Swartz, J.S.: Performance of an index predicting the response of patients with acute bronchial asthma to intensive emergency department treatment. New England Journal of Medicine 310: 573 (1984).

Rossing, T.J.; Fanta, C.H.; Goldstein, D.M.; Snapper, J.R. and McFadden, E.R. Jnr.: Emergency therapy of asthma: Comparison of acute effects of parenteral and inhaled sympathomimetic and infused aminophylline. American Review of Respiratory Disease 122: 365 (1980).

Rubinfield, A.R. and Pain, M.C.F.: The perception of asthma. Lancet 1: 882 (1976).

Schoeffel, S.E.; Anderson, S.D. and Altounyan, R.E.: Bronchial reactivity in response to inhalation of ultrasonically nebulised solutions of distilled water and saline. British Medical Journal 283: 1285 (1981).

Shenfield, G.M.; Hodson, M.E.; Clarke, S.W. and Paterson, J.W.: Interaction of corticosteroids and catecholamines in the treatment of asthma. Thorax 30: 430 (1975).

Shim, C.S. and Williams, M.H.: Evaluation of the severity of asthma: patient versus physicians. American Journal of Medicine 68: 11 (1980).

Speight, A.W.P.; Lee, D.A. and Hey, E.N.: Underdiagnosis and undertreatment of asthma in childhood. British Medical Journal 286: 1253 (1983).

Spiro, S.G.; Johnson, A.J.; May, C.S. and Paterson, J.W.: Effect of intravenous injection of salbutamol and asthma. British Journal of Clinical Pharmacology 2: 495 (1975).

Stewart, M.F.; Barclay, J. and Warburton, R.: Risk of giving intravenous aminophylline to acutely ill patients receiving maintenance treatment with theophylline. British Medical Journal 288: 450 (1984).

Ward, M.J.; Fentem, P.H.; Roderick Smith, W.H. and Davies, D.: Ipratropium bromide in acute asthma. British Medical Journal 282: 598 (1981).

Webber, B.A.; Collins, J.V. and Branthwaite, M.A.: Severe acute asthma: a comparison of three methods of inhaling salbutamol. British Journal of Diseases of the Chest 76: 69 (1982).

Wilson, J.D.; Sutherland, D.C. and Thomas, A.C.: Has the change to beta-agonists combined with oral theophylline increased cases of fatal asthma? Lancet 1: 1235 (1981).

Woodcock, A.A.; Johnson, M.A. and Geddes, D.M.: Theophylline prescribing, serum concentration and toxicity. Lancet 2: 610 (1983).

Chapter XI

The Role of Bronchodilators in the Management of Chronic Bronchitis and Emphysema

G.M. Cochrane and J.G. Prior

The rationale for the use of bronchodilator drugs in asthma is clear, but their place in the management of chronic obstructive bronchitis and emphysema is less obvious. However, in the United Kingdom bronchodilators are more frequently prescribed for chronic bronchitis and emphysema than for asthma, even though the former conditions are often associated with apparently irreversible airflow obstruction. Perhaps all patients with airflow obstruction have some asthmatic component which can be reversed by bronchodilator therapy. If this is so, should those with chronic obstructive airways disease be treated as though they were asthmatic, without establishing a clear diagnosis? Many physicians would support such an idea but care must be taken for otherwise patients who are not helped by bronchodilators and corticosteroids will be given unnecessary therapy. Furthermore, identification of the major factors contributing to airflow obstruction provides a rational basis for the choice of treatment. Reversibility, once demonstrated, can be remeasured at intervals to assess the success, or otherwise, of that treatment.

Chronic Obstructive Lung Disease

Definitions

Chronic bronchitis is defined clinically as chronic productive cough for three months during two consecutive years, in the absence of any other cause, such as tuberculosis or bronchiectasis. Emphysema is defined anatomically as a disease associated with distension of the alveoli, usually due to dilatation and destruction of the air spaces distal to the terminal bronchiole. These definitions are not particularly helpful in clinical practice and they do not indicate the existence of severe, persistent airflow obstruction. In chronic bronchitis, the airflow obstruction is probably a result of intrinsic airway narrowing and distortion, and in emphysema of the loss of elastic recoil and collapse of the airways (Macklem, 1971). Most patients with chronic obstructive lung disease have both chronic bronchitis and emphysema, although the symptoms of one or other condition may predominate and asthma may also be present (fig. 11.1). In a recent editorial Fletcher and Price (1984) reviewed the usefulness of the definitions of emphysema, chronic bronchitis and asthma.

Pathology

Chronic Bronchitis

Chronic bronchitis is associated with an increase in mucus secretion, hyperplasia of submucosal glands and an increased number of goblet cells within the respiratory mucosa of the airways (Reid, 1961). Although mucous gland hyperplasia is typical of bronchitis, it does not correlate well with the severity of the airflow obstruction. Airways become narrowed and distorted. Initially these

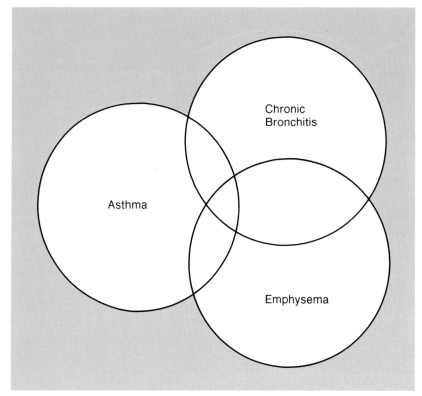

Fig. 11.1. The overlap of clinical types of chronic obstructive lung disease.

changes are seen in the small airways ($< 2mm$ in diameter) [Cosio et al., 1980], but later the larger airways are also affected. The mucociliary escalator functions less efficiently than in normal subjects and the respiratory epithelium can be devoid of cilia.

Emphysema

Emphysema is seen in two major forms; centriacinar and panacinar. Centriacinar emphysema, which occurs almost exclusively in smokers and predominantly in the upper lobes, affects the respiratory bronchiole, leaving the distal alveoli intact. It is frequently associated with chronic bronchitis. Panacinar emphysema is characterised by a more uniform dilatation and destruction of the entire acinus. It is seen in the rare condition of alpha$_1$-antitrypsin deficiency emphysema and as an incidental pathological finding in the elderly. Thurlbeck (1980) has suggested that the loss of elastic recoil in emphysema patients is not a direct effect of emphysema itself but is due to widespread alteration and loss of sclero-protein in the lung, possibly as a reaction to tobacco smoke.

History and Examination

History

The development of chronic obstructive lung disease is slowly progressive and patients seldom present with serious loss of exercise tolerance before the age of 45. However, for many years before presenting with dyspnoea (which is often so severe that normal activity is restricted) many have experienced recurrent acute chest infection, especially in winter. Some patients with chronic obstructive lung disease have increased bronchial hyper-reactivity to histamine and a previous history of childhood asthma (Taylor et al., 1983).

Initially mucoid sputum is produced only in the morning as part of the 'smoker's cough'. The mechanism for early morning sputum production is unclear. The mucociliary escalator may be inhibited by cigarette smoke and in smokers would only function overnight when the excess sputum is transported to the central airways. The first cigarette of the morning stimulates the cough reflex and sputum is expectorated from the central airways. With progression of the disease sputum production increases and is more persistent through the day.

In contrast, patients with predominant emphysema often produce little sputum. They tend to present later in life with a short history of breathlessness, although they have advanced lung disease and gross impairment of respiratory function.

Classically, two comparatively distinctive clinical groups have been described: the 'blue bloaters' and the 'pink puffers'. It is suggested that the pathological changes of chronic obstructive bronchitis occur in the 'blue bloaters', whilst severe emphysema is the predominant finding in 'pink puffers' (Burrows et al., 1966). Although in practice, patients cannot always be conveniently categorised on the basis of pathological findings (Thurlbeck, 1980), some do indeed conform to these clinical descriptions.

'Blue Bloaters'
(Burrows type B)

These tend to be obese individuals who are polycythaemic and cyanosed. Their respiration is characterised by loud breath sounds with audible wheezing and the use of accessory muscles with tracheal tug. Intercostal recession is obvious at rest. During an acute exacerbation *cor pulmonale* frequently develops. In patients with carbon dioxide retention the limbs tend to be warm and there is a wide pulse pressure. Diminished levels of consciousness with muscle flap or twitching are seen in severe cases. Sleep hypoxaemia may be a feature of 'blue bloaters' (Douglas et al., 1979).

'Pink Puffers'
(Burrows type A)

In contrast, 'pink puffers' tend to be thin and anxious looking with gross lung hyperinflation and raised shoulders. Polycythaemia and cyanosis do not occur and the signs of *cor pulmonale* are only evident terminally. Breath sounds are quiet, but the patient exhales against partially closed lips (pursed lip breathing). This pattern of expiration is believed to prevent early closure of the small airways and appears to be a form of positive end-expiratory pressure. There may be little or no evidence of respiratory disturbance at rest, but after the mildest exertion there is severe shortness of breath. Sleep hypoxaemia is unusual (Douglas et al., 1979).

Many patients do not conform to these clinical categories, having some features of each, and these have been described as the Burrows type X.

Investigation of Patients with Chronic Obstructive Lung Disease

Arterial Blood Gases

Arterial hypoxaemia is common in severe chronic bronchitis and emphysema, and is most pronounced in the 'blue bloaters'. Carbon dioxide retention with a compensated chronic respiratory acidosis is common. During an acute infective exacerbation of chronic obstructive bronchitis, the PaO_2 may be further decreased and uncontrolled oxygen therapy may lead to severe carbon dioxide retention and death. Bronchitics are particularly susceptible to respiratory depressants (such as sedatives) during acute infections

Table 11.1. Typical respiratory function tests in patients with asthma and those with smoking-induced chronic airflow obstruction[1]

Diagnosis	PEFR (peak expiratory flow rate)	FEV$_1$ (forced expired volume)	RVC (relaxed vital capacity)	TLC (total lung capacity)	KCO (transfer coefficient for carbon monoxide)
Asthma	Highly variable	Variable	Variable	Increased	Raised/normal
Chronic obstructive bronchitis	Reduced with little diurnal variation	Reduced. Variable over hours or days	Moderately reduced. Variable with therapy	Often normal	Normal
Clinical emphysema	Occasionally surprisingly high. No diurnal variation	Severely reduced with little spontaneous variation over hours	Variable and may change with therapy	Very raised; may be reduced with bronchodilators	Markedly reduced

1 – Patients with 'chronic obstructive bronchitis' and 'emphysema' represent extremes of the clinical spectrum of chronic airways obstruction. Emphysema, small airways disease and hypertrophy of the mucus glands in the large airways are present in most patients in varying degrees. Domiciliary monitoring of PEFR is very useful in assessing response to bronchodilators and steroids in patients with asthma. Airflow obstruction in patients with chronic obstructive bronchitis may reverse with high dose inhaled bronchodilator therapy (even when conventional doses are ineffective) and corticosteroids. Cumulative dose-response curves to inhaled β_2-agonists (measuring FEV$_1$ and RVC as well as PEFR) are a useful guide to the optimal dose of bronchodilator. In patients with emphysema, little change occurs in PEFR or FEV$_1$ following inhaled bronchodilator, although large increases in RVC may be demonstrated. Occasionally, response to bronchodilators in patients with emphysema is indicated by a fall in thoracic gas volume in the absence of changes in spirometry.

and these drugs should be avoided whenever possible. Hypoxaemia is associated with pulmonary vasoconstriction and pulmonary hypertension. 'Pink puffers' maintain near normal partial pressures of arterial oxygen and carbon dioxide, although hypercapnia may occur during acute exacerbations.

Chest X-ray

The chest x-ray of patients with chronic obstructive lung disease may be normal. With the development of *cor pulmonale,* upper lobe vein blood diversion occurs, and the heart size tends to increase. Chest x-rays in patients with emphysema may show (a) hyperinflation with the apex of the right diaphragm below the anterior end of the sixth rib, (b) flattening of the dome appearance of the diaphragm, (c) a long thin heart, and (d) reduced peripheral vascular markings. Lateral chest x-ray shows an enlarged hyperlucent retrosternal air space. Radiographically, emphysema in patients with alpha$_1$-antitrypsin deficiency is greatest in the lower zones while in 'smoker's' emphysema it is predominantly in the upper zones. The chest x-ray may be normal even when severe pathological emphysema is present (Thurlbeck and Simon, 1978).

Respiratory Function

Most patients with chronic obstructive lung disease have combined pathology with intrinsic narrowing of the small airways and distortion of the alveolar spaces with some loss of elastic recoil. There may also be some bronchiolar smooth muscle hypertrophy. Bronchodilator therapy may produce significant reversibility of airflow obstruction. Table 11.1 outlines the typical respiratory function profiles associated with the different clinical conditions. The measurements recorded in asthma are suggestive of changes both in airway calibre and, to a lesser extent, in elastic recoil of lung tissue. In severe emphysema, the very high total lung capacity value and the marked reduction in transfer factor are attributable to loss of elastic recoil of the lung and gross destruction of alveolar and capillary surfaces.

Bronchodilators in Chronic Obstructive Lung Disease

Do They Work?

Although patients with chronic obstructive lung disease experience improvement in symptoms and exercise tolerance with bronchodilators, clinicians are sometimes reluctant to prescribe them. The reason given for withholding bronchodilators is that the airflow obstruction is 'irreversible', as demonstrated by measuring the PEFR before and after the inhalation of 2 puffs from a standard β_2-agonist aerosol. The apparent failure of the bronchodilator could be because a) the dose is inadequate for the severity of the airflow obstruction, b) the reference test is inappropriate to the predominant pathological lesion (see table 11.1), or c) airflow obstruction is indeed irreversible.

Trial of Bronchodilators

Drug Dosage

When the response to bronchodilator drugs in severe chronic lung disease is tested a dose response assessment should be undertaken. Inhaled β-agonists are more suitable for this type of study than the oral methylxanthines as the response can be measured every 10 to 15 minutes and the dose can be increased rapidly without producing unacceptable side effects. Inhaled ipratropium bromide* may also be used but it takes much longer to obtain a significant effect. Barclay and her colleagues demonstrated that a group of chronic obstructive bronchitics were non-responsive to $200\mu g$ of inhaled salbutamol (albuterol), but by gradually increasing the dose a response was obtained in all patients (Barclay et al., 1980). Maximal bronchodilatation was achieved with a very wide dose range of inhaled drug. Similar results were reported by other workers (Prior and Cochrane, 1982).

Lung Function Tests (table 11.1)

As bronchodilator dose is increased improvement in one test of airflow obstruction may occur despite a lack of response in others (Prior and Cochrane, 1982). Therefore, what tests should be used to assess bronchodilators? Except in the situation of clinical research it is unrealistic to measure all variants of airflow obstruction. Drug treatment usually produces an obvious improvement in PEFR in asthmatics but has a less marked effect on PEFR or FEV_1 in patients with chronic bronchitis or emphysema. Relaxed vital capacity (RVC) is often the most useful indicator of bronchodilator response in chronic obstructive lung disease. Patients with predominant loss of elastic recoil may have a reasonably good PEFR despite a very low FEV_1. The explanation appears to be that the PEFR is mainly determined by the sudden flow of gas from the trachea and large airways before the more peripheral airways close and limit gas flow. There is often a good subjective response to bronchodilator therapy even though simple respiratory function testing does not show any improvement. Usually the thoracic gas

---

* For product availability in the USA, see appendix B.

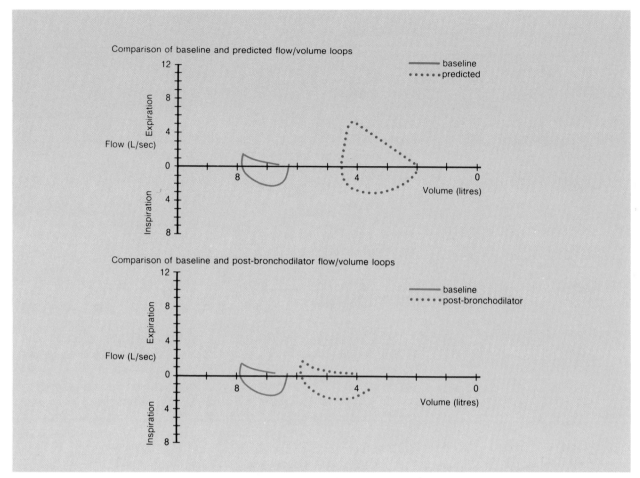

Fig. 11.2. Maximal flow volume loops (MFV) plotted on absolute lung volume measured using a body plethysmograph; taken from a patient with severe obstructive lung disease of the 'pink puffer' type.

The upper tracing shows pre-bronchodilator MFV loop compared with predicted, while the lower trace shows the reduction in lung volume and increase in vital capacity following 800μg of salbutamol administered via a 'Rotahaler'. The PEFR did not change significantly.

volume is greatly increased and the effect of bronchodilatation is to reduce this volume and consequently the work of breathing (which is considerably increased at high lung volumes). In this situation measurement of thoracic gas volume before and after bronchodilator therapy is the most appropriate test (figure 11.2) [Jennings and Cochrane, 1984].

Exercise Testing

The patient's major complaint is the loss of exercise performance, and obviously some test of exercise should be used when assessing the response to treatment. The '12-minute free walking test' has been introduced for this purpose (McGavin et al., 1978). Patients are asked to walk as far as they can in 12 minutes and the distance is measured. Although an objective test, it has a subjective element and it has been considered to best correlate with changes in FVC. Walking for 12 minutes can be too much for the more severely disabled and in this situation a 6 minute test is probably adequate. Alternatively, the patient may time a route he walks regularly before and after treatment to see if therapy confers benefit.

Table 11.2. Possible actions of bronchodilator drugs in patients with chronic obstructive lung disease

Action	Selective β_2-agonists	Methylxanthines	Anticholinergics
Bronchodilatation	Yes	Yes	Yes
Increased mucociliary clearance	Yes	?	No, but no ill effects with ipratropium bromide
Reduced pulmonary hypertension	Yes (not via inhaled route)	Yes	No
Reduced diaphragmatic fatigue	?	Yes	No
Mast cell stabilising action	Yes	Yes	?

Assessment of Dyspnoea

Occasionally, the patient claims benefit from therapy when objective tests show no improvement. Visual analogue scales may be useful to document any improvement in breathlessness following treatment. Diary cards (on which symptoms such as cough and wheeze are recorded using a simple numerical scoring system) help the clinician to assess any subjective benefit from bronchodilator drugs. A large symptomatic improvement in the absence of a definite objective response justifies continuation of therapy.

Bronchodilator Therapy

Advantages and Disadvantages of the Available Drugs

The bronchodilator drugs used in chronic bronchitis and emphysema are the same as those whose use in asthma is described in earlier chapters. In addition to their bronchodilator action other effects of these drugs may be of benefit in the chronic airways diseases (table 11.2). The clinical pharmacology of the bronchodilator drugs is described in chapter II .

β-Agonists

When administered in low doses by inhalation the β-agonists are comparatively poor bronchodilators in chronic bronchitis but in higher inhaled doses (Barclay et al., 1980; Connellan and Wilson, 1978) they may be more effective. Oral therapy is associated with a high incidence of muscle tremor but patients are frequently prepared to tolerate these side effects because of the increased exercise performance obtained. Selective β_2-agonists, e.g. terbutaline, increase mucociliary clearance rates in obstructive lung disease (Santa Cruz, 1974). Although there is a little evidence to suggest that reducing the volume of sputum within the airway decreases airways resistance (Cochrane et al., 1977) the action of β-agonists in increasing sputum clearance is a theoretical rather than a clinical benefit.

Cor pulmonale is a form of right-sided heart failure which develops as a consequence of an elevated pulmonary artery pressure. The effect of chronic hypoxia on the pulmonary vasculature is a progressive increase in pulmonary artery pressure but this mechanism alone does not account for the development of *cor pulmonale* and studies of right heart failure associated with chronic obstructive pulmonary disease suggest that at least part of the oedema is due to fluid accumulation (Finlay et al., 1983). However, there is still a clear correlation between survival and the magnitude of the rise in pulmonary artery pressure (Wietzenblum et al., 1981) – the higher the pulmonary artery pressure, the shorter the survival, although this may be improved by using long term oxygen therapy (Howard, 1983).

Selective β_2-agonists such as salbutamol may modify cardiovascular haemodynamics. When given intravenously to patients with chronic bronchitis, salbutamol improved cardiac output and produced a small fall in pulmonary vascular resistance (Iodice et al., 1980). Intravenous terbutaline has been reported to have an even greater effect in reducing pulmonary vascular resistance, but a direct comparison of the two drugs has not been conducted. In short term studies in patients with chronic obstructive lung disease, pirbuterol, a recently introduced β_2-agonist, reduced pulmonary vascular resistance and increased cardiac output without a significant fall in arterial oxygen tension (Peacock et al., 1983; MacNee et al., 1983); oral salbutamol had similar effects (Winter et al., 1984). However, until further long term studies with systemic β_2-agonists confirm their beneficial effect on pulmonary vascular resistance, these drugs should preferably be administered by inhalation.

Anticholinergic Drugs

The vagal component of bronchoconstriction appears to be more prominent with increasing age and airflow obstruction (Ullah et al., 1981). The side effects of systemic anticholinergic drugs are unacceptable but ipratropium bromide, an atropine derivative (appendix A, fig. 6), is a potent anticholinergic inhibitor of vagal bronchoconstriction (see p.32). Given by inhalation, ipratropium bromide is an effective bronchodilator, especially in patients with chronic airflow obstruction (Douglas et al., 1979). Ipratropium bromide has no inhibitory effect on mucociliary clearance (Rebuck et al., 1982) and side effects are rare although many patients find the bitter taste unpleasant. Maximal bronchodilatation may be delayed for up to 2 hours, a factor frequently overlooked when assessing bronchodilator response. The standard inhaled dose of 40μg four times a day may be inadequate in chronic airflow obstruction and patients may need up to 6 puffs (120μg) at each inhalation to achieve adequate bronchodilatation (Gomm et al., 1983). The possibility of an additive or synergistic effect between anticholinergic agents, β_2-agonists and methylxanthines is discussed elsewhere (see p.89).

Methylxanthines

It is difficult to conduct acute bronchodilatation studies with oral methylxanthines because of the need to establish therapeutic blood levels (see p.39). There are surprisingly few studies of the efficacy of the methylxanthines in chronic bronchitis, although it has been shown that they may produce additional bronchodilatation to that of salbutamol (provided salbutamol alone has had some effect) [Barclay et al., 1981] but one long term study has shown them to be effective in improving the exercise tolerance of chronic bronchitics (Leitch et al., 1981). A further action of theophylline is that it may improve the mechanical performance of the diaphragm, but this has yet to be confirmed or proven to have any therapeutic value in chronic obstructive bronchitis.

In patients with chronic bronchitis and emphysema theophylline metabolism may be modified by factors such as age, cigarette smoking, cardiac failure, acute bacterial infections, and use of drugs such as cimetidine and erythromycin (see p.34). A more complete catalogue of contraindications to the use of methylxanthines is difficult to imagine. It is possible that methylxanthines might reduce pulmonary hypertension and increase cardiac output but any potential benefit may be outweighed by the risk of cardiac arrhythmias and falls in arterial oxygen tensions due to altered ventilation perfusion ratios. For these reasons, the use of methylxanthines in chronic obstructive lung disease requires careful monitoring of theophylline plasma levels (Editorial, 1983) and appreciation of the dangers by both patients and physician (Mountain and Neff, 1984).

Treatment of Patients with Chronic Obstructive Bronchitis and Emphysema

Frequently, the reaction of the physician to the patient with chronic obstructive bronchitis is 'Well, he smoked himself to this' or 'There is nothing I can do to help'; although the former may well be correct, the latter is not necessarily true (figure 11.3).

Bronchodilators

The aim of bronchodilator therapy in patients with chronic bronchitis and emphysema is to treat any airflow obstruction which is reversible. The advantages of the inhaled route over oral administration have already been considered. Inhaled β_2-agonists are first-line therapy; the maximally effective dose should be determined and administered regularly every 4 to 6 hours. Frequently, because inhaler technique is poor, or a large number of puffs are necessary to administer the required dose a pressurised inhaler is unsatisfactory. Other inhaler devices such as the 'Rotahaler', 'Nebuhaler', or a nebuliser may be tried (see appendix C). An objective assessment of response to long term therapy should be made using symptom scores, spirometry and exercise testing. The addition of ipratropium bromide (80 to 120μg i.e. 4 to 6 puffs, every 6 hours) [Gomm et al., 1983; Flenley, 1983] may confer additional benefit and should be given a trial.

When patients are unable to use pressurised aerosol inhalers or other inhalation devices, oral β_2-agonists or methylxanthines should be tried. When methylxanthines are used the dosage must be adjusted to maintain theophylline plasma concentrations within the 10 to 20 mg/L range. Assessment of response to therapy should be made as described above.

Combinations of Bronchodilator drugs

When small responses to individual drugs occur, combination therapy may provide additive benefit. Inhaled β_2-agonists and ipratropium bromide may be prescribed together; 'Duovent' is an aerosol preparation containing both ipratropium bromide and fenoterol. Such a combination may be of value in patients whose airflow obstruction responds to both β-agonists and atropinic agents but whose drug compliance is poor. Alternate 2-hourly inhalations of β-agonists and ipratropium bromide may also be useful. Combinations of bronchodilator drugs are considered in detail in chapter V.

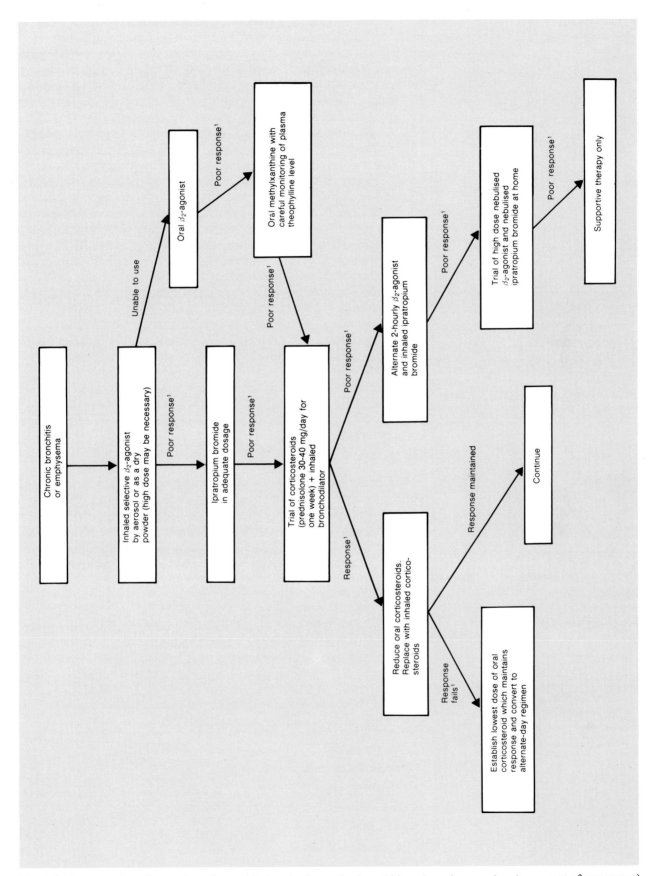

Fig. 11.3. An approach to therapy in patients with chronic obstructive bronchitis and emphysema. 1 = Assessment of response: a) appropriate objective lung function test; b) symptoms scores; c) exercise test.

Trial of Corticosteroids

The rationale for a trial of corticosteroids following failure of bronchodilator therapy is that a few patients may respond to steroid therapy and others may have asthma which has not been diagnosed – if asthma is present it is quickly detected by a corticosteroid trial, but if there is no response the drug should be stopped. By using a short trial of oral prednisolone inappropriate long term therapy and the potential side effects are avoided.

Corticosteroid trials have recently been reviewed (Cochrane, 1983). The majority of patients who have a significant response to steroids will respond to a week's treatment with prednisolone 30 to 40mg daily (Webb et al., 1981). Refractory patients occasionally respond to higher doses but the response is often not maintained when the dose is reduced to realistic levels. The corticosteroid regimen described above can be stopped abruptly with only minimal disturbance in adrenal function (Webb and Clark, 1981) which lasts less than 72 hours. During the corticosteroid trial bronchodilator therapy should be continued.

Assessment of response should include symptom scoring, regular spirometry (together with RVC) and exercise testing. Even when there is a good response to oral corticosteroids it is advisable to substitute inhaled therapy, e.g. beclomethasone dipropionate. In those with previously severe airflow obstruction higher doses of inhaled corticosteroids are usually recommended (steroid responders are treated in a similar way to asthmatics). Very rarely a patient who obtained benefit from systemic treatment fails to respond to inhaled corticosteroid therapy and needs regular oral corticosteroids.

Corticosteroids are of least value in emphysema.

High Dose Inhaled Bronchodilators at Home

Occasionally, patients whose airflow obstruction responds poorly to high dose bronchodilator therapy delivered by pressurised aerosol or 'Rotahaler' achieve considerable benefit from nebulised drugs (e.g. salbutamol 5mg, ipratropium bromide 500μg). An objective trial of domiciliary nebulised bronchodilator (employing jet nebulisers driven by air compressors – see appendix C) is always justifiable before airflow obstruction is said to be 'irreversible'.

Supportive Therapy

The treatment of chronic obstructive bronchitis and emphysema is not limited solely to bronchodilator drugs and corticosteroids, and additional supportive therapy is required (table 11.3).

Table 11.3. Supportive measures for patients with chronic obstructive bronchitis and emphysema

1. Stopping smoking

2. Exercise and breathing programmes

3. Diuretics and digoxin

4. Oxygen therapy

5. Venesection if haematocrit > 50%

6. Anti-breathless drugs

7. Psychotherapy and antidepressants

Health Education and Advice on Stopping Smoking

The rate of decline of FEV_1 in patients with chronic bronchitis or emphysema who smoke is approximately twice that of non-smokers. On stopping smoking this rapid rate of decline is dramatically reduced and further deterioration in FEV_1 is little different from that of a non-smoker. Despite the obvious incentives for stopping smoking many find this difficult. Enthusiastic general practitioners can be as effective as anti-smoking groups in helping patients to stop. High dose 'Nicorette' chewing gum has been shown to be effective in stopping some patients from smoking but as the slow absorption from the buccal mucosa of the nicotine in the gum does not duplicate the smoker's 'high' which is caused by the rapid absorption of inhaled nicotine from cigarettes this therapy is not often successful.

Rehabilitation

There is increasing interest in the use of programmed training exercises in patients with respiratory impairment and the initial results suggest that it is possible to improve exercise performance. However, the improvement in exercise appears to be related more to improved voluntary muscle training than to improvement in respiratory performance itself. Breathing exercise programmes have been tried for many years, but there is disagreement about their efficacy. Those with gross hyperinflation may be helped by altering their pattern of respiration and using abdominal muscles in support of accessory respiratory muscles. All patients should be encouraged to take regular exercise.

Diuretics and Digoxin in Cor Pulmonale

As has been stated, *cor pulmonale* is a form of right-sided heart failure associated with the pulmonary hypertension of chronic hypoxaemia. However, cardiac index may be normal, or even high, even in the presence of gross peripheral oedema. In chronic hypoxaemia and hypercarbia plasma aldosterone concentrations may be increased, and this may account for the gross oedema in the absence of right heart failure (Brown et al., 1970). Although loop diuretics, such as frusemide and bumetanide are usually considered first-line therapy, the addition of spironolactone, especially during an episode of acute-on-chronic respiratory failure, may be particularly effective. Arguments continue over the role of digoxin but it is usually indicated when rapid atrial fibrillation is present. The most logical supportive therapy for patients with *cor pulmonale* is to alleviate the hypoxia which is the primary cause.

Oxygen Therapy

Domiciliary oxygen, administered at a low flow rate of 1 to 3 L/min via nasal prongs for at least 15 hours a day (and preferably for 24 hours), improves survival in severe chronic obstructive bronchitis and emphysema (Nocturnal Oxygen Therapy Trial Group, 1980; Medical Research Council Working Party, 1981). These studies indicate that all patients with a PaO_2 of 50mm Hg (6.6pKa) or less breathing air, should receive continuous oxygen therapy (Flenley, 1981). Obviously, other considerations such as age, social circumstances and current smoking habits must be taken into account. The introduction of oxygen concentrators (a machine converting room air into a stream of 90% oxygen) allows oxygen therapy to be given in a relatively economical fashion. Patients need careful education in the use of these machines and follow-up is required to ensure maximum therapeutic benefit.

Respiratory stimulant drugs such as nikethamide and doxapram have not been successful in improving arterial oxygen tension, except in acute exacerbations of chronic respiratory failure. A recent report from France (Arnaud, 1982) has suggested that long term oral almitrine bismesylate is a safe and effective way of increasing arterial oxygen and reducing carbon dioxide tensions in hypoxic *cor pulmonale*. Short term trials in the United Kingdom support the effectiveness of almitrine.

For many years patients have persuaded their family practitioners to provide domiciliary oxygen for use as a short burst before and after exertion. Some hospital clinicians have considered this practice dangerous (especially in 'blue bloaters') and as having no therapeutic value. Woodcock and his colleagues have shown that pre-exercise oxygenation can increase exercise performance, especially in 'pink puffers' (Woodcock et al., 1981). Prudence is required in using oxygen therapy – it is essential to establish which patient will benefit from long term, low flow oxygen and which from short pre-exercise use. The former may require an oxygen concentrator, the latter, oxygen supplied from cylinders.

Venesection

Chronically hypoxic patients with *cor pulmonale* often, but not invariably, develop polycythaemia. Although polycythaemia will result in improved oxygen transport to tissues, an excessive increase in the haematocrit adversely affects the circulation. In this situation, reduction of the haematocrit is associated with a fall in pulmonary vascular resistance and, occasionally, in pulmonary artery pressure, together with improvement in mental state and exercise tolerance. There are usually no effects on static or dynamic lung volumes. Although PaO_2 may improve one hour after venesection, there is rarely any long term change in PaO_2, $PaCO_2$ or pH. The aim should be to keep packed cell volume at, or just below 50% (Harrison and Stokes, 1982).

Anti-breathless Agents for 'Pink Puffers'

Severe breathlessness is a common complaint in 'pink puffers'. The mechanism for this apparent excessive dyspnoea is not fully understood, but the following have been proposed: (a) excess catecholamine levels due to impaired removal from the lung, (b) excessive stretch receptor and muscle spindle activity and (c) breathing at high static lung volumes. Although β-adrenoceptor blocking drugs and benzodiazepines are generally considered to be contraindicated in chronic airflow obstruction, they have been used therapeutically in a few patients with severe 'clinical emphysema' with apparent success – some claim an improved quality of life (Mitchell-Heggs et al., 1980). Dihydrocodeine has also been shown to reduce breathlessness and increase exercise tolerance in 'pink puffers' (Johnson et al., 1983). Such treatment should be considered only in patients without oedema, whose arterial $PaCO_2$ is less than 40mm Hg (5.6pKa), and who are very severely incapacitated by breathlessness.

Psychotherapy and Antidepressants

A positive approach (including the treatment of depression which is often present) can improve exercise tolerance and decrease distress in patients with chronic obstructive lung disease. Occasionally, the vagal side effects of tricyclic antidepressant compounds may cause bronchodilatation, but an improvement of mood is more important.

In Summary

All patients with chronic bronchitis and emphysema should be given a trial of bronchodilators. A β_2-agonist, by inhalation, is likely to be most effective and best tolerated, especially as these patients frequently need higher doses of bronchodilators than asthmatics. Some patients respond well to vagal blocking agents, and occasionally, corticosteroids are of benefit. However, additional therapy such as diuretics, venesection, domiciliary oxygen and drugs to relieve the sensation of breathlessness may be appropriate. Exercise should be encouraged and every effort should be made to persuade patients to stop smoking; an accusatory stance however is never justified.

References

Arnaud, F.: Almitrine bismesylate in long term treatment of patients with chronic bronchitis. Bulletin European de Physiopathologie Respiratoire 18 (Suppl 4): 737 (1982).

Barclay, J.; Whiting, B. and Addis, G.J.: Salbutamol – theophylline interaction: Results of adding maximal effective doses of theophylline to the maximal effects obtainable from salbutamol in chronic bronchitis. Clinical Science 59: 13 (1980).

Barclay, J.; Whiting, B.; Meredith, P.A. and Addis, J.G.: Theophylline – salbutamol interactions: Bronchodilator response to salbutamol at maximally effective plasma theophylline concentrations. British Journal of Clinical Pharmacology 11: 203 (1981).

Brown, J.; Davies, D.L.; Johnson, V.W.; Lever, A.F. and Robertson, J.I.S.: Renin relationships in congestive cardiac failure treated and untreated. American Heart Journal 80: 329 (1970).

Burrows, B.; Fletcher, C.M.; Heard, B.E.; Jones, N.L. and Wootliffe, J.S.: The emphysematous and bronchial types of chronic airways obstruction. Lancet 1: 930 (1966).

Cochrane, G.M.: Systemic steroids in asthma; in Clark, T.J.H. (Ed.): Steroids in Asthma; pp. 103-120 (ADIS Press, Auckland 1983).

Cochrane, G.M.; Webber, B.A. and Clarke, S.W.: Effects of sputum on pulmonary function. British Medical Journal 2: 1181 (1977).

Connellan, S.J.B. and Wilson, R.S.E.: Nebulised salbutamol in adult asthma. Lancet 1: 662 (1978).

Cosio, M.G.; Hale, K.A. and Niewoehner, D.E.: Morphologic and morphometric effects of prolonged cigarette smoking on the small airways. American Review of Respiratory Disease 122: 265 (1980).

Douglas, N.J.; Calverley, P.M.A.; Leggett, R.J.E.; Brash, H.M.; Flenley, D.C. and Brezinova, V.: Transient hypoxaemia during sleep in chronic bronchitis and emphysema. Lancet 1: 1 (1979).

Douglas, N.J.; Davidson, I.; Sudlow, M.F. and Flenley, D.C.: Bronchodilation and the site of airway resistance in severe chronic bronchitis. Thorax 34: 51 (1979).

Editorial: Theophylline: Benefits and difficulties. Lancet 2: 607 (1983).

Finlay, M.; Middleton, H.C.; Peake, M.B. and Howard, P.: Cardiac output, pulmonary hypertension, hypoxaemia and survival in patients with chronic obstructive airways disease. European Journal of Respiratory Diseases 64: 252 (1983).

Flenley, D.C.: Oxygen therapy. Pharmaceutical Journal 227: 741 (1981).

Flenley, D.C.: New drugs in respiratory disorders. British Medical Journal 286: 871 (1983).

Fletcher, C.M. and Pride, N.B.: Definitions of emphysema, chronic bronchitis, asthma and airflow obstruction: 25 years on from the Ciba symposium. Thorax 39: 81 (1984).

Gomm, S.; Keaney, M.P.; Hunt, L.P.; Allen, S.C. and Stretton, T.B.: Dose response comparison of ipratropium bromide from metered dose inhaler and by jet nebulisation. Thorax 38: 297 (1983).

Harrison, B.D.W. and Stokes, T.C.: Secondary polycythaemia, its causes, effects and treatment. British Journal of Diseases of the Chest 76: 313 (1982).

Howard, P.: Drugs or oxygen for hypoxic cor pulmonale? British Medical Journal 287: 1159 (1983).

Iodice, F.; Rufolo, L.; Piscione, F. and De Michele, G.: Haemodynamic and ventilatory effects of intravenous salbutamol in patients affected by COLD. Respiration 40: 272 (1980).

Jennings, S. and Cochrane, G.M.: Respiratory function reporting. Chest: In Press (1984).

Johnson, M.A.; Woodcock, A.A. and Geddes, D.M.: Dihydrocodeine for breathlessness in pink puffers. British Medical Journal 286: 675 (1983).

Leitch, A.G.; Morgan, A.; Ellis, D.A.; Bell, G.; Haslett, C. and McHardy, G.J.R.: Effect of oral salbutamol and slow-release aminophylline on exercise tolerance in chronic bronchitis. Thorax 36: 787 (1981).

Macklem, P.T.: Airway obstruction and collateral ventilation. Physiological Review 51: 368 (1971).

MacNee, W.; Walten, C.G.; Hannan, W.J.; Flenley, D.C. and Muir, A.L.: Effects of pirbuterol and sodium nitroprusside on pulmonary haemodynamics in hypoxic cor pulmonale. British Medical Journal 287: 1169 (1983).

McGavin, C.R.; Artvinli, M.; Naoe, M. and McHardy, G.J.R.: Dyspnoea disability and distance walked: Comparison of estimates of exercise performance in respiratory disease. British Medical Journal 2: 241 (1978).

Medical Research Council Working Party: Long term domiciliary oxygen therapy in chronic hypoxic cor pulmonale complicating chronic bronchitis and emphysema: A clinical trial. Lancet 1: 681 (1981).

Mitchell-Heggs, P.; Murphy, K.; Minty, K.; Guz, A.; Patterson, S.E.; Minty, P.S.B. and Rosser, R.M.: Diazepam in the treatment of dyspnoea in the 'pink puffer' syndrome. Quarterly Journal of Medicine 49: 9 (1980).

Mountain, R.D. and Neff, T.A.: Oral theophylline intoxications. A serious error of patient and physician understanding. Archives of International Medicine 144: 724 (1984).

Nocturnal Oxygen Therapy Trial Group: Continuous or nocturnal oxygen therapy in hypoxaemic chronic obstructive lung disease: A clinical trial. Annals of Internal Medicine 93: 391 (1980).

Peacock, A.; Busst, C.; Dawkins, K. and Denison, D.M.: Response of pulmonary circulation to oral pirbuterol in chronic airflow obstruction. British Medical Journal 287: 1178 (1983).

Prior, J.G. and Cochrane, G.M.: Assessment of optimum dose of inhaled terbutaline in patients with chronic asthma: The use of simple cumulative dose-response curves. British Journal Diseases of the Chest 72: 266 (1982).

Rebuck, A.S.; Chapman, K.R. and Braude, A.C.: Anticholinergic therapy of asthma. Chest 82: 555 (1982).

Reid, L.: The pathology of chronic bronchitis. British Journal of Clinical Practice 15: 409 (1961).

Santa Cruz, R.; Landa, J.; Hirsch, J. and Sackner, M.A.: Tracheal mucous velocity in normal man and patients with obstructive lung disease; effects of terbutaline. American Review of Respiratory Disease 109: 458 (1974).

Taylor, R.G.; Gross, E.; Joyce, H.; Holland, F. and Pride, N.B.: Bronchial reactivity and rate of decline in FEV_1 in smokers and ex-smokers. Thorax 38: 710 (1983).

Thurlbeck, W.M.: Smoking, airflow limitation and the pulmonary circulation. American Review of Respiratory Disease 122: 183 (1980).

Thurlbeck, W.M. and Simon, G.: Radiographic appearances of the chest in emphysema. American Journal of Roentgenology 130: 429 (1978).

Webb, J. and Clark, T.J.H.: Recovery of plasma corticotrophin and cortisol levels after a three week course of prednisolone. Thorax 36: 22 (1981).

Webb, J.; Clark, T.J.H. and Chilvers, C.: Time course response to obstruction. Thorax 36: 18 (1981).

Wietzenblum, E.; Hirth, C.; Duculone, A.; Mirham, R.; Rasaholinjarsahary, J. and Ehrhart, M.: Prognostic value of pulmonary artery pressure in chronic obstructive pulmonary disease. Thorax 36: 752 (1981).

Winter, R.J.D.; Langford, J.A. and Rudd, R.M.: Effects of oral and inhaled salbutamol and oral pirbuterol on right and left ventricular function in chronic bronchitis. British Medical Journal 288: 824 (1984).

Woodcock, A.A.; Gross, E.R. and Geddes, D.M.: Oxygen relieves breathlessness in 'pink puffers'. Lancet 2: 907 (1981).

Ullah, M.I.; Newman, G.B. and Saunders, A.B.: Influence of age on response to ipratropium and salbutamol in asthma. Thorax 36: 523 (1981).

Appendix A

Structure-Activity Relationship of Bronchodilator Drugs

J.G. Prior

Three classes of bronchodilator drugs are used in the management of patients with airflow limitation: the sympathomimetic agents, the methylxanthines and the atropine-like agents. The calcium channel blockers, such as verapamil, and α-adrenoceptor blocking agents, such as phenoxybenzamine, although of considerable research interest, do not at present have a defined role in the management of airflow limitation and are not considered here further. Sodium cromoglycate (cromolyn sodium) has not been convincingly shown to have bronchodilator activity and is not described in this section. The pharmacology of the bronchodilator drugs is discussed in detail in chapter II.

Sympathomimetic Agents

Although the usefulness of ephedrine (the active principle from an extract of the plant *ma huang*) has been known to Chinese physicians for over 5000 years, sympathomimetic drugs have been used in the Western world only since the end of the nineteenth century. This section considers the chemistry of the sympathomimetic drugs and the alterations to molecular configurations which result in β_2-adrenoceptor specificity, increased duration of action, and activity by the oral route.

β-Phenylethylamine – the Parent Compound

β-Phenylethylamine is the parent compound of the sympathomimetic drugs (fig. 1). It consists of a benzene ring, conjugated to the aliphatic compound ethylamine. Substitutions may be made, on the benzene ring, the α and β carbon atoms and the terminal amino group, to produce a wide range of chemicals with sympathomimetic activity (figs 2 and 3). The catecholamines (so-called because they have a common O-dihydroxybenzene nucleus, known as catechol) comprise agents such as adrenaline (epinephrine), isoprenaline (isoproterenol), isoetharine and rimiterol*. The resorcinols (orciprenaline [metaproterenol], fenoterol and terbutaline) all have the resorcinol aromatic nucleus. Salbutamol is a saligenin and has a hydroxymethyl substitution on the aromatic nucleus of carbon atom 3. Pirbuterol is a recently introduced synthetic sympathomimetic drug.

---

* For product availability in the USA, see appendix B.

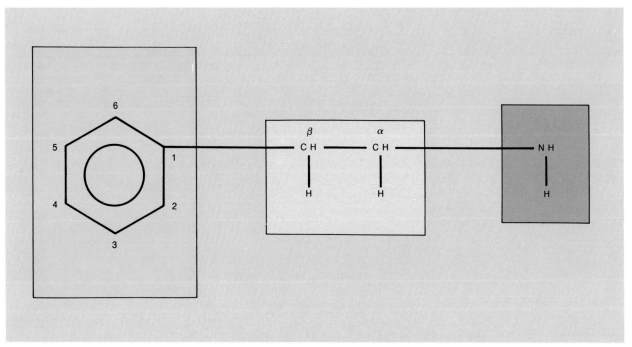

Fig. 1. β-Phenylethylamine–parent compound of the sympathomimetic agents. Substitutions may be made on the benzene ring (blue), α or β carbon atoms (cream), or the terminal amino group (brown). The carbon atoms of the benzene ring are numbered 1 to 6.

Metabolism of Sympathomimetic Agents

Catecholamines are metabolised principally by catechol-*O*-methyl transferase (COMT) and monoamine oxidase (MAO) [see p.23]. Absence of one or both of the hydroxyl groups on the benzene ring prevents the action of COMT, and substitution on the α atom prevents metabolism by MAO.

Non-selective Sympathomimetic Agents

Adrenaline has α_1-, β_1- and β_2-adrenoceptor activities. It is not effective when given orally because of extensive metabolism by MAO in the gastrointestinal tract. The drug has a short duration of action, because of rapid inactivation by COMT and MAO. Isoprenaline is similar to adrenaline but differs by possession of an isopropyl group on the terminal amine nucleus. This eliminates α-adrenoceptor activity. Since isoprenaline has both β_1 and β_2 activities, undesirable effects on the cardiovascular system may occur. Isoprenaline is metabolised within the gut and is irregularly absorbed when given orally or by the sublingual route; when given as a metered dose inhalation, it produces bronchodilatation with rapid onset, but short duration (about 2 hours) of action. However, the non-selective β-agonists have now been replaced in everyday practice by the selective β_2-agonist drugs.

Selective β_2-Sympathomimetic Agents

Modifications of the phenylethylamine nucleus have helped to increase (a) β_2-specificity; (b) duration of action (by decreasing metabolism), and (c) oral efficacy (fig. 3). Several drugs, including fenoterol, pirbuterol, reproterol, rimiterol, salbutamol and terbutaline have predominantly β_2 activities. They may be considered as modifications of the isoprenaline molecule.

Alteration of the hydroxyl groups on the benzene ring (e.g.

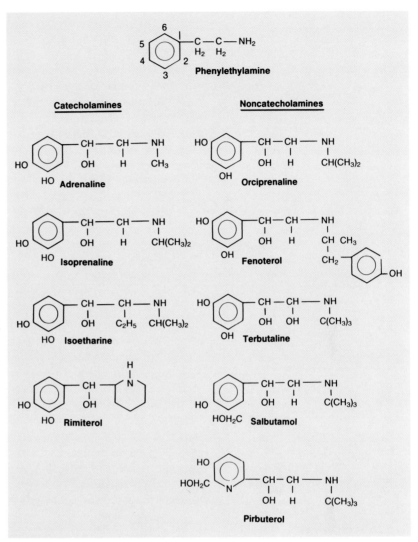

Fig. 2. Sympathomimetic agents used in the management of airflow limitation.

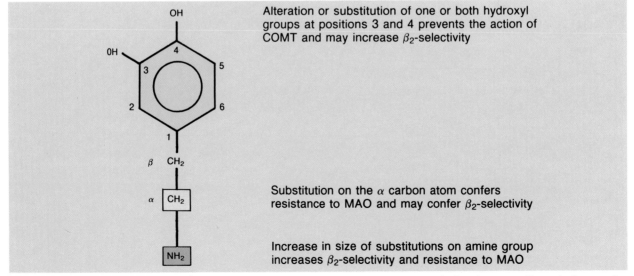

Fig. 3. Effects of substitutions on the benzene ring (blue), α carbon atom (cream) and terminal amino group (brown) of sympathomimetic agents.

orciprenaline, terbutaline and fenoterol) prevents the action of COMT and may increase β_2-specificity. Substitution at position 3 in the benzene ring (e.g. salbutamol) also prevents the action of COMT. Increasing the size of the substitutions on the amine group confers resistance to MAO and enhances β_2-selectivity. Substitution on the α carbon atom (e.g. as in isoetharine) has a similar effect. Such alterations which confer resistance to MAO and COMT greatly enhance the oral efficacy of these drugs and increase their duration of action. Isoetharine is effective when given by inhalation or by the oral route but it has a short duration of action. Rimiterol is inactive orally, as it is metabolised by MAO and COMT. Given by inhalation, it has a short duration of action, although it was shown to be more β_2-selective than salbutamol, when given in equipotent doses by intermittent positive pressure breathing (Cooke et al., 1974). Orciprenaline, being resistant to both COMT and MAO, is orally active, and has comparable activity to salbutamol and terbutaline, although it may cause a greater rise in heart rate. By inhalation, the bronchodilator effect is similar to that of isoprenaline, although of longer duration.

Salbutamol and terbutaline are the most frequently prescribed selective β_2-agonists. Both have a tertiary butyl substituent on the terminal amine group. They are orally active and may also be administered by inhalation or parenterally. Other selective β_2-agonists include fenoterol, reproterol and pirbuterol. Fenoterol and reproterol are administered by inhalation and are claimed to produce slightly more prolonged bronchodilatation than salbutamol. They may be given 8-hourly, although the longer duration of effect with fenoterol is achieved by delivering a relatively high dose, increasing the risk of side effects (Anderson et al., 1979). In practice, however, there is little to choose between the selective β_2'-agonists as they are all effective bronchodilator agents.

Methylxanthines

Caffeine, theophylline and theobromine are 3 closely related alkaloids occurring in plants throughout the world. They are all members of the methylxanthine group of compounds. The basic xanthine structure, derived from uric acid, is shown in figure 4.

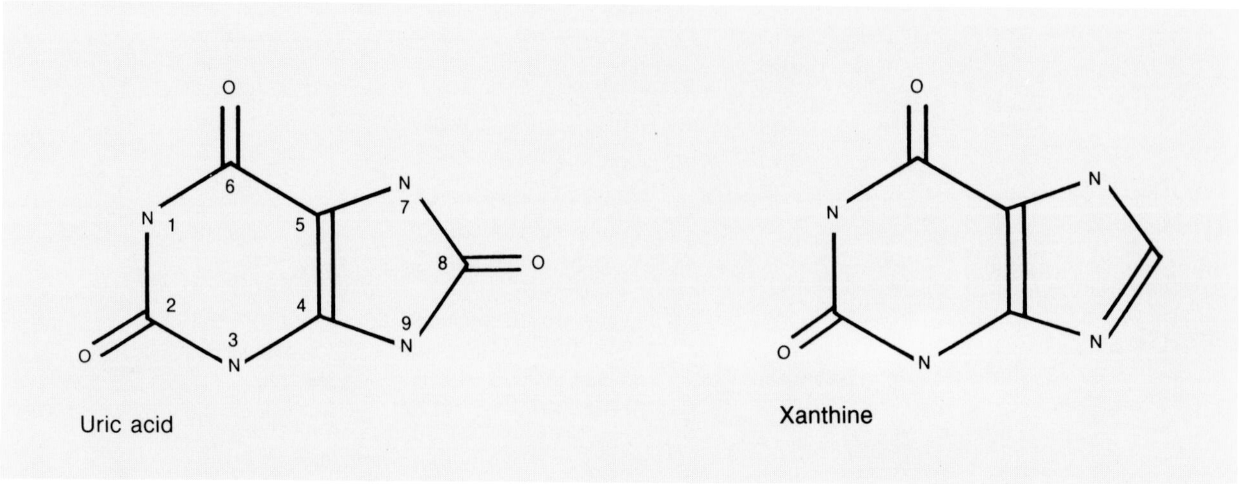

Uric acid   Xanthine

Fig. 4. Xanthine and its relationship to uric acid.

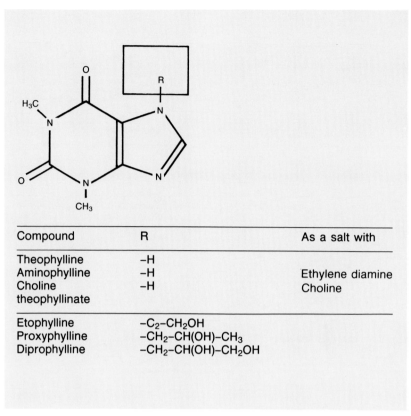

Compound	R	As a salt with
Theophylline	–H	
Aminophylline	–H	Ethylene diamine
Choline theophyllinate	–H	Choline
Etophylline	–C$_2$–CH$_2$OH	
Proxyphylline	–CH$_2$–CH(OH)–CH$_3$	
Diprophylline	–CH$_2$–CH(OH)–CH$_2$OH	

Fig. 5. Methylxanthine derivatives. The parent compound, theophylline, is 1,3-dimethylxanthine. Substitutions may be made at position 7 (R). When -R is -H, the compound is theophylline, which may be conjugated with ethylene diamine or choline. Etophylline, proxyphylline and diprophylline are all derivatives of theophylline, little used today.

The structure is characterised by a heterocyclic 6-membered ring and a heterocyclic 5-membered ring. Substitution is possible on 3 of the 4 nitrogen atoms, thus, caffeine is 1,3,7-trimethylxanthine, theobromine is 3,7-dimethylxanthine, and theophylline is 1,3-dimethylxanthine. In the 1940s it became popular to develop theophyllines substituted at the 7-nitrogen position (with better solubility than that of theophylline), such as diprophylline (dyphylline), etophylline and proxyphylline. Theophylline salts (for example aminophylline, choline theophyllinate, or oxytriphylline), all of which are converted to the theophylline *in vivo,* were synthesised in order to increase the solubility of theophylline, and to decrease its gastrointestinal toxicity. Figure 5 shows some of these compounds.

Enprophylline (3-propylxanthine) is a non-methylated xanthine bronchodilator which is presently undergoing clinical trial.

Atropine and Atropine-like Agents (fig. 6)

Atropine is a plant alkaloid, found in *Atropa belladonna* (deadly nightshade), and *Datura stramonium* (thorn apple). It acts by competitive inhibition at cholinergic receptors. When given by high dose injection, the effects of the non-selective action of atropine will include tachycardia, bronchodilatation, urinary retention etc. At lower doses, bronchodilatation occurs without tachycardia, but this selectivity is dose-dependent. Atropine is most selective

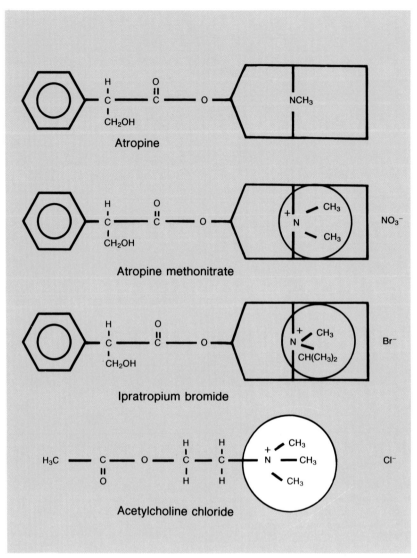

Fig. 6. Atropine and the quaternary ammonium derivatives. Increasing substitution on the nitrogen atom results in the quaternary compounds atropine methonitrate and ipratropium bromide. The quaternary nitrogen atom is shown within the open circle.

when given by inhalation, giving bronchodilatation which is slower in onset than that from adrenaline, but of longer duration.

The quaternary derivatives of atropine, atropine methonitrate and ipratropium bromide, are poorly absorbed from the gastrointestinal tract and do not readily penetrate the central nervous system. They are more bronchoselective than atropine, particularly when given by inhalation, and have fewer systemic side effects.

References

Anderson, G.; Wilkins, E. and Jariwalla, A.G.: Fenoterol in asthma. British Journal of Diseases of the Chest 73: 81 (1979).

Cooke, N.J.; Kerr, J.A.; Willey, R.F.; Hoare, M.V.; Grant, I.W.B. and Crompton, G.K.: Response to rimiterol and salbutamol aerosols administered by intermittent positive-pressure breathing. British Medical Journal 2: 250 (1974).

Appendix B

Dose Equivalents of Bronchodilator Drugs

J.G. Prior

Table I. Recommended doses of selective β_2-agonists given by inhalation. The preparations listed are currently available in the United Kingdom, but availability will vary elsewhere

Approved name (trade name)	Form	Strength	Recommended dosage for regular therapy
Fenoterol hydrobromide[1] ('Berotec')	Aerosol Nebuliser solution	200 μg/puff 5 mg/ml	200-400μg, 3-4 times daily 0.5-2.5mg, up to 4 times daily (as 0.025-0.125% solution)
Orciprenaline sulphate ('Alupent')	Aerosol[2]	750 μg/puff	750-1500μg, 4-6 times daily
Pirbuterol hydrochloride ('Exirel')	Aerosol	200 μg/puff	400μg, 3-4 times daily
Reproterol hydrochloride ('Bronchodil')	Aerosol Nebuliser solution	500 μg/puff 10mg/ml	1000μg, 3 times daily 10-20mg, diluted, as required
Rimiterol hydrobromide ('Pulmadil')	Aerosol[3] Nebuliser solution capsules	200 μg/puff 12.5mg per capsule	200-600μg, repeated after 30 minutes if required to a maximum of 8 inhalations per 24 hours 12.5mg as 0.5% solution, as required
Salbutamol ('Ventolin')	Aerosol[2] 'Rotacaps' Respirator solution Nebuliser solution unit dose	100 μg/puff 200, 400 μg/capsule 5 mg/ml in 20ml vial 2.5mg/2.5ml	200μg, 3-4 times daily 400μg, 3-4 times daily 2.5-5mg (diluted to 0.1 or 0.2% solution), 3-4 times daily
Salbutamol + beclomethasone dipropionate ('Ventide')	Aerosol	100μg + 50 μg/puff	200μg + 100μg, 3-4 times daily
Terbutaline sulphate ('Bricanyl')	Aerosol, 'Spacer' or 'Nebuhaler' Nebuliser solution	250 μg/puff 2.5 mg/ml and 10 mg/ml	250-500μg, 3-4 times daily 2.5-10mg, diluted, 3-4 times daily

1 – Also available as dry powder 'Inhalets' in some countries.
2 – Preparation is available in the USA.
3 – Rimiterol is also available as 'Pulmadil Auto', a breath-actuated inhaler (see appendix C).

β_2-Agonists

Tables I, II and III show the approximately equivalent doses of commonly used β_2-agonist drugs when given by the inhaled, oral or parenteral routes, together with the recommended doses for regular inhaled or oral therapy. These regimens are relevant only to adults and the manufacturer's literature should be consulted when prescribing for children (see also chapter VI). These tables repre-

Table II. Recommended doses of selective β_2-agonists given orally

Approved name (trade name)	Form	Strength	Recommended dosage for regular therapy
Isoetharine hydrochloride ('Numotac')	Tablet	10mg	10-20mg, 3-4 times daily
Orciprenaline sulphate ('Alupent')[2]	Tablet[1]	20mg	20mg, 4 times daily
Pirbuterol hydrochloride ('Exirel')[2]	Capsule	10mg, 15mg	10-15mg, 3-4 times daily
Reproterol hydrochloride ('Bronchodil')[2]	Tablet	20mg	10-20mg, 3 times daily
Salbutamol ('Ventolin')[2]	Tablet[1] Tablet (slow-release formulation)	2mg, 4mg 8mg	2-4mg, 3-4 times daily 8mg, at night or twice daily
Terbutaline sulphate ('Bricanyl')[2]	Tablet[1] Tablet (slow-release formulation)	5mg 7.5mg	5mg, 2-3 times daily 7.5mg, at night or twice daily

1 – Preparation available in the USA.
2 – Available as elixir, suitable for paediatric use. The manufacturer's literature should be consulted for dosage information in children.

sent only a guide to initial therapy. As discussed in earlier chapters, the response to bronchodilators in patients with chronic airflow limitation may be dose-dependent (Prior and Cochrane, 1982; Ruffin et al., 1978). Conventional doses of bronchodilator may not provide benefit where larger doses do (Prior et al., 1982). Thus, to obtain maximum benefit, it is most important that in long term maintenance therapy both the dosage and the frequency of administration should be tailored to each individual patient.

Methylxanthines

Some of the methylxanthine drugs may be given parenterally and aminophylline, by intravenous injection, is the most commonly used. All methylxanthines may be administered orally. Pharmaceutical innovations have led to the manufacture of microcrystalline anhydrous theophylline, which has high bioavailability but little direct irritant action on the gastric mucosa. Theophylline may be administered orally as the anhydrous form, as a salt (e.g. choline theophyllinate), or as a slow-release preparation (incorporating either pure drug or the ethylene diamine conjugate, aminophylline). Several methylxanthines are also marketed in elixir form, suitable for paediatric use.

Slow-release preparations are becoming increasingly popular in the management of chronic asthma because of the convenient twice-daily dosage. Several commercial preparations of methylxanthines contain a mixture of drugs (e.g. aminophylline or theophylline with phenobarbitone, ephedrine, phenylephrine or caffeine). Some may even be purchased 'over the counter'. Such fixed-dose combinations have little to recommend them and those with sedative components should be avoided. Some methylxanthines, e.g. aminophylline, acepifylline, diprophylline, etamiphylline, proxyphylline, and theophylline are also available as rectal suppositories. Rectal absorption of methylxanthines is variable.

Table IV gives dosage equivalents of theophylline and aminophylline. Theophylline is a difficult drug to use safely and effectively. It has a low therapeutic index, and plasma theophylline

Table III. Recommended doses of selective β_2-agonists for parenteral use in severe acute asthma

Approved name (trade name)	Form	Strength	Usual dosage
Orciprenaline sulphate ('Alupent')	Ampoule	0.5 mg/ml	500μg by deep intramuscular injection, repeated after 30 minutes if necessary
Salbutamol ('Ventolin')	Ampoule	0.5 mg/ml and 50 μg/ml for intravenous, intramuscular or subcutaneous injection	500μg (or 8 μg/kg bodyweight) intramuscularly or subcutaneously, repeated 4-hourly as required. 250μg (or 4 μg/kg) intravenously, repeated if necessary
		1 mg/ml for intravenous infusion, diluted appropriately	3-20 μg/min; dosage adjusted according to response
Terbutaline sulphate ('Bricanyl')	Ampoule[1]	0.5 mg/ml	250-500μg intramuscularly, subcutaneously or by slow intravenous injection, repeated 6-hourly as required
			1.5-5 μg/min as continuous intravenous infusion; dosage adjusted according to response

1 – Preparation is available in the USA.

Table IV. Dosage equivalents of theophylline and aminophylline

Drug	Form	Dosage	Comments
Theophylline	Tablet[1]	1-4 mg/kg 3-4 times daily, adjusting dose according to clinical response and plasma theophylline concentration	'Round-the-clock' dosing necessary. Less convenient than slow-release preparations
	Slow-release tablet or capsule[1]	Start with low dose (e.g. 4mg theophylline free acid/kg twice daily. Adjust dose according to clinical response and plasma theophylline concentration[2]	225mg aminophylline equivalent to 200mg theophylline Slow-release preparations can be given twice-daily and are also useful in treating nocturnal asthma[3]
Aminophylline	Slow-release tablet[1]		
	Ampoule 25 mg/ ml[1] and 250 mg/ml	5.6 mg/kg IV over 15 minutes and continue with infusion of 0.5 mg/kg/hour not exceeding 1g in 24 hours unless plasma theophylline concentrations available[4]	Omit loading dose if patient taking oral theophylline preparations. Reduce maintenance dose in conditions where theophylline clearance reduced. Measurement of plasma theophylline concentrations advisable

1 – Preparation is available in the USA.
2 – Prior et al., 1980.
3 – Barnes et al., 1982.
4 – Hendeles et al., 1978.

concentrations must be kept within the 10 to 20 mg/L range (see p.80). With levels above this, serious toxicity may occur (Jacobs et al., 1976). The drug is extensively metabolised in the liver and wide interindividual variations in theophylline metabolism occur (see p.34). Smoking can induce hepatic microsomal enzymes, which will result in more rapid clearance, and dosage may have to be increased. Similarly, dosage should be decreased in patients with liver dysfunction or cardiac failure. Gradual adjustment of dosage, with monitoring of plasma theophylline concentrations, is important to achieve optimal dosage (Prior et al., 1980; see also chapter V).

Ipratropium Bromide

Ipratropium bromide* is the most commonly used anticholinergic agent. In common with the β_2-agonists, the degree of bronchodilatation achieved varies with the dose of ipratropium (Allen and Campbell, 1980; Gomm et al., 1983). These studies indicate that doses of 80 to 120μg will achieve the maximum bronchodilatation which can be produced with atropinic agents, and that this will persist for 6 hours. The metered dose inhaler** delivers 20μg ipratropium bromide per actuation. Thus, 4 to 6 puffs, 6-hourly, is likely to achieve the maximum effect.

References

Allen, C.J. and Campbell, A.M.: Dose response of ipratropium bromide assessed by two methods. Thorax 35: 137 (1980).

Barnes, P.J.; Greening, A.P.; Neville, L.; Timmers, J. and Poole, G.W.: Single-dose slow-release aminophylline at night prevents nocturnal asthma. Lancet 1: 299 (1982).

Gomm, S.; Keaney, N.P.; Hunt, L.P.; Allen, S.C. and Stretton, T.B.: Dose-response comparison of ipratropium bromide from a metered-dose inhaler and by jet nebulisation. Thorax 38: 297 (1983).

Hendeles, L.; Weinberger, M. and Bighley, L.: Deposition of theophylline after a single intravenous infusion of aminophylline. American Review of Respiratory Disease 118: 97 (1978).

Jacobs, M.H.; Senior, R.M. and Kessler, G.: Clinical experience with theophylline. Relationships between dosage, serum concentration and toxicity. Journal of the American Medical Association 235: 1983 (1976).

Prior, J.G. and Cochrane, G.M.: Assessment of optimum dose of inhaled terbutaline in patients with chronic asthma: the use of simple, cumulative dose response curves. British Journal of Diseases of the Chest 76: 266 (1982).

Prior, J.G.; Berry, D. and Cochrane, G.M.: Serum theophylline concentrations during multiple dosing with two sustained release methylxanthine preparations in normal subjects. Postgraduate Medical Journal 56: 638 (1980).

Prior, J.G.; Nowell, R.V. and Cochrane, G.M.: High-dose inhaled terbutaline in the management of chronic severe asthma: comparison of wet nebulisation and tubespacer delivery. Thorax 37: 300 (1982).

Ruffin, R.E.; Obminski, G. and Newhouse, M.T.: Aerosol salbutamol administration by IPPB: Lowest effective dose. Thorax 33: 689 (1978).

Ward, M.J.; Fentem, P.H.; Roderick-Smith, W.H. and Davies, D.: Ipratropium bromide in acute asthma. British Medical Journal 282: 598 (1981).

---

* At present, ipratropium bromide is not on general release in the USA.

** Ipratropium bromide is also available as a respirator solution (250 μg/ml) which may be as effective as nebulised salbutamol in acute severe asthma (see p.180) [Ward et al., 1981].

Appendix C

Inhalation Devices

J.G. Prior

For the management of patients with airflow limitation, drugs are best given by inhalation since this route provides maximum therapeutic benefit with minimum side effects. To reach the airways, drugs must be delivered in particle sizes of 2 to 5μm. Larger particles are deposited in the throat and swallowed whilst those below 1μm either settle in the alveoli or are exhaled. Several inhalation systems are available: pressurised inhalers and their modifications, 'Rotahalers' for inhalation of dry powder and devices for nebulisation of respirator solutions.

Pressurised Inhalers and their Modifications

Pressurised Inhalers (fig. 1)

All pressurised inhalers have a simple valve mechanism, delivering a metered dose of between 25 and 100μl. The active component is dissolved or suspended in fluorcarbon propellants. The volume delivered per dose determines the canister lifetime. Sal-

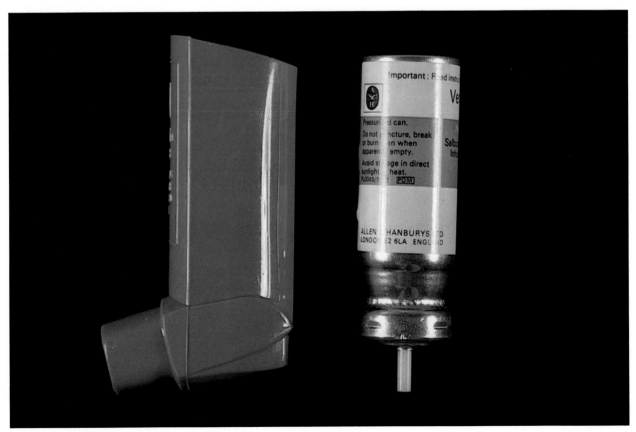

Fig. 1. Pressurised inhaler, container and canister.

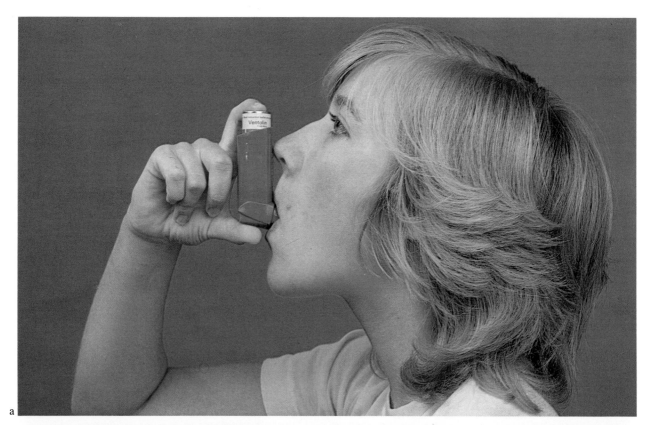

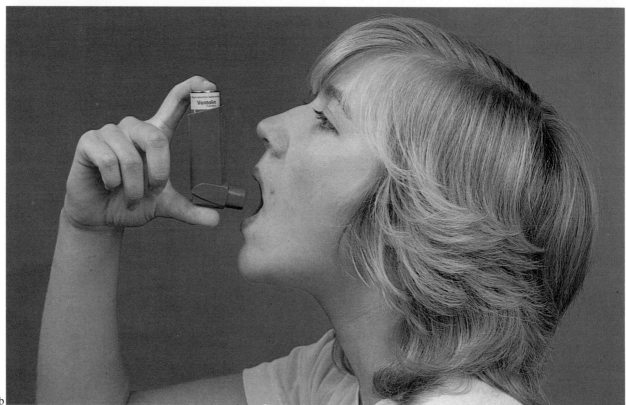

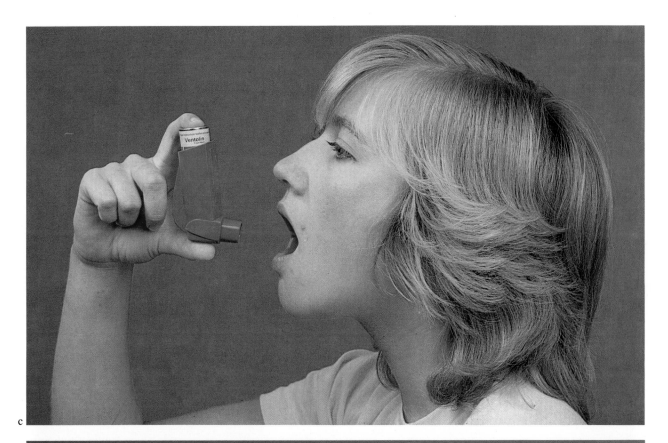

c

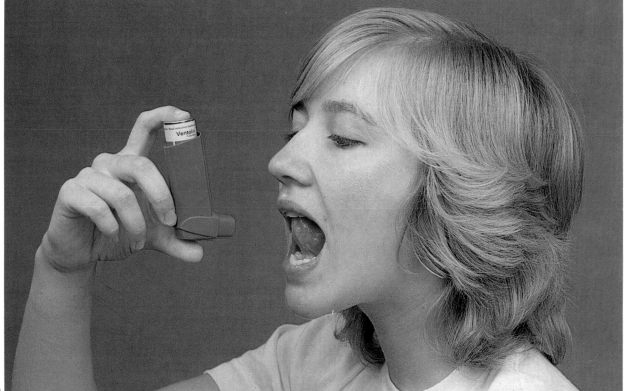

d

Fig. 2. Position of pressurised inhaler relative to the mouth. The mouthpiece is held firmly between the lips ('orthodox position', a), placed between the lips with mouth open (b) or held some distance from the mouth (c). Increase in lung deposition of aerosol may be achieved with the latter two methods (Dolovitch et al., 1981). Obstruction of the aerosol spray by the tongue (d) will offset this effect.

butamol (albuterol) inhalers deliver $50\mu l$ and each canister contains 200 doses, while for terbutaline the volume is $25\mu l$ and each canister contains 400 doses. Less than 10% of a correctly administered dose from a pressurised inhaler reaches the bronchial tree (Davies, 1975), and even to achieve this in practice the physician must repeatedly check and correct the patient's inhaler technique (Patterson and Crompton, 1976). Unfortunately, considerable controversy exists in published literature as to the 'correct' technique for using pressurised aerosols, and even manufacturers' advice varies although recently there has been an attempt to standardise instructions to those shown below. Factors such as position of the inhaler in relation to the lips, lung volume at which the drug is inhaled, inspiratory flow rate, and breath-holding after inhalation may all modify drug deposition within the lungs (Newman, 1983).

Maximum drug deposition in the lungs will be achieved if the following rules are observed:

1) Remove the cap from the mouthpiece, and shake the inhaler vigorously.

2) Hold the inhaler upright, breathe out gently (but not fully).

3) Place mouthpiece in the mouth and close lips around it. Start breathing in slowly and deeply through the mouth, press the inhaler to release the drug and continue to breath in.

4) Hold breath for at least 10 seconds, or as long as is comfortable.

5) If you are to take a second inhalation you should wait at least 1 minute (see p.60) before repeating steps 2, 3 and 4.

Alternatively this technique may be used with the mouth open (fig. 2).

Unfortunately, despite repeated instructions, up to one-third of all patients fail to use a pressurised inhaler correctly (Saunders, 1965) and this proportion is likely to be higher in the very young, the elderly, and the arthritic.

Modifications of the Pressurised Aerosol

In patients unable to coordinate actuation of the aerosol with inhalation, several modifications of the pressurised inhaler may be of value, e.g. a device using light or sound to indicate that inspiration is occurring, may be incorporated. Breath-actuated pressurised aerosols are also in use (D'Arcy and Kirk, 1971). The 'Pulmadil Auto' is one such device, releasing a dose of rimiterol only when the patient inspires (fig. 3). A spring mechanism is incorporated whereby inspiration triggers aerosol actuation. However, the sharp click which occurs during actuation is unacceptable to some patients.

When a 'spacer' device is used, coordination of actuation with inspiration is less critical although with the 'tube spacer' the dose is lost if the patient exhales at the wrong time. Terbutaline may be administered by a 'tube spacer', consisting of a pressurised aerosol canister connected to a 10cm extension tube (fig. 4). Actuation of the canister releases the drug into the extension tube and the dose may then be inhaled. These extension tubes reduce drug deposition within the mouth and increase penetration into the lungs [from 7.8% for standard pressurised aerosol to 11.5% for 'tube spacer' (Newman et al., 1981)]. Long term use of the 'tube spacer' may improve lung function over and above that achieved with

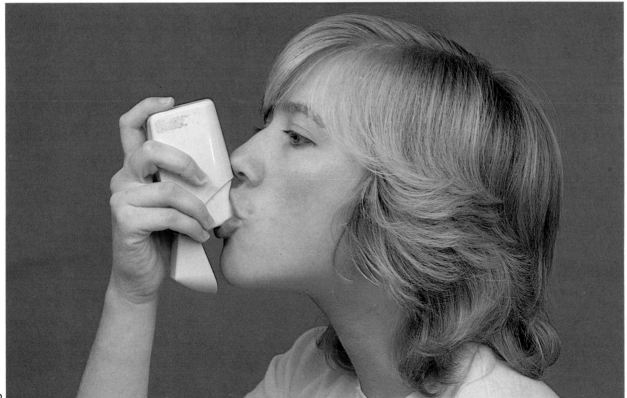

Fig. 3. A breath-triggered inhaler. Closure of the cap resets the trigger mechanism (a) which actuates the canister when the patient inspires (b).

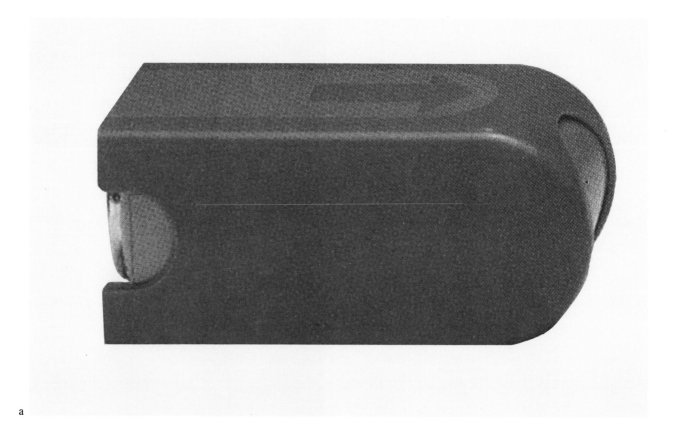

a

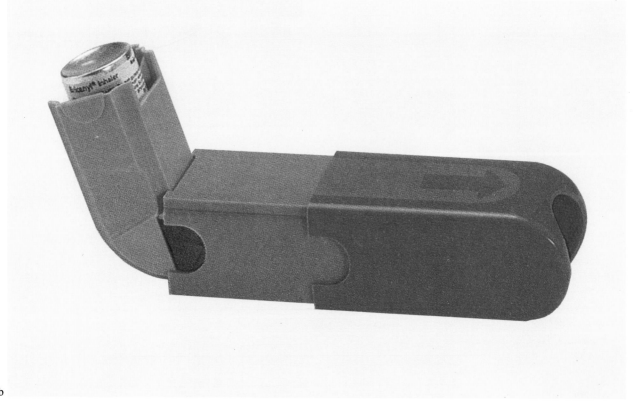

b

Fig. 4. Tube spacer. This folds neatly for convenient carriage in handbag or pocket (a). It is opened by pulling out the two lighter blue segments which lock into position (b). The mouthpiece is held firmly by the lips, the canister is actuated and the drug inhaled from the tube. Coordination of inhalation with actuation is not necessary.

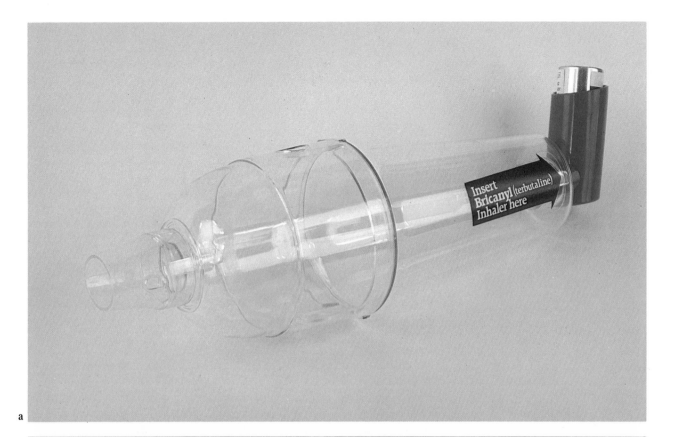

Fig. 5. 'Nebuhaler'. The 'Nebuhaler' is a 750ml plastic cone, incorporating a one-way valve at the mouthpiece. A terbutaline (or budesonide) aerosol will attach to the other end (a). Actuation of the aerosol enables drug to enter the cone from which it is inhaled (b).

conventional pressurised inhalers (Langaker and Hidinger, 1982). However, this device is probably of most benefit in those patients whose conventional inhaler technique is suboptimal (Godden and Crompton, 1981).

The pear 'spacer' or 'Nebuhaler' (fig. 5) is a plastic pear-shaped tube of 750ml volume, which is designed to contain the shape of the aerosol cloud when it leaves the canister. At the front, near the mouthpiece, is a one-way valve and a terbutaline pressurised inhaler is attached to the other end.

Although coordination of inspiration and actuation is normally unnecessary the one-way valve must close to prevent the patient breathing out through the 'spacer' and wasting the drug. A recent report describes a patient who failed to obtain relief from her inhaler and 'Nebuhaler' when her expiratory flow became too low to close the one-way valve (Cox et al., 1984). Lung deposition is improved because a dense, slowly moving cloud of small drug particles is held in the chamber and may be inhaled over several seconds. In one study, whole lung deposition of a radio-labelled aerosol increased from 7.8% with a standard pressurised aerosol, to 13% with the pear 'spacer' (Newman et al., 1981). In severe acute asthma, terbutaline delivered by the 'Nebuhaler' was as effective as nebulisation of terbutaline respirator solution (Morgan et al., 1982). Additionally, the 'Nebuhaler' is cheaper and more convenient than systems for nebulisation of respirator solution and does not require a power source for operation. It should prove to be a valuable device for inclusion in the general practitioner's emergency bag but its size limits patient acceptability.

Dry Powder Inhalation
(fig. 6)

The 'Rotahaler' enables salbutamol to be inhaled as a dry powder. It is useful in patients who cannot coordinate actuation of the conventional pressurised inhaler with inspiration, and has been used successfully in young children (Lenney et al., 1978). The rear loading version of the 'Rotahaler' (fig. 6) is easier to use than the original, but as it has to be charged before each inhalation, it is less convenient to use than the pressurised inhaler. The active component is contained within a gelatin capsule in a lactose base. In humid conditions the gelatin capsules soften and the powder may clog and it is important that the storage recommendations are followed. Other drawbacks are that the lactose vehicle may cause hypersensitivity, and some patients dislike the sensation of a dry powder impacting on the back of the pharynx. The proportion of drug entering the lung when using a 'Rotahaler' is probably no greater than that achieved with a pressurised inhaler but this device does allow the use of inhaled bronchodilators in patients for whom this might otherwise have been impractical.

Respirator Solutions

Bronchodilators available as respirator solutions include some of the β_2-agonists (appendix B), and ipratropium bromide. After nebulisation, they can be administered to the patient as an aerosol. This form of bronchodilator therapy is used for acute exacerbations of asthma or chronic bronchitis and emphysema, and also in patients who have very severe chronic airflow limitation which has not responded to conventional doses of bronchodilator (Prior et al., 1982). The dose of bronchodilator given by nebulisation is much greater than that delivered by pressurised inhalers or 'Ro-

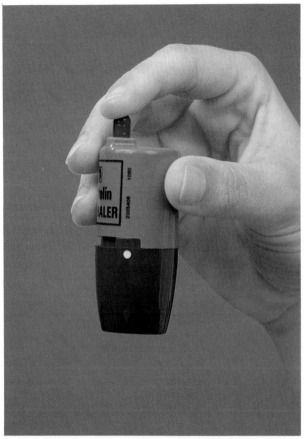

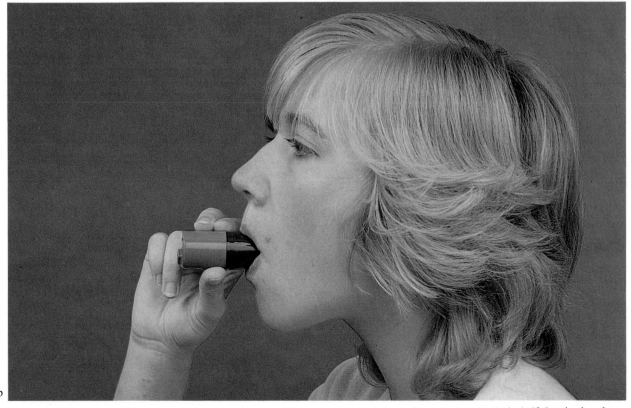

Fig. 6. 'Rotahaler'. The 'Rotahaler' is loaded at its rear end (a). A half turn of the device cuts the capsule in half. Inspiration draws drug into the lungs (b).

tahalers'. About 80% of the initial dose fails to reach the patient (being lost in the nebuliser or atmosphere), but approximately 10% enters the lungs (Lewis et al., 1982). Higher plasma concentrations of drug are achieved with this form of therapy, and as a consequence, side effects, such as tremor and tachycardia, are more common than with conventional pressurised aerosols.

Administration of a respirator solution is achieved by using a nebuliser. Several different types of nebuliser are available, but the principle employed is common to all. Nebulisers are small (usually plastic) containers into which a diluted bronchodilator solution is placed (fig. 7). An aerosol is produced by one of two methods. In the simpler systems ('jet' nebulisers) air or oxygen is passed through the solution and the resulting aerosol is inhaled, either through a mouthpiece or by mask (fig. 8). In hospital, piped

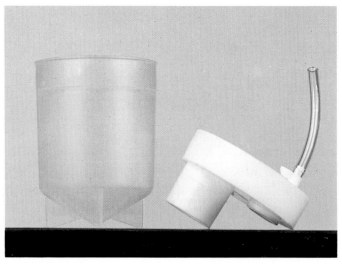

Fig. 7. Different types of jet nebuliser: 'Acorn' (a); 'Hudson' (b); 'Monaghan' (c).

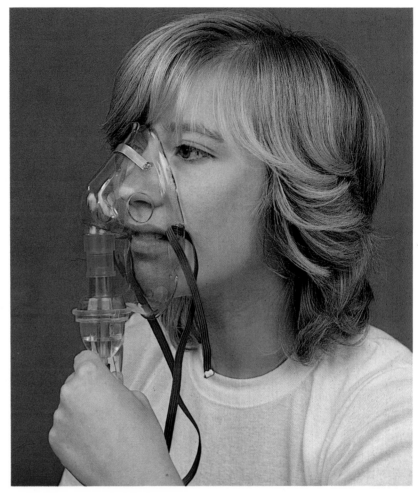

Fig. 8. Inhalation of nebulised bronchodilator by facemask. The mask may be held to the face by hand or strapped around the head.

air or oxygen is used for nebulisation, but for domiciliary use, portable air compressors (fig. 9) are more convenient (and cheaper). To achieve optimal particle size, a flow rate of at least 8 L/min is required (Clay et al., 1982). The drug solution is diluted with saline to an appropriate volume. There is an advantage in using a well diluted solution, as all nebulisers have a 'dead' space or volume (see p.86). With a dilute solution a lower proportion of the dose is lost in the 'dead' volume', than if a more concentrated solution were used. Increasing the initial volume of the solution will, however, increase nebulisation time and a total volume of 4ml would seem a reasonable compromise (Clay et al., 1982).

Ultrasonic nebulisers employ ultrasound to atomise the particles and the resultant aerosol may be carried to the patient by air or oxygen. In general, these devices are more efficient than conventional jet nebulisers, but are also more costly.

Pressure cycled ventilators, such as the Bird ventilator, may be used to deliver bronchodilator respirator solution to patients. The ventilator can be cycled automatically or triggered by the patient's inspiration [intermittent positive pressure breathing (IPPB)]. The sensitivity may be altered such that even the weakest inspiratory effort will trigger the ventilator. The respirator solution is nebulised either by air or oxygen and may be inhaled through a facemask or mouthpiece. Using IPPB, nebulised respirator solution is not wasted during expiration and this method may be of particular value to the physiotherapist treating the semiconscious patient with acute on chronic respiratory failure.

Nebulisers used for domiciliary aerosolisation of respirator solution have a lifespan of 2 to 3 months if used carefully. It is important that the interior of the container is cleaned thoroughly after use to avoid bacterial contamination with organisms such as *Pseudomonas aeruginosa*. The filters and air intake grill on the air compressor should be cleaned regularly since *Aspergillus* species have been cultured from fluff at these locations (George and Gillet, 1980). Inhalation of such organisms could cause serious problems.

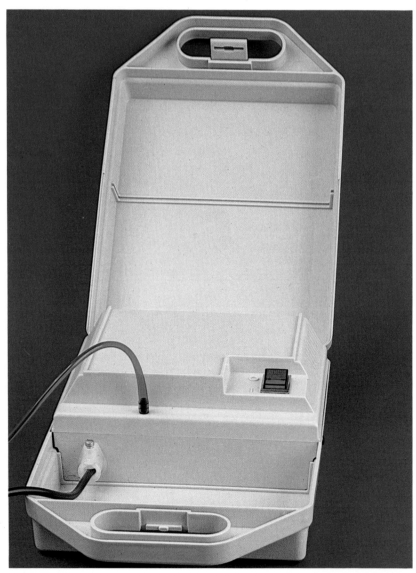

Fig. 9. A portable air compressor. This will fold up neatly for convenient carriage. The green tubing connects the air source to the nebuliser.

References

Cox, I.D.; Wallis, P.J.W. and Apps, M.C.P.: Potential limitations of a conical spacer device in severe asthma. British Medical Journal 288: 1044 (1984).

Clay, M.; Pavia, D.; Newman, S.P. and Clarke, S.W.: Efficiency of jet nebulisers in the production of therapeutic aerosols. Thorax 37: 788 (1982).

D'Arcy, P.F. and Kirk, W.F.: Development of a new device for inhalation therapy. Pharmaceutical Journal 206: 306 (1971).

Davies, D.S.: Pharmacokinetics of inhaled substances. Postgraduate Medical Journal 51 (Suppl. 7): 69 (1975).

Dolovitch, M.; Ruffin, R.E.; Roberts, R. and Newhouse, M.T.: Optimal delivery of aerosols from metered dose inhalers. Chest 80 (Suppl): 911 (1981).

George, R.H. and Gillet, A.P.: Allergic bronchopulmonary aspergillosis. Archives of Disease in Childhood 55: 910 (1980).

Godden, D.J. and Crompton, G.K.: An objective assessment of the tube spacer in patients unable to use a conventional pressurised aerosol efficiently. British Journal of Diseases of the Chest 75: 165 (1981).

Langaker, K.E. and Hidinger, K.G.: Long-term effects of a tube extension on bronchodilator treatment with a pressurised aerosol. European Journal of Respiratory Diseases 63: 498 (1982).

Lenney, W.; Millner, A.D. and Hiller, E.J.: Use of salbutamol powder in childhood asthma. Archives of Disease in Childhood 53: 958 (1978).

Lewis, R.A.; Cushley, M.J.; Fleming, J.S. and Tattersfield, A.E.: Is a nebuliser less efficient than a metered dose aerosol and do pear-shaped extension tubes work? American Review of Respiratory Disease 25: 94 (1982).

Morgan, M.D.L.; Singh, B.V.; Frame, M.H. and Williams, S.J.: Terbutaline aerosol given through pear spacer in acute severe asthma. British Medical Journal 285: 849 (1982).

Newman, S.P.: The correct use of inhalers; in Clark, T.J.H. (Ed.) Steroids in Asthma. p.210 (ADIS Press, Auckland 1983).

Newman, S.P.; Moren, F.; Pavia, D.; Little, F. and Clarke, S.W.: Deposition of pressurised suspension aerosols inhaled through extension devices. American Review of Respiratory Disease 124: 317 (1981).

Patterson, I.C. and Crompton, G.K.: Use of pressurised inhalers by asthmatic patients. British Medical Journal 1: 76 (1976).

Prior, J.G.; Nowell, R.V. and Cochrane, G.M.: High-dose inhaled terbutaline in the management of chronic severe asthma: comparison of wet nebulisation and tube-spacer delivery. Thorax 37: 300 (1982).

Saunders, K.B.: Misuse of inhaled bronchodilator agents. British Medical Journal 1: 1037 (1965).

Index

A

Acetylcholine 18, 208
Acetylglyceryletherphosphorylcholine 9
Adenosine 9,12
Administration routes 209-212
  comparison
    severe acute asthma 173-175
  inhalation (see also Inhalers)
    cf oral 28
    cf parenteral 174
    anticholinergics 33
    β_2-agonists 27, 84, 97-101
    corticosteroids 65-66, 102-103, 184
    dosage 209-210
    order 60
    severe asthma 174, 178-185
    side effects 28, 79
    sodium cromoglycate 72, 103, 124-125
    theophylline 84
  oral 59, 86, 96
    cf inhalation 28
    β_2-agonists 29
    corticosteroids 67-69, 177, 184, 198
    dosage 210-211
    slow-release preparations 38, 75, 97, 142-144
    theophylline 37, 53-54, 64-65, 82, 104
  parenteral 28, 211
    cf inhalation 174
    aminophylline 37, 101, 211
    β-agonists 101, 179, 181, 211
    severe asthma 174, 178-181
    side effects 176
  rectal
    methylxanthines 38
Adrenaline 22, 176
Adrenergic receptors
  distribution function 18, 23, 78
  subtypes 17, 23, 78
Adrenoceptor agonists 17, 78
  β-phenylethylamine 203-205
  catecholamine derivatives 24, 203-204
  mechanism of action 18
  metabolism 23, 204
  pharmacology 22-31
  structure-relationship activity 204-206
β-Adrenoceptor agonists (see also individual drugs) 23
  adenyl cyclase activation 19

administration routes 25
efficacy 24, 27, 29
metabolism 24
pharmacodynamics 23
receptor activity 23, 78
side effects 29
β_2-Adrenoceptor agonists, selective 23, 27
  chemical structure 205
  children < 2 years 105
  children > 2 years 53-54, 96-105
  chronic obstructive lung disease 194-197
  dosage 88
  duration of effect 25, 27, 29, 63, 79, 206
  elderly 161
  exercise-induced asthma 63, 127
  formulations 209-211
  inhalation 27
  + inhaled steroids 88, 102
  + ipratropium bromide 42, 89
  nocturnal asthma 142
    high dose 144
  'on-demand' 62, 76, 97
  onset of effect 25, 27
  parenteral administration 28, 101, 179, 181, 211
  regular therapy 97
  safety 63
  severe asthma 174-175
    diminished response 172-174
  side effects 79, 161, 176
  slow-release preparations 75, 97, 142, 184
  syrups 86, 89
  + theophylline 42, 89
  tolerance 31, 79
β-Adrenoceptor blockers 200
Age (see also Elderly)
  bronchodilator response 105, 160, 195
  theophylline clearance 162
Airway calibre 11
  circadian rhythm 134
  in asthma 4
Airway narrowing 188
Airway obstruction 115, 156
  mechanism 3, 4
  reversibility 156, 157, 188
Albuterol (see Salbutamol)
Allergens 1, 51, 94
Almitrine 200
Alpha$_1$-antitrypsin deficiency 189

Aminophylline 34
  injection 39, 174
    chemical incompatability 37
    dosage regimen 178, 181, 211
    toxicity 65
  nocturnal asthma 143, 145
  slow-release preparations 64, 211
Angina 79, 161, 176
Antibiotics 69, 177, 183
Anticholinergics (see also Atropine, Ipratropium bromide) 18, 31, 82
  cf β-agonists 32
  chronic bronchitis 32, 195
  mechanism of action 18
  mucociliary clearance 22, 83
Arachidonic acid 6
Arrhythmias 79
Arterial carbon dioxide tension 4, 172, 192
Arterial oxygen tension 4, 79, 172, 190, 191
  β_2-agonists 31
Aspirin 9
Asthma (see also Childhood asthma, Exercise-induced asthma, Nocturnal asthma, Severe acute asthma)
  age of onset 93, 153-154
  atopy 88-89
  classification 1
  death 131, 134, 136, 167-170
  deteriorating control 55, 68, 79, 110, 172-174, 177
  diagnosis 47
  drug-induced 1, 9
  immediate reaction 4
  inflammatory changes 3, 4
  late reaction 4, 10
  occupational 1
  pathogenesis 3-16
  prevalence 47-49
    children 93
    elderly 152
  symptomatic relief 49, 62, 76
  trigger factors 1, 50, 52, 94
Asthma crisis plan 51, 59, 64, 67
Asthma features of
  cf chronic bronchitis 165
  elderly 154-155
Asthma monitoring 69
  clinical review 73
  inhaler technique 59
  lung function 55, 73, 109, 183-184
  patient record cards 73
Asthma prevention 48, 64, 65, 76-92

β_2-agonists 53, 54, 87
  child 53, 54
  choice of bronchodilator 77-78, 87
  inhaled steroids 54
  sodium cromoglycate 53, 54
  theophylline 54, 87
  treatment aims 49
Atropine 18, 32, 206-208
  chemical structure 208
  exercise-induced asthma 124, 126
  side effects 83
Atropine methonitrate 11, 32, 208
  side effects 82

B

Barbiturates 160, 178
Beclomethasone dipropionate 50, 65, 198
  + β_2-agonists 55
  children 102
    < 2 years 108
  nebulised 108
  nocturnal asthma 144
Benzodiazepines 200
Bradykinin 9, 12
Bronchial hyper-reactivity 2, 189
  challenge testing 2, 10
  mechanism 11
  suppression 53
Bronchial smooth muscle
  contraction 3, 10, 115
  tone
    vagal innervation 11
Bronchiolitis 95
Bronchoconstriction 1-16
Bronchodilators (see also β-
    Adrenoceptor agonists,
    Anticholinergics, Methylxanthines
    and individual drugs)
  administration
    (see also Administration routes)
    intermittent 62-63, 76
    'on-demand' 53
    regular 50, 64, 76, 77-83
  availability
    geographical differences 48
  clinical trial assessment 25
  dosage 209-212
    children 95
  choice 50, 87
  combination therapy 39, 88-90
    clinical trial assessment 41
    factors affecting choice 88, 90
  factors influencing bronchodilator
    response 26, 42, 105, 192
  historical development 17, 78
  mechanism of action 18-22
  pharmacology 17-46
  structure-activity relationship 203-208
  treatment aims 49
Budesonide 125

C

Caffeine 34, 83, 178
Calcium channel blockers 203
Calcium ion flux 6, 8, 21
  methylxanthines 21
Catecholamines 21, 119, 139
Charcot Leyden crystals 3
Childhood asthma
  allergy 94
  diet 94
  exercise 95
  home nebulisers 100, 105
  inhalers 53, 97
  oral therapy 53, 96
    + inhaled β_2-agonists 102
  parents 108
  symptoms 93
  treatment 53, 105
    children < 2 years 105-108
Chronic bronchitis (see also chronic
    obstructive lung disease)
  definition 151, 188
  features of cf asthma 165, 191
  pathology 188-189
Chronic obstructive lung disease 188-202
  airway obstruction 188
    reversibility 188, 192
  arterial oxygen tension 190
  bronchodilators 192-198
    actions 193-196
    combination therapy 196
    dose 196
    inhaled β_2-agonists 192-197
    ipratropium bromide 195-197
    nebulised 198
    theophylline 195-197
    trial of 192
  clinical features 189-190
    'blue bloaters' (Burrows type B) 190
    Burrows type X 190
    'pink puffers' (Burrows type A) 190
  cor pulmonale 194-195, 199
  corticosteroids 197, 198
  exercise testing 193, 198
  lung function tests 191-193
  oxygen therapy 195, 199, 200
  smoking 189, 199, 202
  supportive therapy 198-202
    antibreathlessness agents 200
    respiratory stimulants 200
Circadian rhythm
  airway calibre 134
Coffee 36, 78
'Cold freon' effect 60
Complement 9
Cor pulmonale 194-195, 199
Corticosteroids, inhaled (see also
    Beclomethasone) 64
  asthma prevention 53, 66
  + β_2-agonists 55, 88
  children 102-103
  chronic obstructive lung disease 198
  exercise-induced asthma 125

nocturnal asthma 55
  side effects 66
    adrenal function 102
    hoarseness 102
    oral candidiasis 66, 102
    sore throat and hoarse voice 66, 102
Corticosteroids, systemic 105, 108
  oral 67, 68, 69
    chronic obstructive lung disease 68, 197-198
    chronic worsening asthma 177
    indications for 68
    self treatment 69
    short course 68
    side effects 67
  parenteral
    severe asthma 169, 179, 181-192
Coughing
  in asthma 93, 155
  in chronic bronchitis 189
Cromolyn sodium (see Sodium
  cromoglycate)
Curschmann's spirals 4
Cyanosis 171, 190
Cyclooxygenase 8
Cyclic AMP 19, 20
Cyclic GMP 19

D

Dermatophagoides pteronyssinus and
  D. farinae (see also House dust mite)
Diary cards 50, 73, 194
Diet
  food sensitivity 94
  theophylline clearance 36, 83
Digoxin 199
Dihydrocodeine 200
Diprophylline 34, 206-207
Diuretics 199
Doctor/patient relationship 52, 58
Doxapram 200

E

Eczema 94
Elderly 151-166
  airways obstruction 151, 157
  asthma 151
    clinical features 154
    diagnosis 152, 155
    management 163, 164
    prevalence 152
    symptoms 154
  bronchodilator response 157, 160
    β_2-agonists 160
    ipratropium bromide 161
    theophylline 161
  corticosteroids 159, 160, 164
Emphysema (see also Chronic
  obstructive lung disease)

definition 188
pathology 189
Enprophylline 34
Eosinophils 10, 12, 155
Ephedrine 17, 23, 78, 160, 178, 203
Epinephrine (see Adrenaline)
Etophylline 206-207
Exercise 52, 127
    testing 193
    tolerance 171, 189
Exercise-induced asthma 95, 112-130
    cf hyperventilation-induced asthma
       117, 120, 123
    definition 116
    drug effects 119, 121, 125
       anticholinergics 124
       assessment 121
       β-agonists 122, 123
       ketotifen 126
       nifedipine 125
       sodium cromoglycate 119, 124
       steroids 125
       theophylline 124
    factors affecting 118
       allergy 115, 122
       airway cooling 119
       environmental factors 119
    lung function 113
    management 127
    mechanism 115
       neutrophil chemotactic factor 115,
        119
    pattern 113
       early reaction 115
       late reaction 155
       refractory period 119
    prevalence 116

F

Fenoterol 51
    chemical structure 205
    dosage 209
       child 98
FEV_1 191
    normal values in elderly 157, 158
    severe acute asthma 172
Forced expiratory volume (see FEV_1)
Forced vital capacity (see FVC)
Δ FEV_1 (see Percent fall index)
FET 157
Forced expiratory time (see FET)
FVC 191
    normal values in elderly 157, 159

G

Glaucoma 82, 161

H

Heart rate 156, 172
Hexoprenaline 24
Histamine 5, 9, 10, 12
HMW - NCF (see Neutrophil
    chemotactic factor)

House dust mite 94
Hydrocortisone 170, 179
Hyperglycaemia 29, 79
Hyperventilation 4, 172
Hyperventilation-induced asthma 120,
    123
Hypokalaemia 29, 79, 161, 176, 183
Hypoxaemia 4, 31, 176, 190

I

IgE
    mast cell activation 5, 6, 9
Immunotherapy 52
Inflammatory cell infiltration 10, 12
Inflammatory changes 115
Inflammatory mediators (see Mast cell)
Inhalation (see Administration routes)
Inhaler technique 85
    children 97, 109
    elderly 162
    instructions 59, 214-219
    monitoring 59
    patient education 60-61
Inhalers (see also Administration
    routes) 84-86, 213-225
    aerosol abuse 53
    dry powder inhalers 27, 53, 85, 98,
       210
       β_2-agonists 209
       problems with 61, 210
       sodium cromoglycate 103
       severe asthma 175, 183
    metered dose aerosols 27, 53, 84, 97
       β_2-agonists 209
       design 213, 216-217, 220
       efficacy cf nebulisers 86
       ipratropium bromide 212
       problems with 60
       severe asthma 175, 177
    nebulisers 27, 108, 220, 222-224
       cf metered dose aerosols 86, 87,
        222
       β_2-agonists 209
       beclomethasone dipropionate 108
       children 98, 99, 108
       design 222
       home use 56, 100, 145, 164, 177
       ipratropium bromide 180, 212
       microbial contamination 224
       severe asthma 175, 178
       sodium cromoglycate 100
    particle size 213
    'spacer' devices 27, 66, 85, 100, 162
       'coffee cup' system 100, 110
       efficacy 216, 220
       severe asthma 175, 179, 183
Intermittent positive pressure
    ventilation (see IPPB)
IPPB 98, 175, 223
Ipratropium bromide 11, 54, 62, 83
    + β_2-agonists 42, 89
    chemical structure 208
    children 104
       < 2 years 106-108

chronic obstructive lung disease 195-
    197
    dosage 212
    efficacy 32, 89
       asthma 83
       chronic bronchitis 89
    elderly 161
    exercise-induced asthma 124
    nebulised 180, 212
    onset of effect 33
    pharmacokinetics 32
    severe asthma 176, 180-182, 184-185
    side effects
       bronchoconstriction 33, 61, 83,
        176
    therapeutic selectivity 32
Irritant fibres 11
Isoetharine
    dosage 210
    chemical structure 205
Isoprenaline
    asthma deaths 17, 169
    chemical structure 204-205
    metabolism 24
    tolerance 79
Isoproterenol (see Isoprenaline)

K

Ketotifen 104, 126

L

Leukotrienes 8, 11, 12, 21
5-Lipoxygenase 8, 11
Lung
    elastic recoil 4, 115, 188-189
    collapse 95
Lung function assessment 56, 74, 158
    home monitoring 73, 185
    records 73, 194

M

Mast cell
    activation 5
    inflammatory mediators 5, 6, 9, 119,
       120
    'leaky' mast cell theory 140
    role in bronchoconstriction 5
    stabilisation 21, 194
Metaproterenol (see Orciprenaline)
Methylxanthines (see also Theophylline
    and Aminophylline) 18, 33-39, 80,
    210-211
    absorption 37
    administration routes 37
    chemical structures 206-207
    mechanism of action 20
Milk
    childhood asthma 94
Mucociliary clearance 22, 188, 193
Mucosal oedema 3, 12, 22
Mucus
    plugging 3, 174, 188
    secretion 3, 12, 22
Muscarinic receptors 31-32

N

NCF (see Neutrophil chemotactic factor)
'Nebuhaler' (see Inhalers, 'Spacer' devices)
Neutrophil chemotactic factor 10, 119, 120
Neutrophils 10, 12
New Zealand 49, 170
Nifedipine 125
Nikethamide 200
Nocturnal asthma
  allergens 134, 141
  body temperature 139
  bronchial challenge 134, 135, 141
  circadian rhythm
    airways calibre 136
    biological clock 137
    catecholamines 140
    mechanisms 137, 138
  drug treatment 141-145
    antihistamines 149
    β_2-agonists 142, 144
    children 146
    choice 145
    frequency of administration 141, 143
    inhaled steroids 144, 147
    ipratropium bromide 148
    oral steroids 148
    side effects 142, 143
    sodium cromoglycate 147, 148
    theophylline 143
    timing 147
  lung function 132, 135
    diurnal variation 132
  mast cells 140
  morbidity and mortality 131, 132, 134
  prevalence 133
  severity 133, 135
  shift work 137
  sleep 138

O

Orciprenaline
  chemical structure 205
  dosage 209-211
    child 96, 98, 102
Oxygen therapy
  chronic obstructive lung disease 190-191
  severe acute asthma 179-182, 195

P

PaCO$_2$ (see Arterial carbon dioxide tension)
PaO$_2$ (see Arterial oxygen tension)
Patient compliance 50
Patient education 51, 61-73
  card 69
Percent fall index 114, 116
PEFR 73, 116
  children

normal values 109
'morning dip'
  nocturnal asthma 132
  severe acute asthma 172
Phosphodiesterase 19, 20
Physiotherapy 52
Pirbuterol
  chemical structure 205
  dosage 209-210
Polycythaemia 190, 200
Prednisolone 67, 177, 181, 197-198
Psychotherapy 52
Prostaglandins 8, 10, 12, 21
Prostanoids 9
Prostatic disorders 162, 176
Proxyphylline 206-207
Pulmonary hypertension 193-194
Pulsus paradoxus 156, 172
Pursed lip breathing 190

R

Ramadan 75
Relaxed vital capacity (see RVC)
Reproterol
  dosage 209-211
    child 96, 98
Respiration rate 171, 172
Respirator solutions (see also Inhalers) 220
  β_2-agonists 179, 209
  dilution 223
  ipratropium bromide 176
Respiratory infections 69, 94, 154
Rimiterol
  chemical structure 205
  dosage 209
    child 98
'Rotahaler' (see Inhalers dry power) 85
RVC
  chronic obstructive lung disease 191

S

Salbutamol 50, 51
  by injection 174-175, 179, 181, 211
  chemical structure 205
  chronic obstructive lung disease 193-195
  dosage 96, 98, 99, 101, 102, 106, 209-211
    children 96, 98, 99, 101, 102, 105, 106, 110
  exercise-induced asthma 122, 123, 126
  nocturnal asthma 55, 142, 144, 145
  severe acute asthma 174-175, 179-185
  slow-release preparations 142
  cf IV infusion 142
Severe acute asthma 167-187
  assessment of severity 171-172
  deteriorating control 177
  drug treatment
    administration route 174-175
    aminophylline 178, 181

at home 178
  β_2-agonists 178-185
  corticosteroids 179, 181-185
  ipratropium bromide 180-182, 184-185
  recovery period 183-185
  theophyllines 183-185
  oxygen therapy 179-183
Shunt effect 31
Smoking 38, 189, 199
  theophylline clearance 83
Sodium cromoglycate 64, 88
  asthma prevention 53
  children 100, 103
    < 2 years 108
  exercise-induced asthma 119, 124, 126
'Spacers' (see Inhalers)
Sputum 155, 189
SRS-A 5, 8
Suppositories 38, 211
Suppressor T cells 21
Sympathomimetic bronchodilators (see Adrenoceptor agonists)
Synergy (see Bronchodilators combination)

T

Tachycardia 29
Tachyphylaxis (see Tolerance)
Taste 62
Terbutaline 51
  by injection 174, 179, 211
  chemical structure 205
  dosage 209-211
    child 96, 98, 99, 102
  exercise-induced asthma 122
  nocturnal asthma 144
  severe acute asthma 174, 179
Theophylline 18, 33
  children 53, 104
  chronic obstructive lung disease 195-196
  clearance, factors affecting 34, 83, 147, 162
  combination therapy 42, 89
  contraindications 82
  dosage 82, 143, 211
    children 104
    maintenance regimen 82
  efficacy (cf β-agonists) 87
  elderly 161, 162
  exercise-induced asthma 124, 126
  nocturnal asthma 143
  pharmacodynamics 80
  pharmacokinetics
    absorption 37, 38
    at night 38, 144
    elimination 36
    half life 83
    metabolism 34, 162
  plasma concentrations 37, 104
    bronchodilator response 38, 81
    monitoring 38, 39, 82, 181
    therapeutic range 39, 81

side effects 81
  toxicity 39, 82
side effects 39, 65, 81, 88, 104, 176
  behavioural disorders 104
  convulsions 81
  death 82, 88
  incidence 82
  learning disorders 104
  slow-release preparations 37-38, 80,
    143, 170
  once-daily administration 143
Therapeutic selectivity 28, 32
Tolerance 31, 64, 79
Tremor

skeletal muscle 29, 161, 176
  tachycardia 63, 97
'Tube-spacer' (see Inhalers) 100

U

Urinary retention 82, 160, 162

V

Vagus nerve
  antagonism 18
  bronchial smooth muscle tone 11,
    195

reflex activity 11, 79
Venesection 200
Ventilation-assisted 183
Ventilation-perfusion mismatching 4,
  31
Viral infection 36, 69, 74, 83
Visual analogue scales 194

W

Walking tests 193